C000003192

Intelligence Theory

This edited volume brings together a range of essays by individuals who are centrally involved in the debate about the role and utility of theory in intelligence studies.

The volume includes both classic essays and new articles that critically analyse some key issues: strategic intelligence, the place of international relations theory, theories of 'surprise' and 'failure', organisational issues, and contributions from police studies. It concludes with a chapter that summarises theoretical developments, and maps out an agenda for future research. This volume will be at the forefront of the theoretical debate and will become a key reference point for future research in the area.

This book will be of much interest for students of Intelligence Studies, Security Studies and Politics/International Relations in general.

Peter Gill is Research Professor in Intelligence Studies at the University of Salford. **Stephen Marrin** is Assistant Professor in the Intelligence Studies Department at Mercyhurst College in Erie, Pennsylvania. **Mark Phythian** is Professor of Politics in the Department of Politics and International Relations at the University of Leicester.

Studies in intelligence series
General Editors: Richard J. Aldrich and Christopher Andrew
ISSN: 1368-9916

Intelligence Theory

Key questions and debates

**Edited by Peter Gill, Stephen Marrin
and Mark Phythian**

LONDON AND NEW YORK

First published 2009
by Routledge
2 Park Square, Milton Park, Abingdon, Oxon, OX14 4RN

Simultaneously published in the USA and Canada
by Routledge
270 Madison Ave, New York, NY 10016

Routledge is an imprint of the Taylor & Francis Group, an informa business

Transferred to Digital Printing 2009

© 2009 Selection and editorial matter, Peter Gill, Stephen Marrin and
Mark Phythian; individual chapters, the contributors

Typeset in Times by Wearset Ltd, Boldon, Tyne and Wear

British Library Cataloguing in Publication Data
A catalogue record for this book is available from the British Library

Library of Congress Cataloging in Publication Data
Intelligence theory : key questions and debates / edited by Peter Gill,
Stephen Marrin and Mark Phythian.
p. cm. – (Studies in intelligence)
1. Intelligence service. 2. National security. I. Gill, Peter, 1947–
II. Marrin, Stephen. III. Phythian, Mark.
JF1525.I6I58 2008
327.1201–dc22   2008004409

ISBN10: 0-415-42947-1 (hbk)
ISBN10: 0-415-55337-7 (pbk)
ISBN10: 0-203-89299-2 (ebk)

ISBN13: 978-0-415-42947-4 (hbk)
ISBN13: 978-0-415-55337-7 (pbk)
ISBN13: 978-0-203-89299-2 (ebk)

Contents

[handwritten annotation: STRUCT REALISM]

Contributors

Richard K. Betts is the Arnold A. Saltzman Professor and Director of the Saltzman Institute of War and Peace Studies at Columbia University. He has also taught at Harvard University and Johns Hopkins' Nitze School of Advanced International Studies, and was a Senior Fellow at the Brookings Institution in Washington for fourteen years. For six years in the 1990s he was a member of the National Security Advisory Panel of the Director of Central Intelligence. Betts has published numerous articles and is author of four books – *Soldiers, Statesmen, and Cold War Crises*; *Surprise Attack*; *Nuclear Blackmail and Nuclear Balance*; and *Military Readiness* – and co-author or editor of *The Irony of Vietnam; Cruise Missiles: Technology, Strategy, and Politics*; *Conflict After the Cold War*; and *Paradoxes of Strategic Intelligence*.

Philip H.J. Davies has published extensively on emerging intelligence and security trends such as information warfare and infrastructural security. Dr Davies has taught and conducted research in the UK, Singapore and Malaysia, and, during two-and-a-half years at the University of Malaya, regularly taught on intelligence policy and analytical methods for elements of the Malaysian intelligence community. He is the author of *MI6 and the Machinery of Spying* (2004), co-author of *Spinning the Spies: Intelligence, Open Government and the Hutton Inquiry* (2004) and also co-author of *The Open Side of Secrecy* (2006), a history to date of the UK Intelligence and Security Committee. He is convenor of the Security and Intelligence Studies Group, a specialist working group of the UK Political Studies and the British International Studies Associations/

Peter Gill is Research Professor in Intelligence Studies at the University of Salford, UK. He has taught courses in political science and criminal justice with particular emphasis on policing, security and intelligence. In addition to a number of journal articles on policing and intelligence issues, he is the author of *Policing Politics* (1994) and *Rounding Up the Usual Suspects?* (2000) that provide comparative analyses of, respectively, security and police intelligence processes in North America and the UK. He is also the co-editor of *Democracy, Law and Security* (2003) and *Transnational Organised Crime* (2003) that both deal primarily with European developments. Most recently, he has co-authored *Intelligence in an Insecure World* (2006). His current interests are concerned with the democratic control of intelligence and policing in both 'old' and 'new' democracies in the context of the so-called 'war on terror'. Between 1998 and 2006 he was convenor of the Security and Intelligence Studies Group.

Glenn P. Hastedt holds a PhD in political science from Indiana University. Formerly the chair of the political science department at James Madison University, he is now the director of the Justice Studies department. He is the author of *American Foreign Policy: Past, Present, Future* (7th edn, 2008) His recent articles on intelligence have appeared in *Intelligence and National Security, Defense Intelligence Journal* and *American Diplomacy.*

Loch K. Johnson is the Regents Professor of Public and International Affairs at the University of Georgia and author of over 100 articles and many books on US national security, most recently *Seven Sins of American Foreign Policy* (2007), *Handbook of Intelligence Studies* (2007) and *Strategic Intelligence* (5 vols; 2007). He has served as special assistant to the chair of the Senate Select Committee on Intelligence (1975–6), as the first staff director of the House Subcommittee on Intelligence Oversight (1977–9), and as special assistant to Chairman Les Aspin on the Aspin–Brown Commission on Intelligence (1995–6).

David Kahn is a historian of intelligence, especially communications intelligence, or code-breaking. He has practised and taught journalism as well as publishing widely on intelligence matters. His book, *The Codebreakers*, was first published in 1967, his PhD was published as *Hitler's Spies* in 1978 and *Seizing the Enigma* followed in 1991. He retired from *Newsday* in 1998 but continued to write on military and intelligence matters.

Stephen Marrin – a former analyst with the CIA and the congressional Government Accountability Office – is an assistant professor in Mercyhurst College's Intelligence Studies Department. He is a doctoral candidate at the University of Virginia, and has written many articles on various aspects of intelligence studies, including one that led to the creation of CIA University. In 2004, the *National Journal* described him as one of the US's top ten experts on intelligence reform. He is also a member of the editorial advisory board of the *International Journal of Intelligence and Counterintelligence*, the editorial review board of the National Military Intelligence Association's *American Intelligence Journal*, a member of American Military University's Intelligence Advisory Council, and on the Board of Directors of the International Association for Intelligence Education.

Mark Phythian is Professor of Politics in the Department of Politics and International Relations, University of Leicester. He is the author or editor of several books on security and intelligence issues, including: *Arming Iraq* (1997); *The Politics of British Arms Sales Since 1964* (2000); *Intelligence in* *an Insecure World* (with Peter Gill, 2006); *The Labour Party, War and International Relations, 1945–2006* (2007); *Intelligence and National Security Policymaking on Iraq: British and American Perspectives* (edited with James P. Pfiffner, 2008); and *PSI Handbook of Global Security and Intelligence: National Approaches* (2 vols; edited with S. Farson, P. Gill and S. Shpiro, 2008), as well as numerous journal articles and book chapters.

James Sheptycki is Professor of Criminology at York University, Toronto Canada. He was editor of the international scholarly journal *Policing and Society* from 1997 to 2003. He has published more than fifty refereed journal articles, book chapters and review essays in scholarly journals including the *British Journal of Criminology*, the *International Journal of the Sociology of Law*, the *European Journal and Crime, Criminal Law and Criminal Justice* and *International Political Sociology*. His edited collections include *Issues in Transnational Policing* (2000), *Transnational and Comparative Criminology* (with Ali Wardak, 2005) and *Crafting Global Policing* (with Andrew Goldsmith, 2007) together with his single authored research monograph *In Search of Transnational Policing* (2003) have helped to stake out the empirical and theoretical connections necessary for the interdisciplinary study of global crime and insecurity, policing and governance.

Jennifer Sims is a visiting professor with the security studies programme at Georgetown University. She has served on the Senate Select Committee on Intelligence and in the Department of State as a senior intelligence officer. She is the author of *Icarus Restrained: An Intellectual History of Nuclear Arms Control, 1945–60* and numerous articles on intelligence-related topics.

B. Douglas Skelley teaches public management courses to graduate and undergraduate students at James Madison University while coordinating its Master of Public Administration programme. He has published widely on public administration theory, public management, and retiree-migration policy, including in *Public Administration, American Review of Public Administration* and *Public Administration and Management.*

Michael Warner is Chief Historian for the Office of the Director of National Intelligence. He has written and lectured extensively on intelligence history, theory and reform. His recent publications include *The Intelligence Community, 1950–1955*, a volume co-edited with Douglas Keene in the Department of State's Foreign Relations of the United States series (Washington, DC. Government Printing Office, 2007); 'Building a Theory of Intelligence Systems', in Gregory Treverton, ed., *Mapping the State of Research on Intelligence* (Cambridge: Cambridge University Press, forthcoming in 2008); 'Sources and Methods for the Study of Intelligence', in Loch K. Johnson, ed., *Handbook of Intelligence Studies* (New York: Routledge, 2007), and 'The Divine Skein: Sun Tzu on Intelligence', *Intelligence and National Security* 21:4 (August 2006).

James J. Wirtz is a Professor at the Naval Postgraduate School in Monterey, California. He is the editor of the Palgrave Macmillan series, *Initiatives in Strategic Studies: Issues and Policies*; he has also been a section chair of the Intelligence Studies Section of the International Studies Association and President of the International Security and Arms Control Section of the American Political Science Association. He received his PhD in Political Science from Columbia University.

Acknowledgements

Each of us owes a multitude of intellectual debts in getting us to the point of contemplating this book, commissioning contributors, commenting on drafts and, finally, completing the editing. It has been a fascinating and challenging process and we have learnt a great deal. Our thanks are due, first, to all the contributing authors who have kept to our deadlines better than we have! Thanks also to Andrew Humphreys and his colleagues at Routledge for their encouragement and work in the book's production. We are grateful to Pen Gill, Angela Marrin and Diane Evans for their continuing support in our efforts to make sense of intelligence. Finally, we acknowledge the following:

Betts, Richard. 'Analysis, War, and Decision: Why Intelligence Failures Are Inevitable' was first published in *World Politics* 31:1 (October 1978), 61–89. ©The Johns Hopkins University Press. Reprinted with permission of The Johns Hopkins University Press.

Johnson, Loch. 'Bricks and Mortar for a Theory of Intelligence,' *Comparative Strategy* 22:1 (2003), 1–28. ©Routledge, part of the Taylor & Francis Group, LLC. A modified version of this article is reprinted as Chapter 3 of the present volume with permission of Taylor & Francis. www.taylorandfrancis.com.

Kahn, David. 'An Historical Theory of Intelligence' was first published in *Intelligence and National Security* 16:3. (2001), 79–92. ©Taylor & Francis Group, LLC. Reprinted with permission.

Wirtz, James. 'Theory of Surprise' was first published in Richard K. Betts and Thomas G. Mahnken (eds), *Paradoxes of Intelligence: Essays in Honor of Michael I. Handel* (London: Frank Cass, 2003). ©Taylor & Francis Group, LLC. Reprinted with permission.

Introduction

Peter Gill, Stephen Marrin and Mark Phythian

This book results from a number of influences. Each of the editors has been studying and/or involved in the intelligence business for some time and, in their work, has sought to develop conceptual thinking as the study of intelligence has become a more mainstream activity than it was thirty years ago. At that time the literature on intelligence, such as it was, was dominated by two main sources: in the United States there was much writing around the consequences of the 'year of intelligence' in 1975, when extensive congressional inquiries produced revelations that led to much soul-searching regarding the propriety of intelligence activities both at home and abroad. These inquiries were mirrored to a lesser extent in Australia and Canada. In Western Europe, particularly the UK, there were no such inquiries and the literature was dominated by historical issues, especially those relating to the role of intelligence in the Second World War. Elsewhere, communist or military authoritarian regimes were the order of the day and there was really no literature at all.

Since then, much has changed. The waves of democratisation across Latin America and Eastern Europe have brought significant changes in intelligence communities, though not always as far-reaching as may appear on the surface from the plethora of new intelligence laws. However, democratisation has meant that academics and other researchers are able to write and publish about intelligence with a new freedom. Research and writing in the 'old' liberal democracies has also developed, in part because of the release of further historical files, but also because of the questions posed by the 11 September 2001 attacks on New York and Washington, DC, followed by others in Madrid, Casablanca, Istanbul and London. These attacks and US and Western responses, framed as the 'war on terror', injected an urgency into debates about intelligence, forcing it even further out of the shadows from which it had begun to emerge after the end of the Cold War. The failure to prevent these attacks raised questions about the effectiveness of intelligence. The apparently fundamental failures in relation to Iraqi weapons of mass destruction meant that intelligence was placed under a critical spotlight twice in a very short period of time.

At the same time, however, the editors share the view that, while the writing of intelligence history, discussions of organisational change and appropriate legal frameworks, and journalism have all increased tremendously, these have not been matched by developments in conceptual and theoretical thinking about intelligence activities and processes. This concern has been most evident in the United States, where not just the intelligence community, but also the community of intelligence scholars, is larger than anywhere else. To that extent, this book is a direct descendant of an effort on the part of the US intelligence community to understand the conceptual and theoretical foundations of intelligence as – to use Sherman Kent's terms – knowledge, organisation and activity. This is reflected in the fact that most of the contributors to this volume are American. However, our aim has been to produce a book that does not simply address issues relating to US intelligence, but rather one that is seen as relevant by scholars of intelligence wherever they are based.

The specific origins of this volume lie in a workshop convened by the RAND Corporation and the Office of the Director of National Intelligence on the subject of intelligence theory, in which the editors and several contributors to this volume participated.[1] The driving force behind this workshop was Deborah Barger, the then-Assistant Deputy Director of National Intelligence for Strategy, Plans, and Policy, who had written a paper investigating the possibilities of transforming intelligence through a 'Revolution in Intelligence Affairs'.[2]

But transformation cannot occur effectively unless a better understanding exists of what is being transformed. Hence, Barger suggested assessing the conceptual foundations of intelligence; to include its definitions and theory. In sponsoring the workshop, she had three goals: first, to begin a series of debates about the future of intelligence writ large; second, to lay the intellectual foundations for revolutionary change in the world of intelligence; and third, to bridge the divide that has long separated intelligence scholars and practitioners. Many of those who attended the workshop believed that it met all three of these goals.

In 2006, Stephen Marrin organised a panel at the International Studies Association's (ISA) annual conference in San Diego on the subject of intelligence theory. This was followed by another organised by Peter Gill and Mark Phythian at the British International Studies Association conference in Cork December 2006 and a further panel at the March 2007 ISA conference in Chicago. This volume grew out of those meetings and discussions. In selecting and inviting contributions the editors have sought to represent a range of the most significant writing on intelligence theory to date and to represent a range of views and approaches that will encourage further consideration and debate by illuminating paths via which future scholars and practitioners may take the debate forward. Our hope is that the contributions here will encourage (and/or provoke) students of intelligence in Africa and Asia and elsewhere in the Americas and Europe to respond with their own writings that can form a future collection that will provide a better representation of global thinking on an issue that is so significant for people's safety, security and liberty.

Peter Gill
Stephen Marrin
Mark Phythian
December 2007

Notes

1 Gregory F. Treverton, Seth G. Jones, Steven Boraz and Philip Lipscy, *Toward a Theory of Intelligence: Workshop Report* (Santa Monica, CA: RAND, 2006).
2 Deborah G. Barger, *Toward a Revolution in Intelligence Affairs* (Santa Monica, CA: RAND, 2005).

1 An historical theory of intelligence

David Kahn

Intelligence has been an academic discipline for half a century now. Almost from the start, scholars have called for a theory of intelligence. None has been advanced. Although some authors entitle sections of their work 'theory of intelligence,' to my knowledge no one has proposed concepts that can be tested. I propose here some principles that I believe warrant being called a theory of intelligence because they offer explanations or predictions that can be seen to be true or untrue. I believe that the facts I give validate the theory; other scholars may adduce facts that disprove it.

I define intelligence in the broadest sense as information. None of the definitions that I have seen work. It is like the term 'news.' Though all but impossible to define, every journalist knows what it is: when something newsworthy is said in a court or a legislative hearing, all the reporters start taking notes.

My principles seek to deal with the past, the present, and the future of intelligence by accounting for the rise of intelligence to its current importance, explaining how it works, and specifying its main unsolved problems.

The past

The roots of intelligence are biological. Every animal, even a protozoan, must have a mechanism to perceive stimuli, such as noxious chemicals, and to judge whether they are good or bad for it. At that level intelligence is like breathing: essential to survival, but not to dominance. To this primitive capacity for getting information from physical objects, humans have joined the ability to obtain it from words. This verbal ability has led to a form of intelligence far more powerful than the kind used by animals or men to hunt prey or flee predators. It has driven the rise of intelligence to its present significance.

For intelligence has not always been as important or as ubiquitous as it is today. Of course, rulers in all times have used it, and have even paid tribute to it. Rameses II beat prisoners of war to make them reveal the location of their army.[1] The Hebrews spied out the land of Canaan before entering it.[2] Sun Tzu wrote, 'Now the reason the enlightened prince and the wise general conquer the enemy wherever they move and their achievements surpass those of ordinary men is foreknowledge.'[3] Ancient India's Machiavellian treatise on kingship, the *Arthasastra*, declares: 'My teacher says that between power (money and army) and skill in intrigue, power is better [...]. No, says Kautilya, skill for intrigue is better.'[4] Caesar's legions scouted their barbarian foes.[5] In the age of absolutism, ambassadors paid informants, while specialists in curtained, candlelit black chambers slid hot wires under wax seals to open diplomats' missives – and then decoded them.[6] Before the Battle of Prague, Frederick the Great observed his enemies' dispositions from a steeple.

But these and similar episodes were sporadic. Most did not stem from an organized effort to gain intelligence. Usually, generals won battles without much more information about their foes than seeing where they were. Cannae, the classic victory of warfare, in which Hannibal encircled a larger Roman force and annihilated it, owed nothing to intelligence. Though rulers outlined campaigns, they did not detail mobilization and battle plans, leaving intelligence little to discover. That is why, in fourteen out of Sir Edward Creasy's *Fifteen Decisive Battles of the World: from Marathon to Waterloo* (1851), victory was decided by strength, brains, and will – with knowledge of the enemy playing an insignificant role. The exception was the Battle of the Metaurus River in Italy in 207 BC. The Romans, having intercepted a Cathaginian message, were able to concentrate their forces, defeat Hasdrubal before his brother Hannibal could reinforce him,[7] and become the chief power of the Western world.

The French and industrial revolutions begat new conditions. In shaping the modern world, they created modern intelligence. The desire of Frenchmen to defend their new democratic nation against the invading armies of monarchist states, and the need to counter the professionalism of these states' forces with a superiority in numbers, led to armies far larger than those of the past. By 1794, France had a million men under arms. The *levée en masse* called for a war economy to support it. Crops were requisitioned. Industrial output was nationalized. Suddenly, factors that had never counted in war became significant. It mattered little to a medieval king how much coal and iron his enemy could produce; such knowledge was vital to a modern head of state. Railroads made possible the rapid mobilization, concentration, and supply of large bodies of troops. These deployments called for war plans far more detailed than any ever envisioned by Caesar or Frederick. At last, intelligence had targets that gave it a chance to play a major role in war.

The industrial and political revolutions also expanded the sources that enabled intelligence to gain access to these new targets. I divide these sources into two kinds.

One consists of information drawn from things, not words. It is seeing marching troops, fortifications, supply dumps, campfire smoke; hearing tank-motor noise, smelling cooking, feeling ground vibrations. I call it physical intelligence. For centuries it came only from the observations of the common soldier, patrols, the cavalry. But the balloon, the Zeppelin, the airplane provided more physical intelligence more quickly than the deepest-driving horsemen. The camera saw more than the eye and reproduced its vision for others. Radar detected oncoming bombers long before humans, even aided by searchlights, could spot them. In addition, larger armies meant more prisoners who might report on, say the supply situation or artillery positions. All these sources provided more physical intelligence than armies had ever been able to get before.

But this increase was greatly outstripped by the growth of the second source, verbal intelligence. This acquires information from a written or oral source, such as a stolen plan, a report on troop morale, an overheard order, even a computerized strength report.[8] Verbal intelligence made intelligence as important as it is today.

Verbal intelligence had long been relatively sparse. But the two revolutions engendered new sources. Larger armies yielded more documents for seizure. Parliamentary government, with its debates and public reports, exposed many specifics about a nation's military strength and programs. A daily press reported on these as well as on the economic situation. The tapping of telegraph wires and the interception of radio messages furnished far more verbal intelligence than the occasional waylaying of a courier ever did.

This growth is significant because verbal intelligence can furnish more valuable information than physical. Understanding this must begin with an acknowledgment that war has both a material and a psychological component. The material elements consist of such tangibles as troops, guns, and supplies. The psychological comprises such matters as a commander's will, his tactical ability, and the morale of his troops. The material factors dominate: the most brilliant, most determined commander of a regiment cannot withstand an army.[9] And this factor is served by verbal intelligence, while the less important psychological component is served by physical intelligence. The reason is this: the men and weapons that are the sources of physical intelligence affirm the likelihood of an encounter with greater probability than a plan, for men cannot move guns or troops as easily as they can rewrite orders. Greater probability is another way of saying less anxiety, and anxiety is a psychological factor. Physical intelligence, by lessening anxiety, steadies command. On the other hand, verbal intelligence deals with intentions, and just as the enemy needs time to realize those plans, so a commander who knows about them gains time to prepare against them. He can shift his forces from an unthreatened flank to an endangered one, for example. In other words, verbal intelligence magnifies strength – or, in the current jargon, is a force multiplier. Thus it serves the material component of war, and because that component is the more decisive, verbal intelligence influences more outcomes than physical.[10]

For the first 4,000 years of warfare, up to the start of World War I, nearly all information came from physical intelligence. That is why intelligence played a relatively minor role: physical intelligence does not often help commanders to win battles. Then, when the guns of August began firing, radio, which in effect turns over a copy of each of its messages to the foe, and the trench telephone, which lets indiscreet chatter be easily overheard, generated enormous quantities of verbal intelligence. These two new sources helped important commanders win important victories.

In August 1914, Germany's interception of a radioed plain-language Russian order told General Paul von Hindenburg and his deputy, General Erich Ludendorff, that they would have time to shift troops from a northern front in East Prussia, where the Russians were advancing slowly, to a southern one, where the Germans could outnumber them. The Germans made the move – and won the Battle of Tannenberg, starting Russia into ruin and revolution.[11] In 1917, Britain's cryptanalysis and revelation of the Zimmermann telegram – in which Germany's foreign minister, Arthur Zimmermann, promised Mexico her 'lost territory' in Texas, New Mexico, and Arizona if she would join Germany in a war against America – helped bring the United States into the war, with all that that has entailed.[12] It was the most important intelligence success in history. Britain's knowledge of Germany's naval codes enabled the Royal Navy to block every sortie of Germany's High Seas Fleet – and so, some have argued, keep it from winning the war in an afternoon.

Verbal intelligence served on the tactical level as well. It helped the Germans when, in 1916, the British fought to take the adjoining villages of Ovilliers and La Boiselle on the Somme. The British suffered casualties in the thousands. In a captured enemy dugout, they found a complete transcript of one of their operations orders. A brigade major had read it in full over a field telephone despite the protest of his subordinate that the procedure was dangerous. 'Hundreds of brave men perished,' the British signal historian related, 'hundreds more were maimed for life as the result of this one act of incredible foolishness.'[13]

At last the admirals and generals understood. Intelligence had made its influence clear to them in the way they knew best. Despite their reluctance to share power and glory with intelligence officers, they realized that to spurn intelligence might cost them a battle or even a war – and their jobs. They and their governments drew the appropriate conclusions. Britain, Germany, Italy, and the United States, none of which had had codebreaking agencies before the war, established them after it. Germany, the most conservative state, whose General Staff had long subordinated intelligence to planning, created for the first time in its history a permanent peacetime military agency to evaluate all information.[14] Intelligence had arrived as a significant instrument of war.

And in the next war, verbal sources made intelligence even more useful to commanders. It sped victory, saving treasure and lives. The reading of U-boat messages enciphered in the Enigma machine shortened the Battle of the Atlantic, the most fundamental struggle of the war, by months. Other Enigma solutions disclosed some of the Wehrmacht's tactical plans, particularly in France in 1944. Cracking the Japanese 'Purple' machine enabled the Allies to read, for example, the dispatches of the Japanese ambassador in Germany, giving them what US Army Chief of Staff General George C. Marshall called 'our main basis of information regarding Hitler's intentions in Europe'.[15] The Battle of Midway, which turned the tide of the war in the Pacific, was made possible by intelligence from codebreaking. Marshall described its value:

Operations in the Pacific are largely guided by the information we obtain of Japanese deployments. We know their strength in various garrisons, the rations and other stores continuing available to them, and what is of vast importance, we check their fleet movements and the movements of their convoys. The heavy losses reported from time to time which they sustain by reason of our submarine action largely result from the fact that we know the sailing dates and routes of their convoys and can notify our submarines to lie in wait at the proper points.[16]

Generals actually praised intelligence. Marshall said the solutions 'contribute greatly to the victory and tremendously to the saving in American lives.'[17] General Dwight D. Eisenhower wrote to the head of the British secret service, whose best information came from codebreaking, that 'the intelligence which has emanated from you [...] has been of priceless value to me.'[18] Their tributes crowned the ascent of intelligence from its humble biological origins as a mere instrument of survival to its supreme capability: helping a nation win a war.

The present

The theory of verbal and physical intelligence explains, I believe, how intelligence grew – its past. But it also describes the present, by showing how physical intelligence steadies command and verbal intelligence magnifies strength. So I believe it can be incorporated into the principles that a theory of intelligence should offer. Indeed, it forms the first of three. This first principle defines the function of intelligence. Magnifying strength and steadying command may be compressed into this: Intelligence optimizes one's resources. I call it O'Brien's Principle, after Patrick O'Brien, an economic historian, who casually remarked to me before lunch one day at St Antony's College, Oxford, 'Well, David, isn't all intelligence just optimizing one's resources?' This is the fundamental, the ultimate purpose of intelligence.[19]

O'Brien's Principle, like any logical proposition, may be obverted. A unit may not have intelligence and thus may not optimize its resources. It may be overwhelmed or, in intelligence terms, surprised. Surprise is the obverse of O'Brien's Principle.

Another corollary of O'Brien's Principle explains what a commander does when he has no intelligence, or faulty intelligence: I have dubbed this the null hypothesis. In the physical realm, he creates a reserve. The purpose of a reserve, Clausewitz said, is 'to counter unforeseen threats [...]. Forces should be held in reserve according to the degree of strategic uncertainty.'[20] In the mental realm, the commander must remain firm in his decisions. He 'must trust his judgment and stand like a rock on which the waves break in vain [...]. The role of determination is to limit the agonies of doubt.'[21] In other words, when a commander lacks the information that can optimize his resources, he must replace it with force and will. These are the counterparts of intelligence in the physical and psychological components of war.[22]

The second permanent principle of intelligence holds that it is an auxiliary, not a primary, element in war. Some writers say loosely that intelligence has won this battle or that, but this is hyperbole. Battles and wars are won by men and guns, brains and will. Intelligence merely serves these. It is secondary to disposing one's forces, obtaining supplies, inspiring the troops. When I asked a general once whether he would rather have a good intelligence man on his staff or a good commander for one of his division's three regiments, he laughed, and his wife said that even she knew the answer to that one. The regimental commander, they said, was far more important. Colonel David Henderson, one of the first military men to study modern intelligence, declared in *The Art of Reconnaissance* (1907) that information cannot be classed with such matters as tactics, organization, discipline, numbers, or weapons because 'its influence is indirect, while theirs is direct.'[23] It is indeed a force multiplier and facilitator of command, but it cannot always make up for insufficient strength or inadequate leadership. It is a service, not an arm.

The third principle is perhaps the most interesting. It came to me when, while working on a book, I was looking for cases in which intelligence helped win battles. I noticed that I was finding many more defensive victories than offensive. These ranged from battles of worldwide importance, such as those of the Metaurus, Tannenberg, and Midway, to smaller operational clashes, such as the German Ninth Army's rebuff of a Soviet offensive south of Rzhev in November 1942 on the basis of all-source intelligence,[24] down to tactical actions, such as the repulse of a Soviet counterattack out of Sevastopol on 21 January 1942, to which wiretaps had alerted the German 24th Infantry Division.[25] In all of these, intelligence helped award victory to the defenders. On the other hand, when intelligence helped win offensive victories, it rarely served directly, as by ascertaining enemy strength or intentions. Rather, as at D-Day, it aided deception – a doubly indirect service. Wondering why intelligence seemed to play so much more significant a role in the defense than in the offense, I looked up the definitions of these two modes to see if they offered a clue. Clausewitz's seemed to, and eventually I propounded a hypothesis. It maintained that intelligence is essential to the defense but not the offense. This theory seemed to explain several phenomena, suggesting that it might be valid.

Intelligence exists, of course, in both the offense and the defense, but in different ways. The difference is that between an accompanying and a defining characteristic. All elephants are gray, but grayness is not a defining characteristic of elephants, merely an accompanying one. Intelligence is a defining characteristic of the defensive; it is only an accompanying characteristic of the offense.

'What is the concept of defense?' asked Clausewitz. 'The parrying of a blow. What is its characteristic feature? Awaiting the blow.'[26] Now, an army can await a blow only if it expects one, and it can expect one only on the basis of information or belief, right or wrong, about the enemy. There can be, in other words, no defense without intelligence. And Clausewitz says the same thing contrapositively when he asserts that surprise is needed for an offensive victory.[27]

To defend is to acknowledge that the initiative comes from the enemy. And, indeed, the offense acts, the defense reacts. The offense prescribes to the enemy; it makes the basic decisions. It is 'complete in itself,'[28] said Clausewitz. Thus, information about enemy intentions, while helpful and to a certain degree always present (an army must see its enemy to fight it), is not essential to an offensive victory. An invading force can march about the countryside, imposing its will, without needing to know where the enemy is. If it learns that the enemy plans to counterattack, it shifts to a defensive mode – and then it requires intelligence. Military theorist Barry Posen has observed, in the terms of information theory, that the offensive, by seizing the initiative and thereby structuring the battle, reduces uncertainty[29] (one reason commanders love it). And less uncertainty means less need for intelligence – which, in one of its functions, steadies command.[30]

What all of this says is this: while intelligence is necessary to the defense, it is only contingent to the offense. The validity of this principle[31] is demonstrated, I believe, by two data. One is the relative frequency of defensive intelligence successes over offensive ones – the phenomenon that started me on the search. The second is that the nations that are aggressive tend to neglect intelligence, while nations in a defensive posture emphasize and rely on it. A clear example is Poland between World Wars I and II. In 1932 her fear of being gobbled up by one or the other of her powerful neighbors motivated her – alone of all the powers – to crack the German Enigma cipher machine. Another case is Britain. She long based her foreign policy on the balance of power, which is a reactive technique; it needs intelligence to succeed – and Britain's secret services were legendary. An example that proves the irrelevance of intelligence to the offensive is Nazi Germany. Hitler expected to dictate (and for a while did dictate) to others as he began to conquer the world; for this he did not need intelligence, so he neglected his espionage and cryptanalytic organs to concentrate instead on Stukas, Panzers, and elite divisions – and when the war came, his inadequate intelligence failed him.[32] During the Cold War, the United States, worried about Soviet aggression, enormously extended its intelligence agencies. And the Soviet Union, almost paranoid about encirclement and subversion, developed the largest intelligence system on earth.

The future

These three principles of intelligence – it optimizes resources, it is an auxiliary function in war, and it is essential to the defense but not to the offense – seek to explain intelligence's operation and its place in the universe, just as the theory of the rise of verbal intelligence seeks to explain how intelligence became as important as it is. But what must intelligence do to improve? What problems must it resolve? What is its future?

I ask this in the largest sense. It is not a question of whether the end of the Cold War will decrease intelligence activity or whether the need to watch a multiplicity of nations, ethnic groups, economic institutions, and terrorists will increase it. Nor is it a question of techniques and their constant seesaw struggle with countermeasures. In response to the pervasiveness of this century's intelligence, a technology of stealth – the silent submarine, the bomber almost invisible to radar – has emerged. These, in turn, have given rise to ever more refined techniques of detection, such as instruments that spot the gravitational anomalies created by a mass of metal underwater. But none of these issues raise fundamental questions about the future of intelligence – nor does the perennial difficulty that these sensors collect far more raw data than the agencies can evaluate in usable time.

Intelligence faces two all-encompassing, never-ending problems. Both are ultimately unsolvable. But intelligence must strive for a solution in the way that a graphed function reaches for – but never actually meets – its asymptote. The first problem is how to foretell what is going to happen. The goal, of course, is to predict everything. And certainly prediction is better in many cases that it ever was before. The new ability springs from the growth in intelligence tools. During World War II, Allied codebreaking revealed many more U-boat operations than it did in World War I. Wellington said, 'All the business of war … is … guessing what was at the other side of the hill.'[33] Today, the near blanketing of the theater of war with Buck Rogers collection devices – over-the-horizon radar, television cameras in the noses of drones and smart bombs, wide-ranging and detailed surveillance by satellite – renders the other side of the hill almost as visible as this side. It is hard to imagine an invasion like that of D-Day surprising any nation possessing today's observation tools. Still, not everything can be known in advance. Camouflage conceals men and weapons. Commanders change their plans. Accidents happen. These hindrances are multiplied a thousandfold in dealing not with a confined though complex activity like a single battle but with the major events of the post-World War II world, such as, for example, the fall of the Shah of Iran. Many more factors, many more people come into play than in a limited action. Even without secrecy, the interaction of these elements is all but incalculable. As Clausewitz said of the difficulty of evaluating another state's capabilities and intentions, 'Bonaparte was quite right when he said that Newton himself would quail before the algebraic problems it would pose.'[34]

This is why intelligence did not foretell North Korea's gamble in attacking South Korea, the Soviet emplacement of nuclear missiles in Cuba, the end of the Cold War itself. Prediction may be getting better, but it can never be perfect.

Even if it were, it would confront intelligence's other basic problem: how to get statesmen and generals to accept information that they do not like. This problem – which may be called the Cassandra complex – is as old as mankind. Pharaoh slew the bearers of ill tidings. Stalin ignored dozens of warnings that Germany was about to attack his country. Hitler swept aerial photographs from his desk when that indisputable evidence showed overwhelming enemy strength. The problem was clearly seen by Germany's pre-World War I Chief of the General Staff, Field Marshal Count Alfred von Schlieffen:

The higher commander generally makes himself a picture of friend and foe, in the painting of which personal wishes provide the main elements. If incoming reports appear to correspond with this picture, they are accepted with satisfaction. If they contradict it, they are discarded as entirely false.[35]

When Secretary of the Navy Frank Knox was told that the Japanese had bombed Pearl Harbor, he said, 'My God, this can't be true. This must mean the Philippines.'

This condition, which psychologists call denial, is not limited to military or political affairs. People often reject reality. An investor does not want to hear all the reasons that a project may fail. A husband insists that his wife, coming home late, is faithful. As Rod Stewart sings (or croaks), 'Still I look to find a reason to believe.' Shakespeare long ago set out the phenomenon in *Troilus and Cressida*: 'yet there is a credence in my heart,/An esperance so obstinately strong,/That doth invert th' attest of eyes and ears.'[36] Edna St. Vincent Millay asked her readers to 'Pity me that the heart is slow to learn/What the swift mind beholds at every turn.'[37] And a little boy begged of Shoeless Joe Jackson, upon hearing that he had betrayed a World Series for money, 'Say it ain't so, Joe.'

Can this very human disposition be changed? Can the facts and logic of intelligence ever overcome wishful thinking? At present, they can only do so if the feelings are not deep-seated. If the consequence of facing the facts is too painful, the evidence will be ignored, suppressed, denied.

Where then is intelligence headed? A new factor darkens its future. Intelligence owes its success to the growth of verbal information. But as the cheap, miniaturized, unbreakable systems of cryptography proliferate, they will increasingly deprive cryptanalysts of the opportunities that data banks and the Internet and cellular telephones offer. As America's first modern cryptologist, Herbert O. Yardley, said in 1929 of AT&T's unbreakable one-time tape cipher machine, 'Sooner or later all governments, all wireless companies, will adopt some such system. And when they do, cryptography [codebreaking], as a profession, will die.'[38] The amputation of intelligence's right arm will cripple it. Just how serious this problem will be, however, no one yet knows.

But other factors counter this one and brighten the promise of intelligence. People see the advantage of permitting intelligence – in both its politico-military and its personal meanings – to rule emotion. They know that reason usually produces better solutions to problems than feelings do. This explains the growth of psychotherapy. This is part of what St. Paul meant in his profound statement to the Corinthians: 'For we cannot do anything against the truth, but only for the truth.'[39] This is why intelligence is so useful. As David Hume wrote in *An Enquiry Concerning Human Understanding*: 'We may observe, in every art or profession, even those which most concern life or action, that a spirit of accuracy, however acquired, carries all of them nearer to that perfection.' He calls this 'the genius of philosophy,' making intelligence a branch of that high domain, and says that from this accuracy, 'the politician will acquire greater foresight and subtlety, [...] and the general more regularity in his discipline, and more caution in his plans and operations.'[40] Reason also produces technologies superior to those stemming from tradition or charisma, and these technologies allow their societies to dominate others. Witness the subjugation of China at the turn of the twentieth century, the conquest of Native Americans, Europeans' grab of colonies in Africa, the rise of post-Perry Japan. The very establishment of intelligence agencies indicates a tendency toward greater reliance on facts and logic. The trend's success suggests that it will continue.

Accentuating this trend is an aspect of man's nature. Aristotle opened his *Metaphysics* by stating, 'All men by nature desire to know.' The first man is the first example. Adam wanted to know what God told him he should not know, so he ate of the fruit of the tree of the knowledge of good and evil, and thus brought death, sin, and sorrow into the world. Like Adam, like Faust, every intelligence service strives to realize what the evangelist Luke put into words: 'For nothing is hid that shall not be made manifest, nor anything secret that shall not be known and come to light.'[41] None achieves it. 'It will always be a certain tragedy of every intelligence service,' wrote the first head of Germany's post-World War I spy service, 'that even the best results will always lag behind the clients' desires.'[42] But the absence of perfection does not keep leaders, political and military, from letting intelligence serve them, any more than they let the absence of perfection keep them from using any other resource they have. Evidently they believe intelligence's results are worth its costs. Should they always follow its sometimes implied advice? No. It may be wrong. It is almost certainly incomplete. But they should at least take it into account.

The universal tendency toward least effort[43] will further enlarge intelligence. As an optimizer of resources, intelligence saves money by reducing the need to buy military equipment – though, as merely an auxiliary element of war, it cannot reduce this need to zero. Since it is integral to the defense, intelligence will be increasingly seen as essential to nonaggressive nations. Yet it must improve its predictions and must convince leaders to accept them if it is to fully realize its potential.

That potential spreads beyond the military. Like the benefactions of knowledge, of which it is a form, the benefactions of intelligence touch all humankind. In war, intelligence shortens the struggle, sparing gold and blood. In peace, it reduces uncertainty and so relaxes tensions among states, helping to stabilize the international system. These are the ultimate human goods of intelligence; these are the ways this servant of war brings peace to man.

Notes

1 Sir Alan Gardiner, *The Kadesh Inscriptions of Ramesses II* (Oxford: OUP 1960) pp. 28–30.
2 Numbers 13.
3 Sun Tzu, *The Art of War*, trans. Samuel Griffith (Oxford: Clarendon Press 1963) xiii: 3 (p. 144).
4 *Kautilya's Arthasastra*, trans. R. Shamasastry, 4th edn (Mysore: Sri Raghuveer 1951) p. 637 (Bk IX, Ch. 1).

5 *The Gallic War*, ii.17.

6 The most detailed description of the workings of a black chamber, that of Austria, is by Harald Hubatschke in his 1973 dissertation for the University of Vienna, 'Ferdinand Prantner (Pseudonym Leo Wolfram), 1817–1871: Die Anfänge des Politischen Romans sowie die Geschichte der Briefspionage und des Geheimen Chiffredienstes in Österreich', at pp. 1269–1328, 1445–60.

7 Livy XXVII.xliii.1–8; *Cambridge Ancient History* rev. edn (Cambridge: CUP 1961–71), Vol. 8, pp. 91–6.

8 It is important to understand that it is the source that matters, not the method of acquisition or the method of transmission. The presence of tanks can be ascertained by a spy and reported by telephone, but this information remains physical intelligence. Enemy plans can likewise be discovered by a spy and relayed by a photograph, but the information is verbal intelligence. The difference rests solely on the objects of intelligence themselves. Verbal objects mean verbal intelligence; nonverbal, physical intelligence.

9 The Allies beat the Germans in World War II primarily because of their overwhelming material superiority. See John Ellis, *Brute Force: Allied Tactics and Strategy in the Second World War* (London: André Deutsch 1990).

10 Of course physical intelligence can also reveal enemy capabilities, but doing so requires an inference – an extra step. Verbal intelligence reveals intentions without that mediation. To simplify, I have reduced this to the preceding formulation.

11 Germany, Reichsarchiv, *Der Weltkrieg: 1914 bis 1918* (Berlin: Mittler & Sohn), Vol. 2 (1925), pp. 136–7, 351; Max Hoffman, *War Diaries and Other Papers*, trans. Eric Sutton (London: Martin Secker 1929), Vol. 2, pp. 265–7, 332.

12 David Kahn, 'Edward Bell and His Zimmermann Telegram Memoranda,' *Intelligence and National Security* 14/3 (Autumn 1999) pp. 143–59, contains the latest scholarship.

13 R. E. Priestly, *The Signal Service in the European War of 1914 to 1918 (France)* (London 1921) p. 106.

14 David Kahn, *Hitler's Spies: German Military Intelligence in World War II* (New York: Macmillan 1978) p. 418.

15 United States, Congress, Joint Committee on the Investigation of the Pearl Harbor Attack, *Pearl Harbor Attack*, Hearings, 79th Congress (Washington, DC: Government Printing Office 1946) Vol. 3, p. 1133.

16 Ibid.

17 Ibid.

18 Eisenhower to Menzies, 12 July 1945, Folder MELO-MEN (Misc.), Box 77 Principal File, Pre-Presidential Papers 1916–52, Dwight D. Eisenhower Library, Abilene, Kansas.

19 This means successful intelligence, not perfect intelligence. Failed intelligence is not considered here as intelligence.

20 Carl von Clausewitz, *On War*, trans. Michael Howard and Peter Paret (Princeton, NJ: Princeton University Press 1976) p. 210.

21 Ibid. pp. 117, 102–3.

22 I have discussed this more fully in 'Clausewitz and Intelligence,' *The Journal of Strategic Studies* 9/2 and 3 (June/Sept. 1985) pp. 117–26, later republished as *Clausewitz and Modern Strategy*, ed. Michael I. Handel (London and Portland, OR: Frank Cass 1986).

23 David Henderson, *The Art of Reconnaissance* (New York: Dutton 1907) p. 2.

24 David Kahn, 'The Defense of Osuga, 1942', *Aerospace Historian* 28 (Winter 1981) pp. 242–50.

25 Germany, Bundesarchiv-Militärarchiv, 24. Infanterie Divison, 22006/11, 19 Jan. 1942, 22006/1, 21 Jan. 1942; 50. Infanterie Division, 22985/4, 20 and 21 Jan. 1942; Hans von Tettau und Kurt Versock, *Geschichte der 24. Infanterie-Division*

1933–1945 (Stolberg, Germany: Kameradschaftsring der ehemaligen 24. Infanterie-Divison 1956) p. 24.

26 Clausewitz (note 20) p. 357.

27 Ibid. p. 198.

28 Ibid. p. 524.

29 Barry R. Posen, *The Sources of Military Doctrine: France, Britain, and Germany Between the World Wars* (Ithaca, NY: Cornell UP 1984) pp. 47–8.

30 As Hamlet says, in a line generals would love, 'We defy augury' (*Hamlet*, V.ii.23). For intelligence does not always resolve problems, does not always eliminate uncertainty. In a footnote above, I excluded failed intelligence from any definition of intelligence. But partial or erroneous information certainly exists in the world, and is sometimes included in the term 'intelligence.' It is in this sense that one German officer explained that what went through generals' minds when the intelligence officer approached was 'Here comes the intelligence officer with his same old stuff. But I'm going to do it like this anyway.' See Kahn, *Hitler's Spies* (note 14) p. 415. Hamlet also maintained that uncertainty weakens determination. Referring to man's incomplete knowledge (in this case of death), he soliloquized, using 'conscience' to mean thinking, 'Thus conscience does make cowards of us all,/And thus the native hue of resolution/Is sicklied o'er with the pale cast of thought,/And enterprises of great pith and moment/With this regard their currents turn awry,/And lose the name of action.' (*Hamlet*, III.i.83–8).

31 George J. A. O'Toole, 'Kahn's Law: A Universal Principle of Intelligence,' *International Journal of Intelligence and CounterIntelligence*, 4 (Spring 1990) pp. 39–46.

32 This is developed at greater length in *Hitler's Spies* (note 14) pp. 528–31.

33 John Wilson Croker, *The Croker Papers*, ed. Louis J. Jennings (London: John Murray 1884), Vol. 3, p. 275.

34 Clausewitz (note 20) p. 586.

35 Generalfeldmarschall Graf Alfred von Schlieffen, *Gesammelte Schriften* (Berlin: Mittler 1913), Vol. 1, p. 188.

36 *Troilus and Cressida*, V.ii.120–2.

37 Edna St. Vincent Millay, 'Pity Me Not,' a sonnet.

38 Herbert O. Yardley, *The American Black Chamber* (Indianapolis, IN: Bobbs-Merrill 1931), p. 365.

39 2 Corinthians 13:8.

40 David Hume, *An Enquiry Concerning Human Understanding* (1777) §1:4.

41 Luke 8:17.

42 Fritz Gempp, 'Geheimer Nachrichtendienst und Spionageabwehr des Heeres.' Im Auftrag der Abwehrabteilung des Reichswehrministeriums (US National Archives microfilm T-77, Rolls 1438–1440, 1442, 1507–1509), II:7:162.

43 George K. Zipf, *Human Behavior and the Principle of Least Effort* (Cambridge, MA: Addison-Wesley 1949).

2 Intelligence as risk shifting

*Michael Warner**

The French, advis'd by good intelligence
Of this most dreadful preparation,
Shake in their fear; and with pale policy
Seek to divert the English purposes.
 Shakespeare, *King Henry V*, Act 2, scene 1

Say from whence
You owe this strange intelligence
Shakespeare again, *Macbeth*, Act 1, scene 3

O, Where hath our intelligence been drunk?
Where hath it slept?
            and again, *King John*, Act 4, scene 2

Shakespeare left us no play set in an intelligence agency. Surely he had his reasons for missing such an opportunity, but had he seized it, he might well have written another tragedy. Certainly his characterizations of intelligence (good, strange, and drunk) would sound fresh to modern practitioners, familiar with concerns over the reliability of sources and complaints about warning dogs that failed to bark. Indeed, that familiarity points to a remarkable stability in this corner of English usage since Shakespeare's time. The word 'intelligence' seems to mean roughly what it meant in 1600; we still use it to denote (among other things) a counselor to sovereign power, a type of privileged information, and the activity of acquiring, producing, and possibly acting on that information.

Yet even a cursory survey of the ways that officials and scholars define the term 'intelligence' quickly exposes a problem. Their definitions tend to group themselves in one of two camps. One follows twentieth-century American military nomenclature and holds that intelligence is information for decisionmakers; it is anything from any source that helps a leader decide what to do about an adversary.[1] The second camp defines intelligence as warfare by quieter means.[2] In sum, one definition emphasizes intelligence as something that informs decisionmaking; the second sees it as clandestine activity that assists both the informing and execution of decisions.[3]

This impasse has frustrated attempts to explain why nations build the intelligence systems they do. Without a clear sense of the dependent variable in the equation, we find it difficult to understand which independent factors cause and affect intelligence phenomena. Nonetheless, this impasse may be abating. Seemingly contradictory definitions of intelligence in recent years unwittingly yield an interesting area of agreement. This chapter builds on them to offer a speculative explanation of what intelligence is for sovereign powers, and thereby to establish the characteristics of that dependent variable.

New approaches

Arguments over the definition of intelligence resemble perhaps nothing so much as a trademark dispute. Each camp admits that 'intelligence' commonly signifies private information or knowledge while also serving as a synonym for espionage. In essence, the debate among scholars and even practitioners is over which of these two senses gets to be called the right one. Recent insights on both shores of the Atlantic have illuminated different aspects of our notions of intelligence that collectively suggest a way to transcend this debate.

The place to begin is with an understanding that is not new. Several scholars over the last generation have explained in passing that intelligence helps decisionmakers cope with the ambiguity of a chaotic world.[4] Kristan J. Wheaton and Michael T. Beerbower of Mercyhurst College follow them and seek to add system to this notion. In their view, intelligence is 'a process, focused externally and using information from all available sources, that is designed to reduce the level of uncertainty for a decisionmaker.' For Wheaton and Beerbower, 'intelligence is more than information'. It is 'something that happens, not something that just is'; intelligence is made to happen for the benefit of decisionmakers, who want assurance or 'certainty regarding the future', but who often have to accept 'something [else] that is based in fact but allows them to plan.' The purpose of the intelligence professional 'should be to reduce the decisionmaker's level of uncertainty to the minimum possible.'[5]

Jennifer E. Sims of Georgetown University looks to international relations theory (specifically to Neo-Realism) for insights that emphasize intelligence as an inevitable facet of inter-state competition. Intelligence, for her, is not simply the process of serving senior officials; it is more accurately the interaction between decisionmakers and their subordinates that allows them collectively to best their opponents. Her fundamental understanding of intelligence (as 'the collection, analysis, and dissemination of information on behalf of national security decision makers') echoes American military usage and resembles Wheaton and Beerbower's position, but contains a key difference.[6] Sims emphasizes that intelligence enhances the effectiveness of decisions made by actors who are working in opposition to other actors (who may well be employing their own intelligence assets). 'If politics involves the competition for power, "intelligence" may be best understood as a process by which competitors improve their decision-making relative to their opponents.'[7] It provides 'decision advantage', either by making our decisions better, or theirs worse. 'Success is not getting everything right, it is getting enough right to beat the other side.' Intelligence methods can foster decision advantage by stealing opponents' secrets, or adulterating the information available to rivals – or both.[8]

Reading Sims in conjunction with Wheaton and Beerbower generates two insights that would seem faithful to both of their definitions. First, intelligence is not a product or something tangible; it is a process, a service, or an interaction between leaders and their subordinates that provides a sort of additive to enhance decisionmaking. Second, that decisionmaking is done to further a collective interest in improving (for the leader and his followers) an environment that is fluid and even dangerous. Wheaton and Beerbower, as well as Sims, emphasize that such a milieu makes certainty impossible. The best that can be hoped for is the attainment of greater assurance on the part of the decisionmaker (Wheaton and Beerbower), or the making of 'better' decisions than the adversary makes (Sims).

Can these insights be combined, especially in a way that transcends a problem that dogs them both: the difficulty of distinguishing intelligence *per se* from other all the organized activities that help leaders make decisions about their environments?[9] After all, much of what any government does on a day-to-day basis is in fact action to gain or hold decision advantage, or to reduce uncertainty. Routine diplomatic ties, for instance, would seem to do both. Yet we do not commonly call such activities 'intelligence'. How then to understand intelligence and how it differs from other functions that serve decisionmakers?

Several British authors have explored a path around this latter dilemma. Len Scott of the University of Wales, for instance, has noticed that 'much contemporary study of intelligence concerns how knowledge is accepted, generated and used.' While granting the value of such a focus on knowledge, Scott has nonetheless found insight in 'a different focus that treats secrecy, rather than knowledge, as an organizing theme.' The boundary to put around intelligence is the secrecy of it. After all, many things serve decision, but intelligence is the one that serves it in ways unseen by adversaries.[10]

Peter Gill (University of Salford) and Mark Phythian (University of Leicester) echo Scott in their recognition that secrecy is a key to understanding the essence of intelligence. They begin from Michel Foucault's concept of *surveillance*: a term to denote the interrelationship between knowledge and power as they are sought and employed by states (though Gill and Phythian also see non-state actors wielding *surveillance*). States as such are understood to pursue power and knowledge to protect and advance their interests, however defined; the notion of *surveillance* sets aside questions of whether leaders have properly understood those interests. For states, intelligence is that special mode of *surveillance* that deals with security, secrecy, and resistance. It comprises

> the range of activities – from planning to information collection to analysis and dissemination – conducted in secret, and aimed at maintaining or enhancing relative security by providing forewarning of threats in a manner

that allows for the timely implementation of a preventive policy or strategy, including, where deemed desirable, covert activities.[11]

Intelligence thus does more than provide forewarning; often it serves to establish conditions in which threats are eliminated or kept at a distance. Gill and Phythian agree with Scott that secrecy is perhaps the salient feature that delineates intelligence from related fields, like diplomacy and security. In addition, they (like Wheaton and Beerbower) incorporate a temporal dimension that helps to distinguish intelligence from other 'information management activities' like scholarship, and from 'forensic' forms of law enforcement. Their definition insists that intelligence serves the future; that its utility lies in prediction or intervention to alter adversaries' moves do or to minimize the harm they do.

Several insights follow from Gill and Phythian's definition. It cannot be regarded as dispositive, unfortunately, due to its focus on the defensive uses of intelligence (to wit, its emphasis on 'security' can be seen to neglect the offensive or aggressive uses of intelligence to gain or expand power). This qualification notwithstanding, viewing intelligence as Gill and Phythian do from the vantage point of the concept of *surveillance* both complements Sims' emphasis on competition and bridges the illusory domestic/foreign divide; intelligence is both a domestic bulwark and a foreign policy tool, protecting regimes from internal as well as external threats.[12] In addition, Gill and Phythian, like Sims, understand that the security purchased via intelligence is only a relative one, depending as it does on an adversary's reactions (and vice versa). Thus they place intelligence in a dynamic system of complex actions and reactions, where cause and effect cannot be clearly discerned, where impacts may be disproportionate to intentions, and were consequences can rarely be calibrated.

By coincidence or not, these ideas of intelligence move via different paths into a common intellectual space. Wheaton and Beerbower provide one insight with their notion that intelligence is a tool to reduce ambiguity. Sims introduces the concept of relative decision advantage. Gill and Phythian more firmly place intelligence in the context of our understanding of states as such, and more closely follow the historical record by including 'covert activities' under the term. They also rightly emphasize that secrecy is a logical dividing line between intelligence activities per se and the myriad other (and vital) informational, administrative, and operational tasks that states routinely perform. All three definitions, moreover, suggest that intelligence helps leaders act to control or improve their environment. These definitions would all seem to agree, whether explicitly or implicitly, that intelligence is a service or interaction with leaders to help them manage, by privileged means, the hazards they face in dealing with rival powers.

Risk and uncertainty for sovereign actors

The insight sparked by these definitions leads to another: that the locus of intelligence is not the state as such but rather *sovereignty*. The late Adda Bozeman observed in 1988 that the state 'is not the decisive working unit in intelligence studies.' Rather, she noted, '[i]nternationally relevant decision making ... emanates increasingly from scattered, often dissimulated command posts of liberation fronts, terrorist brigades, provisional governments, or international Communist parties.'[13] These actors and the true states with which they interact may be understood as *sovereignties*, distinguishable and divided from another by their competitive willingness to use violence to hold or gain control over people, resources, and territory. That employment of lethal force raises the competition to a level qualitatively different than the rivalry between corporations or sports teams that might steal one another's secrets. Indeed, its lethality compels leaders to act in dangerous and provocative ways to protect themselves and ultimately to prevail. It remains now to explain the dynamics of the competition between sovereignties – the *why* of what they do when they perform intelligence activities.

Let us begin with the commonplace that life is a struggle against scarcity and danger that continually demands choices among competing alternative uses of resources and their associated hazards. Gamblers and amateur scientists long ago devised ways to calculate risk: it equals the impact of a potential event multiplied by its probability of occurrence. With the rise of the social sciences, however, scholars applied insights from several disciplines to study the ways in which people and organizations choose among alternatives and strive to mitigate their potential effects (and to maximize the opportunities they offer). Economist Frank Knight's classic *Risk, Uncertainty, and Profit* (1921) introduced the distinction between *risk* proper ('a known chance', for which we can calculate probabilities) and *uncertainty* (for which we can predict neither an outcome nor its probability). Businesses manage risk through insurance or diversification, Knight explained, but uncertainty is a different thing altogether, and riding its waves requires leadership and entrepreneurial skill. Profit is the economic premium paid for such leadership.[14]

Frank Knight's insights helped guide a veritable literature that now spans several disciplines, from sociology to finance to organizational theory and strategic planning.[15] His original distinction between risk and uncertainty has blurred somewhat after decades of experimentation, but it holds explanatory power even for scholars who over the last generation have examined how 'social organization fundamentally *creates* and *distributes* risk and uncertainty', in the words of the late Yale sociologist Albert J. Reiss, Jr.[16] Proponents of this newer, 'constructivist' approach to the 'social construction of risk' acknowledge that our growing knowledge of risk and uncertainty has aided the spread of the economic and social conditions that we call modern life. Yet they also note that institutions (and even components of institutions) not infrequently – wittingly or not – 'manage' risk and uncertainty in ways that can harm themselves and others.

Private and public institutions have their ways of doing so. They study competitors, clients, and customers, and their techniques can get elaborate. Indeed, the analyses they employ can look remarkably like the work that intelligence officers perform. The entire 'intelligence cycle' can be found here: requirements, collection, processing, analysis, and dissemination to decisionmakers for action. Its linear pathologies abide here as well: organizations can choke on surfeits of data, and internal problems can distort information flows and result in poor choices.[17] Another way they 'do something with' risk and uncertainty is to transfer them to the less organized or less powerful – with or without their knowledge and consent.[18] Bankruptcy proceedings, for instance, have been studied as a process of 'risk shifting', a strategy for the stronger actors and creditors to unload risk and uncertainty on their weaker counterparts.[19]

Such insights, however, have had little impact on intelligence studies. This would seem a missed opportunity, because sovereign powers in their role as international actors routinely 'distribute' the burdens of risk and uncertainty. Indeed, managing risk and uncertainty through collective burden sharing is the essence of what sovereignties try to do; they make each subject pay something for the upkeep of armies and governments, and pledge to defend those subjects in return. Governments as such can be thought of as specialized instruments for gauging and refining risk and uncertainty in order to protect and advance their interests.

Managing risk and uncertainty becomes more craft than science, however, when applied to international relations. Sovereign actors have always dealt with an ever-shifting cloud of neighbors, rivals, allies, and enemies, and sought advantages in doing so. Every actor around them, every relationship, and every circumstance is in some sense unique and unrepeatable. In relations between sovereignties there are no practice rounds, and no leader or counselor can personally observe enough 'outcomes' to gauge probabilities and outcomes rightly all the time. The penalties for a mistaken judgment, moreover, can be fatal. How then can a leader tell risk from uncertainty, and assess the probabilities and impacts of alternative decisions?

Sovereign leaders face this dilemma every single day. They cope in several ways. Sovereignties frequently distribute risk and uncertainty 'outward', sharing it with allies, who are those other sovereignties that opt to carry some of 'our' risk because they want 'us' to bear some of theirs. But sovereignties possess another way of sharing risk and uncertainty that it is unique to them. They can impose it on others via the threat of violence against a victim or adversary that resists, or persists.

This insight is hardly new. Sun Tzu's *The Art of War*, for instance, is essentially a treatise on imposing risk and uncertainty on one's enemies. *The Art of War* teaches a ruler to conquer by lowering his own risks and raising his opponent's. War, after all, is less about fighting than about winning: 'What is of supreme importance in war is to attack the enemy's strategy. Next best is to disrupt his alliances. The next best is to attack his army. The worst policy is to attack cities.'[20] Confound your enemy or steal his allies, counsels Sun Tzu, and you may never have to fight because your opponent perceives war as too dangerous, and either capitulates or refrains from provocations.

Since the penalty for a sovereign's failure can be death to himself and everyone around him, he seeks any means he can to slant the odds in his favor.

Intelligence helps him manage risk and uncertainty – and to shift them to his rivals via espionage and subterfuge. Sun Tzu therefore had much to say about spies. Indeed, *The Art of War*'s rhetorical climax is its final chapter, on their use; it concludes that spies and their operations 'are essential in war; upon them the army depends to make its every move.' Spies can fortify a commander with 'foreknowledge', cloak his plans and movements, and harry his enemy in secret, dividing his councils and even killing his officers.[21] To put this in modern management terms, spies help a sovereign to shift uncertainty into risk, to assess and manage probabilities, and to mitigate hazards. Convince an enemy that he cannot win, counsels Sun Tzu. If he insists on fighting, then beat him by the safest means. He may not know that his risk calculus has changed, or he may see that it has shifted but not understand how. The ability to force that dilemma on an enemy by stealth is the genius of intelligence.

Reflecting on Sun Tzu and another ancient author helps us understand how intelligence was and is performed by 'non-states'. After all, *The Art of War* long predates our Westphalian era, and it describes sovereignties rather than states. Sun Tzu wrote of principalities, clans, and even armed bands that acquired and defended territory by force. Sovereignties like these had enemies within their territories as well as without; indeed, their intelligence organs surely spent as much effort (or more) monitoring seditious ministers, pretenders to the throne, and local malcontents, as they did in deploying or catching spies for work abroad. The Indian author Kautilya, a near-contemporary of Sun Tzu, wrote extensively on the domestic uses of intelligence. Spies perform many functions for the wise and ruthless king in Kautilya's monumental treatise on governance, the *Arthasastra*. Mostly, however, spies form a variegated internal secret service that watches everyone and stifles plots and dissensions by fair means and foul.[22]

Both Sun Tzu and Kautilya insisted that sovereigns were not blind puppets of Fate, or the gods, or the stars – especially if they employed spies. The wise king, according to Sun Tzu, mastered the dangers around him through sagacity and 'foreknowledge', which 'cannot be obtained from spirits, nor from gods, nor by analogy with past events, nor from [astrological] calculations. It must be obtained from men who know the enemy situation.'[23] For Kautilya, spies not only brought information, they magnified the king's authority by making him seem god-like in his command of news and events, and they could even pretend to be gods themselves, hiding inside idols and speaking prophecies to frighten and mislead the king's enemies.[24]

These ancient reflections on the employment of intelligence by proto-states implicitly suggest why it is that entities that are not states nonetheless employ intelligence in many ways identical to the ways in which modern states employ it. By the dawn of the modern era 500 years ago, we see in the historical record (and, more compellingly, in Shakespeare's plays) a mix of these sovereign powers alongside the newly emerging states that would soon, at least in the West, tame and supplant the feudal baronies and virtually monopolize the legitimate use of force. These new states organized their intelligence functions in their own ways, as we shall see, but the missions that they gave their secret operatives – to understand and influence rivals and enemies – would endure across cultures and epochs.

In contests between sovereign powers, the life-or-death nature of the competition has convinced many a leader to pay high premiums for 'foreknowledge' and the capability to manipulate rivals in secret. Assuming that his intelligence operatives have rendered him good information and efficient operations (always a big assumption to begin with), the price that a sovereign pays for intelligence is accounted in three ways: direct costs ('a few hundred pieces of gold', to quote Sun Tzu), inefficiency, and the hazards of disclosure. The first is straightforward and need not be discussed in detail here. The second type of cost, however, merits a closer look.

In dealing with opponents, most sovereignties surely prefer 'overt' methods of understanding or influencing an adversary. Secrecy, after all, is not cheap; it imposes costs in terms of resources and speed, which is why overt means are generally preferred to secret ones. Police work, diplomacy, or direct military action are instruments of power that are, in many (or most) cases, *comparatively* safer, faster, and surer (and thus more efficient) than the clandestine sources and methods employed by intelligence operatives. Anything done in secret, by contrast, imposes a degree of 'friction' on a sovereignty's decisionmaking processes. Many of the means that intelligence employs are only effective if they are secret; once spotted, they are extinguished by their target and cease to be of any use for mitigating risks – their loss might even leave their master blind. Sovereignties thus employ secret efforts against neighbors and rivals who lie at or beyond the reach of their juridical powers. In other words, intelligence operations (as opposed to passive analysis) are typically employed where law enforcement is impotent or overmatched, where open diplomacy cannot be employed (or requires help from supplementary activities conducted clandestinely), and where overt military power would be counterproductive (or even suicidal) to unsheathe.

The third cost of intelligence can be called 'the hazards of disclosure'. No sovereign, however powerful, wishes to provoke hostilities with the wrong enemy or at an inopportune time. Here is the dilemma for intelligence. Since time immemorial, those who catch a spy put him death, and regard his employer with suspicion or even enmity. Thus intelligence work is rarely a purely 'informational' activity; anything other than the most passive and innocuous ways of gathering data is in fact a conscious act of policy. Indeed, the action of scrutinizing a competitor, especially by secret means, can itself be viewed as a hostile act; it may even magnify risk and uncertainty by provoking a rival into taking dangerous responses. Intelligence operations are inherently risky and unreliable – and thus tend to be used only where 'doing something' seems better than the alternative: doing nothing. 'For where the lion's skin will not reach', noted Plutarch, 'you must patch it out with the fox's.'[25]

Understanding this point helps in transcending a side debate over the relationship between 'intelligence' and 'operations'. Some advocates of the 'intelligence = information for decision' formulation insist that intelligence, as a form of information, only *informs* policy – and never *executes* it – and thus must be kept separated from what they see as the corrupting influence of 'policy execution'.[26] In contrast, Len Scott and others count activities like covert action and clandestine diplomacy as well within the fold of 'secret intelligence services'.[27] Scott *et al.* would seem to have the better of this argument.

To sum up, intelligence promises to help sovereignties to manage risk and uncertainty by reducing the probability of setbacks, controlling their impact, or both. In practical terms, intelligence informs and executes decision; it helps to make leaders more confident that they understand the hazards surrounding them and their regimes; and it helps them to reassure their friends, to make them new allies, and to confuse or injure their enemies. Intelligence is thus one of the crafts for redistributing risks from one's own regime and allies to one's competitors, and it is that particular craft that does so by stealth, so that an opponent may know that his own risk calculus has changed – but may not know why it has.

Yet intelligence itself is a risky means of shifting risks; risky in the sense that its product is often of ambiguous value, and its fragile methods can provoke angry and dangerous responses from their targets. 'Delicate indeed! Truly delicate!', says Sun Tzu.[28] This helps us to understand how and why such secret means are likely to be employed: i.e., in situations when the stakes are high, the price of failure is steep, and other means are also being used – but (so far) without decisive results. That is why fragile and risky means are employed – because the more obvious and reliable ones are not fully working. This would explain why sovereigns choose *not* to employ intelligence in certain situations or against particular rivals, or why they might employ only specific intelligence means at their disposal, leaving others in reserve for emergencies.

National and departmental

In Shakespeare's time the modern state was barely emerging. Kings and princes vied for power with proud nobles and their private armies. That changed, even before the Industrial Revolution, with the advent of the modern era; indeed, the supplanting of feudal sovereignties by true states and national governments is a characteristic of modernity *per se*. In overawing the barons and monopolizing (and rationalizing) the functions of statecraft, the new nations minimized the power of the all-purpose but geographically localized 'public services' that the barons had provided. Modern nations moreover grew, in the Industrial Revolution, to depend on new, nationally distributed but functionally specialized professions (especially military officer cadres, diplomatic corps, civil servants, and police).

Intelligence changed at the same time, and it is important to understand how. The barons, being minor sovereignties theoretically owing allegiance to a central authority, had surely employed their own spies to watch over rivals and local discontent. As the national state supplanted the barons and came to rely on the new professionals and their bureaus, however, the state's intelligence needs (and consequently its arrangements for meeting those needs) did not necessarily grow fewer or simpler. Each of the professional functions serving the regime required information for its own purposes. A commander preparing for war or a minister executing his sovereign's mandate needed information, however gained, to help him make decisions in defending and implementing national policies. Beginning in the nineteenth century, these ministries, at least in the major powers, built up their own ways of gaining and using privileged information.[29] For the sovereign who made national policies, or his proconsuls in direct contact with their sovereign's enemies, however, intelligence remained what it had always been: an instrument to help him understand *and influence* others who were sources of risk and uncertainty for the state.

As the great powers compartmentalized foreign and domestic policies, military and diplomatic functions, and the 'departmental' and 'national' focuses of their intelligence elements, they created the divergence between the two definitions of intelligence noted above. To wit, the intelligence services of the military, diplomatic, and security functions focused on collecting and processing information that served their own ministers and officials first, and attended to the intelligence needs of the national leadership only secondarily. The twentieth century saw, in several larger states, a recognition that the autonomous but subnational intelligence services of the military, diplomatic, and law enforcement bureaus now had to be coordinated to serve larger, national interests. That has been a difficult task, and it remains incomplete.

This bifurcation of national and departmental intelligence functions in the early twentieth century also explains the development of the rival intelligence definitions. In short, the 'intelligence-equals-information' camp has described intelligence for ministers, the 'silent warfare' camp has described it for sovereigns, and the two sides have talked past one another. How this process developed is important for understanding modern intelligence systems.

The United States represents an almost Petri dish-perfect sample of this evolution in action. America came late to the processes of modernization in the intelligence realm, but once they began in the US Government they operated with great speed and clarity in ways that the European powers had already experienced. Thus their path can be seen as somewhat representative of the development of modern intelligence systems outside the United States as well. In addition, the way in which the US Army's intelligence function became doctrinally self-aware and confident in its understanding coincidentally helps to explain the origin of the two definitional camps noted above. This point is important enough to merit a brief historical detour.

The emergence and evolution of 'military intelligence' in the US Army began in earnest with the experience of World War I. The Army had no fixed definition or doctrine for intelligence work before 1917; military intelligence had led an impoverished and precarious existence in the rudimentary General Staff, and the Army's standard reference on the topic (Arthur Wagner's *Service of Security and Information*, reprinted fifteen times between 1893 and 1916) still included chapters on cavalry patrolling and Indian scouts. Commanders of the American Expeditionary Force (AEF) learned swiftly under British and French tutelage, however, adopting the French army's staff system, borrowing intelligence regulations and doctrine from the British, and building a G-2 of its own, called the Military Intelligence Division (MID), in Gen. John J. Pershing's General Headquarters. MID grew rapidly into a capable service, functioning rather like a modern Combatant Command's J-2 to provide 'theater-level' intelligence services. Pershing's officers brought this experience back to Washington when the war ended, reforming the War Department's own MID along the lines they had utilized in France.[30]

The US Army's modern understanding of military intelligence flowed directly from this World War I experience. In 1918 a West Point instructor of tactics named Edward Farrow had felt no need to define intelligence per se in his reference work *A Dictionary of Military Terms*, though he conceded that a commander in drafting a 'Plan of Action' had need of 'information of the enemy and of the terrain obtained by reconnaissance' – preferably undertaken by the commander himself.[31] By 1924 a former AEF G-2 lieutenant colonel named William Sweeney had taken this thought (or something similar) and fashioned of it an understanding of military intelligence, which he defined as

> information of the enemy or military forces of the enemy that has been collected, tabulated, measured as to its possible value, classified as to its reliability and made ready for use in military plans or operations. It is to be emphasized that information of the enemy does not become Military Intelligence until it has been subjected to these processes.

Sweeney, it bears noting, employed 'intelligence' and 'military intelligence' interchangeably.[32] Constructivist scholars of our time might also observe that Sweeney was positing a rationalistic, linear knowledge cycle that failed to account for the ongoing and cyclical internal discussions about investigative processes and theoretical foundations that always accompany the investigation process.[33] Indeed, by drawing a bright line between intelligence and operations, Sweeney had perhaps overlooked the fact that intelligence activities *are* operations in that they act upon an active adversary, and that all operations stir and change the perceptions and data that are the stuff of intelligence. But these are later considerations. Sweeney may not have decisively influenced War Department thinking on intelligence in the inter-war years, but he was certainly representative of its tenor.

By the onset of World War II, the US Army had firmly reached two conclusions about military intelligence. First, it is essentially information – it is whatever form or manner of knowledge might help a commander make plans and decisions. Second, intelligence is *not* operations, which are the province of a separate (and more powerful) division of the commander's staff and the staffs of his lieutenants in the 'line' components. The Army's self-awareness of its intelligence function at this time can be seen in two examples of doctrine written just before America's entry into the war. In 1940, War Department Basic Field Manual FM 30–5 ('Military Intelligence') called military intelligence evaluated and interpreted information concerning a possible or actual enemy, or theater of operations, together with the conclusions drawn therefrom. It includes information concerning enemy capabilities or possible lines of action open to him, as well as all that relates to the territory controlled by him or subject to his influence.

A year later, the authors of the Army's field manual on 'Operations' (FM 100–5) harked back more directly to Sweeney and through him to Farrow, defining military intelligence in this roundabout fashion:

Information of the enemy and of the terrain over which operations are to be conducted must be evaluated to determine its probable accuracy, and, together with other items of information, it must be interpreted to determine its probable significance. It then becomes military intelligence. From adequate and timely military intelligence the commander is able to draw logical conclusions concerning enemy lines of action. Military intelligence is thus an essential factor in the estimate of the situation and in the conduct of subsequent operations.[34]

These two, parallel definitions of military intelligence would soon be edited into a form that more or less endures to this day. In February 1946, just after World War II had ended, the Army issued a new FM 30–5, with an updated definition: 'Military intelligence is evaluated and interpreted information concerning a possible or actual enemy, or theater of operations including terrain and weather, together with the conclusions drawn therefrom.'

Almost simultaneously, a team of Army and Navy officers, under the aegis of the Joint Chiefs of Staff, convened to standardize terms across the armed services. The Army's definition for military intelligence carried the day, minus its adjective and its emphasis on terrain (both of which to Navy ears sounded too specifically Army-related), becoming almost by default the basis for a broader definition in the Joint Chiefs' new *Joint Dictionary of Military Terms for Army-Navy Use*. Issued in May 1946, that tome defined intelligence first and foremost as 'evaluated and interpreted information of value to the armed forces concerning a possible or actual enemy, or theater of operations.'

The *Joint Dictionary*'s definition stuck. By the time of its Second Revision in April 1953, it had reached essentially its modern form:

[I]ntelligence – The product resulting from the collection, evaluation, analysis, integration and interpretation of all available information which concerns one or more aspects of foreign nations or of areas of operations and which is immediately or potentially significant to planning.

For the sake of comparison, the latest edition of the Joint Chiefs' *Dictionary of Military and Associated Terms* calls intelligence

The product resulting from the collection, processing, integration, evaluation, analysis, and interpretation of available information concerning foreign nations, hostile or potentially hostile forces or elements, or areas of actual or potential operations. The term is also applied to the activity which results in the product and to the organizations engaged in such activities.[35]

The Joint Chiefs' definition of intelligence, which had grown from something originally tailored to denote intelligence for US Army field commanders, soon started turning up as an quasi-authoritative definition of the intelligence function for the nation as a whole. A blue-ribbon study panel chartered by Congress and known to history as the Clark Task Force in June 1955 cited the *Joint Dictionary* as a guidepost used in developing its own understanding of the American intelligence system.[36] Since then the *Joint Dictionary* definition or some derivative of it has been cited countless times – at least by American authors – as the standard definition of intelligence. By 1986 it had become essentially the standard NATO definition as well.[37]

Ironically, the Clark Task Force had studied only a portion of the US intelligence system. President Dwight Eisenhower had not wanted General Clark and his colleagues to examine clandestine operations run by the Central Intelligence Agency – a significant, national-level component of the American intelligence system. The CIA's covert activities were instead surveyed concurrently by a separate team led by Lt. Gen. James H. Doolittle (USAFR), whose famous report thus assumed (and found) intelligence of a very different sort from that sponsored by the Pentagon.[38]

This detour through definitions suggests that the evolution of usage mirrors the evolution of systems, and vice versa. The twentieth century saw, in several larger states, the maturation of large and quasi-autonomous 'departmental' intelligence establishments (like that of the US Army) constructed to serve the purposes of ministers and commanders. It also witnessed a recognition (again shared in several nations) that these sub-national intelligence services assembled by the military, diplomatic, and law enforcement ministries had to be coordinated to serve larger, national interests. That has been a difficult task, and it remains unfinished. The United States illustrates the point (albeit on an exaggerated scale). Its departmental intelligence services were confederated in a national system in 1946 nominally overseen by a Director of Central Intelligence (revised in 2004 to place the oversight role under a Director of National Intelligence).

The larger point here is that the twentieth century did not see the invention of a new form of intelligence for sovereigns. That remains what it has been since the time of Sun Tzu, though now it is fulfilled (in part, and in some larger states) through sophisticated ministries and departments. Nonetheless, the overall lack of historical understanding of how these national and departmental components created and adapted conscious notions of their purposes (and doctrine to support them) has exacerbated a 'national' and 'departmental' divide, especially in the United States. The US intelligence system has seen long-running debates over who controls scarce 'national' collection assets (which by definition cannot be acquired and employed in numbers sufficient to satisfy both national and departmental demands simultaneously). We need a wider and deeper understanding of how other components of the American intelligence system conceived of what they were doing, and, more important, how the intelligence components and systems of other nations developed their own definitions and doctrine.[39] In our American example above, we saw how one service fashioned a concept of intelligence for its own needs that, through an almost accidental process, came to be interpreted by some as authoritative for *national* missions as well. This is not the place to explain how the resulting confusion over the nature and limits of intelligence has or has not affected decisionmaking for the US Intelligence Community. It is appropriate, however, to note that usage matters, because definitions and systems influence one other – for good and for ill. Definitions make it easier, or harder, to understand what is, and what can be.

What does it all mean?

> The King hath note of all that they intend,
> By interception which they dream not of.
>   Shakespeare, *Henry V*, Act 2, scene 2

Shakespeare used the word 'intelligence' in his tragedies, and thus we should not be surprised that fundamental questions still confront us. Intelligence is a service function for security, diplomacy, and war; we would expect it to influence them all; but is it more, or less, important for policy success? Is it a force for stability and peace, or for instability, tyranny, and war? Answering such a question from the historical record is surprisingly difficult. What we can say without hesitation is that, for most of history, intelligence has been used to oppress, and to maintain systems of oppression. Sovereignties, moreover, may poorly understand the risks around them, and actually heighten them by premature or promiscuous uses of intelligence methods.

Understanding intelligence as one means for a sovereignty to gauge risk and uncertainty (and shift them quietly to adversaries) seems fitting in light of this unhappy historical record. Secrets and secret activities would seem inevitable in any system of competition between sovereignties. Do the stability and assurance gained by individual states through the employment of secret means outweigh the collectively greater tension and conflict in the overall system that intelligence can abet? Intelligence provides real (and illusory) benefits to leaders and imposes costs on their regimes, as we noted above, and grasping these phenomena as benefits and costs provides a template for determining when, and where, and what price has been paid for what measure of security and effectiveness, how that price been measured and born, and what price is too high. Studying such questions can also help us see how to organize intelligence, and how to determine which activities should be its alone, and which others can and should be done if at all by other (non-secretive) organs of government. Intelligence, if we understand it, might some day be more clearly a force for good. If intelligence is ever to be a force for good, then it must be studied. We can bet that, if we remain ignorant of it, intelligence will certainly be a force for ill.

Notes

* The opinions in this essay are his alone and do not represent the official views of the ODNI or any other entity of the US Government.

1 The Department of Defense *Dictionary of Military and Associated Terms*, for instance, calls intelligence

> The product resulting from the collection, processing, integration, evaluation, analysis, and interpretation of available information concerning foreign countries or areas. Nations, hostile or potentially hostile forces or elements, or areas of actual or potential operations. The term is also applied to the activity which results in the product and to the organizations engaged in such activity.
>
> Joint Publication 1–02, 12 April 2001, amended through 4 March 2008

2 James Der Derian called intelligence 'the continuation of war by the clandestine interference of one power into the affairs of another.' *Antidiplomacy: Spies, Terror, Speed, and War* (Cambridge, MA: Blackwell, 1992), p. 21.

3 Michael Warner, 'Wanted: A Definition of Intelligence', *Studies in Intelligence* 46:3 (2002). Abram N. Shulsky and Gary J. Schmitt also compare the 'traditional' and 'American' views, in *Silent Warfare: Understanding the World of Intelligence* (Washington, DC: Potomac Books, 2002 [1991]), pp. 159–67.

4 For example, Richard K. Betts states that 'It is the role of intelligence to extract certainty from uncertainty and to facilitate coherent decision in an incoherent environment. (In a certain and coherent environment there is less need for intelligence.)' 'Analysis, War, and Decision: Why Intelligence Failures Are Inevitable', *World Politics* 31 (October 1978), p. 69, and in this volume, p. 93. Wheaton and Beerbower cite with approval Robert M. Clark's finding that 'Intelligence is about reducing uncertainty in conflict by obtaining information that the opponent in a conflict wishes to deny you. Intelligence is information to act upon and take action from.' See *Intelligence Analysis: A Target-centric Approach* (Washington, DC: Congressional Quarterly Press, 2004), p. 13.

5 Kristan J. Wheaton and Michael T. Beerbower, 'Towards a New Definition of Intelligence', *Stanford Law & Policy Review* 17:2 (2006), p. 329.

6 Jennifer E. Sims, 'Understanding Friends and Enemies: The Context for American Intelligence Reform', in Jennifer E. Sims and Burton Gerber, eds., *Transforming US Intelligence* (Washington, DC: Georgetown University Press, 2005), pp. 15–16.

7 Jennifer E. Sims, 'Smart Realism: A Theory of Intelligence in International Politics', delivered at the International Studies Association conference in Chicago, 28 February 2007, p. 2.

8 Office of the Director of National Intelligence (Strategy, Plans, and Policy Office), 'Exploring the Doctrinal Principle of Integration', proceedings of a workshop in Washington, DC, 12 October 2006, p. 19. The quoted passage paraphrases a remark by Dr. Sims at that event.

9 Wilhelm Agrell amplifies this point in his critique of the widespread 'application of the *concept* or perhaps the *illusion* of intelligence analysis to various information-processing activities that are not really intelligence in the professional sense of the word.' See 'When Everything Is Intelligence – Nothing Is Intelligence', Central Intelligence Agency (Sherman Kent Center for Intelligence Analysis), Occasional Papers: Volume 1, Number 4, 2002, p. 4. Emphases in the original.

10 Len Scott, 'Secret Intelligence, Covert Action and Clandestine Diplomacy', in L.V. Scott and P.D. Jackson, eds., *Understanding Intelligence in the Twenty-First Century: Journeys in Shadows* (London: Routledge, 2004), pp. 162–3.

11 Peter Gill and Mark Phythian, *Intelligence in an Insecure World* (Cambridge, UK: Polity, 2006), pp. 7, 29.

12 The foreign/domestic divide can be found in the thinking of many authors. Gill and Phythian (*Intelligence in an Insecure World*, p. 29) cite Sherman Kent's seminal treatise on analysis, *Strategic Intelligence for American World Policy* (Princeton, NJ: Princeton University Press, 1949), p. 3.

13 Adda Bozeman, 'Political Intelligence in Non-Western Societies: Suggestions for Comparative Research', in Roy Godson, ed., *Comparing Foreign Intelligence: The US, the USSR, the UK, and the Third World* (Washington, DC: Pergamon-Brassey's, 1988), p. 135.

14 Frank H. Knight, *Risk, Uncertainty, and Profit* (New York: Sentry Press, 1964 [1921]), pp. 19, 230–2.

15 Michael Fitzsimmons recently noted, for instance, that rational choice theorists still dispute the border between risk and uncertainty. See 'The Problem of Uncertainty in Strategic Planning', *Survival* 48 (Winter 2006–7), p. 134.

16 Albert J. Reiss, Jr., in James F. Short, Jr., and Lee Clarke, eds., *Organizations, Uncertainties, and Risk* (Boulder, CO: Westview, 1992), pp. 299–307. Emphases in the original.

17 Tomas Hellstrom and Merle Jacob, *Policy Uncertainty and Risk: Conceptual Developments and Approaches* (Norwell, MA: Kluwer Academic Publishers, 2001), pp. 37–46. See also Reiss, 'The Institutionalization of Risk', in Short and Clarke, eds., *Organizations, Uncertainties, and Risk*, p. 305.

18 James F. Short, Jr., and Lee Clarke, 'Social Organization and Risk', in Short and Clarke, eds., *Organizations, Uncertainties, and Risk*, pp. 309, 321.

19 Kevin J. Delaney, 'Shifting Risk in Business Bankruptcy', in ibid., p. 115.

20 This passage comes from Samuel B. Griffith's translation *Sun Tzu: The Art of War* (New York: Oxford University Press, 1971 [1963]) see Chapter III, on Offensive Strategy.

21 Michael Warner, 'The Divine Skein: Sun Tzu on Intelligence', *Intelligence and National Security* 17:4 (August 2006).

22 The *Arthasastra* has several English translations. R. Shamasastry's 1915 version is available online; see *Kautilya's Arthasastra* (Mysore: Sri Raghuveer 1956), particularly Book I, Chapter 12, at www.mssu.edu/projectsouthasia/history/primarydocs/Arthashastra/index.htm4. A recent translation is by L.N. Rangarajan ed., *Kautilya: The Arthashastra* (New Delhi, India: Penguin Classics, 1992).

23 *The Art of War*, 13:4.

24 *Arthasastra*, Book XIII, Chapters 1 and 2.

25 'Lysander', in Plutarch's *Lives of the Noble Greeks and Romans*. John Dryden, trans. (New York: Modern Library).

26 William W. Kennedy, for example, laments that

> the intelligence function has been besmirched by activities that have nothing to do with intelligence, as such.... To the extent to which they have any legitimacy at all, such functions are properly described under the heading of political and military 'operations.' The mischief lies in failing to maintain a distinct organizational boundary. In short, intelligence is one thing: operations are something else.

See *Intelligence Warfare: Penetrating the Secret World of Today's Advanced Technology Conflict* (New York: Crescent Books, 1987), p. 16.

27 Len Scott, 'Secret Intelligence, Covert Action and Clandestine Diplomacy', in Scott and Jackson, *Understanding Intelligence in the Twenty-First Century*, pp. 162–3.

28 *The Art of War*, 13:14.

29 Peter Jackson, 'Historical Reflections on the Uses and Limits of Intelligence', in Peter Jackson and Jennifer Siegel, eds., *Intelligence and Statecraft: The Use and Limits of Intelligence in International Society* (Westport, CT: Praeger, 2005), pp. 19–26. See also Olivier Forcade and Sebastien Laurent, *Secrets d'Etat: Pouvoir et renseignement dans le monde contemorain* (Paris: Armand Colin, 2005), pp. 53–64.

30 Bruce W. Bidwell, *History of the Development of the Military Intelligence Division, Department of the Army General Staff: 1775–1941* (Frederick, MD: University Publications of America, 1986). pp. 250–6. See also Jim Beach, 'Origins of the Special Intelligence Relationship? Anglo-American Intelligence Co-operation on the Western Front, 1917–18', *Intelligence and National Security* 22: 2 (April 2007), pp. 231–9.

31 Edward S. Farrow, *A Dictionary of Military Terms* (New York: Thomas Y. Crowell, 1918).

32 Walter C. Sweeney, *Military Intelligence: A New Weapon in War* (New York: Frederick A. Stokes, 1924), pp. 13–15.

33 See, for an example of this hypothetical critique, Hellstrom and Jacob, *Policy Uncertainty and Risk*, p. 36.

34 War Department Field Manual FM 100–5, 'Operations', 22 May 1941.

35 Joint Publication 1–02, 12 April 2001, amended through 4 March 2008.

36 The Clark Task Force, so named for its chairman, Gen. Mark Clark (USA ret.), contributed to the work of the second Commission on Organization of the Executive Branch of the Government, which former President Herbert Hoover chaired. The *Joint Dictionary*'s definition appeared on p. 26 of the Task Force's public report, issued in June 1955. For more on the Clark Task Force, see Michael Warner and J. Kenneth McDonald, *US Intelligence Community Reform Studies since 1947* (Washington: Central Intelligence Agency, 2005), pp. 15–17.

37 See Joint Chiefs of Staff, *Department of Defense Dictionary of Military and Associated Terms*, JCS Publication 1, 1 January 1986. The NATO definition is listed below its American counterpart and reads as follows:

> 1. The product resulting from the processing of information concerning foreign countries, hostile or potentially hostile forces or elements, or areas of actual or potential operations. The term is also applied to an activity which results in the product and to the organizations engaged in such activity.

38 Warner and McDonald, *US Intelligence Community Reform Studies*, pp. 15–16.

39 I examine the variables in the intelligence systems of the United States and other nations at more length in 'Building a Theory of Intelligence Systems', in Greg Treverton, ed., *Mapping the State of Research on Intelligence* (Cambridge: Cambridge University Press, forthcoming in 2008).

3 Sketches for a theory of strategic intelligence

Loch K. Johnson

Intelligence theory and human nature

For too long the role of strategic intelligence in world affairs has stood in the shadows of traditional research on international relations.[1] What a pity that it takes events like Pearl Harbor in 1941, the domestic spy scandals of 1975 (Operations Chaos and COINTELPRO), the terrorist attacks of 9/11, and the faulty estimates on Iraqi weapons of mass destruction (WMDs) in 2002 to underscore the importance of this subject. At last, though, the public – and perhaps even hide-bound IR theorists – seem ready to acknowledge the need to understand the hidden side of foreign and security policy.

Good theory should have explanatory power, parsimony, and the attribute of falsifiability. A starting point on the road to a theory of intelligence is the consideration of basic human nature. The human species is motivated by two dominant motivations. The first is fundamental: the survival instinct. The second is also important: the desire for prosperity, or what economists refer to as "maximizing personal economic utility." Survival is associated with a fear of life-threatening dangers; prosperity is associated with a sense of ambition. In both instances, information is vital to success. At the level of national decision-making, government leaders seek information about both threats and opportunities.

A certain amount of the information sought by governments is hidden by rivals. Thus, rather than rely on the Library of Congress as a sole reservoir of knowledge, the government of the United States has established intelligence agencies to ferret out the secret information the nation needs to enhance its security and its quest for political and economic opportunities. Moreover, nations seek to shield their own secrets from the prying eyes of adversaries; therefore, they create a counterintelligence service. As well, nations look for whatever edge they can find against competitors and, thus, are drawn to covert action – secret methods, such as unattributable propaganda, for shaping history to one's advantage. Here are the three key intelligence missions: collection-and-analysis (the heart and soul of intelligence), along with counterintelligence and covert action (subsidiary intelligence activities).[2] Further, democracies have a related interest in the protection of citizens against the possible abuse of power by their own secret agencies. This function of government is usually referred to as intelligence accountability or "oversight."

A theory of intelligence will need to take into account each of these considerations. In these early stages of theory development, we should not be dogmatic about approaches and methodologies; we must insist only on the accuracy of data, the clarity of definitions, and a rigor in hypothesis-testing. Braithwaite defines a theory as a "set of hypotheses which form a deductive system."[3] The greatest initial challenge for intelligence theory-builders will be to fashion a set of coherent, testable hypotheses that takes into account the fundamentals examined in this volume.

Propositions for a theory of intelligence

Central to a theory of intelligence will be a set of core propositions about intelligence organizations and activities. The purpose of the propositions will be to impart a sense of the dimensions that a theoretical framework must encompass, particularly with respect to one of the most central concerns in the field: When is intelligence likely to succeed or fail? Most of the propositions presented below are from the American experience, although they are framed in such a manner as to invite testing in other societies as well.

The intelligence cycle

Any theory of strategic intelligence must take into account the so-called intelligence cycle, a model that describes the sequence of activities that carries intelligence from the initial planning stages all the way to a finished product ready for the consideration of decision-makers at the highest councils of government. The cycle consists of five phases: planning and direction, collection, processing, production and analysis, and dissemination. Each phase involves behavior that must be taken into account by intelligence theorists.

In reality, the intelligence "cycle" is less a series of smoothly integrated phases, one leading to another, than a complex matrix of back-and-forth interactions among intelligence officers (the "producers" of intelligence) and the policy officials they serve (the "consumers"). This matrix – a composite of intricate human and bureaucratic relationships – is characterized by interruptions, midcourse corrections, and multiple feedback loops.[4] Even though reductionist, the concept of a cycle remains analytically useful, drawing attention to the *process* of intelligence. Conceptually, the cycle provides at least a rough approximation of how intelligence professionals think of their work.

Planning and direction

In the first phase of the cycle, intelligence managers and policy officials must decide what information should be gathered from around the world. The goal is to provide the president and other top leaders with knowledge – ideally, foreknowledge – helpful for their policy deliberations, on the assumption that facts and insight are better than ignorance in charting a nation's course. Two features of this phase are particularly notable: the choices made regarding the scope of collection, and the distortions that arise as a result of flawed communications between intelligence professionals and decision-makers about the kinds of information that need to be gathered.

Scope refers to the breadth of intelligence requirements assigned ("tasked") by policy officials. Large, affluent nations with extensive international commercial transactions, widespread political alliances, and worldwide rivalries are likely to want a far-flung network of intelligence capabilities, in the form of assets on the ground (human intelligence or "humint") as well as machines that can listen and watch from land, sea, or air (technical intelligence or "techint"). This breadth of coverage allows, for those fortunate nations (or groups) that can afford the luxury, a good chance of acquiring valuable "heads up" information about world affairs – information that lies far beyond the reach of the less affluent.

During the first Persian Gulf War (1991), the United States enjoyed a remarkable battlefield transparency in Kuwait and Iraq, thanks to its extensive fleet of surveillance satellites and reconnaissance aircraft, while the Iraqi forces gathered information largely on foot in the deserts – not much differently than their ancestors had 1,000 years before. Superior battlefield awareness explains much of the dramatically disproportionate casualty rates that favored the United States during this conflict, by a ratio of some 1,000:1 (or as high as 3,000:1, according to some estimates).

In a paradox, though, well-heeled nations with behemoth intelligence services are also likely to suffer acute information failures. Because of the breadth of their concerns, not even expenditures in the range of $44 billion a year (the widely reported figure for US intelligence in recent years) can offer transparency for the entire globe – especially when adversaries choose to conceal their activities and weapons systems in deep underground caverns, with camouflage, deception operations, or by other methods of stealth to avoid the prying lens of satellite cameras orbiting above them. In contrast, the intelligence objectives of smaller nations are much more limited, say, to a single region or even a solitary enemy. Some may view this comparison as self-evident, but contrasts among the intelligence systems of different countries are often made without taking into account the differences in their funding abilities and targeting needs.

Consider the intelligence focus of the United States compared to New Zealand, or even Israel in its hostile setting. America's intelligence failures have been extensive in recent years, including the terrorist attacks on the World Trade Center and the Pentagon in 2001; the mistaken targeting of the Chinese embassy in Belgrade in 1999; the inability to find the Iraqi leader Saddam Hussein in 1991, the Somali warlord Mohamed Farah Aidid in 1993, or the al-Qaeda leader Osama Bin Laden; and a series of miscalculations related to Iraq in 2002–6, among them flawed estimates on: the likelihood of WMDs in the nation; the expected greeting of American soldiers as liberators; the strength of the insurgency; and, generally, the ease of establishing a democracy in Iraq to replace the Hussein dictatorship. While New Zealand may falter from time to time in its efforts to track illegal Japanese fishing for tuna in its seas, and Israel may suffer the more hurtful inability to anticipate the next suicide bombing, the tasks of the intelligence services in these smaller nations are much more focused and manageable. As a result, the percentage rate of success for a given list of targets is apt to be better for them and other small nations with a concentrated threat assessment than for a wide-ranging great power. The more focused nations, however, are not immune from major failures either, as when Israel reeled from the rash and unanticipated Egyptian attack on its territory at the onset of the Yom Kippur War in 1973.

In the form of a general proposition (P), we can say:

> *P1: The more affluent and globally oriented a nation, the larger its agenda of intelligence objectives and its institutional apparatus for espionage, and the more likely its chances for a large number of successes as a result of this saturated world coverage.*

> *P2: Yet, paradoxically, the more affluent and globally oriented a nation, the more it is apt to experience intelligence failures as well, because its broader global objectives cannot be completely satisfied in a world that is too large and complex for full transparency.*

At the very beginning of the intelligence cycle, a basic difficulty often arises that distorts all the subsequent phrases: policy officials are unable or unwilling to articulate clearly their intelligence priorities. This happens for a number of reasons. Some officials do not know much about intelligence as a cluster of agencies and resource; therefore, they fail to use intelligence properly. "I need information about Burundi," for example, is too diffuse an intelligence request to elicit the precise data required to address a specific policy problem that may have arisen with respect to that African nation.

Or, in some cases, policy officials believe that their own personal sources of information (whether the *New York Times*, club colleagues, or visits with foreign dignitaries) are better and more timely than the sometimes sluggish responses of large bureaucracies like the Central Intelligence Agency (CIA) or its fifteen companion agencies that comprise the US "intelligence community." In other cases, the policy officials simply may be too harried to find time for consultation with intelligence professionals. Moreover, at times, those in high office wear ideological blinders that cause them to eschew any information that fails to fit comfortably into their policy preconceptions, or that contradicts a decision or speech they made just last week. Thus:

> *P3: To the extent that policy-makers focus and clearly delineate their foreign policy objectives and informational needs, the chances for intelligence collection successes correspondingly rise.*

Collection

Once a nation's leaders communicate to intelligence managers their intelligence requirements, however imperfectly, this tasking must be translated by the managers – in the United States, the DNI and subordinates – into specific targets: nations (civilized or rogue), terrorist cells, drug cartels, multinational corporations, individuals ("bad actors," like Bin Laden), or some topic of interest, say, the efficiencies of North Korean rocket fuel. The managers must decide, too, what methods ("tradecraft") will be used to gather the information, from human to technical.

Every new administration in Washington, DC, goes through a "threat assessment" exercise in which a list of priority intelligence targets is developed. The list, a tableau of friends and foes, is subject to rapid alterations as fresh threats suddenly arise: Burundi today, Rwanda tomorrow, Somalia the next day – each of these particular crises ("flavors of the month") unanticipated by the Clinton Administration. Mostly, though, the list is fairly easy to predict and, even though the threat-list is highly classified, the average undergraduate history or political science major could guess what they might be, since – logically enough – the list concentrates on those nations and groups that can cause the most harm to the United States or its interests abroad. Russia, one suspects, is likely to have a reserved spot on the list despite the end of the Cold War, for the simple reason that its missiles can still destroy the United States in thirty minutes, in the witch fire of a nuclear holocaust. This capability draws one's attention. Other nations known or suspected to have nuclear, biological, and chemical (NBC) weapons, coupled with a history of tension with the United States, are duly accorded prominence in the threat assessment. So are non-state groups that blow up American embassies, ships, and military barracks, or fly planes into skyscrapers and government buildings. Generally, then:

P4. The greater a perceived threat (especially military, but also political and economic) from a nation or group, the larger the amount of intelligence collection resources that will be dedicated to that threat – although unanticipated crises frequently divert resources from the formal threat-assessment list.

Even affluent nations will fall short of achieving perfect global transparency, since the world is large and the number of adversaries and competitors is copious. The intelligence services of affluent nations with superpower aspirations are likely to pursue a policy of "global presence," that is, having permanent assets in most of the world's countries. Poorer nations have to settle for a more limited reach, relying on a policy of "global surge," that is, sending assets temporarily into a new area of the world that has flared up (to the extent a nation has an interest there and intelligence assets to deploy). Even nations with extensive intelligence capabilities must sometimes resort to a policy of global surge, as when Rwanda and Somalia (where the United States had few assets) suddenly became important during the Clinton Administration, then just as quickly faded off its radar screen. Global presence is a more effective approach, because it allows a nation to establish over time a reliable ring of spies and to put into place technical surveillance hardware. In contrast, sending assets and their CIA handlers into a location unfamiliar to them, moving satellites into new orbits, and flying reconnaissance airplanes over unfamiliar territory is more difficult – and often too late and ineffectual.

> *P5. Affluent nations with great power aspirations will seek an intelligence policy of global presence; but, since resources are finite even for the affluent, they will rely on a global-surge capacity for regions of the world that are considered less threatening.*

Affluent and poor nations alike, but especially the latter, will have gaps in their collection capabilities. These gaps may be a result of failing to properly identify emerging interests or threats, or because of an insufficient dedication of intelligence resources to the region in question. Even if the threat assessment has been accurate and the financial resources are available to purchase the desired intelligence coverage, the nation may have too shallow a pool of potential operational officers who can live abroad in the places of interest and effectively recruit indigenous assets. Successful recruitment requires the development of rapport between an operations officer and a potential agent, which in turns means the operations officer must speak the local language and know something about its culture and mores. The United States has a dearth of operational officers with Middle East or South Asia training and, in order to track and eradicate terrorist cells in those regions, its intelligence agencies have sought recently to bolster the hiring of American citizens with the requisite skills and knowledge – notably young Arab-American citizens with Middle Eastern and South Asian language abilities and unquestioned loyalty to the United States.

> *P6. A nation – however affluent – may suffer from a lack of well-trained operational officers with strong foreign language and cultural skills and, as a result, will have limited success in recruiting assets in some parts of the world.*

As for tradecraft, technical means of spying has a special magic within the inner sanctums of Washington, DC, where decisions are made about questions of intelligence funding and *modus operandi*. When intelligence briefers visit Capitol Hill, the National Security Council (NSC), or budget analysts in the Office of Budget and Management, they come equipped with impressive photographs of foreign military bases snapped by US satellite cameras (imagery intelligence or "imint"); with fascinating design renderings of the shiny, metallic "birds" (satellites) themselves, orbiting deep in space; still more photographs of Unmanned Aerial Vehicles (UAVs, like the low-altitude, rocket-equipped Predator used in the anti-Taliban war in Afghanistan and to hunt down suspected terrorists in places like Yemen); and accounts of successful telephone and email intercepts, compliments of the technical services of the CIA and the National Security Agency (NSA). Audiences are impressed, as well they should be. During the Cold War, America's intelligence machines watched the military activities of the Soviets, allowing great confidence in Washington that Moscow's armies, bombers, and missiles could not be used against the United States in a successful surprise attack – an invaluable, reassuring capability both then and since.

In comparison, human intelligence comes across in briefings as less flashy. The identities of assets must be kept a tight secret; no slide shows to dazzle legislators. And even though humint has scored some remarkable successes, as when documents given to the CIA by the Soviet asset Col. Oleg Penkovsky helped to detect the presence of the Soviet missiles in Cuba in 1962. Nonetheless, during the Cuban missile crisis few of the hundreds of humint reports provided accurate information about the presence of Soviet missiles.[5] Worse still, throughout the Cold War, indigenous counterintelligence services managed to double every CIA asset recruited in Cuba and in East Germany, sending them back against the United States to sow disinformation.[6]

So in the inner councils of intelligence planning and funding, techint has drawn more favorable attention; machines neither lie nor come down with the flu and miss two weeks of work. Yet satellites and reconnaissance aircraft have their weaknesses. Imagery intelligence is most effective in identifying the *capabilities* of an adversary (how many missiles he has), rather than his *intentions* (will he fire those missiles and, if so, exactly when?). Cameras on satellites and UAVs cannot see through mud hut roofs, into the labyrinth of caves where al-Qaeda terrorists hide in Afghanistan and Pakistan, or inside the vast caverns in North Korea where the government of P'yongyang is thought to be constructing atomic bombs. This takes a human agent. In addition, nations and terrorist cells have become more clever at avoiding the scrutiny of satellite cameras, timing their orbits and using camouflage to conceal activities on the ground.[7]

The NSA's signals intelligence ("sigint," such as telephone taps) can be an important techint source of information about intentions, although adversaries will sometimes use this channel for disinformation and sigint intercepts must be handled gingerly. Moreover, adversaries have begun to use more advanced encoding devices for their telephone, fax, and email communications, and have turned to new technologies (like fiber-optic telephone cables) that – for the time being at least – greatly complicate the challenge of intercepting the communications of adversaries. These technical problems notwithstanding, intelligence "hardware" consistently attracts a preponderance of the total expenditures for spying.

Looking more broadly at intelligence resources, the US example suggests that national spending on espionage operations by affluent nations will occur at the rate of about 10 percent of the total defense budget – although data on this subject is hard to acquire, even in open societies.

P7. In the collection of intelligence, techint will be strongly emphasized by nations that can afford it, while poorer nations will be more restricted to humint.

P8. In the United States, intelligence activities attract resources at the rate of approximately 10 percent of the funds dedicated to overall defense spending.

Collection failures occur, too, because of a tendency by some nations to place their operational officers inside the limited confines of their embassies overseas, giving them an identity ("cover") as diplomats or military personnel – so-called "official cover" (OC). By all accounts, these spies are relatively easy for local counterintelligence services to identify. Moreover, case officers under official cover are often content to limit their information gathering to the embassy cocktail circuit. To some extent this approach succeeded for the United States during the Cold War, since Communist diplomats and spies attended embassy parties and could be courted, in hopes of recruiting them to the Western cause. Members of al-Qaeda, though, are unlikely to be part of the embassy cocktail circuit.

More successful than official cover for most countries has been the use of individual spies operating outside the embassy, employing non-official cover (thus, the acronym NOC, pronounced "knock"), say, as a bartender, oil rigger, or freelance writer. These assets blend into local society more effectively and, unlike government officials abroad, are not automatically suspected as spies – although, if caught in *lèse majesté*, they lack the protection of diplomatic immunity.

P9. Nations employing a system of non-official cover will have more success – although face greater danger – in gathering intelligence abroad than those that rely on official embassy cover.

Another method used by nations to fill in their intelligence gaps is the development of liaison relationships with foreign intelligence services.[8] The classic example is the espionage cooperation between the United States and the United Kingdom, which has led to a high level of information sharing.[9] The British benefit from America's imagery intelligence; and the United States is pleased to receive from its "cousins" information based on the UK's humint networks that extend back to the days of empire, along with the first-rate sigint and code-breaking abilities of Her Majesty's Secret Service. While a helpful addition to one's own collection activities, foreign intelligence liaison is treated cautiously; after all, the interests of one's allies are rarely fully congruent with one's own. Moreover, too much sharing might reveal technical tradecraft that might be used against the home nation one day by an erstwhile ally.

P10. Nations participate in intelligence sharing with allies, but only with a sense of ambivalence and caution, less than full cooperation, and a realization that today's partner can become tomorrow's competitor.

Affluent nations, or at least those that are militarily powerful and have global interests, have displayed since the end of the Cold War a willingness to move beyond narrow "realist" pursuits to define their interests more broadly as well, in terms of international humanitarian objectives. Intelligence tradecraft has been relied upon to provide evidence for international judicial proceedings against war criminals, as when US satellites detected the mass graves of Bosnians slaughtered by Serbian paramilitary troops in the 1990s or when an American-piloted U-2 aided searches conducted by the United Nations for weapons caches in Iraq following the first Persian Gulf War. Slowly, more international intelligence sharing is beginning to take place, not just between close allies but with less friendly countries, too, and even international organizations, as nations are drawn together by a common interest in thwarting terrorism and other world-wide threats.[10]

> *P11. As the world moves further toward globalization, intelligence services are increasingly targeting nations or other entities that threaten the common good and sharing information with a wider set of coalitions than usual, including international organizations.*

Processing

Information collected by intelligence agencies is often in a form decision-makers would find unreadable. The tiny black-and-white squiggles on satellite photographs require an expert eye to discern the specifications of weapons systems and other valuable data; the Farsi telephone transcript and the Chinese military manual must be translated into English. This process of conversion can be daunting. Satellite photos pour into the National Reconnaissance Office (NRO) in Virginia at the rate of over 400 a day. Moreover, hundreds of humint reports flow into the CIA each week and millions of sigint intercepts inundate the NSA. The processing of this information cannot keep up with the incoming volume and a majority of the data must be stored for later "mining," should its subject matter become of particular importance to policy-makers.

> *P12. In affluent nations that collect large volumes of secret information from around the world, the processing of this information will lag far behind ongoing collection, leading to an extensive warehousing of unexamined data.*

Analysis

Intelligence seldom speaks for itself; it must be interpreted by smart, well trained people who understand the country, group, or topic at question. This effort at analysis ("assessment," in British terminology) amounts to a search for insights into the meaning of "raw" or unevaluated data. Information collected overseas by intelligence assets and machines must be placed into the context of what the analyst knows or can learn from public sources, whether archives at the Library of Congress, the internet, or the *Washington Post*. Once the analyst mines the open-source intelligence ("osint"), he or she can then supplement this broad framework of understanding with "value-added" information derived from clandestine sources. In this sense, analysts proceed in the manner of academic researchers, with the additional step of integrating secret sources of data into their work. These extra "nuggets" may (or may not) add value to the findings that a university scholar could just as well provide to the president, based on a scouring of sources in the campus library or on the Web.

> *P13. The overwhelming percentage of information in intelligence reports comes from open-source searches, augmented by a small percentage of clandestinely derived data.*

Even though osint is predominant in intelligence reports, the secret add-ons are sometimes of great significance. On occasion, intelligence assets have access to data that newspaper correspondents, scholars, and others writing openly on world affairs simply do not have, especially with respect to terrorist organizations, the political and military machinations that occur within closed societies, and the specifications of weapons systems possessed by foreign regimes. Conversely, at times, writers in open organizations – like the media and the academy – may have information sources superior to the intelligence agencies, as when a journalist or a scholar has spent years in a foreign nation and knows its culture, language, and politics inside out (unlike most US intelligence officers, who rotate frequently from one country to another). That is why a blend of osint, techint, and humint – what the professionals call the "all-source fusion" of intelligence – is vital and can produce important synergies.

> *P14. A blend of the intelligence "ints" – osint, humint, techint – produces valuable "all-source" synergies, leading to a more complete understanding of world affairs.*

> *P15. Clandestine collection is particularly important for the information it provides about terrorist organizations and activities, events and conditions within closed regimes, and the inventory and capabilities of foreign weapons systems.*

In a similar fashion, interagency cooperation (not just a blending of all-source tradecraft inside separate agencies, a common phenomenon known as "stovepiping") usually leads to a more complete picture than a reliance for information on any single agency. In 1947, President Harry S. Truman created the CIA in response to the intelligence disaster at Pearl Harbor and the rising threat of the Soviet Union. The Pearl Harbor failure stemmed in part from a lack of coordination among US intelligence agencies. By establishing a *Central* Intelligence Agency, the President hoped to bring about better integration of the secret agencies and a more fused intelligence product – an agency that would assemble in a timely manner all of the pertinent information the White House needed to make an informed decision. The supposition was that many "heads" (agencies) could think better than one; and that their findings, including dissents, should be presented to policy officials in a coherent whole: one-stop shopping.

> *P16. In contrast to a loose confederation of secret agencies, a true intelligence community with strong institutional integration increases the chances of full reporting and, therefore, the delivery of more comprehensive information to policy officials.*

The integration of a nation's espionage resources requires, though, a strong intelligence manager with authority over spending and personnel for each secret agency in the government. Instead, in the United States, the intelligence "community" still remains a loose confederation – even though reformers made a concerted effort in 2004 to bring about greater integration under the new Office of the Director of National Intelligence.[11] Eight agencies are organizationally wired to have dual supervisors: the DNI and the Secretary of Defense (SecDef). The SecDef dominates this relationship, in part because of his higher status as a member of the NSC. Even more significant are the Pentagon's longstanding ties to the congressional defense and appropriations committees, which give the SecDef great leverage over intelligence spending on Capitol Hill (since funding decisions for intelligence are not made by the Intelligence Committees alone, but in conjunction with these other congressional panels).

Seven other agencies also enjoy the protection from control by the DNI, because they report as well to such luminaries as the Secretaries of State, Treasury, Energy, Homeland Security, and the Attorney General. The only agency over which the DNI supposedly has full authority is the independent CIA in Langley, Virginia. Yet even the CIA's component directorates have proven resistant to control from the DNI or even their own director.[12] This absence of institutional integration has interfered with the all-source intelligence fusion envisioned by President Truman.

> *P17. Generally, in the absence of full budget and appointment authority for a national intelligence chief over a nation's cluster of secret agencies, the institutions of the "community" will exhibit strong centrifugal forces that lessen the degree of interagency cooperation and comprehensive intelligence reporting to policy officials on both military and civilian topics.*

And an important corollary in the United States:

> *P18. A nation's defense secretary will attempt to dominate intelligence resources for military purposes, resisting efforts that might lead to greater civilian (DNI) control and better civilian-military analytic synergism.*

This tilting of intelligence toward military concerns (often known as support for military operations or SMO), understandable in time of war, has the effect in peace time of weakening support for diplomatic operations (SDO: political, economic, and cultural activities) that might help ward off the outbreak of war or terrorist attacks in the first place. In light of the DNI's difficulties in gaining formal control over all of the secret agencies in the United States, the Director is likely to seek less formal means for bringing about greater institutional integration, informational synergism, and a better balance between military and civilian intelligence priorities.

> *P19. To improve the degree of coordination and synergism in the intelligence community, as well as to bring about more of a civilian focus to intelligence priorities, DNIs will resort to the establishment of informal institutional arrangements, such as special integrative task forces and centers that draw together personnel on temporary assignment from throughout the community.*

Whether a president or a prime minister, a dictator or a king, leaders want to know about threats to their regimes, as well as opportunities for advancing their interests. Ideally, they hope to be forewarned by their intelligence services about every twist of fate. For better or worse, though, the gift of clairvoyance lies beyond the ken of human beings. Intelligence officers confront a world of secrets and mysteries. The secrets they may discover, with good tradecraft and some luck: information like the number of Chinese ICBMs (from NRO imagery) or the fallback position of Japanese automobile negotiators (from NSA intercepts). In contrast, mysteries – events and conditions that elude empirical verification – can defy the best efforts at collection and analysis. Who will succeed President Vladimir V. Putin in Russia? How long will al-Qaeda remain an attractive career option for disenchanted Muslims?

Even with respect to secrets, all the pieces of the jigsaw puzzle are rarely found; the analyst must try to discern the full picture from the few parts he or she may have acquired from osint, humint, and techint sources. Moreover, the fragmentary evidence is often filled with contradictions ("noise") rather than relevant and accurate information ("signals"), forcing the intelligence professional to make hard choices that move analysis into the realm of speculation.

The best an analyst can hope for is reasonably complete and reliable data about secrets, which must then be augmented with educated guesses about the world's mysteries. Given humankind's "incapacity to pierce the fog of the future,"[13] intelligence analysts will always be subject to failure – an existential reality of espionage.

> *P20. Since data about secrets are rarely complete and since humans are unable to predict the future (mysteries), intelligence analysts will fail from time to time in their efforts to anticipate and comprehend the meaning of world events.*

Good analysis depends on having a stable of well-educated minds – PhDs and others with special skills, whether individuals who speak Pashto and have a deep knowledge about the politics, economics, culture, and military affairs of places like Afghanistan, or scientists with insights into global disease surveillance or the effects of radiological bombs. Such training is expensive and not all nations have the luxury of drawing on the wellspring of a well-educated populace for the recruitment of intelligence analysts.

> *P21. The more affluent the nation and the more extensive its global interests, the greater its pool of potential intelligence recruits with advanced training in world affairs.*

Even affluent nations will have trouble tapping into expertise for the whole planet, especially nations like the United States and Australia that are removed by oceanic moats from close proximity to other continents with a diversity of languages and cultures. Relatively isolated nations, however well-heeled, will find themselves deficient in knowledge when it comes to many corners of the globe, especially territories that have not traditionally posed a threat to them. Such has been the case with the United States in its recent wars in the Middle East, the Balkans, and South Asia. This liability of distance from Europe and Asia (though often a blessing in the nation's earlier history) was mitigated to some extent with respect to the Soviet Union during the Cold War, as Washington poured massive intelligence resources into learning about the heavily-armed Eurasian power.

> *P22. Even affluent nations with global aspirations will display gaps in their collection and analytic capacities, until sufficient new resources are dedicated to overcome the knowledge deficits.*

Some critics have charged that intelligence analysis has been, all too often, an exercise in crying wolf. Military analysts are notorious for portraying their adversaries as ten feet tall, armed to the hilt, and ready to storm the home front at any moment – the "worst-case" scenario. "The armed services always want more funds than are available," notes intelligence scholar Harry Howe Ransom, "producing a tendency to exaggerate the threats to each of the armed services separately."[14] The end result of too many worse-case scenarios is a mushrooming intelligence budget based on groundless speculation about the supposed strength of an enemy.

> *P23. Military intelligence analysts are inclined to exaggerate the nature of the threat.*

Sometimes an analyst will succumb to a different temptation, known as "politicization," that is, putting a spin on or "cooking" intelligence to serve the political needs or beliefs of an intelligence manager or policy official – the danger of "intelligence to please."[15] Rejection of the honored intelligence tradition of objectivity is a cardinal sin of the profession. British intelligence scholar Michael Herman has observed that politicization is rampant in authoritarian regimes. "Despite its collection successes, Soviet intelligence selected and interpreted its material to suit the preconceptions of the regime of which it was an integral part," he writes, "and encouraged misleading estimates of Western intentions."[16] This happens from time to time in democratic regimes as well; but a stronger sense of professional ethics seems to tether intelligence analysts in open societies closer to the norm of objectivity.

P24. Intelligence can become politicized in democratic regimes, but because of the countering influence of professional integrity this happens far less frequently than in authoritarian regimes.

Dissemination

The best intelligence reporting in the world would not be worth much if it remained bottled up within the secret agencies; it must make its way into the hands of the men and women who make decisions, or become nothing more than a "self-licking ice cream cone."[17] This end stage is often the most difficult step in the intelligence cycle, because the information must have certain key attributes before it will be appreciated and used by policy officials.

First, the finished intelligence must be relevant. If it fails to help extinguish fires that have flared up in the policy-maker's in-box, it will be ignored. Incisive reporting on political elections in Estonia has its place; however, what the White House really wants to know these days is the location and the plans of al-Qaeda leaders, the nature of weaponry in Iraq and North Korea, and how Turkey and Iran are likely to respond to a full-blown civil war in Iraq. Timeliness is equally vital. One of the most disconcerting acronyms an analyst can see scrawled across his intelligence report is OBE – "overtaken by events." Further, the importance of accuracy is self-evident in the information business, and underscored vividly in the embarrassing US misidentification in 1999 of a suspected arms warehouse in Belgrade that turned out to be the Chinese Embassy. Once proven irrelevant, late, or unreliable, intelligence officers will find it much harder to gain access to decision councils in the future.

A corollary of this proposition has to do with intelligence liaison inside the Washington Beltway (as opposed to foreign intelligence liaison). If the secret agencies have liaison personnel assigned to the various policy departments in the government, these individuals can attend staff meetings and be a part of the informal hallway or watercooler discussions about policy concerns (what intelligence officers jokingly refer to as "rumint" or rumor intelligence). At the close of business, they can return to their respective agencies (CIA, NSA...) to inform analysts more confidently about what kind of information is most needed by policy-makers the next day.

P25. If intelligence is irrelevant to current crises, or if it is late or inaccurate, it will be ignored by policy officials, with a concomitant diminishment of access for intelligence officers to key decision councils.

P26. Intelligence agencies with a liaison team in a policy department or agency will be in a better position to provide relevant and timely information to inform policy deliberations.

Another important attribute of good intelligence reports is the degree to which they are "actionable," that is, contain specific information that allows policymakers to respond in a precise and concrete manner. What officials in the United States needed to know prior to the 9/11 attacks was when they would occur, how, and against what targets. Equipped with this information, law enforcement officials could have arrested the nineteen hijackers before they boarded the airplanes that struck New York City and Washington, DC. At the same time, it must be acknowledged that acquiring this level of specificity is very difficult, requiring close access to key decision-makers in the adversary's camp.

P27. The most valued intelligence provides actionable information, allowing policy officials to carry out operations with confidence, precision, and a high likelihood of success.

P28. The most difficult challenge of intelligence reporting is to include actionable information.

At the end of this intelligence pipeline, policy-makers have often been more responsible for "intelligence failures" than the secret agencies. Just as at the very beginning phase of planning and direction, office holders at this final stage sometimes display a distorting ideological or political bias against information that may be disagreeable. Or they may be too busy, or arrogant, to read intelligence reports. Speaking truth to power is notoriously difficult, because power often refuses to listen.

P29. Policy-makers will sometimes ignore intelligence reports, no matter how relevant, timely, and accurate, because the reports may fail to pass an ideological litmus test; or because policy-makers are too busy to read the reports, or deem themselves already sufficiently well informed.

Further, policy-makers may never act on important intelligence assessments, because the policy-makers have too many other concerns to consider or may decide that taking action might be too difficult or expensive. As early as 1995 (six years before the airplane attacks against the World Trade Center), the CIA's Counterterrorism Center was reporting to high-level policy-makers that "aerial terrorism seems likely at some point – filling an airplane with explosives and dive-bombing a target."[18] Yet nothing was done to improve airport security or to monitor individuals in the United States receiving flight training.[19]

> *P30. Policy-makers may ignore important intelligence findings, because acting on this information is perceived as too difficult or expensive, or because the information is crowded out by other pressing concerns.*

Covert action

Some intelligence agencies engage in the aggressive mission called covert action: the secret manipulation of events aboard to advance a nation's interests. Its primary forms are propaganda, political and economic action, and paramilitary operations. These clandestine activities can include, respectively, planting stories in foreign media outlets, bribing politicians overseas, sowing economic disruption, and providing weapons to a favored side in a civil war.

Presidents often find covert action an appealing "quiet option," less noisy than sending in the Marines and more apt to produce quick results than the glacial pace of diplomacy. For the United States, covert action led to rapid successes (at least over the short run) in Iran in 1953 and in Guatemala in 1954, where anti-US regimes were easily toppled and replaced with friendly dictators. The supply of shoulder-held Stinger missiles to the *mujahideen* in Afghanistan for their war against Soviet invaders (1979–89) also produced (again, over the short run) a useful outcome for the United States – although this particular intervention was more of an "overt-covert action," closely covered by the media.

Presidents are persistently drawn to covert action (called, too, the "Third Option" – between reliance on the Marines and diplomats), even those like Jimmy Carter, who in 1976 railed against this approach in presidential campaign rhetoric as a corruption of American values. Covert action is notably appealing to presidents engaged in an ideological or military struggle against an aggressive global competitor. Carter turned to this instrument of foreign policy when the Soviet Union invaded Afghanistan; and, throughout his two terms in office, President Ronald Reagan employed covert action against the Soviet "evil empire" as it intruded into the developing world, a response labeled the "Reagan Doctrine" by the media. American presidents who find themselves relatively free of major military provocations or ideological confrontations overseas are inclined to leave covert action on the shelf. Presidents may also, Ransom suggests, turn to covert action when no national consensus exists for open military intervention against a target.[20]

> *P31. Covert action is used most frequently by presidents engaged in an ideological or military struggle against an adversary, or when no national consensus exists for open military intervention.*

Money is a consideration, too, since covert action can be costly – especially major, long-term paramilitary operations. In Laos, the CIA and its local Hmong

(Meo) assets fought a secret war for a decade (1963–73); and the supply of weapons to the *contras* in Nicaragua and the *mujahideen* in Afghanistan kept Uncle Sam's cash register ringing during the 1980s. Only a well-to-do nation can undertake such sponsorships, although the successful 9/11 paramilitary attack by the al-Qaeda terrorist organization demonstrates that extensive short-term damage can be inflicted against a target without much financial cost. More prolonged covert actions, however, are expensive.

Even with the money to support significant covert actions, most will be successful only within modest parameters. Successes are most likely to occur when a targeted regime is weak to begin with (as in Iran in 1953 and Guatemala in 1954); when paramilitary surrogates are dedicated, experienced fighters with widespread indigenous support (as in Laos in 1963–73 and in Afghanistan in 2001–2); or when a quick, dramatic use of limited paramilitary force is carried out against civilian or military targets (like the al-Qaeda strikes against the United States or the *USS Cole* in the Yemeni port of Aden, in 2000). The great success of the CIA's paramilitary operations in Afghanistan in 2001–02 enjoyed the support of the indigenous Northern Alliance, tough anti-Taliban fighters who knew the terrain of their own country well, as well as support from the Pentagon's Special Forces and pinpoint bombing by the US Air Force – a rare array of aligned forces.

P32. Affluent nations can afford to conduct more extensive covert actions than poorer nations, especially when it comes to major paramilitary operations – although even weak states or groups can inflict considerable damage through limited surprise paramilitary attacks.

P33. Major covert actions (and especially those with a paramilitary component) conducted over a longer period of time are most likely to succeed when a target regime is weak, when local surrogates are dedicated fighters with indigenous support, and when complemented as well by air force bombing and coordinated military "special forces."

Counterintelligence

The third core mission of intelligence agencies is the protection of a nation against hostile intelligence services and other adversaries, a practice known as counterintelligence. The defensive side of this mission depends on barbed wire fences around agency buildings, patrolled by armed guards; polygraph tests; identification badges; and encoded communications. Counterintelligence has an offensive side, too: the penetration of the opposition with a mole of one's own, to discover what operations the adversary has running against the homeland and to foil those attacks. Again, money is important. Sophisticated telephone and personal computer safeguards are costly, as is the wide gamut of defensive barriers from fences to well-trained security guards. Yet, even wealthy nations have experienced counterintelligence failures, such as the Cambridge spy ring in

England or the cases of Ames (CIA), Hanssen (FBI), and the Walker family (Navy Intelligence) in the United States. When failures come to light, investigations are carried out and counterintelligence is usually provided additional resources to enhance security.

> *P34. The more affluent the nation, the less porous its counterintelligence defenses are apt to be.*

> *P35. Some counterintelligence failures are inevitable; however, their frequency is likely to decline in the aftermath of a major security breach, because the victimized nation then takes steps to tighten its defenses.*

Intelligence oversight

A theory of intelligence must take into account efforts to maintain supervision over the conduct of secret operations, at least in those open societies where accountability has been attempted in this hidden domain. Even in the United States, which is among the nations that have given intelligence oversight the most attention, the experiment is of relatively recent vintage. From 1789 until 1975, America's intelligence agencies were considered a separate government whose sensitive operations would have to be sheltered from the normal checks and balances of the US Constitution. Improper domestic spying led to a scandal in 1974, however, which produced strong pressure to bring the principles of accountability into the secret side of government.[21]

> *P36. Within democracies, intelligence scandals – especially if they involve domestic spying – stimulate efforts to establish greater accountability over secret agencies.*

Short of a scandal, the vigor with which intelligence accountability is carried out will be related to the degree of consensus behind a nation's foreign policy; and that consensus is likely to be highest in times of perceived external threat. The efficiency of a nation's war and espionage capabilities are of greatest concern in times of danger, with questions of civil liberties and the close legislative supervision of intelligence a secondary consideration as the nation rallies behind its leader and the executive branch of the government in times of peril.[22] In contrast, during periods of normalcy a nation (if it enjoys basic freedoms) will be more inclined to engage in vigorous debate about policy directions, permit criticism of its chief executive, and concentrate on the safeguarding of civil liberties and democratic procedures.

The political science literatures reminds us, though, that the legislative supervision of executive branch agencies can fail even during times of normalcy, as a result of co-optation.[23] Over time, law-makers become the advocates and protectors of the very agencies they are meant to oversee.

P37. In times of military crisis, a nation tends to rally behind its leader in favor of an efficient intelligence and military response to the threat, placing at a lower level of concern questions of civil liberties and intelligence accountability.

P38. Over time, intelligence oversight committees are apt to become co-opted by the agencies they are assigned to supervise.

Although in the United States some intelligence officers initially looked with horror on the prospect of having to submit to normal governmental oversight procedures, most national intelligence chiefs since 1975 have come to appreciate the new partnership with Congress and a chance to share their weighty responsibilities with law-makers. (DCI William J. Casey, 1981–87, is the exception.) They have also expressed few concerns about the diminution of intelligence effectiveness as a result of the new oversight procedures. Moreover, although intelligence oversight has displayed some of the usual weaknesses of co-optation, some legislators have take accountability seriously and provided a check on many (if not all) misguided intelligence initiatives. The executive "energy" that Alexander Hamilton extolled remains important in government and especially within the national security domain; but, as James Madison countered at the founding, safeguards against the overzealous use of executive power are even more vital.

P39. Nations that have experimented with procedures for greater intelligence accountability have found that this approach allows some semblance of policy debate and a healthy "look over the shoulder" by elected representatives – in a word, the advantages of democracy in providing a check on ill-conceived intelligence activities.

Most of the data needed for a rigorous test of the propositions presented above are locked up in government vaults. Given this situation, one must resort to the only possible remedies: sifting through published government reports and other open literature on intelligence, which has become quite voluminous, and interviewing officials involved in intelligence work.[24]

Conclusion

These research propositions offered here provide a series of sketches for a theory of intelligence, although the inventory is not meant to be exhaustive. Each proposition requires extensive empirical testing as more information on intelligence becomes available to the public. The large amount of work that remains to be done in this field of inquiry should whet the scholarly appetites of those with an interest in the hidden side of foreign and security policy.

A final word: intelligence scholars should resist "physics envy," longing for a grand field theory of intelligence or a wonderful formula like $e = mc^2$ that explains all of intelligence. After all, human beings are much more complicated than atoms and it will take us longer to unravel the secrets of intelligence behavior. We must bring to bear the findings and methodologies of such disciplines of history, psychology, economics, public administration (notably organizational theory), anthropology, and political science. And the experiences of practitioners in the field will continued to be of great value, as will normative theorizing. Let a thousand flowers bloom.

Notes

1 This chapter draws upon the author's earlier works on intelligence theory, including "Preface to a Theory of Strategic Intelligence," *International Journal of Intelligence and Counterintelligence* 16 (Winter 2003–04): 638–63; "Bricks and Mortar for a Theory of Intelligence," *Comparative Strategy* 22 (Spring 2003): 1–28; and "Is There an American Theory of Intelligence?" presentation, Workshop on Theories of Intelligence, RAND Corporation (Crystal City, VA, June 15, 2005).
2 See Loch K. Johnson, ed., *Strategic Intelligence*, vols. 1–5 (Westport, CT: Praeger, 2007).
3 R.B. Braithwaite, *Scientific Explanation: A Study of the Function of Theory, Probability and Law in Science* (Cambridge: Cambridge University Press, 1955), cited in Claire Selltiz, Marie Johoda, Morton Deutsch, and Stuart Cook, *Research Methods in Social Relations* (New York: Holt, Rinehart and Winston, 1967): 480.
4 On the intelligence cycle, see Arthur S. Hulnick, "The Intelligence Producer-Policy Consumer Linkage: A Theoretical Approach," *Intelligence and National Security* 1 (May 1986): 212–33, and "What's Wrong with the Intelligence Cycle," in Johnson, ed., *Strategic Intelligence*, Vol. 2, op. cit.; and Johnson, *America's Secret Power: The CIA in a Democratic Society* (New York: Oxford University Press, 1989).
5 Thomas Powers, *The Man Who Kept the Secrets: Richard Helms and the CIA* (New York: Simon & Schuster, 1979): 447, note 6.
6 See Johnson, *Secret Agencies: U.S. Intelligence in a Hostile World* (New Haven, CT: Yale University Press, 1996).
7 See, for example, the case of the surprise Indian nuclear tests in 1998, in Johnson, "The CIA's Weakest Link," *Washington Monthly* 33 (July–August 2001): 9–14.
8 See H. Bradford Westerfield, "America and the World of Intelligence Liaison," *Intelligence and National Security 11* (July 1996): 523–60; Michael Herman, "11 September: Legitimizing Intelligence?" *International Relations* 16 (August 2002): 227–41.
9 Jeffrey T. Richelson and Desmond Ball, *The Ties that Bind: Intelligence Cooperation Between the UKUSA Countries* (Winchester, MA: Allen & Unwin, 1986).
10 See Loch K. Johnson, *Bombs, Bugs, Drugs, and Thugs: Intelligence and the Quest for Security* (New York: New York University Press, 2000).
11 Loch K. Johnson, "A Centralized Intelligence System: Truman's Dream Deferred," *American Intelligence Journal* 23 (Autumn/Winter 2005), pp. 6–15.
12 Johnson, *Bombs, Bugs*, op. cit.
13 The phrase is from former Secretary of State Dean Rusk, in a conversation with the author (July 4, 1984), Athens, GA. On why analysts unavoidably err, see Richard K. Betts, "Analysis, War and Decision: Why Intelligence Failures Are Inevitable," *World Politics* 31 (October 1978): 61–89.
14 Letter to the author (January 30, 2002).
15 See Harry Howe Ransom, "The Politicization of Intelligence," in Stephen J. Cimbala, ed., *Intelligence and Intelligence Policy in a Democratic Society* (Dobbs Ferry, NY: Transnational Press, 1987): 25–46.
16 Herman, "11 September": 229.

17 A saying sometimes used by CIA analysts when their work is ignored by policy-makers.
18 Loch K. Johnson, "The Aspin–Brown Intelligence Inquiry: Behind the Closed Doors of a Blue Ribbon Commission," *Studies in Intelligence* 48 (Winter 2004): 1–20.
19 The 9/11 Commission Report, *Final Report of the National Commission on Terrorist Attacks Upon the United States* (New York: Norton, 2004).
20 Ransom, correspondence to the author (January 30, 2002).
21 See Loch K. Johnson, "Intelligence Oversight in the United States," in Steve Tsang, ed., *Intelligence and Human Rights in the Era of Global Terrorism* (Westport, CT: Praeger, 2007): 54–66.
22 See Ransom, "Politicization, op. cit."
23 Joel D. Aberbach, "The Development of Oversight in the United States Congress: Concepts and Analysis," paper, American Political Science Association Annual Meeting (September 1977), Washington, DC; Harry Howe Ransom, *The Intelligence Establishment* (Cambridge, MA: Harvard University Press, 1970).
24 For an summary of some preliminary findings regarding the specific propositions offered here, see, Johnson, "Bricks and Mortar," op. cit.: 15–22; for a guide to the broader literature and its research findings, see Johnson, *Strategic Intelligence*, Vol. 1, op. cit.; Loch K. Johnson and James J. Wirtz, *Intelligence and National Security: The Secret World of Spies*, 2nd edn (New York: Roxbury/Oxford University Press, 2008); and Mark M. Lowenthal, *The U.S. Intelligence Community: An Annotated Bibliography* (New York: Garland, 1994).

4 Intelligence theory and theories of international relations

Shared world or separate worlds?

Mark Phythian

Introduction

Writing shortly before the events of 11 September 2001 (9/11), historian of intelligence David Kahn observed that:

> Intelligence has been an academic discipline for half a century now. Almost from the start, scholars have called for a theory of intelligence. None has been advanced. Although some authors entitle sections of their work 'theory of intelligence', to my knowledge no one has proposed concepts that can be tested.

Since then considerable work has been done on both sides of the Atlantic with a view to developing a solid theoretical basis from which the study of strategic intelligence, in the post-9/11 world more visibly central to our lives than at any previous time, can proceed.[1]

In part, this is a consequence of a general anxiety within the Intelligence Studies (IS) academic community that such a body of theoretical work needs to be generated in order to confer legitimacy on this developing subject area. Work to date has generated key questions about the role of theory, and whether the aim should be to seek an overarching 'theory of intelligence' or to generate theoretical bases for a number of key areas of inquiry. A related question concerns the relationship between attempts to theorize about strategic intelligence and existing theories of and within International Relations (IR). The aim of this chapter is to focus on this latter question, the role of theory, and its implications for the IS research agenda.

If IS is to further establish itself as a distinct subject area it clearly needs to develop those areas of study that are distinctive to it. Writing in 1993, Wesley Wark did much to define the subject area in identifying eight approaches to the study of intelligence, of which social science theorizing, somewhat vaguely termed the 'fourth perspective' by Wark, was but one (the others were: the research project; the historical project; the definitional project; memoirs; the civil liberties project; investigative journalism; and the popular culture project).[2] What, then, is the place of theory in IS? There seems little prospect of a unifying theory of intelligence because of the scope and complexity of the subject area and, moreover, little need in that a significant part of the frame that this would provide already exists in the form of structural realist analyses. It is also worth noting that existing efforts to highlight links and commonalities between IS and IR have not got us very far. The starting point should be the definitional debate, one of Wark's eight 'projects', but one closely linked to the theory-building project by virtue of the fact that a solid definitional foundation is a necessary pre-requisite for theory-building. Indeed, it can be argued that this project itself borders on the theoretical.[3]

The meaning of theory

At the outset, though, it is worth discussing what we mean by 'theory'. There is much debate within IR over what constitutes a theory or theoretical approach, and whether or not IR as a discipline should be based on scientific principles. This debate has been variously characterized as being one between explaining and understanding, positivism and post-positivism, and rationalism and reflectivism. Within this, the form of theorizing that most closely approximates to the professional world of intelligence is explanatory or problem-solving theory. These are the theories most concerned with isolating and identifying the causal role of a given element and going on to draw conclusions and predictions from analysis. In this, explanatory theories have greater policy relevance than the critical approaches to be found in, for example, post-structuralism. Whether policy relevance should be an aim of IR theorizing is a separate debate,[4] but it seems logical that the professional world of intelligence should be drawn to theories that seek to explain the world it is tasked with monitoring and analysing, which employ a similar positivist methodology to that used in intelligence analysis, and which hold out the possibility of predicting state behaviour.[5]

Explanatory theory is based on firmly positivist foundations which emphasize the importance of vigorous scientific method, which can lead its advocates to question how far alternative approaches to IR actually constitute 'theory'. As Kenneth Waltz put it: 'Students of international politics use the term "theory" freely, to cover any work that departs from mere description and seldom to refer only to work that meets philosophy-of-science standards.'[6]

From this perspective, then, the purpose of theory is to facilitate understanding of the past and present and, through its predictive capacity, act as a guide to the future.[7] A theory serves to isolate the relevant factors and highlight the relationship between them, thereby constructing a theoretical reality. This isolation of a segment of activity in order to better explain it is fundamental to this approach to theorization. Isolation serves to expose patterns otherwise concealed by the mass of facts that exist around any phenomena. Where such isolation is impossible, theorization cannot proceed.[8] As understood by Waltz:

> Reality emerges from our selection and organization of materials that are available in infinite quantity ... since empirical knowledge is potentially infinite in extent, without some guidance we can know neither what

information to gather nor how to put it together so that it becomes comprehensible. If we could directly apprehend the world that interests us, we would have no need for theory. We cannot. One can reliably find his way among infinite materials only with the guidance of theory.[9]

For positivists like Waltz, theories exist to explain laws. In the social sciences these laws take the form of hypotheses derived from observation and/or measurement. We can distinguish between two different levels. First, there are 'laws' themselves, based on proven and inevitable links. Second, there are 'law-like statements'. These latter are probabilistic, derived from observation that demonstrates that a proposition is often and reliably proven but is still not inevitable, and therefore falls short of constituting a 'law'. Theory is then required to help us understand these observations. This is precisely the pattern – generating hypotheses ('laws') which call for theories to provide explanation and which can lead to corollaries or modifications to the hypotheses – that a number of IS academics have followed. For example, one of the leading figures in IS, Loch Johnson, in a series of writings including 'Bricks and Mortar for a Theory of Intelligence'[10] and (Chapter 3 of this volume) 'Sketches for a Theory of Strategic Intelligence', has developed propositions that require theoretical explanation. The titles of these pieces accurately convey the pre-theoretical nature of the propositions being outlined. The key point is that it is necessary to proceed from law to theory, by proposing hypotheses and then developing explanations of them.[11] As Waltz notes: 'A theory is born in conjecture and is viable if the conjecture is confirmed.'[12]

This kind of positivist approach also emphasizes that the use of models can be fundamental in facilitating theorization. The advantage of a model is that it, 'pictures reality while simplifying it, say, through omission or through reduction of scale.'[13] The model at the core of IS – the intelligence cycle – does just this. Moreover, 'this is how intelligence professionals conceptually think of their work',[14] notwithstanding the fact that the reality is inevitably more complex and qualified than the model suggests. Hence, it seems reasonable to suggest that the intelligence cycle should be at the heart of much of the theoretical work that marks IS out as a distinctive subject area.

From definitions to theoretical approaches

Following on from this, I want to argue that when the IS community considers the areas where theorization should be prioritized so as to continue to develop this distinctive subject area, there are some areas where it need not become bogged down, because the work has, in effect, already been done by an existing theoretical approach to IR. In order to get to this point, however, it is necessary to proceed from some discussion of the definitional debate.

There is considerable debate as to how intelligence should be defined. For example, should a definition embrace covert action, or does this constitute an 'allied activity'?[15] Is secrecy essential to it? To take just a few examples, for

Michael Warner, 'intelligence is secret, state activity to understand or influence foreign entities'[16] For Abram Shulsky and Gary Schmitt, it is 'information relevant to a government's formulating and implementing policy to further its national security interests and to deal with threats to those interests from actual or potential adversaries.'[17] For his part, Loch Johnson has defined intelligence as 'the knowledge – and, ideally, foreknowledge – sought by nations in response to external threats and to protect their vital interests, especially the well-being of their own people.'[18] For Gill and Phythian:

> Intelligence is the umbrella term referring to the range of activities – from planning and information collection to analysis and dissemination – conducted in secret, and aimed at maintaining or enhancing relative security by providing forewarning of threats or potential threats in a manner that allows for the timely implementation of a preventive policy or strategy, including, where deemed desirable, covert activities.[19]

While all of these vary, one thing that a number have in common is not just the idea of providing security, but also, implicitly or explicitly, that intelligence is sought and intelligence agencies organized so as to secure *relative advantage*. On this basis, if we were to ask why states regard intelligence as being necessary, we could answer that intelligence is the agency through which states seek to protect or extend their relative advantage. In this, intelligence and structural realism share a common core concern and, to an extent, employ a common language.[20] It is no accident that Shulsky and Schmitt titled their book *Silent Warfare* or that then Director of Central Intelligence Robert Gates should tell junior CIA officers that the 'nation is at peace because we in intelligence are constantly at war.'[21]

Intelligence and structural realism

Hence, there is a close relationship between intelligence and structural realism. Security and securing relative advantage are the job of intelligence and structural realism is the explanatory approach to IR most centrally concerned with security. The requirement for the former arises out of the latter's analysis of the international system and the understanding it invites of the likely behaviour of states under conditions of anarchy. This means that structural realism already provides a theoretical explanation for certain key questions in IS, such as why intelligence is necessary and why, particularly in the case of the US, intelligence agencies did not wither away with the passing of the Cold War.

It has been suggested that intelligence has attracted little attention from IR scholars.[22] However, intelligence actually occupies a central place in structural realist thinking, albeit one that is sometimes more implicit than explicit.[23] As noted above the need for it arises out of the core assumptions about the nature of the international system that structural realists make. For offensive realists, and as outlined by John Mearsheimer, these are that:

1   great powers are the main actors in world politics, and operate in an anar-
    chic international system;
2   all states possess some offensive military capability;
3   states can never be certain about the intentions of other states;
4   the main goal of states is survival;
5   states are rational actors.[24]

It is the combination of these factors that, for structural realists, generates an
unending security competition. In particular, it is the third of these assumptions
that explains the need for intelligence, as is clear from Mearsheimer's discussion
of it:

> States ultimately want to know whether other states are determined to use
> force to alter the balance of power, or whether they are satisfied enough
> with it that they have no interest in using force to change it. The problem,
> however, is that it is almost impossible to discern another state's intentions
> with a high degree of certainty. Unlike military capabilities, intentions
> cannot be empirically verified. Intentions are in the minds of decision-
> makers and they are especially difficult to discern.
>
> One might respond that policy-makers disclose their intentions in
> speeches and policy documents, which can be assessed. The problem with
> that argument is policy-makers sometimes lie about or conceal their true
> intentions. But even if one could determine another state's intentions today,
> there is no way to determine its future intentions. It is impossible to know
> who will be running foreign policy in any state five or ten years from now,
> much less whether they will have aggressive intentions. This is not to say
> that states can be certain that their neighbours have or will have revisionist
> goals. Instead, the argument is that policy-makers can never be certain
> whether they are dealing with a revisionist or status quo state.[25]

Hence, acceptance of the validity of these assumptions underpins state investment in intelligence. The job of intelligence, through collection and analysis, is
to reduce this uncertainty about other states' current and future intentions, to
attempt to uncover 'impossible' knowledge, and thus to provide advance
warning of any trouble ahead and so reduce fear. State investment in intelligence
is premised on the existence of international anarchy wherein trust among states
is low and, as Kenneth Waltz puts it, wars can occur, 'because there is nothing
to prevent them.'[26] It is also premised on the fact that the international system is
a self-help one where, as Mearsheimer puts it, 'there is no higher authority to
come to [states'] rescue when they dial 911'.[27] Because of this, states that can
will organize agencies to act as needed, and as secretly as necessary. This will
include engaging in covert actions designed to protect or extend relative
advantage.

As this suggests, a structural realist perspective also provides an explanation
for the centrality of secrecy to intelligence. In a self-help system secrecy is

essential to the success of operations, the prospects of their successful repetition, and to minimizing the risk of reaction from other states (or non-state actors), given that states can rely on no one else to provide for their security. In an inherently competitive realm secondary states will seek to imitate and emulate the intelligence practices and innovations of the leading states no less than they will their military innovations.

Why are secrets secret? In any realm secrecy is related to the desire to secure advantage or avoid the development of disadvantageous situations. In this context secrecy is essential because the knowledge it conceals is considered a constituent part of a state's relative advantage, which could be eroded by disclosure. Hence, a structural realist prism serves to highlight how both covert action and secrecy are fundamental to intelligence, an issue of some debate within IS.

Moreover, structural realism can provide explanations as to why even the strongest state(s) must maintain significant intelligence capabilities, by suggesting that where secondary states have a choice they will

BANDWAGONING

flock to the weaker side; for it is the stronger side that threatens them. On the weaker side, they are both more appreciated and safer, provided, of course, that the coalition they join achieves enough defensive or deterrent strength to dissuade adversaries from attacking.[28]

This holds out the risk of the emergence of a balancing coalition, early warning of the development of which is essential to its prevention and the maintenance of relative advantage.

Although there are clear differences between how offensive and defensive realists see the world, the need for intelligence is writ large in both approaches. The principal difference lies in the fact that the defensive realism of Waltz rests on just two assumptions – that the international system is anarchic and that states seek to survive. It does not assume that states always act rationally. However, the absence of this assumption simply makes the need for accurate intelligence all the more pressing. Hence, just as structural realism can provide explanations of other phenomena, for example, the conditions under which states seek to engage in nuclear proliferation, so it can also explain the conditions that give rise to the need for intelligence.[29]

If the growth of foreign intelligence communities in the leading Western states was premised on the Soviet threat, why did they survive the Cold War largely intact? Structural realism explains this by reference to the uncertainty principle discussed above and through highlighting how, regardless of the existence of any specific threat, the strongest and wealthiest states will invest most heavily in intelligence because they have the strongest interest in the maintenance of the existing configuration of forces in the international system, the one that gives rise to their relative strength.[30] Even in an environment where a preponderant power, such as the contemporary United States, feels relatively secure because of the limited likelihood that another state will attack it directly, it will still require a broad-based intelligence capability, because:

war among the lesser great powers is still possible, because the balance of power between any two of them will at least sometimes be roughly equal, thus allowing for the possibility that one might defeat the other. But, even then, if the preponderant power believes that such wars might upset a favourable international order, it should have the wherewithal to stop them, or at least make them unusual events.[31]

Intelligence, then, is also the early warning means by which such powers seek to manage the international system to their continued advantage. Such international management is essentially reactive and, as such, good intelligence is of fundamental importance. This logic also suggests that preponderant powers are the most likely to intervene in areas of instability, with all of the attendant costs – human and financial, but also political – and so have the strongest incentive to gather the best and most extensive (not always the same thing) intelligence on these areas, allowing for a timely and effective policy response to potential or actual instability, and thereby minimizing the costs. This need provides the context for Loch Johnson's invitation to:

> Consider the intelligence focus of the United States compared to New Zealand, or even Israel in its hostile setting. America's intelligence failures have been extensive in recent years, including (most painfully) the terrorist attacks on the World Trade Center and the Pentagon in 2001, the mistaken targeting of the Chinese embassy in Belgrade in 1999, and the inability to find the Iraqi leader Saddam Hussein in 1991, the Somali warlord Mohamed Farah Aidid in 1993, or the Al Qaeda leader Osama Bin Laden in 2001–2002. While New Zealand may falter from time to time in its efforts to track illegal Japanese fishing for albacore tuna in its seas, and Israel may suffer the more hurtful inability to anticipate the next suicide bombing, the tasks of the intelligence services in these smaller nations are much more focused and manageable.[32]

A few caveats are in order. Firstly, structural realism was not conceived as an explanation of all international activity. Especially in its offensive realist variant, it is designed to be a parsimonious theory which, because it omits a broad range of actors and factors from its explanatory apparatus, has clear limits. Increased international co-operation at various levels presents a challenge to the theory, especially in the form of the European Union. Because it is a theory about state behaviour, structural realism has little to say about the post-9/11 'war on terror', a not insignificant omission. As John Mearsheimer concedes; 'there are limits to what realism can tell us about al-Qaeda, because it is a non-state actor, and there is no room for non-state actors in structural realism.'[33] Similarly, it has little to say about the security challenges posed by transnational organized crime, about environmental politics, or about intelligence co-operation and the role of intelligence in support of UN operations and war crimes prosecutions. Secondly, to anticipate some of the discussion to come, there is the question of whether structural realism, especially in its offensive variant, accurately describes the world as seen by everyone or is an approach which best describes it from a US perspective and in light of US interests. Structural realism may not be a theory *of* US foreign and security policy, but there is a sense in which it is a theory *for* US foreign and security policy; the prescriptions that arise from it are intended to secure or enhance US hegemony.

Nevertheless, in practice, both intelligence customers and practitioners tend to view the world through a realist/idealist dichotomy that does not easily accommodate or see the immediate policy relevance of post-structuralist or reflectivist approaches. Practitioners are unlikely to be highly receptive to approaches to IR which deny the possibility of uncovering objective truth when their task is to deliver the most objective analysis possible ('best truth'), and where failure can result from compromising this effort and, instead of telling 'truth to power', tailoring analysis to suit real or imagined customer preferences.

None of this is intended to exaggerate the claims that can be made for the explanatory power of structural realism. There are other approaches that can help explain, for example, the failure of intelligence agencies to wither away with the passing of the Cold War – bureaucratic politics, for one. Rather it is simply intended to show why in practice it is the foundation from which the practice of intelligence arises and the framework that *best* describes the world as seen, implicitly or explicitly, from the point of view of the intelligence professional and at least some leading figures in the IS field.

Two important final points emerge from this. First, if it is the case that intelligence activity is underpinned by either defensive or offensive realist assumptions, then intelligence clearly has a built-in offensive as well as defensive role. Second, if one or more of the core assumptions underpinning structural realism can be disproved, then the theory collapses. As Mearsheimer puts it, 'if you knock out an assumption, you cripple the theory.'[34] This has serious implications for intelligence. If the theory is flawed, there is no need for such a large, expensive, unwieldy intelligence community as that which exists in the contemporary US. More funding should be allocated instead to public diplomacy. Hence, intelligence professionals have a vested interest in general acceptance of the logic of structural realism. If it collapses, they might lose their jobs.

Theorization and intelligence studies: towards a research agenda

Structural realism, then, provides a theoretical basis for addressing key questions, but also has clear limits which IS needs to move beyond in developing its instinctive research agenda. In doing this, it needs to bear in mind Peter Gill's distinction between theories *of* intelligence and theories *for* intelligence.[35] In part this is a consequence of the need to bear in mind the difficulties generated for the outsider academic by the secrecy that attaches to its practice. The outsider academic can never hope to be as well-informed as the practitioner. This is no different from the realities that exist in the field of Strategic Studies. With regard to this, Lawrence Freedman has suggested that:

> In terms of defining a field of study, the vantage point of a student of strategy is quite different from that of a practitioner. Efforts by the former to display some superior wisdom may well deserve to be treated with contempt. The most helpful role remains that which can be properly described as 'academic' (even though in the policy world this is all too often synonymous with irrelevant). The task is to conceptualize and contextualize rather than provide specific guidance. If it is done well, then the practitioner should be able to recognize the relevance for whatever may be the problem at hand.[36]

This does, however, also raise the question of the audience for whom the IS academic is writing. The natural assumption with regard to Strategic Studies is that this is the practitioner. This can, and probably should, be true *in part* for IS academics, but their role should go beyond this to educate publics and foster and engage in debate on issues of ethics, accountability and the liberty/security trade-off. IS and IS academics do not exist simply to be of assistance to intelligence agencies, their responsibilities are broader.[37] While intelligence can be a force for good by ensuring the security and well-being of the citizens in whose name it operates, history is littered with examples where, acting in secrecy, agencies have exceeded their mandate and violated human rights and/or civil liberties.

Recognising the utility of structural realism in explaining the emergence, persistence and resilience of intelligence agencies, by moving beyond this, I would suggest that the focus of theoretical work in IS should be on intelligence failure, intelligence ethics, and intelligence oversight and accountability, the first two of which at least hold out the prospect of other theoretical approaches in IR making a substantial contribution.

The core theoretical focus should be on the causes of intelligence failure, the study of which is rooted in the concept of the intelligence cycle and so potentially embraces all intelligence activity. Failure is that which, ideally, shouldn't happen.[38] The 'law' that this theorizing would respond to, if firm positivist foundations need to be sought, is that of Richard Betts on the inevitability of intelligence failure.[39] This focus gives IS theorizing a distinctive, *post mortem*, character. It is also an area where outsider academics are able to contribute in the manner suggested by Freedman in relation to Strategic Studies, drawing on insights from a range of disciplines and approaches including, for example, discourse analysis, cognitive psychology, and economics.[40] This reflects the fact that the existence of a relatively rich vein of case study material, and the increasing norm that acknowledged failures will result in public or other inquiries which publish reports and even the evidence underpinning them, has meant that the obstacle of secrecy is nowhere near as great as it once was, and outsider academics have the potential to make a genuine contribution to debates. This work is far more than a service to the government of the day and its intelligence agencies. It is also important in terms of civic education and in informing debates about the kind of intelligence agencies a state requires and the nature of the oversight required.

This *post mortem* character also lends itself to analyses from a number of IR standpoints which can stimulate fresh thinking about the causes and extent of intelligence failure. Constructivism, for example, with its greater emphasis on agency and the social dimensions of IR and focus on norms, rules, language and the 'how possible' question, can inform thinking about the role of intelligence in, for example, the Iraq failure. From a constructivist standpoint, the causes of the war in Iraq and role of intelligence in this might be explained thus:

It is now known that intelligence communities on both sides of the Atlantic got it wrong, in (falsely) believing that Iraq had weapons of mass destruction. An explanation that the invasion was caused by Iraq's weapons of mass destruction is more accurately stated in the following terms. The reason for the invasion of Iraq, given by foreign-policy elites, was the threat posed by Saddam Hussein's weapons of mass destruction. Whether these actors believed the intelligence or manufactured it, this 'reason' made the invasion possible. The reason was the means for persuading the US public, and US soldiers, that this was a legitimate act by their government. The reason was strengthened by the link made in political discourse between Saddam and the attackers on 9/11. The premise that Saddam had weapons of mass destruction, although based on false data, established the context for making a justification, that is giving a reason for the invasion. The reason was publicly accessible in political language. It constituted an action and a 'reality', that is the invasion. The intention to invade was embedded in these language games and in the act of invasion itself.[41]

This leads to the second area of the proposed IS theoretical focus – intelligence oversight and accountability – aimed at citizens and legislators, and of fundamental importance in a liberal democratic context. Much work has been done here in recent years.[42] Moreover, this is the area where most comparative work within IS has been undertaken, focusing in particular on developments in transition states and treating intelligence oversight as a central component of the democratization process. This work has generated studies not just on the usual suspects, but also on oversight in Poland, Argentina, South Korea, and South Africa, to name but a few. It has also facilitated the generation of propositions as to what effective oversight should look like.[43]

This second focus should be informed by a third, on intelligence ethics. Ethical issues are inseparable from intelligence activities and, like the question of failure, can take in the entire intelligence cycle. Targeting of 'friendly' states, the very notion of covert surveillance, and the more intrusive forms of collection, together with the question of covert action and other intelligence-led policy responses, all raise fundamental ethical questions. There is a growing body of work on this subject,[44] most recently clearly informed by developments in the 'War on Terror', specifically the torture debate in the US[45] and the associated question of extraordinary rendition – in effect, the outsourcing of torture by the US. Hence, more than ever before, there is a need to adapt the just war paradigm to construct a concept of *jus in intelligentia*.[46]

Given their critical posture, there is a potentially important role for post-structuralist writings to play in thinking about intelligence. While subject to criticism on a range of grounds,[47] discourse approaches to intelligence do have the capacity to illuminate issues of key importance to publics in democracies. More a critical approach to IR than a theory or paradigm, post-structuralism generates critiques aimed at exposing assumptions underpinning states of affairs that have come to be regarded as natural or inevitable, thereby demonstrating that in fact they are not, drawing attention to the relationship between power and knowledge in the process. As explained by Michel Foucault:

> A critique is not a matter of saying that things are not right as they are. It is a matter of pointing out on what kinds of assumptions, what kinds of familiar, unchallenged, unconsidered modes of thought the practices that we accept rest. We must free ourselves from the sacralization of the social as the only reality and stop regarding as superfluous something so essential in human life and in human relations as thought.... It is something that is often hidden, but which always animates everyday behavior. There is always a little thought even in the most stupid institutions; there is always thought even in silent habits. Criticism is a matter of flushing out that thought and trying to change it: to show that things are not as self-evident as one believed, to see what is accepted as self-evident will no longer be accepted as such. Practicing criticism is a matter of making facile gestures difficult.[48]

In a sense, then, post-structuralism sees itself carrying out a form of oversight of power at the level of discourse. In the current 'War on Terror' this could involve analysis of the public language used by politicians to achieve the required degree of political and social consensus in using intelligence to justify pre-emptive or preventive war. Such critical approaches also have a clear role to play in the *post mortem* debates about the nature and causes of intelligence failure. A number of writers, such as Richard Jackson, have begun to focus on the construction of the 'War on Terror' in this way, considering the role of intelligence within this, and in so doing performing an educative function that has considerable importance given the context. For Jackson:

> The language of the 'war on terrorism' is not simply an objective or neutral reflection of reality; nor is it merely accidental or incidental. It is not the only way to talk and think about counter-terrorism. Rather, it is a deliberately and meticulously composed set of words, assumptions, metaphors, grammatical forms, myths and forms of knowledge – it is a carefully con-

structed *discourse* – that is designed to achieve a number of key political goals: to normalize and legitimize the current counter-terrorist approach; to empower the authorities and shield them from criticism; to discipline domestic society by marginalising dissent or protest; and to enforce national unity by reifying a narrow conception of political identity. The discourse of the 'war on terrorism' has a clear *political* purpose; it works for someone and for something: it is an exercise of power.[49]

Such perspectives shift the focus of IS from the intelligence cycle and the production of intelligence to its impact, thereby encouraging and informing debates about ethics and oversight and accountability. They also focus attention on the problem of objective truth. Acceptance of the structural realist logic that underpins the existence of intelligence communities rests on the positivist assumption that there is such a thing as objective truth and reality and that, through careful collection and analysis, intelligence agencies exist to arrive at it. Acceptance, instead, of the impossibility of unearthing a single objective truth, of the idea that intelligence agencies through collection and analysis 'create' their own reality, coupled with the secrecy that attaches to intelligence, raises the key question of manipulation.[50]

The premise here, as Fry and Hochstein have noted, is that intelligence is not simply an objective 'eye' seeing and describing reality but one which, for a range of reasons, may introduce distortions with the consequence that intelligence, 'participates in the creation and reproduction of international political reality' and therefore, 'does not merely describe the world in which the state operates, but in fact actively "creates" that world for each state.'[51] This has potentially serious implications for democratic governance, well illustrated by journalist Ron Suskind's account of an encounter with an anonymous 'senior advisor' to President Bush in the build-up to the 2003 invasion of Iraq:

> The aide said that guys like me [i.e., reporters and commentators] were 'in what we call the reality-based community,' which he defined as people who 'believe that solutions emerge from your judicious study of discernible reality.' I nodded and murmured something about enlightenment principles and empiricism. He cut me off. 'That's not the way the world really works anymore,' he continued. 'We're an empire now, and when we act, we create our own reality. And while you're studying that reality – judiciously, as you will – we'll act again, creating other new realities, which you can study too, and that's how things will sort out. We're history's actors ... and you, all of you, will be left to just study what we do.'[52]

There is an irony here, in that the question of trust emerges as being central to the IS agenda twice over. Firstly, at the international level it is the impossibility of permanent inter-state trust arising from the anarchic, 'self-help', international system that does much to create the requirement for intelligence in the first place. Secondly, at the societal level there is the question of how far trust can be placed in intelligence agencies, a consequence of the political cultures of both the US and UK, but reaffirmed by pre-9/11 historical experience and post-9/11 developments around detention, extraordinary rendition, torture, destruction of evidence relating to torture and suspicion that co-operation with official inquiries is limited by a desire to protect intelligence bureaucracies and individuals within them. Hence, a 'trust deficit' leads to the creation of intelligence agencies, but their creation, in turn, generates a 'trust dilemma' at a societal level.[53]

Commonalities with terrorism studies

The above discussion of approaches to the study of intelligence rooted in different theories in and of IR cannot be exhaustive given limitations of space. A more comprehensive account would also have pointed to the various contributions that could be made by feminist, post-colonialist, globalization, and Marxist approaches[54] and, perhaps in particular in the current security environment, the international society approach of the English School. At the same time, intelligence activities represent a challenge for other theoretical approaches, such as democratic peace theory. In thinking about the potential for theorizing about strategic intelligence and the focus of such theorizing it is also useful to briefly consider the similarities in the approach of a related subject area, Terrorism Studies (TS) and the potential that academics in the two fields have to learn from and collaborate with each other.

There are parallels between IS and TS in terms of the definitional debates both have engaged in. As with IS, within TS these 'pre-theoretical' debates have in the past served as a substitute for advancing theoretical frameworks. Just as the focus of theorizing within IS is essentially limited to a small number of core issues, so it is in TS. Here, the key theoretical questions concern the causes of terrorism, and the conditions under which terrorist movements decline. The focus of the theoretical work can be at the level of the individual, societal or international. As with IS, the absence of any general agreement on a definition of the subject has implications for the development of theoretical work. For example, the debate over whether covert action is 'part' of intelligence has its counterpart in debates as to whether TS concerns just terrorism 'from below' or whether it also includes state terrorism. As with IS, it draws on insights from other disciplines – particularly psychology – for its impact. Like intelligence, terrorism is a term that describes a method, a process, a means to an end. It is similarly wide-ranging. As with intelligence, there is no overarching theory that explains the whole field. Indeed, as with intelligence, much writing on terrorism adopts the historically-rooted case study approach rather than seeking to construct theoretical frames to explain terrorist activity. Here too, a small multi-disciplinary field mushroomed in the wake of 9/11. Both academic communities share the need to overcome the obstacle of secrecy. Both embrace concerns that they are not really disciplines in their own right.[55] Here too is concern that 'law-like' statements that have become cornerstones of the subject need further theoretical testing and even qualification (for example, Brian Jenkins' assertion that, 'terrorists like a lot of people watching rather than a lot of people dead'),[56] and that, overall, its study, 'is widely recognized as theoretically impoverished, [and] stands to gain in theoretical scope, precision, and cumulativeness of findings.'[57]

Moreover, IS and TS have a number of concerns in common. Both are agreed on the inevitability of strategic surprise, whether framed as intelligence failure or terrorist occurrence.[58] Both communities have an important role to play in public education about the nature of the terrorist threat and public expectations concerning intelligence. The 'War on Terror' has seen both communities engage in controversies over human rights abuses arising from extraordinary rendition, the operation of black sites, imprisonment without charge or trial at Guantánamo Bay, and the use of torture, in general seeking to support normative principles relating to civil liberties at a time when they are ignored or bypassed in the name of national security. It may well be that these commonalities point to the need for joint research where ideas concerning the theoretical possibilities and limitations that each subject area confronts can be shared to the benefit and advancement of both.

Concluding thoughts

Strategic intelligence is a process, a means to an end. That end is security and the maintenance or enhancement of relative advantage. The overarching theory that explains the need for and persistence of intelligence agencies is the one that explains the prevalence of the threats and uncertainties that intelligence exists to provide early warning of in order to ensure that potential threats do not translate into actual ones. This is not a theory of intelligence, but a theory of international politics. Theorizing within IS, therefore, need not detain itself with these issues, and can instead focus on and further develop those aspects of IS that mark it out as a distinctive subject area – failure, ethics, and oversight and accountability. There is nothing permanent about these, and the research agenda should shift to reflect contemporary developments, but in the current international security environment each is of great importance.

The study of failure involves analysis of all the activities that comprise the intelligence cycle model. This represents the bounded realm within which factors can be isolated and connections made. It would be odd if one of the key areas for theorization did not centre on the model at the heart of the study of intelligence. As Loch Johnson has observed, for IS 'the central issue' concerns 'when intelligence is likely to succeed or fail.'[59] Stephen Marrin makes the point that, 'teasing out the causes of intelligence failure provides the same kind of theoretical foundation for intelligence studies that isolating causes of war does in international relations theorizing.'[60] Much work remains to be done here, particularly in explaining the way in which intelligence seems to remain stubbornly immune to the lessons of the recent past. Hence, even after exhaustive inquiries into failure relating to Iraqi WMD and subsequent reforms, the James

Baker-led Iraq Study Group in December 2006 was still obliged to report on the under-reporting of violence in Iraq by US intelligence officials, who in one instance recorded just 93 'attacks or significant acts of violence' on a day when the actual figure was well over 1,000.[61] Why was this? One possible explanation is that the intelligence–customer interface continues to merit serious attention and that, for whatever reason, politicization remains a major issue. Theorization is called for in order to best explain these phenomena.

At the same time, more comparative work is necessary with regard to failure to establish whether emerging theoretical propositions relate to intelligence *per se*, or whether they are essentially explanations of the US intelligence environment. A good candidate for such consideration is Loch Johnson's proposition that: 'Intelligence can become politicized in democratic regimes, but because of the countering influence of professional integrity this happens far less frequently than in authoritarian regimes.'[62] This also points to the fact that, while the bulk of the work to date with regard to IS theorizing has been undertaken in the US, the next stage will require the focus to shift somewhat to consider other intelligence environments, and thereby generate, test and establish general theories of intelligence that are more than theories of US intelligence. There is a sense in which this is what much writing to date, following on from the lead established by Sherman Kent, in fact represents.

Notes

1 See David Kahn, p. 4 above. Intelligence activities are carried out, and hence intelligence exists, at a number of levels from the international to that of the individual. Because it exists at a number of levels, theorization concerning intelligence can be conceived of as operating vertically, across levels, or horizontally, focusing on a specific level. Peter Gill and I have suggested that surveillance is a useful linking concept that facilitates vertical theorization. See, Peter Gill and Mark Phythian, *Intelligence in an Insecure World* (Cambridge: Polity Press, 2006), Ch. 2. The focus here is the level of strategic intelligence.

2 Wesley K. Wark, 'The Study of Espionage: Past, Present, Future?', *Intelligence and National Security* Vol. 8 No. 3 1993, pp. 1–13.

3 For example, Shulsky and Schmitt's final chapter 'Toward a Theory of Intelligence' merely revisits the definitional debate with which their book opens. See Abram N. Shulsky and Gary J. Schmitt, *Silent Warfare: Understanding the World of Intelligence* (3rd edn, Washington, DC: Potomac Books, 2002), pp. 169–76.

4 On this question, see William Wallace, 'Truth and Power, Monks and Technocrats: Theory and Practice in International Relations', *Review of International Studies*, Vol. 22 No. 3 1996, pp. 301–21; Ken Booth, 'Discussion: A Reply to Wallace', *Review of International Studies*, Vol. 23 No. 2 1997, pp. 371–7; and Steve Smith, 'Power and Truth: A Reply to William Wallace', *Review of International Studies*, Vol. 23 No. 4 1997, pp. 507–16.

5 See, for example, Sherman Kent, *Strategic Intelligence for American World Policy* (Princeton, NJ: Princeton University Press, 1966 [originally 1949]); Isaac Ben-Israel, 'Philosophy and Methodology of Intelligence: The Logic of the Estimate Process', *Intelligence and National Security*, Vol. 4 No. 4 1989, pp. 660–718.

6 Kenneth N. Waltz, *Theory of International Politics* (Reading, MA, Addison-Wesley, 1979), p. 1.

7 In the realm of IR, it is often argued that a theory should be capable of performing four principal tasks: describe; explain; predict; prescribe. See Charles W. Kegley, Jr (ed.), *Controversies in International Relations: Realism and the Neoliberal Challenge* (New York: St Martin's Press, 1995), p. 8.

8 Waltz, *Theory*, p. 8.

9 Ibid., p. 5.

10 Loch K. Johnson, 'Bricks and Mortar for a Theory of Intelligence', *Comparative Strategy*, Vol. 22 2003, pp. 1–28. See also Loch K. Johnson, 'Preface to a Theory of Strategic Intelligence', *International Journal of Intelligence and Counterintelligence*, Vol. 16 2003, pp. 638–63.

11 Waltz, *Theory*, p. 8.

12 Ibid., p. 2.

13 Ibid., p. 7.

14 Johnson, 'Bricks and Mortar', p. 2.

15 See, for example, Michael Herman, *Intelligence Power in Peace and War* (Cambridge: RIIA/Cambridge University Press, 1996), pp. 55–6.

16 Michael Warner, 'Wanted: A Definition of Intelligence', *Studies in Intelligence* Vol. 46 No. 3 2002, www.cia.gov/library/center-for-the-study-of-intelligence/csi-publications/csi-studies/studies/vol46no3/article02.html accessed 18 October 2007.

17 Shulsky and Schmitt, *Silent Warfare*, p. 1.

18 Loch K. Johnson, 'Intelligence', in Bruce W. Jentleson and Thomas G. Paterson (eds), *Encyclopedia of US Foreign Relations* (New York: Oxford University Press, 1997), pp. 365–73.

19 Gill and Phythian, *Intelligence in an Insecure World*, p. 7.

20 A number of academics and practitioners adopt implicitly neo-realist explanations of intelligence rooted in the idea of relative advantage. For example, Loch Johnson writes of how: 'Whether a president or a prime minister, a dictator or a king, leaders want to know about threats to their regimes, as well as opportunities for advancing their interests.' Johnson, 'Bricks and Mortar', p. 10.

21 Cited in Charles E. Lathrop, *The Literary Spy* (New Haven, CT: Yale University Press, 2004), p. 205.

22 See, for example, the discussion in Len Scott and Peter Jackson, 'The Study of Intelligence in Theory and Practice', *Intelligence and National Security*, Vol. 19 No. 2 2004, pp. 146–8.

23 It is not alone in this. For example, structural realism says little explicitly about the force of nationalism, although this is an important consideration in structural realist thinking. See 'Conversations in International Relations: Interview with John Mearsheimer (Part II)' *International Relations*, Vol. 20 No. 2 2006, p. 235.

24 John J. Mearsheimer, *The Tragedy of Great Power Politics* (New York: W. W. Norton, 2001), pp. 30–1.

25 John J. Mearsheimer, 'Structural Realism', in Tim Dunne, Milja Kurki and Steve Smith (eds), *International Relations Theories: Discipline and Diversity* (Oxford: Oxford University Press, 2007), p. 73.

26 Kenneth N. Waltz, *Man, the State, and War: A Theoretical Analysis* (New York: Columbia University Press, 1954), p. 232. See also, Robert Gilpin, 'The Richness of the Tradition of Political Realism', in Robert O. Keohane (ed.), *Neorealism and Its Critics* (New York: Columbia University Press, 1986), pp. 87–8.

27 Mearsheimer, *The Tragedy of Great Power Politics*, p. 33.

28 Waltz, *Theory*, p. 127.

29 See, Scott D. Sagan, 'Why Do States Build Nuclear Weapons? Three Models in Search of a Bomb', *International Security*, Vol. 21 No. 3 Winter 1996/7, pp. 54–87; Scott D. Sagan and Kenneth N. Waltz, *The Spread of Nuclear Weapons: A Debate Renewed* (New York: W. W. Norton, 2003). The reasons why states may be reluctant

to rely on intelligence sharing and the reasons why they may not trust in extended deterrence also bear similarities, rooted in neo-realist explanations.

30 Loch Johnson makes essentially the same point slightly differently in noting that: 'As the world moves further toward globalization, intelligence services are increasingly targeting nations or other entities that threaten the common good and sharing information with a wider set of coalitions then usual, including international organizations.' 'Bricks and Mortar', p. 7.

31 Mearsheimer, 'Structural Realism', p. 81.

32 Johnson, 'Bricks and Mortar', p. 3.

33 'Conversations in International Relations', p. 235.

34 Ibid., p. 234.

35 Peter Gill, 'Theories of Intelligence: Where are we, where should we go and how might we proceed?', in this volume, p. 212.

36 Lawrence Freedman, 'The Future of Strategic Studies', in John Baylis, James Wirtz, Eliot Cohen and Colin S. Gray (eds), *Strategy in the Contemporary World: An Introduction to Strategic Studies* (Oxford: Oxford University Press, 2002), p. 333.

37 This takes us back to the debate referred to in note 4, above.

38 As James Murphy notes:

> The very designation "intelligence failure", when we contrast it with our attitude towards law enforcement, tells us something important about what people expect from intelligence. Police officers enjoy considerable advantages over criminals – they even know most of them – yet they are seldom held responsible for preventing crime: we ask only that they act after the fact to arrest and prosecute the guilty.

> James Murphy, 'How to Judge Which Spies Are Right', *Times Literary Supplement*, 7 June 2006.

39 Richard K. Betts, 'Analysis, War, and Decision: Why intelligence failures are inevitable', *World Politics*, Vol. 31 No. 1 1978, pp. 61–89, and in this volume, pp. 87–111.

40 See, for example, Peter R. Neumann and M. L. R. Smith, 'Missing the Plot? Intelligence and Discourse Failure', *Orbis*, Winter 2005, pp. 95–107; Richards J. Heuer, Jr, 'Limits of Intelligence Analysis', *Orbis*, Winter 2005, pp. 75–94; Ohad Leslau, 'Intelligence and Economics: Two Disciplines with a Common Dilemma', *International Journal of Intelligence and Counterintelligence*, Vol. 20 No. 1 2007, pp. 106–21; Paul Ormerod, *Why Most Things Fail ... And How to Avoid It* (London: Faber & Faber, 2005). See also Gregory F. Treverton, Seth G. Jones, Steven Boraz and Philip Lipscy, *Toward a Theory of Intelligence: Workshop Report* (Santa Monica, CA: RAND, 2006).

41 K. M. Fierke, 'Constructivism', in Dunne *et al.*, *International Relations Theories*, pp. 176–7.

42 Most notably, Hans Born, Loch K. Johnson and Ian Leigh (eds), *Who's Watching the Spies? Establishing Intelligence Service Accountability* (Washington, DC: Potomac Books, 2005); Hans Born and Ian Leigh, *Legal Standards and Best Practice for Oversight of Intelligence Agencies* (Oslo: Publishing House of the Parliament of Norway, 2005); Loch K. Johnson (ed.), *Strategic Intelligence, Volume 5: Intelligence and Accountability – Safeguards Against the Abuse of Secret Power* (Westport, CT: Praeger Security International, 2007).

43 Hans Born and Loch K. Johnson, 'Balancing Operational Efficiency and Democratic Legitimacy', in Born *et al.*, *Who's Watching the Spies?*, pp. 225–39.

44 See, for example, Michael Herman, 'Intelligence and International Ethics', in Herman, *Intelligence Services in the Information Age* (London: Frank Cass, 2001), pp. 201–27; Michael Herman, 'Ethics and Intelligence after September 2001', *Intelligence and National Security*, Vol. 19 No. 2 2004, pp. 342–58; Michael Andregg,

'Intelligence Ethics: Laying a Foundation for the Second Oldest Profession', in Loch K. Johnson (ed.), *Handbook of Intelligence Studies* (New York: Routledge, 2007), pp. 52–63; Alfred W. McCoy, *A Question of Torture: CIA Interrogation, From the Cold War to the War on Terror* (New York: Metropolitan Books, 2006).

45 There is now a significant literature on this. For original documents and a good summary of the debate, see: Karen J. Greenberg, Joshua L. Dratel and Anthony Lewis (eds), *The Torture Papers: The Road to Abu Ghraib* (New York: Cambridge University Press, 2005); Karen J. Greenberg (ed.), *The Torture Debate in America* (New York: Cambridge University Press, 2005).

46 See, Michael Quinlan, 'Just Intelligence: Prolegomena to an Ethical Theory', *Intelligence and National Security*, Vol. 22 No. 1 2007, pp. 1–13.

47 For a discussion of the scope, merits and limitations of post-structuralism, something which is beyond the scope of this chapter, see Fred Halliday, *Rethinking International Relations* (Basingstoke: Macmillan, 1994), pp. 37–46; Steve Smith, 'New Approaches to International Theory', in John Baylis and Steve Smith (eds), *The Globalization of World Politics* (Oxford: Oxford University Press, 1997), pp. 165–90; Jean-François Lyotard, *The Postmodern Condition: A Report on Knowledge* (Manchester: Manchester University Press, 1984); R. K. Ashley, 'The Achievements of Post-Structuralism', in Steve Smith, Ken Booth and Marysia Zalewski (eds), *International Theory: Positivism and Beyond* (Cambridge: Cambridge University Press, 1996), pp. 240–53; and Gill and Phythian, *Intelligence in an Insecure World*, pp. 20–38.

48 Michel Foucault, *Politics, Philosophy and Culture: Interviews and Other Writings 1977–1984* (London: Routledge, 1988), pp. 154–5.

49 Richard Jackson, *Writing the War on Terrorism: Language, Politics and Counter-Terrorism* (Manchester: Manchester University Press, 2005), p. 2. See also, for example, Philip Smith, *Why War? The Cultural Logic of Iraq, The Gulf War, and Suez* (Chicago: University of Chicago Press, 2005), esp. Chs. 5–6.

50 Of course, there is something of the straw man about the idea that intelligence always seeks a single objective truth in holy grail fashion, as suggested by the title of the book by Bruce D. Berkowitz and Allan E. Goodman, *Best Truth: Intelligence in the Information Age* (New Haven, CT: Yale University Press, 2000).

51 Michael G. Fry and Miles Hochstein, 'Epistemic Communities: Intelligence Studies and International Relations', *Intelligence and National Security*, Vol. 8 No. 3 1993, p. 25.

52 Ron Suskind, 'Without a Doubt', *New York Times Magazine*, 17 October 2004, www.ronsuskind.com/articles/000106.html, accessed 18 October 2007.

53 I discuss this 'trust dilemma' in a UK context in Mark Phythian, 'Still a Matter of Trust: Post-9/11 British Intelligence and Political Culture', *International Journal of Intelligence and Counter-Intelligence*, Vol. 18 No. 4 Winter 2005–6, pp. 653–81. For a recent critical history of the CIA which raises the same question, albeit more implicitly, see Tim Weiner, *Legacy of Ashes: The History of the CIA* (London: Allen Lane/Penguin, 2007).

54 For example, building on the analysis of the international system provided by Justin Rosenberg, *The Empire of Civil Society: Critique of the Realist Theory of International Relations* (London: Verso, 1994).

55 For example, see Frank Schorkopf, 'Behavioural and Social Science Perspectives on Political Violence', in Christian Walter, Silja Vöneky, Volker Röben and Frank Schorkopf (eds), *Terrorism as a Challenge for National and International Law: Security Versus Liberty?* (Berlin: Springer, 2004), pp. 3–22.

56 Magnus Ranstorp, 'Mapping Terrorism Research – Challenges and Priorities', in Magnus Ranstorp (ed.), *Mapping Terrorism Research: State of the Art, Gaps and Future Direction* (London: Routledge, 2006), p. 7.

57 Martha Crenshaw, 'Current Research on Terrorism: The Academic Perspective', *Studies in Conflict and Terrorism*, Vol. 15 No. 1 1992, p. 1.

58 For example, in terms of terrorism, see Colin S. Gray, 'Thinking Asymmetrically in Times of Terror', *Parameters*, Spring 2002, pp. 5–14.
59 Johnson, 'Bricks and Mortar', p. 1.
60 Stephen Marrin, 'Intelligence Analysis Theory: Explaining and Predicting Analytic Responsibilities', *Intelligence and National Security*, 22: 6, pp. 821–46.
61 Iraq Study Group, *Report* (Washington, DC, December 2006), p. 62.
62 Johnson, 'Bricks and Mortar', p. 11.

5   Theory of surprise

James J. Wirtz

Why do states, non-state actors, or individuals attempt to surprise their opponents? Why do they often succeed? How does surprise affect strategic interactions, competitions in which the behavior of both sides determine the outcome? Why do some surprise initiatives succeed spectacularly, only to end in disaster for the side that initially benefited from surprise? If we can explain surprise, can we prevent it from occurring?

To answer these questions, one would have to develop a theory of surprise – a unifying explanation of why states, for example, attempt to surprise their opponents with diplomatic or military initiatives, why they succeed and how surprise helps them to achieve their objectives. Some might protest, however, that such a powerful (in the sense that it would apply to people, businesses, bureaucracies, and states) and parsimonious (thrifty in the number of causal factors it highlights) explanation would be impossible to construct because of the many challenges that often bedevil those wishing to avoid surprise.[1] At the heart of the problem are the limits to human cognition that constrain our ability to anticipate the unexpected or novel, especially if the future fails to match our existing analytical concepts, beliefs, or assumptions.[2] Idiosyncratic factors – the 'Ultra syndrome,' the 'cry-wolf syndrome,' denial and deception or an unfavorable signal-to-noise ratio – complicate institutional efforts at intelligence analysis and the production of finished estimates.[3] Compartmentalization, hierarchy, 'group think,' a deference to organizational preferences or an organizational culture that creates 'intelligence to please,' in other words, bureaucracy itself, can impede efforts to avoid surprise.[4] Historians also might note that each instance of surprise is wedded to a unique set of circumstances, institutions and personalities. They would suggest that efforts to surprise an opponent have been present throughout history, but attaining and benefiting from surprise really is embedded in a specific technical, political, or military context.

Given this Pandora's box of cognitive weaknesses, intelligence pathologies and bureaucratic nightmares, it is impossible to say exactly which combination of shortcomings will conspire to assist cunning opponents in surprising their victims. But it is possible to predict when and why that Pandora's box will be opened and why its consequences can be devastating for the victim. It also is possible to explain why the side that achieved surprise can suffer a devastating setback when the box snaps shut. Additionally, the key role played by surprise in asymmetric attacks and special operations can be identified. There are discernable patterns in the history of surprise in warfare and diplomacy, suggesting that surprise is a general phenomenon that can be explained with a general theory.[5]

To the best of my knowledge, the theory of surprise has never been fully articulated elsewhere. The theory is derived largely from Michael Handel's writings, especially his early philosophical musings about the nature of intelligence and surprise. It is no coincidence, therefore, that the theory of surprise is based on Clausewitz's concept of strategy and war. The theory relies on this Clausewitzian vision of war to explain why surprise is attractive to a specific party in a conflict, although it diverges sharply from the great Prussian philosopher's judgment that surprise was over rated as a strategic instrument in war. It then turns to Handel's insights about actors' incentives to base their strategy on the element of surprise and how this inherently risky enterprise increases the likelihood that efforts to achieve surprise will succeed. These insights, what I call 'Handel's risk paradox,' provide an important link between the structure of conflict and the psychology of surprise. The theory, then, explains why those who rely on surprise might win a battle, but rarely achieve overall victory in war. The theory also identifies a way at least to mitigate the threat of being victimized by surprise in the future.

War as administration

Surprise often is described as a force multiplier, something that increases the effectiveness of one's forces in combat. Across cultures and history, military doctrines have encouraged soldiers to incorporate surprise, along with other force multipliers such as the use of cover or maneuver, into their military operations because they increase the prospects for success and reduce casualties. In 1984, Handel summarized the battlefield advantages derived from surprise:

> A successful unanticipated attack will facilitate the destruction of a sizable portion of the enemy's forces at a lower cost to the attacker by throwing the inherently stronger defense psychologically off balance, and hence temporarily reducing his resistance ... the numerically inferior side is able to take the initiative by concentrating superior forces at the time and place of its choosing, thereby vastly improving the likelihood of achieving a decisive victory.[6]

Clearly surprise serves as a force multiplier or, as Handel notes, it allows one side to achieve the temporary numerical superiority needed to launch offensive operations. But Handel only alludes to how surprise produces this force multiplier effect. Surprise temporarily suspends the dialectical nature of warfare (or any other strategic contest) by eliminating an active opponent from the battlefield. Surprise turns war into a stochastic exercise in which the probability of some event can be determined with a degree of certainty or, more rarely, an event in which the outcome can be not only known in advance, but determined by one side in the conflict.

Surprise literally transforms war from a strategic interaction into a matter of accounting and logistics. Probability and chance still influence administrative matters and friction still can bedevil any evolution, whether it is conducted in peacetime or in war. But surprise eliminates war's dialectic: achieving a military objective no longer is impeded by an opponent who can be expected to do everything in their power to make one's life miserable. This has a profound effect on military operations.[7] For example, the amount of time it might take to arrive and seize a destination can be derived from simple calculations about how fast a unit can drive down some autobahn (Of course, those gifted in mathematics might use more elegant algorithms to determine the effects of equipment breakdowns, road conditions, or crew fatigue to estimate probabilities of likely arrival times.). No account need be made for delays caused by roadblocks, blown bridges, pre-registered artillery, or major enemy units astride one's path. 'Without a reacting enemy,' according to Edward Luttwak, 'or rather to the extent and degree that surprise is achieved, the conduct of war becomes mere administration.'[8]

Doctrine and planning guides universally encourage officers to incorporate surprise and other force multipliers into military operations. Even when surprise is virtually nonexistent, military planners appear compelled to explain that they have attained a degree of surprise. US planners, for example, prior to the start of air strikes against Iraq in 1991 and Afghanistan in 2001, claimed they surprised their opponents, even though the attacks were preceded by very public force deployments and diplomacy.[9] But all of the lip service paid to the desirability of utilizing force multipliers hides the fact that surprise really offers a 'silver bullet' in war. Whether it occurs at the tactical, theater, or strategic level of operations, surprise allows weak adversaries to contemplate operations that are simply beyond their capability in wartime.[10] Although surprise usually is a matter of degree,[11] when it approximates its ideal type, surprise literally makes war go away.

For a theory which is avowedly based on Clausewitz's work, it might at first appear a bit odd to reach a conclusion about the potential utility of surprise that diverges completely from the judgment of the great philosopher of war.[12] From a dialectical perspective, there is a cost to everything in war: operational security can prevent proper planning and briefing, diversionary attacks and deception operations can take on a life of their own or draw resources away from the main battle. Even spectacular successes like the 11 September attacks operate on the narrowest margins of success. For instance, there simply were too few al-Qaeda operatives aboard hijacked aircraft to maintain control in the face of determined opposition from the passengers and crew. But inserting more operatives into the United States only would have increased the chances of detection and overall failure of the terrorist attacks.[13] Clausewitz estimated that the costs of obtaining surprise generally outweighed the benefits surprise provided. Clausewitz, however, was more concerned with explaining war's dialectic and the way it shaped the nature, course and outcome of battle. What the theory of surprise posits is that under ideal circumstances that occasionally can be achieved in practice, war's dialectic can be eliminated. In other words, it identifies a way to eliminate one's opposition by pre-empting the 'duel' that is war.

Surprise makes extraordinary kinds of military activity in warfare possible because it eliminates an active opponent from the battlefield. Special Operations or commando raids, for instance, are a good example of a type of activity that is made possible by the element of surprise. Despite their cultivated reputation for ferocity, combat skill and daring, commandos and other types of Special Forces are lightly armed, poorly supplied, and generally outnumbered by their adversaries. In a pitched battle against competent conventional units, they would be quickly surrounded and outgunned. To achieve their objectives, they have become experts in unconventional modes of transportation and operations to enable them to appear and disappear in unexpected ways and at unanticipated times and places. Surprise is the key enabler of all types of unconventional operations because it allows commandos to achieve some objective or attack some target without significant opposition or no opposition at all. Surprise also creates the opportunity for special operations to produce strategic effects. A dozen or so operatives appearing at a crucial command center deep behind enemy lines can affect the course of some battle. But the same commandos would have no discernable impact on the course of a conflict if they joined a divisional engagement on the front line.[14]

Unless it produces complete victory, the ability of surprise to transform conflict is fleeting. Enjoying the benefits of complete surprise, the first wave of Japanese aircraft that attacked Pearl Harbor on 7 December 1941 apparently suffered few casualties. But by the time the second wave left the airspace over Oahu about two hours later, twenty-nine aircraft had been lost, even though the island's defenses had been damaged by the first wave of attacks.[15] When the Japanese returned in June 1942 to ambush the US Navy in the waters around Midway, it had become extremely difficult to surprise Americans with a carrier air strike in the waters around Hawaii. After all, the concept was no longer novel after the attack on Pearl Harbor. An outstanding American intelligence effort denied Japan the element of surprise that was crucial to their success in the engagement. The US Navy then delivered a stunning defeat to the Japanese, making Midway the beginning of the end for Imperial Japan. Similarly, surprise was the crucial element in the 11 September 2001 terrorist attacks against the World Trade Center and the Pentagon. When passengers aboard a fourth hijacked airliner learned of their probable fate in cell phone conversations with loved ones, they stopped the terrorists from completing their mission. Without the surprise needed to prevent the passengers from realizing that they were engaged in a conflict, the terrorists lacked the forces necessary to maintain control of the aircraft.

Surprise is extraordinarily attractive because it allows actors to achieve objectives that would normally be well beyond their reach if they faced an alert and determined opponent. Surprise allows one side to operate with virtually no opposition. Relying on the element of surprise, however, is extraordinarily risky. It is impossible ex ante to guarantee that surprise will occur, or for that matter, exactly when the effects of surprise will begin to wear off, and the inability to achieve surprise will doom the operation to failure. Stronger adversaries always can rely on more predictable attrition strategies to wear down weaker opponents.[16] In fact, stronger adversaries generally do not want to surprise their opponents. They prefer to intimidate them into surrender by announcing clearly their intention to fight if the adversary does not comply with their demands. US officials for example, made clear their intention to attack Afghanistan if the Taliban did not hand over the al-Qaeda ringleaders responsible for the 11 September attacks. The Taliban might have been surprised by the way the US campaign unfolded and by the speed with which their forces collapsed, but they were not really surprised by the war itself.

The risk paradox and surprise

Surprise is attractive to the weaker party in a conflict because it allows it to contemplate decisive actions against a stronger adversary.[17] But because achieving surprise is a risky proposition and because it allows actors to consider initiatives that are beyond their capabilities, the victim of surprise often will dismiss potential surprise scenarios as hare-brained. In other words, even if the victims of surprise detect the beginnings of an initiative, they will have to overcome their existing assumption that the unfolding initiative is beyond the capability of their adversary or will prove to be suicidal. This asymmetry in the perception of what is prudent and what is reckless creates a paradox, identified by Handel, which lies at the heart of the theory of surprise: 'The greater the risk, the less likely it seems, and the less risky it becomes. In fact, the greater the risk, the smaller it becomes.'[18]

Handel is suggesting that there is a direct link between the weaker party's incentive to use surprise and the stronger party's propensity actually to be surprised by the initiative. He offered this insight, however, without fully outlining the causal linkages he was suggesting. Elsewhere, for example, he wrote 'The powerful stronger side conversely lacks the incentive to resort to surprise and thus not only sacrifices an important military advantage but also plays into his enemy's hands.'[19] From this passage it would appear that Handel believes that weakness is a necessary condition for one side to gamble an entire operation on surprise. In this sense, he is probably correct; stronger parties lack the incentive to risk everything on an effort to gain surprise. Stronger parties, however, often hope to achieve and benefit from surprise. American officials thought that the technological surprise suffered by Japan over Hiroshima and Nagasaki would shock the Japanese into surrender, but they did not stop their preparations to launch a bloody attritional invasion of the home islands to force a surrender. They did not risk everything on gaining and benefiting from surprise. In other words, the causal claims made by Handel required some refinement (e.g., the weaker party in a conflict is more likely than the stronger side to attempt operations or strategies that *require* the element of surprise to succeed). Similarly, Handel never really explains how victims of surprise contribute to their own demise. In this sense, he missed an opportunity to offer an important advance in the theory of surprise.

From a political scientist's perspective, what is especially elegant about Handel's risk paradox is that it provides a link between explanatory levels of analysis.[20] The incentives to seek surprise are located at a systemic level of analysis, or in the very structure of the situation we find ourselves in. Without parties in competition, without surprise becoming a priority for the weaker party in its quest for victory, there would be no deliberate efforts to risk everything on strategies that require surprise for success. But surprise is not a systemic or a structural phenomenon; it exists in the mind of the victim. Surprise is about human cognition, perception and psychology. In other words, the different perceptions of risk between the stronger and weaker opponent link the structural setting, which creates the incentive for surprise, with the cognitive setting, which creates the opportunity to surprise an opponent. The weaker party has a stronger interest in basing its plans on the element of surprise, while the more powerful side has reason to over look the danger of enemy attack.

The ex ante divergence in perceptions of risk and opportunity sets the stage for human cognition and psychology to create the phenomenon of surprise. The weaker side becomes mesmerized by the potential opportunity created by surprise (i.e., suspending the dialectic of war), while the stronger side fails to consider possible courses of enemy action based on stochastic estimates because it becomes focused on estimates of the enemy's *wartime* capabilities. This cognitive divergence, for example, sets the stage for the use of denial and deception. It is relatively easy for the weaker side to hide (deny) information from opponents who are not looking for it, or to mislead opponents by feeding them information that confirms their more realistic expectations of what is possible in war. A leading student of denial and deception has even gone so far as to claim that 'deception operations usually have substantial payoffs and never backfire.'[21] Moreover, if accurate information reaches the victim concerning what is about to transpire, it is likely to be dismissed as fantastic or implausible based on the real facts of the situation. In planning surprise, the weaker side, out of desperation, is likely to grasp at straws and to believe that they have opportunities that really do not exist with or without the element of surprise. Prior to the Tet offensive, most American analysts dismissed information that the North Vietnamese and their Viet Cong allies were planning to instigate a revolt among the South Vietnamese population because they accurately perceived that southerners would not rebel against the regime in Saigon.[22] Opponents who are desperate enough to gamble everything on surprise can be expected to ignore data that complicates their planning or calls into question their predictions about how their victims will respond to surprise.[23] Nikita Khrushchev was warned repeatedly by various advisors that even if he surprised Americans with his plan to deploy nuclear weapons and associated delivery vehicles to Cuba, the US reaction to the deployment would erase any gains the Soviets might obtain from the gambit (The Central Intelligence Agency's Special National Intelligence Estimate [SNIE] 85–3–62 that was published in September 1962 also predicted that the Soviets would not place missiles in Cuba because it would be too risky.).[24] The side planning surprise is prone to make mistakes because it walks an extraordinarily fine line between success and failure. This fact creates a real challenge for intelligence analysts: they often have to convince their chain of command that the opponent is about to launch an operation that appears ex ante to suffer from a fundamental flaw, a perception that is likely to undermine the plausibility of their warning.

To prevent surprise the victim must overcome several challenges. It must overcome efforts at denial and deception. It must anticipate how weaker opponents might expect to achieve wildly ambitious objectives aided by surprise. It must anticipate that its opponent's strategy might be riddled with errors of omission or commission, or at least an overly optimistic view of its prospects of success. All of this must occur, however, as analysts and policy-makers are blinded by their own assumptions and theories about how the conflict should unfold, perceptions colored by their conservative, attritional, view of the battlefield. The possibility that the opponent will launch asymmetrical attacks is hard to imagine because of the inherent difficulty in discovering weaknesses in one's own forces or strategies. In the absence of compelling data, mirror imaging – or the use of one's own preferences, culture, and strategy to explain an opponent's behavior – is likely to occur. This tendency to understand the opponent's behavior in light of one's own perception of the situation really constitutes the heart of the surprise problem from the victim's perspective. This is the point at which a host of cognitive biases, intelligence pathologies, or bureaucratic weaknesses will conspire to hide the possibilities for surprise from potential victims.[25] Even more troubling is the fact that evidence of what is about to transpire, or an eerily prophetic analysis, generally can be identified somewhere in the intelligence pipeline in the aftermath of surprise.[26] What is missing from the victim's perspective is the analytical context necessary to use accurate data to generate a useful and timely warning.

The fundamental divergence in the perception of what is possible and what is foolish creates a paradox that leaves open the possibility for surprise to occur. Extraordinarily ambitious initiatives are not only planned, but are often brilliantly executed against opponents who fail to recognize what is happening before it is too late. They succeed because extraordinarily risky operations that require an acquiescent opponent to succeed appear implausible ex ante to the victim. This plausibility assumption will lead the victim to place impending signals of an opponent's unfolding initiative in an analytic context that is likely to be flawed.

The failure of surprise

Much is written about intelligence failure, but little is written about the failure of surprise. Scholars have focused on successful surprise at the operational level of war, not on the effect of surprise in achieving overall victory. Surprise attacks often produce spectacular results temporarily or locally, but surprise rarely wins wars. Successful operational surprise may even hasten defeat by mobilizing the victim (e.g., the American response to the Japanese attack on Pearl Harbor) or by expending scarce assets without achieving a decisive victory (e.g., the fate of the Nazi offensive through the Ardennes forest in the winter of 1944). Even when surprise produces positive strategic consequences, the price can be extraordinarily high. The shock of the Tet attacks or the Egyptian surprise attack at the outset of the 1973 Yom Kippur war can be said to have produced victory in the very important sense that they altered the political balance between the combatants, but from the North Vietnamese or Egyptian perspective, events on the battlefield did not unfold according to plan. In that sense, the shock of surprise itself, not the temporary suspension of war's dialectic, helped to deliver victory. But this political shock effect is rare and in the previously mentioned cases it was an unanticipated, albeit not unwelcome, positive effect produced by a failed military attack. Because they can alter the political balance in a conflict, the consequences of surprise are often unanticipated and unintended by the side launching the initiative. If surprise is an *immediate force multiplier*, then over time it can act as a *resistance multiplier*.[27] The side that achieves surprise may reach the culminating point of attack, thereby achieving some fantastic local victory, without ever reaching the culminating point of victory, thereby hastening its defeat in war.

Surprise attacks often fail disastrously because the side undertaking the initiative miscalculates in several ways. Those contemplating surprise might correctly estimate that surprise is needed to achieve their military objectives, only to find that a successful surprise attack undermines the political or moral basis of their campaign. The Japanese attack on Pearl Harbor was a military tour de force, a feat of professional skill that will be remembered for a thousand years. But the successful surprise attack was a political disaster for Japan because it eliminated the basis of its grand strategy in the Pacific: a 'casualty averse' American public that would negotiate rather than fight over relatively unknown and unwanted territory. The Japanese failed to understand that the military force multiplier they needed to succeed – surprise – would destroy the political basis of their quest for empire. Those launching an attack often fail to understand that surprise can maximize the impact of a specific blow, but that even the most successful surprise attack needs to be integrated into an overall strategy to win the war. Surprise can worsen the weaker side's position once the dialectic of war is reestablished because it can elicit a heightened response from the stronger victim. Successful surprise can make it impossible for the attacker to reach the culminating point of victory in war because it causes the more powerful victim to engage fully in battle.

Failures also occur because of a mismatch between the weaker side's objectives and the degree, duration, or scope of the paralysis induced in the stronger opponent. The attacker might achieve surprise, but not across a large enough front or for a sufficient enough time, allowing the opponent to muster its superior forces to crush the attack. Indeed, when the effects of surprise begin to dissipate, the weaker side risks being caught overextended without the combat power needed to manage even a decent fighting withdrawal. This is what happened to the Nazi counterattack through the Ardennes forest. Nazi forces achieved surprise and punched through the allied line, but the allies had sufficient forces to absorb the attack and launch their own counterattack against the exposed Nazi flanks and lines of communication. If surprise is not linked to some sort of knockout blow or an overall strategy to win the conflict, it often worsens the weaker party's position and accelerates its loss of the war.[28]

The failure of surprise is related to Handel's risk paradox in the sense that it vindicates the stronger side's judgment that a possible operation is extraordinarily risky or simply irrational. It made no sense for the Japanese to attack Pearl Harbor because they lacked the resources to defeat the United States; the sneak attack on 7 December simply guaranteed that superior American resources would be brought to bear against them. Even aided by the element of surprise, operations that appear hare-brained ex ante can actually turn out to be hare-brained. The analysts who predicted in SNIE 85–3–62 that the Soviets would not place missiles in Cuba because it would be too dangerous stated in the aftermath of the Cuban Missile Crisis that their analysis was at least partially vindicated by events. In other words, the Soviets should not have placed missiles in Cuba because the gambit risked superpower war for what were at best marginal benefits. CIA analysts were not alone in this judgment. When Secretary of State Dean Rusk called on Soviet Ambassador Anatoly Dobrynin to inform him that the United States had detected missiles in Cuba, he surprised the Soviet official with the news (Dobrynin had not been privy to the decisions made in Moscow). Rusk stated informally that it was incomprehensible to him how leaders in Moscow could make such a gross error of judgment about what was acceptable to the United States.[29] Years later, he noted that Dobrynin was so shaken by the news that he aged ten years right before his eyes.[30]

Surprise fails because it leads the weaker side in the conflict to reach for goals that are truly beyond their grasp or to forget that when the effects of surprise dissipate, the dialectic of war returns with a vengeance. Indeed, the ultimate paradox of surprise is that it often amounts to a 'Lose–Lose' proposition: it creates a disastrous initial loss for the victim and a painful loss of the war for the attacker. The outcome of the war actually confirms both sides estimate of the pre-war balance of power as the stronger power defeats the weaker side in the conflict. The theory of surprise thus offers an important caveat to Geoffrey Blainey's argument that war is more likely as states near parity.[31] Even though the leaders of the weaker side in a conflict might recognize the disparity in power between them and their opponent, the prospect of surprise can prompt them to believe that they can nullify that disparity and achieve their objectives.

The future of surprise

In the aftermath of 11 September 2001, the idea that the United States, its allies, military forces, or interests are likely targets of surprise attacks or initiatives would not stir much controversy. But this prediction is not based solely on recent events. Instead, the theory of surprise suggests that America's opponents must somehow circumvent its diplomatic, economic, or military might to achieve goals that Washington opposes. The United States' relative strength creates incentives for its opponents to launch surprise initiatives or asymmetric attacks to achieve their objectives before America and its allies can bring their full power to bear. Americans' relative strength also creates an attritional mindset that blinds them to the possibility that enemies will use surprise to attempt to achieve objectives that in war would be beyond their reach.

Evidence exists to support the idea that the problem of surprise is especially acute for the United States. Thomas Christensen, for example, notes that the American academic and policy debate about the potential threat created by the emergence of China as a peer competitor (i.e., a state capable of challenging the United States in a battle of attrition), ignores a more likely road to war. Chinese leaders' perceptions of their own weakness have led them to a search for methods to distract, deter, or bloody the United States.[32] What is particularly chilling is that the thinking emerging in China is eerily similar to Japanese strategy on the eve of Pearl Harbor: a casualty-averse America will seek a negotiated settlement following some military setback. The fact that many American observers fail to realize that China might gamble on surprise rather than work for decades to match US military capabilities also is disturbing. Additionally, al-Qaeda's recent success in the skies over New York and Washington demonstrates that terrorists, fanatics, or syndicates might find the element of surprise attractive because it affords them a way to attack an infinitely more powerful United States. As the information and communication revolution continues to empower individuals, the US intelligence community now has to worry that non-state actors will attempt to capitalize on surprise to achieve their objectives. The stage is set for surprise to occur.

Michael Handel was a pessimist when it came to the future of surprise, agreeing with his colleague Richard Betts that intelligence failures are inevitable.[33] Handel came to this conclusion in his early writings, and the advent of advanced data processing and reconnaissance capabilities did little to alter his judgment. Indeed, what is especially vexing to Handel, Betts, and a host of other scholars is that victims of surprise often had a chance to avert disaster, but cognitive, bureaucratic, or political constraints or pathologies prevented them from capitalizing on these opportunities. Accurate signals of impending attack generally can be discovered in the intelligence pipeline after surprise occurs. Some people even manage to recognize these signals. Intelligence 'dissenters' – individuals who swim against the analytical or policy tide – often issue accurate warnings before disaster strikes only to be ignored by fellow intelligence analysts or policy-makers. Prior to the Tet offensive, for instance, civilian analysts in Saigon developed an accurate estimate of North Vietnamese and Viet Cong intentions, only to have their analysis dismissed as far-fetched by analysts at the headquarters of the Central Intelligence Agency.[34] Occasionally intelligence analysts might even get things right: US intelligence analysts surprised the Japanese Navy at Midway. But the American miracle at Midway was made possible by the American disaster at Pearl Harbor. According to Handel:

> Arrogance and a sense of invincibility blinded the Japanese, who did not consider their opponent worthy of much attention. On the other hand, the Americans, who had been humbled early in the war and who lacked both confidence and ships, knew that learning as much as possible about their enemy was imperative. There is no stronger incentive to encourage the appreciation of intelligence than fear and weakness (whether actual or perceived); conversely, victory and power reduce one's motivation to learn about the enemy, thus bringing about the conditions that may eventually cause defeat.[35]

What changed in the months following Pearl Harbor was that the Japanese had adopted the attritional mindset characteristic of the strong while US analysts and officers recognized that they needed force multipliers to overcome their disadvantage in numbers, equipment, morale, and experience.

The American experience at Midway thus offers some insights into possible ways of avoiding future surprise that American policy-makers and analysts might use to great benefit. The outcome of the Battle of Midway raises an important question: why did the same analysts and intelligence organizations fail so badly in their task prior to Pearl Harbor, yet succeed so well in its aftermath? Was it war alone that concentrated their minds? In the past, most observers have identified cognitive, bureaucratic, or political problems as a source of intelligence failure. But the pathologies and bureaucratic and cognitive limits to analysis often identified as the source of intelligence failure might simply be consequences of a more fundamental causal force. The theory of surprise suggests that it is the initial cognitive framework created by the relative power position of the parties in conflict that sets the stage for surprise to occur. In other words, if strong parties began to view conflict from the weaker party's perspective, while weak actors kept war's dialectic in mind, then surprise would become less likely. Christensen's analysis of the potential Chinese threat ends on a similar note: Chinese officers and officials should be encouraged to visit Pearl Harbor to take note of the fact that it is a mistake to count on a lack of American resolve in war.[36] One might also think about modifying the tour to include the surrender deck of the battleship *Missouri* to suggest that once the effect of surprise fades, the dialectic of war returns.

Clearly, reversing the cognitive predisposition that accompanies one's position in a conflict is no small or simple matter. Midway suggests that it might be possible to alter this fundamental bias quickly, although it is not apparent if this change in mindset can be accomplished quickly enough or completely before disaster strikes. The theory of surprise suggests, however, that at least a 'theoretical' path to reducing the likelihood that surprise will be attempted or succeed is available.

Conclusion

Handel began his 1977 article in *International Studies Quarterly* with the observation that the theory of surprise would be better at explaining, rather than preventing, disaster. He turned to Hegel's famous passage to capture this shortcoming: 'The owl of Minerva begins its flight when dusk is falling ... man can perceive the conception of actuality ... only when the actuality has already been fully unfolded and has indeed become cut and dried.'[37] One can only add the observation that things in fact did become pretty cut and dried on the morning of 11 September when the old bird returned home to roost. Millions of people in real time experienced surprise, which was accompanied by an inability on the part of nearly all concerned to interfere with the airplane hijackers. War, for a moment, became a matter of administration, a phenomenon in which it was possible for a few people to destroy the World Trade Center with the aid of a box cutter in just two hours. The very brilliance of such an audacious surprise attack showed that the assumption that people, groups or states would not dare do such a thing was flawed, if not down right stupid. Osama bin Laden, after all, had established a track record of attacking American interests and targets and made no effort to hide the fact that he intended to attack Americans in the future.[38] The fact that we could have seen the attack coming simply adds insult to injury. Handel would of course suggest that this sort of thing is inevitable, that this is what it means to be a victim of surprise.

It is too much to expect that surprise can be prevented in the future. But the theory of surprise can identify when it is likely to occur, who is likely to find the element of surprise attractive as a basis of policy or strategy and who is likely to be its victim. It also explains why the beginning of the end for al-Qaeda came when the first New Yorker noticed an aircraft heading toward the World Trade Center. The trick now lies in making operational use of the theory of surprise.

Notes

1 A host of factors also bedevils those wishing to achieve surprise. For efforts to organize the body of theory related to intelligence and surprise, see Michael Handel, 'The Politics of Intelligence,' *Intelligence and National Security* Vol. 2, No. 4 (October 1987), pp. 5–46; James J. Wirtz, 'The Intelligence Paradigm,' *Intelligence and National Security* Vol. 4, No. 4 (October 1989), pp. 829–37.

2 Robert Jervis, *Perception and Misperception in World Politics* (Princeton, NJ: Princeton University Press, 1976); and Richards J. Heuer, Jr., *Psychology of Intelligence Analysis* (Washington, DC: Center for the Study of Intelligence, Government Printing Office, 1999).

3 The 'Ultra Syndrome' is the tendency to become overly reliant on a clandestine source of information that has proven to be useful in the past, while the 'cry-wolf syndrome' is the tendency for repeated false warnings to desensitize an audience to subsequent alarms. See Ephraim Kam, *Surprise Attack: The Victim's Perspective* (Washington, DC: Cambridge: Harvard University Press, 1988).

4 Walter Laqueur, *A World of Secrets: The Uses and Limits of Intelligence* (New York: Basic Books, 1985).

5 For a similar argument about the prospects for a theory of deception, see Barton

Whaley and Jeffrey Busby, 'Detecting Deception: Practice, Practitioners, and Theory,' in Roy Godson and James J. Wirtz, *Strategic Denial and Deception* (New Brunswick, NJ: Transaction Publisher, 2002), pp. 181–221.

6 Michael Handel, 'Intelligence and the Problem of Strategic Surprise,' *The Journal of Strategic Studies* Vol. 7, No. 3 (September 1984), pp. 229–30.

7 Surprise, however, cannot overcome gross incompetence (troops that cannot conduct basic maneuvers), or negligence (weapons that will not work or vehicles that will not run) on the part of the attacker.

8 Edward Luttwak, *Strategy: The Logic of War and Peace* (Cambridge, MA: Harvard University Press, 1987), p. 8.

9 Although in both instances US forces can be said to have benefited from technological surprise. On that phenomenon, see Michael Handel, 'Technological Surprise in War,' *Intelligence and National Security* Vol. 2, No 1 (January 1987), pp. 1–53.

10 Handel often made the similar point that 'the weaker side has a very strong incentive to compensate for his weakness by resorting to the use of stratagem and surprise as a force multiplier.' Michael Handel, 'Crisis and Surprise in Three Arab–Israeli Wars,' in Klaus Knorr and Patrick Morgan (eds), *Strategic Military Surprise* (New Brunswick, NJ: Transaction Books, 1983), p. 113.

11 Richard Betts, *Surprise Attack: Lessons for Defense Planning* (Washington, DC: The Brookings Institution, 1982), especially pp. 88–92.

12 In his writings Handel often stated that Clausewitz was no fan of intelligence, deception and surprise, but he also often noted that since the early nineteenth century, changes in technology, logistics, and communications increased the attractiveness of surprise in war. In 1996, for instance, he wrote: 'While for Clausewitz, surprise was rarely achievable on he strategic level but was more feasible on the operational or strategic levels, today the opposite is true ... the development of radars and other sensors have made operational and tactical surprise easier to prevent.' Michael Handel, *Masters of War*, 2nd rev. edn (London: Frank Cass, 1996), p. 131.

13 After all, one of the would-be hijackers apparently was already in police custody prior to 11 September 2001.

14 William McRaven, *Spec Ops Case Studies in Special Operations Warfare: Theory and Practice* (Novato, CA: Presidio Press, 1998).

15 Samuel Eliot Morison, *The Two-Ocean War: A Short History of the United States Navy in the Second World War* (Boston, MA: Little, Brown & Co., 1963), p. 67.

16 In the revised edition of his seminal volume, Luttwak makes the same point: 'military leaders whose forces are altogether superior may be quite justified in spurning surprise, for the sake of ample preparations to use their full strength with the simplest methods, to minimize organizational risk.' Edward Luttwak, *Strategy: The Logic of War and Peace*, rev. edn (Cambridge, MA: Harvard University Press, 2001), p. 13.

17 According to Luttwak, 'In a manner itself paradoxical, it is those who are materially weaker, and therefore have good reason to fear a straightforward clash of strength against strength, who can most benefit by self-weakening paradoxical conduct – if it obtains the advantage of surprise, which may yet offer victory.' Luttwak, *Strategy*, rev. edn, p. 14.

18 Michael Handel, 'The Yom Kippur War and the Inevitability of Surprise,' *International Studies Quarterly* Vol. 21, No. 3 (September 1977), p. 468.

19 Handel, 'Crisis and Surprise in Three Arab–Israeli Wars,' p. 113.

20 Another important effort to link levels of analysis is Robert Putnam, 'The Logic of Two-Level Games,' *International Organization* Vol. 42, No. 2 (Spring 1988), pp. 427–60.

21 Barton Whaley, 'Conditions Making for Success and Failure of D&D: Authoritarian and Transition Regimes,' in Roy Godson and James J. Wirtz (eds), *Strategic Denial and Deception: The 21st Century Challenge* (New Brunswick, NJ: Transaction Books, 2001), p. 67.

22 James J. Wirtz, *The Tet Offensive: Intelligence Failure in War* (Ithaca, NY: Cornell University Press, 1991).

23 According to Jervis, 'A person is less apt to reorganize evidence into a new theory or image if he is deeply committed to the established view.' Jervis, *Perception and Misperception*, p. 196.

24 Special National Intelligence Estimate 85–3–62, *The Military Buildup in Cuba* (September 1962), pp. 1–2, 8–9; and James J. Wirtz, 'Organizing for Crisis Intelligence: Lessons from the Cuban Missile Crisis,' in James G. Blight and David Welch (eds), *Intelligence and the Cuban Missile Crisis* (London: Frank Cass, 1998).

25 Betts, *Surprise Attack*, pp. 87–149. This also is the point at which the theory of surprise can integrate the existing literature and competing theories of surprise into a unified explanation of the phenomenon.

26 Richard Betts, 'Surprise Despite Warning,' *Political Science Quarterly* Vol. 95, No. 4, pp. 551–72; and Michael Handel, *The Diplomacy of Surprise: Hitler, Nixon, Sadat* (Cambridge, MA: Center for the Study of International Affairs, 1981), p. 144. Roberta Wohlstetter's use of a metaphorical 'signal to noise' ratio was an effort to show how accurate 'signals' could always be found in an intelligence system, along with extraneous information described as 'noise.' Signals would have to grow stronger than this background noise before they could be perceived accurately. Ariel Levite offered a dissenting opinion on the issue, that surprise often occurred because of a lack of accurate warning, if not raw data, in an intelligence bureaucracy. See Ariel Levite, *Intelligence and Strategic Surprises* (New York: Columbia University Press, 1987).

27 Surprise can make war go away, but it rarely can prevent it from returning.

28 Stalin offered a similar judgment about the effectiveness of surprise, which provided him with an excuse for the denigration of the disaster of June 1941. For Stalin, surprise was a transient influence in war, not a permanently operating factor that could determine the outcome of a conflict. I would like to thank Dick Betts for offering this observation.

29 State Department Cable on Secretary of State Dean Rusk Meeting with Soviet Ambassador Dobrynin to Give Kennedy's Letter to Premier Khrushchev, 'Announcing Discovery of Missiles in Cuba,' contained in Laurence Chang and Peter Kornbluh (eds), *The Cuban Missile Crisis, 1962* (New York: The New Press, 1982), pp. 146–7.

30 James Blight's interview with Dean Rusk, 18 May 1987, in James G. Blight and David Welch, *On the Brink: Americans and Soviets Reexamine the Cuban Missile Crisis* (New York: Hill and Wang, 1989), p. 185.

31 Geoffrey Blainey, *The Causes of War* (New York: The Free Press, 1988).

32 Thomas J. Christensen, 'Posing Problems without Catching Up: China's Rise and Challenges for U.S. Security Policy,' *International Security* Vol. 23, No. 4 (Spring 2001), pp. 5–40.

33 Handel, 'The Yom Kippur War,' pp. 461–2; and Richard Betts, 'Analysis, War and Decision: Why Intelligence Failures are Inevitable', *World Politics* Vol. 31 (October 1978), pp. 61–89 and in this volume, pp. 000.

34 Wirtz, *The Tet Offensive*, pp. 172–7.

35 Michael Handel, 'Intelligence and Military Operations,' in Michael Handel (ed.), *Intelligence and Military Operations* (London: Frank Cass, 1990), p. 39.

36 Christensen, 'Posing Problems,' p. 36.

37 Handel, 'The Yom Kippur War and the Inevitability of Surprise', p. 462.

38 Kenneth Katzman, 'Terrorism: Near Eastern Groups and State Sponsors' (CRS Report to Congress, 10 September 2001), pp. 9–13.

6 Analysis, war, and decision

Why intelligence failures are inevitable

*Richard K. Betts**

Military disasters befall some states, no matter how informed their leaders are, because their capabilities are deficient. Weakness, not choice, is their primary problem. Powerful nations are not immune to calamity either, because their leaders may misperceive threats or miscalculate responses. Information, understanding, and judgment are a larger part of the strategic challenge for countries such as the United States. Optimal decisions in defense policy therefore depend on the use of strategic intelligence: the acquisition, analysis, and *appreciation* of relevant data. In the best-known cases of intelligence failure, the most crucial mistakes have seldom been made by collectors of raw information, occasionally by professionals who produce finished analyses, but most often by the decision makers who consume the products of intelligence services. Policy premises constrict perception, and administrative workloads constrain reflection. Intelligence failure is political and psychological more often than organizational.

Observers who see notorious intelligence failures as egregious often infer that disasters can be avoided by perfecting norms and procedures for analysis and argumentation. This belief is illusory. Intelligence can be improved marginally, but not radically, by altering the analytic system. The illusion is also dangerous if it abets overconfidence that systemic reforms will increase the predictability of threats. The use of intelligence depends less on the bureaucracy than on the intellects and inclinations of the authorities above it. To clarify the tangled relationship of analysis and policy, this essay explores conceptual approaches to intelligence failure, differentiation of intelligence problems, insurmountable obstacles to accurate assessment, and limitations of solutions proposed by critics.

Approaches to theory

Case studies of intelligence failures abound, yet scholars lament the lack of a theory of intelligence.[1] It is more accurate to say that we lack a positive or normative theory of intelligence. Negative or descriptive theory – empirical understanding of how intelligence systems make mistakes – is well developed. The distinction is significant because there is little evidence that either scholars or practitioners have succeeded in translating such knowledge into reforms that measurably reduce failure. Development of a normative theory of intelligence has been inhibited because the lessons of hindsight do not guarantee improvement in foresight, and hypothetical solutions to failure only occasionally produce improvement in practice. The problem of intelligence failure can be conceptualized in three overlapping ways. The first is the most reassuring; the second is the most common; and the third is the most important.

Failure in perspective

There is an axiom that a pessimist sees a glass of water as half empty and an optimist sees it as half full. In this sense, the estimative system is a glass half full. Mistakes can happen in any activity. Particular failures are accorded disproportionate significance if they are considered isolation rather than in terms of the general ratio of failures to successes; the record of success is less striking because observers tend not to notice disasters that do not happen. Any academician who used a model that predicted outcomes correctly in four out of five cases would be happy; intelligence analysts must use models of their own and should not be blamed for missing occasionally. One problem with this benign view is that there are no clear indicators of what the ratio of failure to success in intelligence is, or whether many successes on minor issues should be reassuring in the face of a smaller number of failures on more critical problems.[2] In the thermonuclear age, just *one* mistake could have apocalyptic consequences.

Pathologies of communication

The most frequently noted sources of breakdowns in intelligence lie in the process of amassing timely data, communicating them to decision makers, and impressing the latter with the validity or relevance of the information. This view of the problem leaves room for optimism because it implies that procedural curatives can eliminate the dynamics of error. For this reason, official post mortems of intelligence blunders inevitably produce recommendations for reorganization and changes in operating norms.

Paradoxes of perception

Most pessimistic is the view that the roots of failure lie in unresolvable trade-offs and dilemmas. Curing some pathologies with organizational reforms often creates new pathologies or resurrects old ones;[3] perfecting intelligence production does not necessarily lead to perfecting intelligence consumption; making warning systems more sensitive reduces the risk of surprise, but increases the number of false alarms, which in turn reduces sensitivity; the principles of optimal analytic procedure are in many respects incompatible with the imperatives of the decision process; avoiding intelligence failure requires the elimination of strategic preconceptions, but leaders cannot operate purposefully without some preconceptions. In devising measures to improve the intelligence process, policy makers are damned if they do and damned if they don't.

It is useful to disaggregate the problem of strategic intelligence failures in order to elicit clues about which paradoxes and pathologies are pervasive and therefore most in need of attention. The crucial problems of linkage between analysis and strategic decision can be subsumed under the following categories:

Attack warning

The problem in this area is timely prediction of an enemy's immediate intentions, and the "selling" of such predictions to responsible authorities. Major insights into intelligence failure have emerged from catastrophic surprises: Pearl Harbor, the Nazi invasion of the USSR, the North Korean attack and Chinese intervention of 1950, and the 1973 war in the Middle East. Two salient phenomena characterizes these cases. First, evidence of impending attack was available, but did not flow efficiently up the chain of command. Second, the fragmentary indicators of alarm that did reach decision makers were dismissed because they contradicted strategic estimates or assumptions. In several cases hesitancy in communication and disbelief on the part of leaders were reinforced by deceptive enemy maneuvers that cast doubt on the data.[4]

Operational evaluation

In wartime, the essential problem lies in judging the results (and their significance) of interacting capabilities. Once hostilities are under way, informed decision making requires assessments of tactical effectiveness – "how we are doing" – in order to adapt strategy and options. In this dimension, the most interesting insights have come from Vietnam-era memoirs of low-level officials and from journalistic muckraking. Again there are two fundamental points. First, within the context of a glut of ambiguous data, intelligence officials linked to operational agencies (primarily military) tend to indulge a propensity for justifying service performance by issuing optimistic assessments, while analysts in autonomous non-operational units (primarily in the Central Intelligence Agency and the late Office of National Estimates) tend to produce more pessimistic evaluations. Second, in contrast to cases of attack warning, fragmentary tactical indicators of *success* tend to override more general and cautious strategic estimates. Confronted by differing analyses, a leader mortgaged to his policy tends to resent or dismiss the critical ones, even when they represent the majority view of the intelligence community, and to cling to the data that support continued commitment.[5] Lyndon Johnson railed at his Director of Central Intelligence (DCI) at a White House dinner:

> Policy making is like milking a fat cow. You see the milk coming out, you press more and the milk bubbles and flows, and just as the bucket is full, the

cow with its tail whips the bucket and all is spilled. That's what CIA does to policy making.[6]

From the consensus-seeking politician, this was criticism; to a pure analyst, it would have been flattery. But it is the perspective of the former, not the latter, that is central in decision making.

Defense planning

The basic task in using intelligence to develop doctrines and forces for deterrence and defense is to estimate threats posed by adversaries, in terms of both capabilities and intentions, over a period of several years. Here the separability of intelligence and policy, analysis and advocacy, is least clear. In dealing with the issue of "how much is enough" for security, debates over data merge murkily into debates over options and programs. As in operational evaluation, the problem lies more in data mongering than in data collecting. To the extent that stark generalizations are possible, the basic points in this category are the reverse of those in the previous one.

First, the justification of a mission (in this case, preparedness for future contingencies as opposed to demonstration of current success on the battlefield) prompts pessimistic estimates by operational military analysts; autonomous analysts without budgetary axes to grind, but with biases similar to those prevalent in the intellectual community, tend towards less alarmed predictions.[7] Military intelligence inclines toward "worst-case" analysis in planning, and toward "best-case" analysis in operational evaluation. (Military intelligence officials such as Lieutenant General Daniel Graham were castigated by liberals for *under*estimating the Vietcong's strength in the 1960's but for *over*-estimated Soviet air deployments in the "bomber gap" controversy of the 1950s, and CIA-dominated National Intelligence Estimates (NIE's) underestimated Soviet ICBM deployments through the 1960s (over-reacting, critics say, to the mistaken prediction of a "missile gap" in 1960).[8]

Second, in the context of peacetime, with competing domestic claims on resources, political leaders have a natural interest in at least partially rejecting military estimates and embracing those of other analysts who justify limiting allocations to defense programs. If the President had accepted pessimistic CIA operational evaluations in the mid-1960s, he might have withdrawn from Vietnam; if he had accepted pessimistic military analyses of the Soviet threat in the mid-1970s, he might have added massive increases to the defense budget.

Some chronic sources of error are unique to each of these three general categories of intelligence problems, and thus do not clearly suggest reforms that would be advisable across the board. To compensate for the danger in conventional attack warning, reliance on worst-case analysis might seem the safest rule, but in making estimates for defense planning, worst-case analysis would mandate severe and often unnecessary economic sacrifices. Removing checks on the influence of CIA analysts and "community" staffs[9] might seem justified by the record of operational evaluation in Vietnam, but would not be warranted by the record of estimates on Soviet ICBM deployments. It would be risky to alter the balance of power systematically among competing analytic components, giving the "better" analysts more status. Rather, decision makers should be encouraged to be more *and* less skeptical of certain agencies' estimates, *depending on the category of analysis involved.*

Some problems, however, cut across all three categories and offer a more general basis for considering changes in the system. But these general problems are not very susceptible to cure by formal changes in process, because it is usually impossible to disentangle intelligence failures from policy failures. Separation of intelligence and policy making has long been a normative concern of officials and theorists, who have seen both costs and benefits in minimizing the intimacy between intelligence professionals and operational authorities. But, although the personnel can be segregated, the functions cannot, unless intelligence is defined narrowly as the collection of data, and analytic responsibility is reserved to decision makers. Analysis and decision are interactive rather than sequential processes. By the narrower definition of intelligence, there have actually been few major failures. In most cases of mistakes in predicting attacks or in assessing operations, the inadequacy of critical data or their submergence in a viscous bureaucracy were at best the proximate causes of failure. The ultimate causes of error in most cases have been wishful thinking, cavalier disregard of professional analysts, and, above all, the premises and preconceptions of policy makers. Fewer fiascos have occurred in the stages of acquisition and presentation of facts than in the stages of interpretation and response. Producers of intelligence have been culprits less often than consumers. Policy perspectives tend to constrain objectivity, and authorities often fail to use intelligence properly. As former State Department intelligence director Ray Cline testified, defending his analysts' performance in October 1973 and criticizing Secretary Kissinger for ignoring them:

> Unless something is totally conclusive, you must make an inconclusive report ... by the time you are sure it is always very close to the event. So I don't think the analysts did such a lousy job. What I think was the lousy job was in bosses not insisting on new preparation at the end of that week [before war broke out] ... the reason the system wasn't working very well is that people were not asking it to work and not listening when it did work.[10]

Basic barriers to analytic accuracy

Many constraints on the optimal processing of information lie in the structure of authority and the allocation of time and resources. Harold Wilensky argues persuasively that the intelligence function is hindered most by the structural characteristics of hierarchy, centralization, and specialization.[11] Yet it is precisely these characteristics that are the essence of any government. A related problem is the dominance of operational authorities over intelligence specialists, and the trade-off between objectivity and influence. Operators have more influence in decision making but are less capable of unbiased interpretation of evidence because they have a vested interest in the success of their operations; autonomous analysts are more disinterested and usually more objective, but lack influence. Senior generalists at the policy level often distrust or discount the judgments of analytic professionals and place more weight on reports from operational sources.[12] In response to this phenomenon, the suggestion has been made to *legislate* the requirement that decision makers consider analyses by the CIA's Intelligence Directorate (now the National Foreign Assessment Center) before establishing policy.[13] Such a requirement would offer no more than wishful formalism. Statutory fiat cannot force human beings to value one source above another. "No power has yet been found," DCI Richard Helms has testified, "to force Presidents of the United States to pay attention on a continuing basis to people and papers when confidence has been lost in the originator."[14] Moreover, principals tend to believe that they have a wider point of view than middle-level analysts and are better able to draw conclusions from raw data. That point of view underlies their fascination with current intelligence and their impatience with the reflective interpretations in "finished" intelligence.[15]

The dynamics of decision are also not conducive to analytic refinement. In a crisis, both data and policy outpace analysis, the ideal process of staffing and consultation falls behind the press of events, and careful estimates cannot be digested in time. As Winston Churchill recalled of the hectic days of spring 1940,

> The Defence Committee of the War Cabinet sat almost every day to discuss the reports of the Military Co-ordination Committee and those of the Chiefs of Staff; and their conclusions or divergences were again referred to frequent Cabinets. all had to be explained or reexplained; and by the time this process was completed, the whole scene had often changed.[16]

Where there is ample time for decision, on the other hand, the previously mentioned bureaucratic impediments gain momentum.[17] Just as information processing is frustrated by constraints on the time that harried principals can spend scrutinizing analytic papers, it is constrained by the funds that a government can spend. To which priorities should scarce resources be allocated? The Schlesinger Report of 1971, which led to President Nixon's reorganization of US intelligence, noted that criticisms of analytic products were often translated into demands for more extensive collection of data, but "Seldom does anyone ask if a further reduction in uncertainty, however small, is worth its cost."[18] Authorities do not always know, however, which issues require the greatest attention and which uncertainties harbor the fewest potential threats. Beyond the barriers that authority, organization, and scarcity pose to intelligence lie more fundamental and less remediable intellectual sources of error.

Ambiguity of evidence

Intelligence veterans have noted that "estimating is what you do when you do not know,"[19] but "it is inherent in a great many situations that after reading the estimate, you will still not know."[20] These observations highlight an obvious but most important obstacle to accuracy in analysis. It is the role of intelligence to extract certainty from uncertainty and to facilitate coherent decision in an incoherent environment. (In a certain and coherent environment there is less need for intelligence.) To the degree they reduce uncertainty by extrapolating from evidence riddled with ambiguities, analysts risk oversimplifying reality and desensitizing the consumers of intelligence to the dangers that lurk within the ambiguities; to the degree they do not resolve ambiguities, analysts risk being dismissed by annoyed consumers who see them as not having done their job. Uncertainty reflects inadequacy of data, which is usually assumed to mean *lack* of information. But ambiguity can also be aggravated by an *excess* of data. In attack warning, there is the problem of "noise" and deception; in operational evaluation (particularly in a war such as Vietnam), there is the problem of overload from the high volume of finished analyses, battlefield statistics, reports, bulletins, reconnaissance, and communications intercepts flowing upward through multiple channels at a rate exceeding the capacity of officials to absorb or scrutinize them judiciously. (From the CIA alone, the White House received current intelligence dailies, Weekly Reports, daily intelligence Information Cables, occasional Special Reports and specific memoranda, and analyses from the CIA Vietnam Working Group.) Similarly, in estimates for defense planning, there is the problem of innumerable and endlessly refined indices of the strategic balance, and the dependence of assessments of capabilities on complex and variable assumptions about the doctrine, scenarios, and intentions that would govern their use.

Because it is the job of decision makers to decide, they cannot react to ambiguity by deferring judgment.[21] When the problem is an environment that lacks clarity, an overload of conflicting data, and lack of time for rigorous assessment of sources and validity, ambiguity abets instinct and allows intuition to drive analysis. Intelligence can fail because the data are too permissive for policy judgment rather than too constraining. When a welter of fragmentary evidence offers support to various interpretations, ambiguity is exploited by wishfulness. The greater the ambiguity, the greater the impact of preconceptions.[22] (This point should be distinguished from the theory of cognitive dissonance, which became popular with political scientists at the time it was being rejected by psychologists.[23]) There is some inverse relation between the importance of an assessment (when uncertainty is high) and the likelihood that it will be accurate. Lyndon Johnson could reject pessimist NIEs on Vietnam by inferring more optimistic conclusions from the reports that came through command channels on pacification, interdiction, enemy casualties, and defections. Observers who assume Soviet malevolence focus on analyses of strategic forces that emphasize missile throw-weight and gross megatonnage (Soviet advantages); those who assume more benign Soviet intentions focus on analyses that emphasize missile accuracy and numbers of warheads (US advantages). In assessing the naval balance, Secretary of Defense Rumsfeld focused on numbers of ships (Soviet lead), and Congressman Les Aspin, a critic of the Pentagon, focused on total tonnage (U.S. lead).

Ambivalence of judgment

Where there are ambiguous and conflicting indicators (the context of most failures of intelligence), the imperatives of honesty and accuracy leave a careful analyst no alternative but ambivalence. There is usually *some* evidence to support *any* prediction. For instance, the CIA reported in June 1964 that a Chinese instructor (deemed not "particularly qualified to make this remark") had told troops in a course in guerrilla warfare, "We will have the atom bomb in a matter of months."[24] Several months later the Chinese did perform their first nuclear test. If the report had been the only evidence, should analysts have predicted the event? If they are not to make a leap of faith and ignore the data that do not mesh, analysts will issue estimates that waffle. In trying to elicit nuances of probability from the various possibilities not foreclosed by the data, cautious estimates may reduce ambivalence, but they may become Delphic or generalized to the point that they are not useful guides to decision. (A complaint I have heard in conversations with several US officials is that many past estimates of Soviet objectives could substitute the name of any other great power in history – Imperial Rome, sixteenth century Napoleonic France – and sound equally valid.) Hedging is the legitimate intellectual response to ambiguity, but it can be politically counter-productive, if the value of intelligence is to shock consumers out of wishfulness and cognitive insensitivity. A wishful decision maker can fasten onto that half of an ambivalent analysis that supports his predisposition.[25] A more objective official may escape this temptation, but may consider the estimate useless because it does not provide "the answer."

Atrophy of reforms

Disasters always stimulate organizational changes designed to avert the same failures in the future. In some cases these changes work. In many instances, however, the changes persist formally but erode substantively. Standard procedures are constant. Dramatic failures occur only intermittently. If the reforms in procedure they have provoked do not fulfill day-to-day organizational needs – or if, as often happens, they complicate operations and strain the organization's resources – they fall into disuse or become token practices. After the post-mortem of North Korea's downing of a US EC-121 monitoring aircraft in 1969, there was, for several months, a great emphasis on risk assessments for intelligence collection missions. Generals and admirals personally oversaw the implementation of new procedures for making the assessments. Six months later, majors and captains were doing the checking. "Within a year the paperwork was spot-checked by a major and the entire community slid back to its old way of making a 'quick and dirty' rundown of the JCS criteria when sending in reconnaissance mission proposals."[26] The downing of the U-2 over the Soviet Union in 1960 and the capture of the intelligence ship *Pueblo* in 1968 had been due in part to the fact that the process of risk assessment for specific collection missions, primarily the responsibility of overworked middle-level officers, had become ponderous, sloppy, or ritualized.[27] At a higher level, a National Security Council Intelligence Committee was established in 1971 to improve responsiveness of intelligence staff to the needs of policy makers. But since the subcabinetlevel consumers who made up the committee were pressed by other responsibilities, it lapsed in importance and was eventually abolished.[28] A comparable NSC committee that *did* serve tangible day-to-day needs of consumers to integrate intelligence and policy – the Verification Panel, which dealt with SALT – was more effective, but it was issue-orientated rather than designed to oversee the intelligence process itself. Organizational innovations will not improve the role of intelligence in policy unless they flow from the decision makers' views of their own needs and unless they provide frequent practical benefits.

None of these three barriers are accidents of structure or process. They are inherent in the nature of intelligence and the dynamics of work. As such, they constitute severe constraints on the efficacy of structural reform.

The elusiveness of solutions

If they do not atrophy, most solutions proposed to obviate intelligence dysfunctions have two edges: in reducing one vulnerability, they increase another. After the seizure of the *Pueblo*, the Defense Intelligence Agency (DIA) was reprimanded for misplacing a message that could have prevented the incident. The colonel responsible developed a careful microfilming operation in the message center to ensure a record of transmittal of cables to authorities in the Pentagon. Implementing this check, however, created a three-to-four-hour delay – another potential source of failure – in getting cables to desk analysts whose job was to keep reporting current.[29] Thus, procedural solutions often constitute two steps forward and one step back; organizational fixes cannot transcend the basic barriers. The lessons of Pearl Harbor led to the establishment of a Watch Committee and National Indications Center in Washington. Although this solution eliminated a barrier in the communication system, it did not prevent the failure of timely alert to the Chinese intervention in Korea or the 1973 October War, because it did not eliminate the ambiguity barrier. (Since then, the Watch Committee has been replaced by the DCI's Strategic Warning Staff.) DIA was reorganized four times within its first ten years; yet it continued to leave most observers dissatisfied. The Agranat Commission's review of Israel's 1973 intelligence failure produced proposals for institutional reform that are striking because they amount to copying the American system of the same time – which had failed in exactly the same way as the Israeli system.[30] Reform is not hopeless, but hopes placed in solutions most often proposed – such as the following – should be circumscribed.

Assume the worst

A common reaction to traumatic surprise is the recommendation to cope with ambiguity and ambivalence by acting on the most threatening possible interpretations. If there is *any* evidence of threat, assume it is valid, even if the *apparent* weight of contrary indicators is greater. In retrospect, when the point of reference is an actual disaster attributable to a mistaken calculation of probabilities, this response is always justifiable, but it is impractical as a guide to standard procedure. Operationalizing worst-case analysis requires extraordinary expense; it risks being counterproductive if it is effective (by provoking enemy countermeasures or pre-emption), and it is likely to be ineffective because routinization will discredit it. Many Israeli observers deduced from the 1973 surprise that defense planning could only rest on the assumption that no attack warning will be available, and that precautionary mobilization should always be undertaken even when there is only dubious evidence of impending Arab action.[31] Similarly, American hawks argue that if the Soviets' intentions are uncertain, the only prudent course is to assume they are seeking the capability to win a nuclear war.

In either case, the norm of assuming the worst poses high financial costs. Frequent mobilizations strain the already taut Israeli economy. Moreover, countermobilization can defeat itself. Between 1971 and 1973, the Egyptians three times undertook exercises similar to those that led to the October attack; Israel mobilized in response, and nothing happened. It was the paradox of self-negating prophecy.[32] The Israeli Chief of Staff was sharply criticized for the unnecessary cost.[33] The danger of hypersensitivity appeared in 1977, when General Gur believed Sadat's offer to come to Jerusalem to be a camouflage for an Egyptian attack; he began Israeli maneuvers in the Sinai, which led Egypt to begin maneuvers of its own, heightening the risk of accidental war.[34] To estimate the requirements for deterrence and defense, worst-case assumptions present an open-ended criterion. The procurement of all the hedges possible for nuclear war-fighting – large increments in offensive forces, alert status, hardening of command-control-and-communications, active and passive defenses – would add billions to the US defense budget. Moreover, prudent hedging in policy should be distinguished from net judgment of probabilities in estimates.[35]

Alternatively, precautionary escalation or procurement may act as self-fulfilling prophecies, either through a catalytic spiral of mobilization (à la World War I) or on arms race that heightens tension, or doctrinal hedges that make the prospect of nuclear war more "thinkable." Since evidence for the "action-reaction" hypothesis of US and Soviet nuclear policies is meager, and arms races can sometimes be stabilizing rather than dangerous, the last point is debatable. Still, a large unilateral increase in strategic forces by either the United States or the Soviet Union would, at the least, destroy the possibility of gains desired from SALT. A surprise attack or defeat make the costs of *under*estimates obvious and dramatic; the unnecessary defense costs due to *over*estimates can only be surmised, since the minimum needed for deterrence is uncertain. Worst-case analysis as a standard norm would also exacerbate the "cry wolf" syndrome. *Unambiguous* threat is not an intelligence problem; rather, the challenge lies in the response to fragmentary, contradictory, and dubious indicators. Most such indicators turn out to be false alarms. Analysts who reflexively warn of disaster are soon derided as hysterical. General William Westmoreland recalled that the warnings that had been issued before the 1968 Tet Offensive were ignored. US headquarters in Saigon had each year predicted a winter–spring offensive, "and every year it had come off without any dire results.... Was not the new offensive to be more of the same?"[36]

Given the experience of intelligence professionals that most peace-time indicators of suspicious enemy activity lead to nothing, what Colonel who has the watch some night will risk "lighting up the board" in the White House simply on the basis of weak apprehension? How many staffers will risk waking a tired President, especially if they have done so before and found the action to be needless? How many distracting false alarms will an overworked President tolerate before he makes it clear that aides should exercise discretion in bothering him? Even if worst-case analysis is promulgated in principle, it will be compromised in practice. Routinization corrodes sensitivity. Every day that an expected threat does not materialize dulls receptivity to the reality of danger. As Roberta Wohlstetter wrote of pre-Pearl Harbor vigilance, "We are constantly confronted by the paradox of pessimistic realism of phrase coupled with loose optimism in practice."[37] Seeking to cover all contingencies, worst-case analysis loses focus and salience; by providing a theoretical guide for everything, it provides a practical guide for very little.

Multiple advocacy

Blunders are often attributed to decision makers' inattention to unpopular viewpoints or to a lack of access to higher levels of authority by dissident analysts. To reduce the chances of such mistakes, Alexander George proposes institutionalizing a balanced, open, and managed process of debate, so that no relevant assessments will be submerged by unchallenged premises or the bureaucratic strength of opposing officials.[38] The goal is unobjectionable, and formalized multiple advocacy certainly would help, not hinder. But confidence that it will help systematically and substantially should be tentative. In a loose sense, there has usually been multiple advocacy in the US policy process, but it has not prevented mistakes in deliberation or decision. Lyndon Johnson did not decide for limited bombing and gradual troop commitment in Vietnam in 1965 because he was not presented with extensive and vigorous counterarguments. He considered seriously (indeed solicited) Under Secretary of State George Ball's analysis, which drew on NIEs and lower-level officials' pessimistic assessments that any escalation would be a mistake. Johnson was also well aware of the arguments by DCI John McCone and the Air Force from the other extreme – that massive escalation in the air war was necessary because gradualism would be ineffective.[39] The President simply chose to accept the views of the middle-of-the-road opponents of *both* Ball and McCone.

To the extent that multiple advocacy works, and succeeds in maximizing the number of views promulgated and in supporting the argumentative resources of all contending analysts, it may simply highlight ambiguity rather than resolve it. In George's ideal situation, the process would winnow out unsubstantiated premises and assumptions about ends–means linkages. But in the context of data overload, uncertainty, and time constraints, multiple advocacy may in effect give all of the various viewpoints an aura of empirical respectability and allow a leader to choose whichever accords with his predisposition.[40] The efficacy of multiple advocacy (which is greatest under conditions of manageable data and low ambiguity) may vary inversely with the potential for intelligence failure (which is greatest under conditions of confusing data and high uncertainty). The process could, of course, bring to the surface ambiguities where false certainty had prevailed; in these cases, it would be as valuable as George believes. But if multiple advocacy increases ambivalence and leaders do *not* indulge their instincts, it risks promoting conservatism or paralysis. Dean Acheson saw danger in presidential indecisiveness aggravated by debate: " 'I know your theory,' he grumbled to Neustadt. 'You think Presidents should be warned. You're wrong. Presidents should be given confidence.' "[41] Even Clausewitz argued that deference to intelligence can frustrate bold initiative and squander crucial opportunities. Critics charged Henry Kissinger with crippling US intelligence by refusing to keep analysts informed of his intimate conversations with foreign leaders.[42] To do so, however, would have created the possibility of leaks and might thereby have crippled his diplomatic maneuvers. It is doubtful that Nixon's initiative to China could have survived prior debate, dissent, and analysis by the bureaucracy.

It is unclear that managed multiple advocacy would yield markedly greater benefits than the redundancy and competitiveness that have long existed. (At best it would perfect the "market" of ideas in the manner that John Stuart Mill believed made liberalism conducive to the emergence of truth.) The first major reorganization of the American intelligence community in 1946–1947 emphasized centralization in order to avert future Pearl Harbors caused by fragmentation of authority; the latest reorganization (Carter's 1977 extension of authority of the Director of Central Intelligence over military intelligence programs) emphasized centralization to improve efficiency and coherence. Yet decentralization has always persisted in the overlapping division of labor between several separate agencies. Recent theorists of bureaucracy see such duplication as beneficial because competition exposes disagreement and presents policy makers with a wider range of views. Redundancy inhibits consensus, impedes the herd instinct in the decision process, and thus reduces the likelihood of failure due to unchallenged premises or cognitive errors. To ensure that redundancy works in this way, critics oppose a process that yields coordinated estimates – negotiated to the least common denominator, and cleared by all agencies before they are passed to the principals. George's "custodian" of multiple advocacy could ensure that this does not happen. There are, of course, trade-off costs for redundancy. Maximization of competition limits specialization. In explaining the failure of intelligence to predict the 1974 coup in Portugal, William Hyland pointed out, "if each of the major analytical components stretch their resources over the same range, there is the risk that areas of less priority will be superficially covered."[43]

The problem with arguing that the principals themselves should scrutinize numerous contrasting estimates in their integrity is that they are constantly overwhelmed by administrative responsibilities and "action items"; they lack the time to read, ponder, and digest that large an amount of material. Most intelligence products, even NIEs, are never read by policy makers; at best, they are used by second-level staffers as background material for briefing their seniors.[44] Consumers want previously coordinated analyses in order to save time and effort. In this respect, the practical imperatives of day-to-day decision contradict the theoretical logic of ideal intelligence.

Consolidation

According to the logic of estimative redundancy, more analysis is better than less. Along this line of reasoning, Senate investigators noted critically that, as of fiscal year 1975, the US intelligence community still allocated 72 percent of its budget for collection of information, 19 percent for processing technical data, and less than 9 percent for production of finished analyses. On the other hand, according to the logic of those who focus on the time constraints of leaders and the confusion that results from innumerable publications, quantity counteracts quality. The size of the CIA's intelligence directorate and the complexity of the production process "precluded close association between policymakers and analysts, between the intelligence product and policy informed by intelligence analysis."[45] For the sake of clarity and acuity, the intelligence bureaucracy should be streamlined.

This view is consistent with the development of the Office of National Estimates (ONE), which was established in 1950 and designed to coordinate the contributions of the various organs in the intelligence community for the Director of Central Intelligence. DCI Walter Bedell Smith envisioned an operation of about a thousand people. But William L. Langer, the scholar Smith imported to organize ONE, wanted a tight group of excellent analysts and a personnel ceiling of fifty. Langer prevailed, and though the number of staff members in ONE crept upwards, it probably never exceeded a hundred in its two decades of existence.[46] Yet ONE could not eliminate the complexity of the intelligence process; it could only coordinate and integrate it for the production of National Intelligence Estimates. Other sources found conduits to decision makers (to Cabinet members through their own agencies, or to the President through the National Security Council). And some policy makers, though they might dislike the cacophony of multiple intelligence agencies, were suspicious of the consolidated NIEs knowing that there was pressure to compromise views in order to gain agreement. Over time, the dynamics of bureaucracy also blunted the original objectives of ONE's founder. From a cosmopolitan elite corps, it evolved into an insular unit of senior careerists from the CIA. The National Intelligence Officer system that replaced ONE reduced the number of personnel responsible for coordinating NIEs but has been criticized on other grounds such as greater vulnerability to departmental pressures. Bureaucratic realities have frustrated other attempts to consolidate the intelligence structure. The Defense Intelligence Agency was created in 1961 to unify Pentagon intelligence and reduce duplicative activities of the three service intelligence agencies, but these agencies regenerated themselves; in less than a decade they were larger than they had been before DIA's inception.[47]

The numerous attempts to simplify the organization of the analytic process thus have not solved the major problems. Either the streamlining exercises were short-lived, and bureaucratization crept back, or the changes had to be moderated to avoid the new dangers they entailed. Contraction is inconsistent with the desire to minimize failure by "plugging holes" in intelligence, since compensating for an inadequacy usually requires *adding* personnel and mechanisms; pruning the structure that contributes to procedural sluggishness or complexity may create lacunae in substantive coverage.

Devil's advocacy

Multiple advocacy ensures that all views held by individuals within the analytic system will be granted serious attention. Some views that should receive attention, however, may not be held by anyone within the system. Virtually no analysts in Israel or the United States believed the Arabs would be "foolish" enough to attack in 1973. Many observers have recommended institutionalizing dissent by assigning to someone the job of articulating apparently ridiculous interpretations to ensure that they are forced into consideration. Establishing an official's devil's advocate would probably do no harm (although some argue that it may perversely facilitate consensus-building by domesticating true dissenters or providing the illusory comfort that all views have been carefully examined;[48] worse, it might delude decision makers into believing that *uncertainties* have been resolved). But in any case, the role is likely to atrophy into a superfluous or artificial ritual. By the definition of the job, the devil's advocate is likely to be dismissed by decision makers as a sophist who only makes an argument because he is supposed to, not because of its real merits. Institutionalizing devil's advocacy is likely to be perceived in practice as institutionalizing the "cry wolf" problem; "There are limits to the utility of a 'devil's advocate' who is not a true devil."[49] He becomes someone to be indulged and disregarded. Given its rather sterile definition, the role is not likely to be filled by a prestigious official (who will prefer more "genuine" responsibility); it will therefore be easier for policy makers to dismiss the arguments. In order to avert intelligence failures, an analyst is needed who tells decision makers what they don't want to hear, dampening the penchant for wishful thinking. But since it is the job of the devil's advocate to do this habitually, and since he is most often wrong (as would be inevitable, since otherwise the conventional wisdom would eventually change), he digs his own grave. If the role is routinized and thus ritualized, it loses impact; but if it is not routinized, there can be no assurance that it will be operating when it is needed.

Despite the last point, which is more important in attack warning than in operational evaluation or defense planning, there is a compromise that offers more realistic benefits: *ad hoc* utilization of "real devils." This selective or biased form of multiple advocacy may be achieved by periodically giving a platform within the intelligence process to minority views that can be argued more persuasively by prestigious analysts outside the bureaucracy. This is what the President's Foreign Intelligence Advisory Board and DCI George Bush did in 1976 by commissioning the "Team B" critique of NIEs on Soviet strategic objectives and capabilities. Dissenters within the intelligence community who were skeptical of Soviet intentions were reinforced by a panel of sympathetic scholars, with a mandate to produce an analysis of their own.[50] This controversial exercise, even if it erred in many of its own ways (as dovish critics contend), had a major impact in promoting the re-examination of premises and methodology in US strategic estimates. The problem with this option is that it depends on the political biases of the authorities who commission it. If it were balanced by a comparable "Team C" of analysts at the opposite extreme (more optimistic about Soviet intentions than the intelligence community consensus), the exercise would approach regular multiple advocacy, with the attendant limitations of that solution. Another variant would be intermittent designation of devil's advocates in periods of crisis, when the possibility of disaster is greater than usual. Since the role would then be fresh each time, rather than ritualized, the advocate might receive a more serious hearing. The problem here is that receptivity of decision makers to information that contradicts preconceptions varies inversely with their personal commitments, and commitments grow as crisis progresses.[51]

Sanctions and incentives

Some critics attribute intelligence failures to dishonest reporting or to the intellectual mediocrity of analysts. Suggested remedies include threats of punishment for the former, and inducements to attract talent to replace the latter. Other critics emphasize that, will or ability aside, analytic integrity is often submerged by the policy makers' demands for intelligence that suits them; "the NIEs ought to be responsive to the evidence, not the policymaker."[52] Holders of this point of view would institutionalize the analysts' autonomy. Unobjectionable in principle (though if analysts are totally unresponsive to the consumer, he will ignore them), these implications cannot easily be operationalized without creating as many problems as they solve.

Self-serving operational evaluations from military sources, such as optimistic reports on progress in the field in Vietnam or pessimistic strategic estimates, might indeed be obviated if analysts in DIA, the service intelligence agencies, and command staffs were credibly threatened with sanctions (firing, nonpromotion, reprimand, or disgrace). Such threats theoretically could be a countervailing pressure to the career incentives analysts have to promote the interests of their services. But, except in the most egregious cases, it is difficult to apply such standards without arbitrariness and bias, given the problem of ambiguity; it simply encourages an alternative bias or greater ambivalence. Moreover, military professionals would be in an untenable position, pulled in opposite directions by two sets of authorities. To apply the sanctions, civil authorities would have to violate the most hallowed military canon by having civilian intelligence officials interfere in the chain of command. In view of these dilemmas, it is easier to rely on the limited effectiveness of redundancy or multiple advocacy to counteract biased estimates.

Critics concerned with attracting better talent into the analytic bureaucracy propose to raise salaries and to provide more high-ranking positions (supergrades) to which analysts can aspire. Yet American government salaries are already very high by academic standards. Those who attribute DIA's mediocrity (compared to CIA), to an insufficient allocation of supergrades and a consequent inability to retain equivalent personnel are also mistaken; as of 1975 the difference in the grade structures of DIA and CIA had been negligible.[53] And the fact that CIA analysts cannot rise to a supergrade position (GS-16 to 18) without becoming administrators is not convincing evidence that good analysts are underpaid; GS-15 salaries are higher than the maximum for most tenured professors.

Non-military analysts, or high-ranking soldiers with no promotions to look forward to, have fewer professional crosspressures to contend with than military intelligence officers. But an analyst's autonomy varies inversely with his influence, and hortatory injunctions to be steadfast and intellectually honest cannot ensure that he will be; they cannot transcend political realities or the idiosyncrasies of leaders. Richard Helms notes that

> there is no way to insulate the DCI from unpopularity at the hands of Presidents or policymakers if he is making assessments which run counter to administrative policy. That is a built-in hazard of the job. Sensible Presidents understand this. On the other hand they are human too.

Integrity untinged by political sensitivity courts professional suicide. If the analyst insists on perpetually bearing bad news, he is likely to be beheaded. Helms himself succumbed to policy makers' pressures in compromising estimates of the MIRV capabilities of the Soviet SS-9 missile in 1969, and the prospects for Cambodia in 1970.[54] The same practical psychological constraints are reflected in an incident in which Chief of Naval Operations Elmo Zumwalt, who had already infuriated Nixon and Kissinger several times with his strategic estimates, was determined to present yet another unwelcome analysis; Secretary of Defense Schlesinger dissuaded him with the warning, "To give a briefing like that in the White House these days would be just like shooting yourself in the foot."[55]

Cognitive rehabilitation and methodological consciousness

The intertwining of analysis and decision and the record of intelligence failures due to mistaken preconceptions and unexamined assumptions suggest the need to reform the intelligence consumers' attitudes, awareness, and modes of perception. If leaders were made self-conscious and self-critical about their own psychologies, they might be less vulnerable to cognitive pathologies. This approach to preventing intelligence failure is the most basic and metaphysical. If policy makers focused on the methodologies of competing intelligence producers, they would be more sensitive to the biases and leaps of faith in the analyses passed to them. "In official fact-finding ... the problem is not merely to open up a wide range of policy alternatives but to create incentives for persistent criticism of evidentiary value."[56] Improvement would flow from mechanisms that force decision makers to make explicit rather than unconscious choices, to exercise judgment rather than engage in automatic perception, and to enhance their awareness of their own preconceptions.[57]

Unlike organizational structure, however, cognition cannot be altered by legislation. Intelligence consumers are political men who have risen by being more decisive than reflective, more aggressive than introspective, and confident as much as cautious. Few busy activists who have achieved success by thinking the way they do will change their way of thinking because some theorist tells them to. Even if they could be forced to confront scholarly evidence of the dynamics of misperception, it is uncertain that they could consistently internalize it. Preconception cannot be abolished; it is in one sense just another word for "model" or "paradigm" – a construct used to simplify reality, which any thinker needs in order to cope with complexity. There is a grain of truth in the otherwise pernicious maxim that an open mind is an empty mind. Moreover, the line between *perception and judgment* is very thin, and consumers cannot carefully scrutinize, compare, and evaluate the methodologies of competing analyses, for the same prosaic reason (the problem of expertise aside) that impedes many proposed reforms: they do not have the *time* to do so. Solutions that require principals to invest more attention than they already do are conceptually valid but operationally weak. Ideally, perhaps, each principal should have a Special Assistant for Rigor Enforcement.

Although most notable intelligence failures occur more often at the consuming than the producing end, it is impractical to place the burden for correcting those faults on the consumers. The most realistic strategy for improvement would be to have intelligence professionals anticipate the cognitive barriers to decision makers' utilization of their products. Ideally, the Director of Central Intelligence should have a theoretical temperament and personal skills in forcing unusual analyses to the attention of principals; he might act as George's "custodian" of the argumentation process. To fulfill this function, the DCI should be not only a professional analyst and an intellectual (of the twelve DCIs since 1946, only James Schlesinger met those criteria, and he served for only three months), but also a skilled bureaucratic politician. These qualifications seldom coincide. The DCI's coordinating staff and National Intelligence Officers should be adept at detecting, making explicit, and exposing to consumers the idiosyncracies in the assessments of various agencies – the *reasons* that the focus and conclusions of the State Department's Bureau of Intelligence and Research differ from those of DIA, or of naval intelligence, or of the CIA. For such a procedure to work, the consumers would have to favor it (as opposed to negotiated consensual estimates that would save them more time). There is always a latent tension between what facilitates timely decision and what promotes thoroughness and accuracy in assessment. The fact that there is no guaranteed prophylaxis against intelligence failures, however, does not negate the value of incremental improvements. The key is to see the problem of reform as one of modest refinements rather than as a systematic breakthrough.

Living with fatalism

Organizational solutions to intelligence failure are hampered by three basic problems: most procedural reforms that address specific pathologies introduce or accent other pathologies; changes in analytic processes can never fully transcend the constraints of ambiguity and ambivalence; and more rationalized information systems cannot fully compensate for the predispositions, perceptual idiosyncracies, and time constraints of political consumers. Solutions that address the psychology and analytic style of decision makers are limited by the difficulty of changing human thought processes and day-to-day habits of judgment by normative injunction. Most theorists have thus resigned themselves to the hope of marginal progress, "to improve the 'batting average' – say from .275 to .301 – rather than to do away altogether with surprise."[58]

There is some convergence in the implications of all three ways of conceptualizing intelligence failures. Mistakes should be expected because the *paradoxes* are not resolvable; minor improvements are possible by reorganizing to correct *pathologies*; and despair is unwarranted because, seen *in perspective*, the record could be worse. Marginal improvements have, in fact, been steadily instituted since World War II. Although many have indeed raised new problems, most have yielded a net increase in the rationalization of the system. The diverisification of sources of estimates of adversaries' military power has grown consistently, obviating the necessity to rely exclusively on military staffs. The resources and influence of civilian analysts of military data (principally in the CIA's Office of Strategic Research but also in its Directorate of Science and Technology) are unparalleled in any other nation's intelligence system. At the same time, the DCI's mechanism for coordinating the activities of all agencies – the Intelligence Community Staff – has grown and become more diverse and representative, and less an extension of the CIA, as more staffers have been added from the outside. In 1972, a separate Product Review Division was established within the staff to appraise the "objectivity, balance, and responsiveness" of intelligence studies on a regular basis. It has conducted postmortems of intelligence failures since then (the Yom Kippur War, the Cyprus crisis of 1974, the Indian nuclear test, and the seizure of the *Mayaguez*).[59] (Previously, postmortems had been conducted by the analysts who had failed, a procedure that hardly guaranteed objectivity.)

Within the Pentagon, capabilities for estimates relevant to planning were enhanced with the establishment of an office for Net Assessment, which analyzes the significance of foreign capabilities in comparison with US forces. (CIA, DIA, and NIEs only estimate foreign capabilities.) Civilian direction of military intelligence was reinforced by an Assistant Secretary of Defense for Intelligence after the 1970 recommendation of the Fitzhugh Commission, and an Under Secretary for Policy in 1978. Experiments in improving communication between producers and consumers have been undertaken (such as, for example, the testing of a Defense Intelligence Board in late 1976). The dominance of operators within the intelligence community has also waned – especially since the phasing out of paramilitary operations in Southeast Asia and the severe reductions in size and status of CIA's covert action branch that began in 1973. Dysfunctions in the military communications system, which contributed to crises involving intelligence collection missions in the 1960s (the Israeli attack on the USS *Liberty* and North Korea's seizure of the *Pueblo*) were alleviated (though not cured) by new routing procedures and by instituting an "optimal scanning system" in the Pentagon.[60] Statistical analyses of strategic power have become progressively more rigorous and comprehensive; as staffs outside the executive branch – such as the Congressional Budget Office – have become involved in the process, they have also become more competitive.[61]

Few of the changes in structure and process have generated more costs than benefits. (Some critics believe, however, that the abolition of the Office and Board of National Estimates and their replacement with National Intelligence Officers was a net loss.) But it is difficult to prove that they have significantly reduced the incidence of intelligence failure. In the area of warning, for instance, new sophisticated coordination mechanisms have recently been introduced, and since the institution at the time of the 1974 Cyprus crisis of DCI "alert memoranda" – "brief notices in a form which cannot be overlooked"[62] – no major warning failure has occurred. But the period of testing is as yet too brief to demonstrate that these adaptations are more effective than previous procedures. In the area of operational evaluation, it is clear that there was greater consciousness of the limitations and cost-ineffectiveness of aerial bombardment during the Vietnam War than there had been in Korea, due largely to the assessments made by the offices of Systems Analysis and International Security Affairs in the Pentagon and Secretary of Defense McNamara's utilization of CIA estimates and contract studies by external analytic organizations.[63] Yet this greater consciousness did not prevail until late in the war because it was not a consensus; Air Force and naval assessments of bombing effectiveness contradicted those of the critical civilian analysts. Nor has the elaboration and diversification of analytic resources for strategic estimates clearly reduced the potential for erroneous planning decisions. Determination of the salience and proper weight of conflicting indicators of strategic power and objectives or of the comparative significance of quantitative and qualitative factors is inextricable from the political debate over foreign policy: uncertainties always remain, leaving the individual's visceral fears or hopes as the elements that tilt the balance of judgment.

Although marginal reforms may reduce the probability of error, the unresolvable paradoxes and barriers to analytic and decisional accuracy will make some incidence of failure inevitable. Concern with intelligence failure then coincides with concern about how policy can hedge against the consequences of analytic inadequacy. Covering every hypothetical vulnerability would lead to bankruptcy, and hedging against one threat may aggravate a different one. The problem is thus one of priorities, and hedging against uncertainty is hardly easier than resolving it. Any measures that clarify the cost-benefit trade-offs in policy hedges are measures that mitigate the danger of intelligence failure.

One reasonable rule in principle would be to survey the hypothetical outcomes excluded by strategic premises as improbable but not impossible, identify those that would be disastrous if they *were* to occur, and then pay the price to hedge against them. This is no more practicable, however, than the pure form of worst-case analysis, because it requires willingness to bear and inflict severe costs for dubious reasons. Escalation in Vietnam, after all, was a hedge against allowing China to be tempted to "devour" the rest of Southeast Asia. The interaction of analytic uncertainty and decisional prudence is a vicious circle that makes the segregation of empirical intelligence and normative policy an unattainable Platonic ideal.

In the simplest situation, the intelligence system can avert policy failure by presenting relevant and undisputed facts to non-expert principals who might otherwise make decisions in ignorance. But these simple situations are not those in which major intelligence failures occur. Failures occur when ambiguity aggravates ambivalence. In these more important situations – Acheson and Clausewitz to the contrary – the intelligence officer may perform most usefully by *not* offering the *answers* sought by authorities, but by offering *questions*, acting as a Socratic agnostic, nagging decision makers into awareness of the full range of uncertainty, and making the authorities' calculations harder rather than easier. Sensitive leaders will reluctantly accept and appreciate this function. Most leaders will not; they will make mistakes, and will continue to bear the prime responsibility for "intelligence" failures. Two general values (which sound wistful in the context of the preceding fatalism) remain to guide the choice of marginal reforms: anything that facilitates dissent and access to authorities by intelligence producers, and anything that facilitates skepticism and scrutiny by consumers. The values are synergistically linked; one will not improve the use of intelligence without the other. (A third value, but one nearly impossible to achieve, would be anything that increases the time available to principals for reading and reflection.)

Intelligence failures are not only inevitable, they are natural. Some are even benign (if a success would not have changed policy). Scholars cannot legitimately view intelligence mistakes as bizarre, because they are not more common and no less excusable than academic errors. They are less forgivable only because they are more consequential. Error in scholarship is resolved dialectically, as deceptive data are exposed and regnant theories are challenged, refined, and replaced by new research. If decision makers had but world enough and time, they could rely on this process to solve their intelligence problems. But the press of events precludes the luxury of letting theories sort themselves out over a period of years, as in academia. My survey of the intractability of the inadequacy of intelligence, and its inseparability from mistakes in decision, suggests one final conclusion that is perhaps most outrageously fatalistic of all: tolerance for disaster.

Notes

* For corrections or comments whose usefulness exceeded my ability to accommodate them within space limitations, thanks are due to Bruce Blaire, Thomas Blau, Michael Handel, Robert Jervis, Klaus Knorr, H. R. Trevor-Roper, and members of the staff of the National Foreign Assessment Center.
1 For example, Klaus Knorr, "Failures in National Intelligence Estimates: The Case of the Cuban Missiles, *World Politics*, XVI (April 1964), 455, 465–466; Harry Howe Ransom, "Strategic Intelligence and Foreign Policy," *World Politics*, XXVII (October 1974), 145.
2 "As that ancient retiree from the Research Department of the British Foreign Office reputedly said, after serving from 1903–1950: 'Year after year the worriers and fretters would come to me with awful predictions of the outbreak of war. I denied it each time. I was only wrong twice.'" Thomas L. Hughes, *The Fate of Facts in a World of Men – Foreign Policy and Intelligence-Making* (New York: Foreign Policy Association, Headline Series No. 233, December 1976), 48. Paradoxically, "successes may be indistinguishable from failures." If analysts predict war and the attacker cancels his plans because surprise has been lost, "success of the intelligence services would have been expressed in the falsification of its predictions," which would discredit the analysis. Avi Shlaim, "Failures in National Intelligence Estimates: The Case of the Yom Kippur War," *World Politics*, XXVIII (April 1976), 378.
3 Compare the prescriptions in Peter Szanton and Graham Allison, "Intelligence: Seizing the Opportunity," with George Carver's critique, both in *Foreign Policy*, No. 22 (Spring 1976).
4 Roberta Wohlstetter, *Pearl Harbor: Warning and Decision* (Stanford, CA: Stanford University Press 1962); Barton Whaley, *Codeword Barbarossa* (Cambridge, MA: The MIT Press 1973); Harvey De Weerd, "Strategic Surprise in the Korean War," *Orbis*, VI (Fall 1962); Alan Whiting, *China Crosses the Yalu* (New York: Macmillan 1960); James F. Schnabel, *Policy and Direction: The First Year* (Washington, D.C.: Department of the Army 1972), 61–65, 83–85, 274–278; Michael I. Handel, *Perception, Deception, and Surprise: The Case of the Yom Kippur War* (Jerusalem: Leonard Davis Institute of International Relations, Jerusalem Paper No. 19, 1976); Shlaim (fn. 2); Abraham Ben-Zvi, "Hindsight and Foresight: A Conceptual Framework for the Analysis of Surprise Attacks," *World Politics*, XXVIII (April 1976); Amos Perlmutter, "Israel's Fourth War, October 1973: Political and Military Misperceptions," *Orbis*, XIX (Summer 1975); US Congress, House, Select Committee on Intelligence [hereafter cited as HSCI], *Hearings, U.S. Intelligence Agencies and Activities: The Performance of the Intelligence Community*, 94th Cong., 1st sess., 1975; Draft Report of the House Select Committee on Intelligence, published in *The Village Voice*, February 16, 1976, pp. 76–81.

5 David Halberstam, *The Best and the Brightest* (New York: Random House 1972); Morris Blachman, "The Stupidity of Intelligence," in Charles Peters and Timothy J. Adams, eds., *Inside the System* (New York: Praeger 1970); Patrick J. McGarvey, "DIA: Intelligence to Please," in Morton Halperin and Arnold Kanter, eds., *Readings in American Foreign Policy: A Bureaucratic Perspective* (Boston, MA: Little, Brown 1973); Chester Cooper, "The CIA and Decision-Making," *Foreign Affairs*, Vol. 50 (January 1972); Sam Adams, "Vietnam Cover-Up: Playing War With Numbers," *Harper's*, Vol. 251 (June 1975); Don Oberdorfer, *Tet!* (Garden City, NY: Doubleday 1971). For a more detailed review, see Richard K. Betts, *Soldiers, Statesmen, and Cold War Crises* (Cambridge, MA: Harvard University Press 1977), chap. 10.

6 Quoted in Henry Brandon, *The Retreat of American Power* (Garden City, NY: Doubleday 1973), 103.

7 Betts (fn. 5), 160–161, 192–195. On bias within CIA, see James Schlesinger's comments in US Congress, Senate, Select Committee to Study Governmental Operations with Respect to Intelligence Activities [hereafter cited as SSCI], *Final Report, Foreign and Military Intelligence*, Book I, 94th Cong., 2nd sess., 1976, 76–77.

8 Ibid., Book IV, 56–59; William T. Lee, *Understanding the Soviet Military Threat: How CIA Estimates Went Astray* (New York: National Strategy Information Center, Agenda Paper No. 6, 1977), 24–37; Albert Wohlstetter: "Is There a Strategic Arms Race?" *Foreign Policy*, No. 15 (Summer 1974); Wohlstetter, "Rivals, But No Race," *Foreign Policy*, No. 16 (Fall 1974); Wohlstetter, "Optimal Ways to Confuse Ourselves," *Foreign Policy*, No. 20 (Fall 1975). There are exceptions to this pattern of military and civilian bias: see *ibid.*, 185–188; Lieutenant General Daniel Graham, USA (Ret.), "The Intelligence Mythology of Washington," *Strategic Review*, IV (Summer 1976), 61–62, 64; Victor Marchetti and John Marks, *The CIA and the Cult of Intelligence* (New York: Knopf 1974), 309.

9 The US intelligence *community* includes the CIA, Defense Intelligence Agency (DIA), National Security Agency, the intelligence branches of each military service, the State Department Bureau of Intelligence and Research, the intelligence units of the Treasury and Energy Departments, and the FBI. Before 1973, coordination for national estimates was done through the Office of National Estimates, and since then, through the National Intelligence Officers. The Intelligence Community Staff assists the Director of Central Intelligence in managing allocation of resources and reviewing the agencies' performance.

10 HSCI, *Hearings* (fn. 4), 656–657.

11 Harold Wilensky, *Organizational Intelligence* (New York: Basic Books 1967), 42–62, 126, 179.

12 Ibid., *passim*. The counterpoint of Cooper (fn. 5) and McGarvey (fn. 5) presents a perfect illustration.

13 Graham Allison and Peter Szanton, *Remaking Foreign Policy: The Organizational Connection* (New York: Basic Books 1976), 204.

14 Quoted in SSCI, *Final Report* (fn. 7), I, 82.

15 Ibid., 267, 276; SSCI, *Staff Report, Covert Action in Chile 1963–1973*, 94th Cong., 1st sess., 1975, 48–49. The Senate Committee deplored the tendency of decision makers to focus on the latest raw data rather than on refined analyses, a practice that contributed to the intelligence failure in the 1974 Cyprus crisis. SSCI, *Final Report* (fn.7), I, 443. But the failure in the October War was largely due to the *reverse* phenomenon: disregarding warning indicators because they contradicted finished intelligence that minimized the possibility of war. HSCI Draft Report (fn. 4), 78; Ben-Svi (fn. 4), 386, 394; Perlmutter (fn. 4), 453.

16 Winston Churchill, *The Gathering Storm* (Boston, MA: Houghton Mifflin 1948), 587–588.

17 "Where the end is knowledge, as in the scientific community, time serves intelligence; where the end is something else – as in practically every organization but

those devoted entirely to scholarship – time subverts intelligence, since in the long run, the central institutionalized structures and aims (the maintenance of authority, the accommodation of departmental rivalries, the service of established doctrine) will prevail." Wilensky (fn. II), 77.

18 Quoted in SSCI, *Final Report* (fn. 7), I, 274.
19 Sherman Kent, "Estimates and Influence," *Foreign Service Journal*, XLVI (April 1969), 17.
20 Hughes (fn. 2), 43.
21 "The textbooks agree, of course, that we should only believe reliable intelligence, and should never cease to be suspicious, but what is the use of such feeble maxims? They belong to that wisdom which for want of anything better scribblers of systems and compendia resort to when they run out of ideas." Carl von Clausewitz, *On War*, ed. and trans. Michael Howard and Peter Paret (Princeton, NJ: Princeton University Press 1976), 117.
22 Robert Jervis, *The Logic of Images in International Relations* (Princeton, NJ: Princeton University Press 1970), 132; Jervis, *Perception and Misperception in International Politics* (Princeton, NJ: Princeton University Press 1976), chap. 4; Floyd Allport, *Theories of Perception and the Concept of Structure*, cited in Shlaim (fn. 2), 358. Cognitive theory suggests that uncertainty provokes decision makers to separate rather than integrate their values, to deny that inconsistencies between values exist, and even to see contradictory values as mutually supportive. John Steinbruner, *The Cybernetic Theory of Decision* (Princeton: Princeton University Press 1974), 105–108.
23 See William J. McGuire, "Selective Exposure: A Summing Up," in R. P. Abelson *et al.*, eds., *Theories of Cognitive Consistency* (Chicago: Rand McNally 1968), and Irving L. Janis and Leon Mann, *Decision Making: A Psychological Analysis of Conflict, Choice, and Commitment* (New York: Free Press 1977), 213–214.
24 CIA Intelligence Information Cable, "Remarks of the Chief of the Nanking Military Academy and Other Chinese Leaders on the Situation in South Vietnam," June 25, 1964, in Lyndon B. Johnson Library National Security Files, Vietnam Country File [hereafter cited as LBJL/NSF-VNCF], Vol XII, item 55.
25 See for example, US Department of Defense, *The Senator Gravel Edition: The Pentagon Papers* (Boston, MA: Beacon Press 1971) [hereafter cited as *Pentagon Papers*], Vol. II, 99; Frances Fitzgerald, *Fire in the Lake* (Boston, MA: Atlantic-Little, Brown 1972), 364; Special National Intelligence Estimate 53–64, "Chances for a Stable Government in South Vietnam," September 18 1964, and McGeorge Bundy's covering letter to the President, in LBJL/NSF-VNCF, Vol. XIII, item 48.
26 Patrick J. McGarvey, *CIA: The Myth and the Madness* (Baltimore, ND: Penguin 1974), 16.
27 David Wise and Thomas B. Ross, *The U-2 Affair* (New York: Random House 1962), 56, 176, 180; Trevor Armbrister, *A Matter of Accountability* (New York: Coward-McCann 1970), 116–118, 141–145, 159, 187–195; US Congress, House, Committee on Armed Services, *Report, Inquiry Into the U.S.S. Pueblo and EC-121 Plane Incidents* [hereafter cited as *Pueblo and EC-121 Report*], 91st Cong., 1st sess., 1969, 1622–1624, 1650–1651; US Congress, House, Committee on Armed Services, *Hearings, Inquiry Into the U.S.S. Pueblo and EC-121 Plane Incidents* [hereafter cited as *Pueblo and EC-121 Hearings*], 91st Cong., 1st sess., 1969, 693–694, 699–700, 703–707, 714, 722, 734, 760, 773–778, 815–816.
28 SSCI, *Final Report* (fn. 7), I, 61–62; HSCI Draft Report (fn 4), 82.
29 McGarvey (fn. 26), 16.
30 Shlaim (fn. 2), 375–377. The proposals follow, with their US analogues noted in parentheses: appoint a special intelligence advisor to the Prime Minister (Director of Central Intelligence) to supplement the military chief of intelligence; reinforce the Foreign Ministry's research department (Bureau of Intelligence and Research); more

autonomy for non-military intelligence (CIA); amend rules for transmitting raw intelligence to research agencies, the Defense Minister, and the Prime Minister (routing of signals intelligence from the National Security Agency); restructure military intelligence (creation of DIA in 1961); establish a central evaluation unit (Office of National Estimates). On the US intelligence failure in 1973, see the HSCI Draft Report (fn. 4), 78–79.

31 Shlaim (fn. 2), 379; Handel (fn. 4), 62–63.
32 Ibid., 55.
33 Shlaim (fn. 2), 358–359. The Israeli command estimated a higher probability of attack in May 1973 than it did in October. Having been proved wrong in May, Chief of Staff Elazar lost credibility in challenging intelligence officers, complained that he could no longer argue effectively against them, and consequently was unable to influence his colleagues when he was right. Personal communication from Michael Handel, November 15, 1977.
34 *Washington Post*, November 27, 1977, p. A17.
35 Raymond Garthoff, "On Estimating and Imputing Intentions," *International Security*, II (Winter 1978), 22.
36 William C. Westmoreland, *A Soldier Reports* (Garden City, NY: Doubleday 1976), 316. See the postmortem by the President's Foreign Intelligence Advisory Board, quoted in Herbert Y. Schandler, *The Unmaking of a President* (Princeton, NJ: Princeton University Press 1977), 70, 76, 79–80.
37 Wohlstetter (fn. 4), 69.
38 Alexander George, "The Case for Multiple Advocacy in Making Foreign Policy," *American Political Science Review*, Vol. 66 (September 1972). My usage of the term multiple advocacy is looser than George's.
39 Henry F. Graff, *The Tuesday Cabinet* (Englewood Cliffs, NJ: Prentice-Hall 1970), 68–71; Leslie H. Gelb with Richard K. Betts, *The Irony of Vietnam: The System Worked* (Washington, DC: Brookings Institution, 1979), chap. 4; Ball memorandum of October 5, 1964, reprinted as "Top Secret: the Prophecy the President Rejected," *Atlantic Monthly*, Vol. 230 (July 1972); McCone, memorandum of April 2, 1965, in LBJL/NSF-VNCF, Troop Decision folder, item 14b.
40 Betts (fn. 5), 199–202; Schandler (fn. 36), 177. George (fn. 38), 759, stipulates that multiple advocacy requires "no major maldistribution" of power, influence, competence, information, analytic resources, and bargaining skills. But, except for resources and the right to representation, the foregoing are subjective factors that can rarely be equalized by design. If they are equalized, in the context of imperfect data and time pressure, erroneous arguments as well as accurate ones will be reinforced. Non-expert principals have difficulty arbitrating intellectually between experts who disagree.
41 Quoted in Steinbruner (fn. 22), 332.
42 Clausewitz (fn. 21), 117–118; HSCI, *Hearings* (fn. 4), 634–636; William J. Barnds, "Intelligence and Policymaking in an Institutional Context," in US Commission on the Organization of the Government for the Conduct of Foreign Policy [hereafter cited as Murphy Commission], *Appendices* (Washington, DC: GPO, June 1975), Vol. VII, 32.
43 HSCI, *Hearings* (fn. 4), 778.
44 SSCI, *Final Report* (fn. 7), IV, 57; Roger Hilsman, *Strategic Intelligence and National Decisions* (Glencoe: Free Press 1956), 40. During brief service as just a low-level staff member of the National Security Council, even I never had time to read all the intelligence analyses relevant to my work.
45 SSCI, *Final Report* (fn. 7). I, 344 and IV, 95 (emphasis deleted).
46 Ray S. Cline, *Secrets, Spies, and Scholars* (Washington, DC: Acropolis 1976), 20.
47 Gilbert W. Fitzhugh *et al.*, *Report to the President and the Secretary of Defense on the Department of Defense, By the Blue Ribbon Defense Panel* (Washington, DC: GPO, July 1970), 45–46.

48 Alexander George, "The Devil's Advocate: Uses and Limitations," Murphy Commission, *Appendices* (fn. 42), II, 84–85; Jervis, *Perception and Misperception* (fn. 22), 417.

49 Ibid., 416.

50 US Congress, Senate, Select Committee on Intelligence, *Report, The National Intelligence Estimates A-B Team Episode, Concerning Soviet Capability and Objectives*, 95th Cong., 2nd sess., 1978; *New York Times*, December 26, 1976, pp. 1, 14; *Washington Post*, January 2, 1977, pp. A1, A4.

51 George H. Poteat, "The Intelligence Gap. Hypotheses on the Process of Surprise," *International Studies Notes*, III (Fall 1976), 15.

52 Cline (fn. 46), 140.

53 SSCI, *Final Report* (fn. 7), I, 352. A valid criticism is that military personnel systems and promotion standards penalized intelligence officers, thus encouraging competent officers to avoid intelligence assignments. This situation was rectified in the service intelligence agencies by the early 1970s, but not within DIA. Ibid.; Betts (fn. 5), 196–197.

54 SSCI, *Final Report* (fn. 7), I, 77–82. See also US Congress, Senate, Committee on Foreign Relations, *Hearings, National Security Act Amendment*, 92nd Cong., 2nd sess., 1972, 14–24.

55 Elmo Zumwalt, *On Watch* (New York: Quadrangle 1976), 459.

56 Wilensky (fn. II), 164.

57 Jervis, *Perception and Misperception* (fn. 22), 181–187.

58 Knorr (fn. I), 460.

59 SSCI, *Final Report* (fn. 7), I, 276, and IV, 85; US Congress, House, Committee on Appropriations, *Hearings, Supplemental Appropriations for Fiscal Year 1977*, 95th Cong., 2nd sess., 1977, 515–621; *Washington Post*, February 15, 1977, p. A6; Paul W. Blackstock, "The Intelligence Community Under the Nixon Administration," *Armed Forces and Society*, I (February 1975), 238.

60 Joseph C. Goulden, *Truth is the First Casualty* (Chicago: Rand McNally 1969), 101–104; Phil G. Goulding, *Confirm or Deny* (New York: Harper & Row 1970), 130–133, 269, *Pueblo and EC-121 Hearings* (fn. 27), 646–647, 665–673, 743–744, 780–782, 802–803, 865–867, 875, 880, 897–899; *Pueblo and EC-121 Report* (fn. 27), 1654–1656, 1662–1667; Armbrister (fn. 27), 196FF, 395; US Congress, House, Committee on Armed Services, *Report, Review of Department of Defense Worldwide Communications: Phase I*, 92nd Cong., 1st sess., 1971, and *Phase II*, 2nd sess., 1972.

61 See, for example, James Blaker and Andrew Hamilton, *Assessing the NAT0/Warsaw Pact Military Balance* (Washington, DC: Congressional Budget Office, December 1977).

62 SSCI, *Final Report* (fn. 7), I, 61; Thomas G. Belden, "Indications, Warning, and Crisis Operations," *International Studies Quarterly*, XXI (March 1977), 192–193.

63 *Pentagon Papers*, IV, III–12, 115–124, 217–232. CIA critiques of bombing results began even before the Tonkin Gulf crisis. CIA/OCI, Current Intelligence Memorandum, "Effectiveness of T-28 Strikes in Laos," June 26, 1964; CIA/DDI Intelligence Memorandum, "Communist Reaction to Barrel Roll Missions," December 29, 1964. But ambivalence remained even within the CIA, which occasionally issued more sanguine evaluations – e.g., CIA Memorandum for National Security Council, "The Situation in Vietnam," June 28, 1965 (which McGeorge Bundy called directly to the President's attention), and CIA/OCI, Intelligence Memorandum, "Interdiction of Communist Infiltration Routes in Vietnam," June 24, 1965. (All memoranda are in LBJL/NSF-VNCF, Vol. I, Item 5, Vol. III, items 28, 28a, 28b, Vol. VI A, items 4, 5, 8.) See also *Pentagon Papers*, IV, 71–74. See also the opposing assessments of the CIA, the civilian analysts in the Pentagon, and the Joint Chiefs in NSSM-I (the Nixon Administration's initial review of Vietnam policy), reprinted in the *Congressional Record*, Vol. 118, part 13, 92nd Cong., 2nd sess., May 10, 1972, pp. 16749–16836.

7 Intelligence in a turbulent world

Insights from organization theory

Glenn P. Hastedt and B. Douglas Skelley

In October 2005 Director of National Intelligence John Negroponte issued the *National Intelligence Strategy of the United States of America*. In the forward he recalled that when President George W. Bush signed the Intelligence Reform and Terrorism Prevention Act in 2004 the president put forward the expectation that 'our vast intelligence enterprise will become more unified, coordinated, and effective.' Negroponte continued that the new approach to intelligence embodied in this strategy represents: 'a far-reaching reform of previous intelligence practices and arrangements. National intelligence must be collaborative, penetrating, objective, and far-sighted.... The time has come for our domestic and foreign intelligence cultures to grow stronger by growing together.'[1]

The primary goal of the intelligence community is to inform and warn. To accomplish this mission the *National Intelligence Strategy* asserts that the intelligence community must become 'a unified enterprise of innovative intelligence professionals.' It asserts that this will be accomplished by a transformation of the intelligence community rooted in the doctrinal principle of integration which in turn will be centered on six mutually reinforcing and interdependent characteristics: (1) results-focused; (2) collaborative; (3) bold; (4) future-oriented; (5) self-evaluating and; (6) innovative.

The critical intelligence community reform which is to allow these goals to be accomplished is the creation of a Director of National Intelligence (DNI). This post was recommended by the bipartisan National Commission on Terrorist Attacks on the United States, more commonly known as the 9/11 Commission.[2] Created in November 2002 it received testimony from 160 witnesses and held 12 public hearings. The commission released its 567-page report on July 22, 2004. That report identified four kinds of intelligence failures that contributed to the 9/11 terrorist attacks and made 41 recommendations for improving US intelligence. The failures were those of imagination, policy, capabilities, and management. In recommending the creation of a DNI the 9/11 Commission called for an individual that would oversee all-source national intelligence centers, serve as the president's principal intelligence advisor, manage the national intelligence program, and oversee the component agencies of the intelligence community. Included in this power would be responsibility for submitting a unified intelligence budget appropriating funds to intelligence agencies and setting personnel policies for the intelligence community. The DNI's office would be in the White House.

The Commission's reform proposals quickly became the center of a political controversy between Congress, the White House, and the families of the 9/11 victims. Congressional leaders promised to move quickly on overhauling the intelligence community's structure while the White House urged caution. Acting CIA Director John McLaughlin, Secretary of Defense Donald Rumsfeld, and Homeland Security Secretary Tom Ridge all spoke out against creating a national intelligence director. With Democratic presidential candidate John Kerry endorsing the Commission's report, the Bush administration came under political pressure to do the same. It came out in favor of a national intelligence director but with authority only to coordinate intelligence. Joseph Lieberman (D-CT) criticized Bush for wanting a 'Potemkin national intelligence director' while Republican Senator Arlen Specter (Pa.) referred to it as a shell game.

On October 8, 2004, the House voted 282–134 to create a new national director of intelligence. The Senate had voted in favor of such a move the week before. Their bills differed on the power to be given to that individual. Under the language of the Senate bill the CIA director 'shall be under the authority, direction, and control' of the national intelligence director. In the House version the CIA director would only 'report' to the national intelligence director. The House bill also only gave the director the power to 'develop' budgets and give 'guidance' to intelligence community members. The Senate bill stated that he or she would 'determine' the budget. The Senate bill would also make the intelligence budget public, require that most of the director's high-ranking assistants be confirmed by the Senate, and create a civil liberties panel to prevent privacy abuses.

By the end of October the House and Senate were deadlocked with some House Republicans led by Rep. Duncan Hunter (R-Calif.), chair of the House Armed Services Committee, being adamant that the Pentagon not lose control over its intelligence budget and that the overall budget remain secret. Family members of the victims of the 9/11 attacks called upon President Bush to break the stalemate in favor of the Senate's version of the bill. He did not. Republican opposition in the House remained firm forcing Speaker J. Dennis Hastert (R-Ill.) to pull the bill from the docket in late November. Behind the scenes negotiations produced a compromise acceptable to House Republicans and the White House.

President Bush signed The Intelligence Reform and Terrorism Prevention Act of 2004 on December 17. Title One of the Act stipulated that the DNI not be located in the Executive Office of the President. It gave the DNI the power to 'develop and determine' an annual budget for the national intelligence program based on budget proposals provided by the heads of intelligence agencies and departments. The DNI is to ensure the 'effective execution' of the annual budget and 'monitor the implementation and execution of the National Intelligence Program.' After consulting with department heads the DNI is authorized to transform or reprogram a maximum of $150 million and no more than 5 percent of an intelligence unit's budget in any one fiscal year, but he or she may not terminate an acquisition program. Larger transfers may take place if the affected department head agrees. In addition the DNI 'establishes objectives and priorities for the intelligence community and manages and directs tasking of collection, analysis, production and dissemination of national intelligence.' He or she is also given the power to develop personnel policies and programs in consultation with the heads of other agencies and elements of the intelligence community. And, the DNI is tasked with establishing a National Counterterrorism Center and National Counterproliferation Center, and assigning individuals to protect the integrity of the analytical process and conduct alternative analysis as appropriate.

Bureaucratic reorganizations such as the one involving the creation of a DNI are highly visible and symbolic acts. They seek to calm public fears and reassure the electorate that policy makers have taken steps to prevent a reoccurrence of the events that prompted the call for reform. A common feature of such reorganizations is an immediate desire to centralize political control in the problem area. The dominant motif of these control-oriented reorganization plans is the need for greater economy of effort and control. Bureaucracies are too decentralized. What is needed is 'strong managerial leadership, clear lines of authority and responsibility, manageable spans of control, meritocratic personnel procedures, and the utilization of modern techniques for management.'[3] As time passes, the managerial orientation to organizational reform often gives way to a political orientation in which talk of effectiveness and centralization are surpassed by concerns that all constituencies are listened to and that there also be political control over new and restructured organizations.

The 9/11 Commission's call for a strong DNI located in the White House is fully consistent with the logic of a centralized management approach to reorganization. Clear lines of accountability would be created and a direct link to the president established. Where the Bush administration supported locating Homeland Security in the White House to keep congressional influence to a minimum, it balked at this proposal because it invited Congress in through its confirmation and budgetary powers. The countering political logic of reorganization emerged here, too, as key Bush administration officials spoke out against the creation of a strong DNI. Even more significantly an alliance between the Pentagon and its congressional overseers asserted itself and imposed its will on the reform process.

There has been no shortage of commentary on the merits of this reform initiative and its ability to prevent future intelligence failures.[4] Where some have criticized its implementation as being counter-productive, others have challenged the very logic of relying on the principle of greater managerial centralization to prevent future intelligence failures. In place of greater managerial centralization many have called for a creating more decentralized or networked organizational structures for the intelligence community. Calls for organizational reform are countered with calls for organizational transformation and even abolition as some advocate the privatization of intelligence.

If the creation of the DNI and the ultimate form it took was understandable in terms of an underlying political logic, then the question remains: does it – or competing proposals – make sense in terms of its underlying organizational logic? The answer to this question is not at all clear because an important limiting dimension to this discussion is the failure to root it in the literature on organizational structure, agency, and the environment. What we find all too often instead are assertions that a given reform proposal will work or that it is superior to competitors that are grounded in little more than references to managerial guides for the business sector, common sense, or some form of inherited wisdom. Missing is an examination of what organization theory tells us about the structure, control mechanisms, and the influence of the organizational environment.

In the following sections we will explore the insights that classical bureaucratic theory, organizational economics, and environmental perspectives on organizational structure and behavior hold for evaluating efforts to prevent strategic surprise by creating a DNI and for informing a broader strategy organizational issues in seeking to prevent strategic surprise.

Interpreting reform: the classical bureaucratic view

'Organization theory' contains a broad range of ideas, some of which are useful in assessing the DNI solution to the post-9/11 intelligence problem. The concentration of authority and control in an additional layer of hierarchy reflects traditional notions of organization. The so called 'classical' school of organization theory is concerned with efficiency and effectiveness. It pursues these meta-goals through a mechanistic model of organization. The organizational features considered important by this school of thought are authority, structure, and process. If these can be rationally applied, then efficient attainment of organizational goals should follow. Bureaucratic hierarchy seeks efficiency through the division of labor and control through the structuring of decision making. Authority, accountability, and rules are requisites of such a structure. Centralization and increased supervision – in the case of the DNI, increased centralized supervision – rationalize the need for control, unity in command, and unity of purpose among the disparate members in the intelligence community who previously served many masters with different purposes.

Organizational structure is not neutral. Without question structure favors certain interests and facilitates specific kinds of communication and control.[5] The division of labor, the *raison d'être* of bureaucratic organizations, reflects the normative preferences of organizers for the distribution of authority, the resulting decision points of the organization, and the communications network believed to support decision making that directs production and responds to clients. Tasks, technology, and clients establish limitations for this structuring. Whether a particular function or staff-support activity is subordinated to another group of decision makers determines their roles and the relevance of those roles. As Meyer observes, 'Organizational structure spells out the contracts and exchanges that link individuals to roles and roles to each other.'[6] Thus the debate in Congress over positioning the Office of the DNI (ODNI) within or without the White House was not only about the relative power of those two institutions in overseeing the ODNI, but it was also central to the authority and communication structure of the intelligence community's reorganization.

Why is structure significant here? As Hammond shows, an organization's structure is like agenda setting. 'It follows that different organizational structures (agendas) should be expected to produce different outcomes.'[7] Assuming an upward flow of issues (e.g., policy choices, intelligence interpretations) from advisory and operating actors with 'bounded rationality,' Hammond demonstrates that recommendations communicated upward can vary depending on structures and who, holding a particular point of view, occupies a decision point in the chain of command. He finds that top-level decision makers are greatly influenced by recommendations filtered through organizational structures. Among his several conclusions about the significance of structure, all of which he submits for further testing, are that structure tends to determine the recommendations top decision makers approve, that different structures will convert the same data differently, and that it is impossible to create a neutral structure that will not influence decisional outcomes passing thorough that structure. Thus more than symbolism is involved in having the DNI displace the DCI as the communications link between the president and the intelligence community.

But is this enough to prevent intelligence failures? The DNI is tasked with giving guidance to a US intelligence community of some 16 organizations embedded to various degrees within other institutions.[8] From a classically focused organization theory standpoint there are two fundamental considerations that are raised by this arrangement. First, DNI must coordinate and establish policy for existing organizations within their own institutional contexts. Second, these organizations must serve two masters – their own organizations and the president through the ODNI. While the ODNI appears to centralize aspects of the intelligence community, enhancing its function, yet the interactions of constituent agencies will have to cross more organizational boundaries than in the past.

Can this new arrangement facilitate informing and warning? There is reason for concern. Organization structure should ' "route" information exchange, coordination processes and conflict resolution.'[9] While the ODNI bears the burden of coordinating 16 agencies, there are structural barriers to success. Boundaries define organizations, distinguishing them from their environments.[10] Within those boundaries any given organization is distinguished by its people who maintain the boundary, perform its functions, carry its peculiar culture, create its structural arrangements in support of functions, and, from an open-system perspective, span its boundaries to relate to clients and stakeholders within its environment.

Egeberg reports that interaction and communication tend to reflect the administrative structure of organizations and that information, while flowing through this structure, is constrained by its boundaries.[11] Boundaries, furthermore, appear to contribute to conflict over policy substance and jurisdiction while discouraging conflict resolution. How permeable will be the boundaries of established defense and civilian institutions? Organization theory suggests that doing away with boundaries facilitates information flow, but ODNI adds a boundary while retaining the ones that have impeded information flow in the past.

Imposing a coordinator (DNI) over organizations is neither a merger nor a divisional reform, but it pushes upward the resolution of disputes over policy substance and jurisdiction.[12] Under the new, but slimly tested, ODNI scheme of exercising authority over resources and intelligence planning, the DNI may become a lightning rod for conflict. Hammond shows that disagreement among officials can push resolution of such questions to the next administrative level and that structure may determine where such a question will be resolved.[13] Further, Hammond suggests that the higher the value of a decision, the more likely it will be referred upward. Where penalties are involved for not making decisions horizontally, however, the less likely questions will be referred upward.

One of the classic structural disadvantages of this reform is the span of control imposed on the DNI. Although technology has enhanced the ability to 'manage' a larger number of subordinate units, the 16 members of the community are quite varied in purpose and scope while dwelling within their own sponsoring organizations' structures. Because of the nature of this large number of subordinate divisions, the DNI may become a referee among competing units that seek resources and the shortest route of influence over presidential decision making. In practical terms does DNI have the power to impose decisions on intelligence organizations that have their bases in established institutions? Ambiguities regarding responsibilities at the departmental levels are likely to be pushed up for resolution at the DNI level. The budget process is always one of competition and conflict. If a single intelligence budget is realized, then DNI would take on major allocation and referee roles. There is evidence, however, that early maneuvers, especially in the Defense Department and FBI sought to shelter intelligence budgets from direct control by the new DNI.

One of the tenets of the classical school is unity of command.[14] In order to prevent conflicting commands, traditional bureaucracies abhor having personnel or divisions answer to more than one authority. Yet as long as intelligence units remain within their home bureaucracies, there would appear to be two lines of authority attached to them. Although ODNI may plan and resource, it is hard to believe that tactical defense intelligence activities will be directed by the ODNI. Under this regime intelligence units appear particularly vulnerable to conflicting objectives, functions, and commands. The FBI and Secret Service, for example, collect intelligence other than strategic information related to terrorism and international espionage. When do the demands of the Attorney General run counter to those of the ODNI? How are such conflicts resolved? Does the DNI have the authority to resolve them or will the president become umpire?

As Simon observed, the classical approach to bureaucratic organization has its internal contradictions.[15] Its pathologies are well recognized.[16] Why, then, did Congress and the president take this organizational approach to resolving what is perceived as poor intelligence performance? Zegart observes, 'American bureaucracy, in short, is a creature of politics.'[17] Similarly, Meier and Krause report Crozier's position 'that organizations reflect imperfect social compromises that arise in bargaining among individuals and groups. Specifically, the organizational design, structure, and operation are not randomly determined but reflect an equilibrium agreement among actors and stakeholders behaving in a purposeful manner.'[18] As a result, no one should expect the DNI or other intelligence operations to epitomize an 'ideal type' agency, but a collection of disparate intentions arrived at in the process of collective – legislative and political – decision making. That the bureaucratic 'solution' should appear rationalistic does not mean that the agency will operate in the rationalistic way intended.

The classical tradition of organization theory would affirm the actions taken in the DNI legislation.[19] Nominally, centralization should enhance control of the intelligence community by high-level authorities, unless the span of control proves unmanageable. The DNI received decision-making authority and control of resources. Weber's legal-rational model of the bureaucratic authority would accommodate such action.[20] But there are limits to bureaucratization. Extended levels of centralization delay responsiveness as communication is transmitted up and down extended chains of command. The DNI imposes a single, filtered, if integrated, channel for information transmitted to the president. Does adding another layer of organization enhance warning and information flow? Probably not. It may impose control and accountability, however. After events in which organizations do not appear to perform as expected, demands for accountability often outweigh the need for sensitivity and responsiveness to environmental change.

Firm boundaries lead to the compartmentalization of information and that in turn promotes secrecy. Secrecy is an essential feature of intelligence organizations, yet sharing secrets are important in the warning function. What provisions of the DNI legislation will enhance warning? What is needed is a responsive organization in which information flows readily to decision makers and doesn't get suppressed. Part of the information function is to parse out useful information from the noise of intelligence, which in many situations can reach high decibels. What model of organization makes for speedy communication and warning, but with accuracy in information collected? Such an organizational structure is unlikely to be the traditional hierarchical bureaucracy. At the same time, the segmented nature of such structures is good for securing secrets and defending against information sharing.

What government may well face is the quandary of contradictory needs. Secrecy and security, on the one hand, and responsiveness and speed in communicating information and warnings on the other. Such a paradox would not surprise those organizational theorists that eschew the rational model on which bureaucracies are premised. Rather they would expect internal contradictions in organizations that lead to 'irrational' behavior – irrational decisions.[21]

Interpreting reform: organizational economics

Organizational economics speaks to the problems of control and accountability by considering 'principal-agent contracts' and 'transaction costs.' The DNI is saddled with the age-old problem of agency: how does a principal (DNI) ensure that agents (members of the intelligence community and their subdivisions) pursue goals as the principal intended? (The agent's failure to do so results in 'agency loss'). Or to put it differently, how can a principal avoid the 'moral hazard' of an agent failing to carry out an agreed upon task?[22] The concomitant burden of monitoring and auditing the performance of agents (transaction costs) must be weighed against the return of the agent's performance.[23] Whether the DNI is a viable contractor in the principal–agent chain should be examined; moreover, the transaction cost of DNI should be judged. Because this approach is derived from economics, it is assumed that actors are motivated by self-interest.

In the case of the ODNI it appears that DNI runs the risk of 'adverse selection' (choosing an unreliable agent) not because the DNI might place untrustworthy people in leadership positions of the various intelligence organizations, but because DNI has either no official role in their selection or only a limited one. In truth, they are selected by either the president, in the case of the CIA, or the heads of departments in which they are embedded. The DNI actually inherited the agents already in place within the intelligence community. As a result the 'contract' between the DNI and agency heads is one of presumption: that these intelligence operations will accept the DNI's leadership as created under the Intelligence Reform and Terrorism Prevention Act of 2004. The DNI does select his/her immediate subordinates, but their agency is secured to some degree by the directness of their dealings with the DNI.

The 'moral hazard' (the risk that an agent will act dishonestly) for the DNI is great. The significance of boundaries for communication received attention above. These boundaries, the indirectness of performance measurement and the great breadth of DNI's span of control make moral hazard likely. Uncertain and inaccurate performance measures may motivate agents to pursue goals that satisfy the performance evaluation system and in so doing displace the goals of policy. Knott and Hammond observe that 'many of the social dilemmas that provide the rationale for hierarchy also plague the operation of the hierarchy once it is created.... Which kind of institution is better at a given task cannot be answered in general.'[24]

One of the reasons to have hierarchy (bureaucracy) is to control transaction costs where policing and enforcement costs are too high to control the opportunistic behavior of agents in the marketplace. In other words, there may be a point in the market where the nature of exchanges is such that hierarchy can reduce uncertainty of agent behavior.[25] Nonetheless, hierarchies themselves are challenged to monitor and control the behavior of agents. In the case of the intelligence community, the centralizing of intelligence in another level of hierarchy is explained by the level of uncertainty regarding the intelligence community's performance in support of national goals. The governance structure, however, challenges the capacity of the ODNI to maintain knowledge and compliance in 16 agencies. ODNI has done several things to try to address this problem, but they are expensive and inconclusive. The DNI has attempted to assert control and direction through the issuance of 'Intelligence Community Directives' regarding budgets, personnel, and information sharing, but response from the community has proved less than enthusiastic.[26] Negroponte sought to intervene in the direction of the CIA by attempting to send desk analysts into the field with operatives; additionally, DNI attempted to move CIA analytical assets into the ODNI.[27] These efforts reflect the desire to reduce moral hazard and transaction costs.

The principal–agent approach offers additional insight into the behavior of agents that have multiple principals.[28] Shapiro observes:

> Theories become much more complex (and interesting) when they allow for the possibility that collections or teams of principals (or agents) disagree or compete over interests and goals.... How do agents understand and reconcile the duties delegated to them when they are receiving mixed messages and conflicting instructions – and incentives – from multiple principals? How do they do so when the contract is exceptionally vague by design, to paper over the irreconcilable differences among principals with conflicting interests – say, controversial legislation that requires implementation? When do these cleavages among and collective action problems faced by principals give agents opportunities to play one principal off against another?[29]

In the case of the intelligence community members, DNI added to their legislative, chief executive, and departmental principals. What are the consequences of agents having to respond to the demands of a variety of principals? Hammond and Knott show that it all depends on the number of principals that can reject (veto) a policy preference and the degree to which the principals are in agreement on policy preferences.[30] The fewer the principals and higher the degree of policy agreement among principals, the less autonomy agents have and vice versa. For the 16 intelligence agencies the DNI is an additional principal. All, but the CIA, function under department heads (e.g., Defense) and many are subordinated to subheads of departments (e.g., Secretary of the Navy). All hold the policy interest of the two houses of Congress, generally, and a number of their specific committees. Most of these principals hold some decision-making authority that impact the intelligence community. The policy interests among these principals are varied, in part, because of the diverse functions distributed among the intelligence community. Principals, moreover, appear, at this point in time, to have different preferences regarding the substantive and administrative policies affecting the intelligence community. The situation appears to be one of heterogeneous policy preferences among a relatively large number of principals. Such a situation allows greater autonomous action of the part of the agent organizations including resistance to directives and unresponsiveness. Shapiro also observes:

> Multiple agents who have been delegated to undertake a task collectively add other wrinkles to the economists' models. Agents, too, have competing

interests; indeed the interests of some agents may be more congruent with those of their principals than with the other agents. Some agents are more risk averse than others; incentives work differently on different agents. Some agents may be free riders. And the existence of multiple principals and multiple agents sometimes increases the informational asymmetries and the difficulties of monitoring.[31]

This characterization could well apply to the state of the intelligence community, which is often described as a community in name only.

Interpreting reform: the environmental perspective

The failure of domestic and international intelligence organizations to detect the 9/11 attack and the subsequent controversy over misidentified weapons of mass destruction, which led to the Iraq war, raise questions about these organizations' adaptation to post-Cold War conditions and their ability to identify new threats arising out of that context. Organizational adaptation is directly linked to organizational environments and the degree to which organizations may be determined structurally and procedurally by their responses to environmental events. Organizational success in dealing with environmental demands is deemed to depend on organizational responsiveness and flexibility as well as the organization's capacity to manipulate its environment.

The external environment of organizations and its influence over organizational structure and behavior has received considerable attention since the 1960s when Burns and Stalker[32] posited organizational types to fit stable and unstable environments and Lawrence and Lorsch[33] found that effective organizations adjust their 'differentiation and integration' to meet changing environmental demands. Two streams of thought have emphasized the importance of the organizational environment: systems theory and institutional theory. Systems theory clearly delineates the organization from its environment and provides a conceptual language with which to speak of their relationship. Institutionalism emphasizes the development of values and interests that, on the one hand, are a reaction to the origins of organizational design and the demands of environmental stakeholders and, on the other, an effort to shape the environment to facilitate organizational needs such as support, legitimacy, survival, etc.

The assumption of the systems perspective is that factors outside the organization are primary determinants of organizational structure and process. The organic metaphor for organization as a living entity, an 'open system,' surviving off its environment, suggests that an organization may face challenges of adaptation if its environment changes. Certain populations of organizations, moreover, have better prospects for surviving change than others. Because rapid environmental change is a given for most organizations, adaptation becomes a major preoccupation of organizational leadership. For organizations to adapt successfully, organizational learning must take place. While learning may be those incremental adjustments in behavior and structure that organizations make to accommodate shifts in service (product) demand and resource supply, large scale, rapid efforts at adaptation – 'punctuated change' – may require a more theoretical understanding of the environment and an organization's connections with it.[34] Such challenges are very real today for the intelligence community. Prior to 9/11 it was still common to refer to the international system as 'post-Cold War,' a phrase that clearly conveyed a lack of firm understanding as to its underlying dimensions. After 9/11 terrorism emerged front and center as the international system's defining feature, yet disagreement continues over its root causes (economic globalization, culture conflict, imperial overreach) and whether or not to replace Cold War strategies of containment and deterrence with new ones such as preemption.

Institutionalism goes beyond systems theory to consider what societal values and commonly held assumptions (culture) dictate and sustain a set of organizational structures. Institutionalism rejects the assumption that structure is simply a response to demands on the organization or the type of technology used to generate its services (products). While these are thought significant, societal beliefs are significant in defining the roles of institutions in society and providing the value base of the institutional organization. Organizational learning and adaptation is constrained by the shared norms of institutional members and their leaderships' efforts to meet the role expectations of others – including other constituent institutions – in society. For example, Johnston in his ethnographic study of the analytic culture of the intelligence community observes that 'often policymakers perceive a change in judgment as though the original opinion was wrong, and although unstated, there are significant internal and external social pressures and consequences associated with being perceived as incorrect.'[35]

The ability of institutional organizations to interpret environmental threats and opportunities in terms of the organization's strengths and weaknesses depends heavily on the perceived 'appropriateness of choices.'[36] In the case of intelligence the consensus on appropriate choice of those outside the CIA prior to 9/11 was to place an increased emphasis on modern technology to obtain information and to downgrade the reliance on human sources. The absence of human intelligence sources would emerge as one of the major weaknesses of the intelligence community in 9/11 post mortems.

Organizational environments, especially turbulent ones, have been addressed in several ways in the organization theory literature. Hult suggests that we can categorize these approaches as focusing on contingencies, resource dependencies, ecology, and institutional features.[37] Contingency theory is based in the assumptions of an 'open system' and addresses how environmental factors impact the structure and performance of the organization. In both instances contingency theory attempts to assess the adaptability of the organization and the appropriateness of that adaptability for sustaining the organization in its environment. Structural investigations appear to analyze decision processes and seek to estimate 'fit' whereas performance assessments look at policy activities and events – frequently implementation.[38] No doubt the ODNI was created with a fairly elaborate internal structure in part because of the complex environment and the multifunctional nature of the intelligence community it was intended to direct. ODNI contains one principal deputy, four deputies, three associate deputies, and more than 19 assistant deputies. Whether this is an appropriate fit with the environment remains to be seen.

Miles and Snow warn of two 'generic' types of organizational misfits: externally initiated misfit and internally initiated misfit.[39] The first of these reflects the failure to respond quickly or appropriately enough to environmental changes. Miles and Snow suggest that organizations may be crippled by their own past history of successes. Thus they are unwilling to change in their beliefs about what they do or how they do it. Others, they contend, are inconsistent in their response to change. Internally initiated misfit stems from 'modifying strategy and/or structure far enough to violate the organization's operating logic.' It is not unreasonable to see external misfit in the intelligence community's inability or reluctance to embrace the notion of open-source intelligence[40] or replacing the search for secrets with a concern for unraveling mysteries as at least in part a product of Cold War successes.[41] The post 9/11 embrace of domestic surveillance and involvement in overseas renditions may in the future be read in the context of internal misfit as intelligence organizations shifted focus away from core missions. Some see the CIA's involvement in renditions as posing a similar threat to its core mission of intelligence analysis.

Resource dependency theory is also based on the open-systems concept. Although it is not particularly distinguishable from the contingency approach, this theory emphasizes exchange issues between an organization and others in its environment. Hult criticizes the products of this approach because 'many resource-based narratives risk becoming little more than *post hoc* reconstructions yielding few generalizations.'[42] A resource, moreover, is variously defined. Nonetheless, these inquiries underscore interdependency among an organization and other actors. A resource dependency perspective on organizational reform of the intelligence community would direct our attention away from narrowly focused questions of structure to ones of capabilities and mission. Is money to be spent on strategic intelligence or tactical intelligence; on human intelligence or technical intelligence-gathering systems; should self-sufficiency be the norm or should it be joint operations; with whom should electronic intercepts be shared? This perspective also brings us back to the question of direction and control. Control over the intelligence budget for the DNI was one of the most sought-after powers by intelligence reformers and was not realized. The DNI's power is limited to developing, determining, and faithfully executing the annual budget for the national intelligence program, based on budget proposals provided by the heads of intelligence agencies and departments. This power is further weakened when directives for new intelligence programs are received from the White House or when funds are hidden or placed in budget accounts beyond the DNI's reach. Building up analytic abilities within the ODNI to evaluate agency budgets as has been done does not substitute for the ability to control the distribution of those funds and thus affect how agencies interact.

The intelligence community, particularly those organizations which previously focused on the Cold War, enjoyed some four decades of a relatively stable environment. Incremental changes occurred, but the intelligence focus and purpose, the Soviet Union and China, their strategic advantage or disadvantage, remained much the same until the collapse of the Soviet empire. This punctuated change, consisting of the loss of Soviet control over Eastern European countries, the collapse of the Berlin Wall, the Communist Party's fall from grace, and the disintegration of the USSR in a brief period of time, demanded a structural response by the intelligence community. Obviously the creation of the DNI is a structural response within government to address failures to deal appropriately with the intelligence environment. This structural change followed the apparent failure to effect change within the CIA and FBI. Hastedt reports that in 2005 'modernization plans being put forward by the FBI and CIA were described as a "business as usual approach to intelligence gathering." '[43] He further notes that Army analysts who contributed to the weapons of mass destruction debacle were rewarded, rather than disciplined, while the CIA avoided any accountability review for its failures. In addition the CIA retained its control over international spy operations. The evidence regarding organizational change points to efforts to avoid innovation and substantive structural change. This resistance lay the foundation for an internal misfit in organizational structure.

'Organizational ecology,' the study of similar organizations in a defined space, draws, like systems theory, on biological concepts as means to examine organizations. Hult finds ecology research emphasizes 'selection,' focusing on survival within an environment rather than adaptation to environmental change.[44] In public administration, Herbert Kaufman's *Time, Chance, and Organizations* represents the classic example of this type of research.[45] The ecology approach addresses the density of populations within a community, the status of the community's 'habitat,' and whether it remains stable and supportive. Much of organizational ecology addresses the tendency of organizations with similar missions to become more like each other – isomorphism. The loss of diversity within a 'species' of organizations may make them vulnerable to impacts on their niches within the environment. Hult observes that this approach has been largely applied in the private sector, but it 'may continue to hold promise for application to a variety of "species" within the governmental, for-profit, and nonprofit sectors.'[46]

The intelligence community may be seen as, not one species of organization, but several operating in different environments. The environment of the FBI, or the Justice Department, is not the same as that of Defense Intelligence or the Department of Energy's Office of Intelligence and Counterintelligence. Some agencies operate largely in secret while others testify openly before Congress. Some agencies operate in the United States while others are forbidden to do so. In truth what exists within the intelligence community is a diversity of organizational functions and varied 'habitat.' Some of these organizations may experience stress amid the changing intelligence environment. The CIA, for example, found itself reporting to congressional intelligence committees that were becoming increasingly politicized and being headed by a succession of

DCIs whose primary mission was to control the agency or at a minimum ensure that the White House's perspective was heard and listened to.

The conditions of the Cold War tended to structure international spy organizations in similar ways. The thrust and parry of intelligence and counterintelligence required similar deployments of personnel and the use of evolving technological devices. The conditions were such that the threats were known and the objects of intelligence were recognized by all involved. While innovation to achieve intelligence breakthroughs was pursued, the nature of the 'game' was understood and operated on established assumptions. It might be argued that isomorphism, a gravitation toward similar organizational structures, took place in organizations such as the CIA, KGB, and MI6.

The surprise of 9/11 and the misinterpretation of weapons of mass destruction illustrate a species of organization undergoing the stress of habitat incursions brought on by environmental changes. While the ecology perspective on organizational environments would suggest that maladaptive organizations would essentially die, we also know that government agencies tend not to die natural deaths. Kaufman has written on the longevity of government organizations in spite of the decline of their functionality.[47] Few government agencies die, and the rate of creation, mid-twentieth century, was high. Interestingly Kaufman found the majority of new government organizations were 'staff' in nature rather than 'line.' In the post-World War II period intelligence organizations proliferated, and they perform a staff function.

Institutionalism moves away from most biological analogies, but remains concerned with environments. Hult observes that legitimacy is a central concern of most institutional studies and may not be unlike resource dependency study when legitimacy is perceived as a resource.[48] Following Scott, she suggests that the use of the institutional approach can be categorized by Scott's 'three' pillars of institutional environments: regulation, norms, and culture.[49] Rules, laws, and sanctions, such as those established by the state, set the conditions for organizations within the institutional context. Norms and values shared by actors within the institutional context guide decision making while prompting or restraining action. Culture serves as a common frame of reference from which institutional actors interpret the world, share a common language and give meaning to the environment and what their organizations do within it.

Institutionalism helps us interpret the inertia of large, established social organizations such as those associated with government, and it also suggests what it may take to effect change. On the one hand, what Thoenig calls thick institutionalization is achieved when some rules or procedures are sanctified, when some units or members of the public agency become semi-autonomous centers of power and develop their own vested interests, when administrative rituals, symbols, and ideologies exist. Expectations, behaviors, beliefs are channeled and stabilized. Moral communities are set up. A public institution develops in a gradual manner, without any explicit design forces behind it. It becomes valued by some of its members and by outside vested interests for the special place it holds in the larger social system.[50]

What makes an institution an institution is the fixing of rules, procedures, norms, beliefs, and behaviors into patterns and structures. The very nature of an institution, then, is that it is hard to change. Resistance to change should be expected as institutional members seek to hold to what is familiar – to the power and influence that existing rules and structures convey and that culture confirms.

There is evidence from the intelligence community of institutional barriers to change. Those analysts who provided the misguided reports of Weapons of Mass Destruction were not disciplined for their lapses and some were rewarded for service. Such acts affirm the existing institutional belief system rather than demonstrate support of institutional change. Continued reluctance by intelligence organizations to share information with local law enforcement reflects persistent prejudices as well as security concerns.

Given the intransigence of institutions, how can they advance to reform? Thoenig reports that some institutionalists argue that 'revolutionary change happens swiftly and affects all the parts of the organization simultaneously.'[51] Such change follows one of two possible scenarios: (1) a new value position is asserted by internal actors who believe their interests are not being addressed; or (2) outside interests push for a change in values. While the 9/11 Commission's recommendations and the subsequent ODNI legislation sought to bring outside pressure for change, it hasn't happened during the time period anticipated by these policy makers. There are signs that where there is change, it is in form and not substance.

Conclusion

Establishing a DNI is an organizational solution to the problem of intelligence failures. It is not the first organizational solution put forward, nor will it be the last. Presidential commissions looking into the quality of intelligence analysis have repeatedly suggested organizational reforms.[52] The position of a DNI is a reoccurring one in their deliberations and recommendations. *The Commission on the Intelligence Capabilities of the United States Regarding Weapons of Mass Destruction* that conducted its investigation after the 9/11 Commission put forward 74 recommendations intended to transform the intelligence bureaucracy.[53]

Students of international politics and practitioners of intelligence view such proposals with skepticism. The former point to the inherent uncertainty and complexity that lies at the core of world politics while the latter root their arguments in the art of intelligence analysis and the realities of bureaucratic life. We share this skepticism but reach our conclusions from a different vantage point, a review of organization theory literature.

Our reading of this literature points to the conclusion that organizational changes will fail to prevent intelligence failures not so much because the resulting organizational arrangement is pre-designed to fail, but because intelligence organizations, like all organizations, operate under the shadow of a series of paradoxes. Efforts to improve managerial control and lines of accountability require boundaries but boundaries block the flow of information. Flexible systems maximize the organization's ability to obtain information but create an environment in which coordination is difficult limiting the effective flow of information. A similar trade-off exists with regard to delegation of authority. Secrecy is highly valued and argues for compartmentalization which, in turn, limits flexibility and information flow while increasing moral hazard and transaction costs. Tightly limited and controlled arrangements best ensure that directives and priorities are followed yet they create impediments to the flow of information and the exercise of initiative. Loosely structured arrangements provide for initiative but invite willful or inadvertent goal displacement.

To be effective, organizations must be created with an eye toward operating in a certain type of environment. But should that environment change its effectiveness will diminish. Hedging organizational structures by building in flexibility to cope with potential environmental changes is expensive because operating environments seldom change rapidly or in an entirely predictable fashion and these resources then cannot be effectively targeted on current organization priorities. For intelligence organizations the environmental challenge is twofold. Not only must they develop a structure that is compatible with the nature of threats emanating from the international system, they must also be structured in such a way that they are compatible with the domestic political/governmental environment in which they operate. The demands from these two environments may not always be easy to reconcile.

Many commentators argue that organizational structure may not be as important as organizational culture to preventing strategic surprise. Yet this observation does not allow one to escape from operating under the shadow of paradox, for while organizational culture is distinct from organizational structure the two are linked. Cultural reform and structural reform are part of a single whole. Organizational culture grows out of how boundaries, authority patterns, and relations with external units are defined. To change structure without an attention to culture is to invite failure just as surely as is the reverse, to change culture without an attention to structure. Complicating any reform effort is the reality that while organization structural changes can be put in place through legislation or fiat, cultural changes cannot. Organizational culture springs spontaneously from the interaction of those who work in organizations.

The presence of organizational reform paradoxes does not negate the wisdom of trying to improve the performance of the intelligence community through organizational change. Rather it points to the need for an organizational reform perspective that begins by emphasizing the contingent and limited nature of organizational changes and ends with the need for constant vigilance. Organizational reforms work at the margins, and their success is as much dependent on the environment in which they operate as it is on the changes themselves. Constant vigilance is needed to ensure that organizational reforms do not become the source of new problems. In the case of the 9/11 reforms concern is already being voiced that changes so heavily focused on preventing future terrorist attacks will leave the US open to strategic surprise in other areas.[54]

Notes

1 *The National Intelligence Strategy of the United States of America*, www.dni. gov/publications/NISCOctober2005.pdf (accessed April 2, 2007), p. 1.
2 The National Commission on Terrorist Attacks Upon the United States, *The 9/11 Report* (New York: St. Martins, 2004).
3 James March and Johan Olson, 'Organizing Political Life: What Administrative Reorganization tells Us about Government,' *American Political Science Review* 77 no. 2 (1983): 283.
4 For a sampling, see Richard Posner, *Preventing Surprise Attacks, Intelligence Reform in the Wake of 9/11* (Lanham, MD: Rowman & Littlefield, 2005); Arthur Hulnick, 'Does the U.S. Intelligence Community Need a DNI?,' *International Journal of Intelligence and CounterIntelligence* 17 no. 4 (2005): 710–730; Michael Turner, 'Intelligence Reform and the Politics of Entrenchment,' *International Journal of Intelligence and CounterIntelligence* 18 no. 3 (2005): 383–397; and Helen Fessenden, 'The Limits of Intelligence Reform,' *Foreign Affairs* 84 no. 6 (2005): 106–120.
5 Morton Egeberg, 'How Bureaucratic Structure Matters: An Organizational Perspective,' in *Handbook of Public Administration*, ed. B. Guy Peters and Jon Pierre (London: Sage Publications, 2003), 116–126.
6 John W. Meyer, 'Conclusion: Institutionalization and the Rationality of Formal Organizational Structure,' in *Organizational Environments: Ritual and Rationality*, 2nd edn, ed. John W. Meyer and W. Richard Scott (Newbury Park, CA: Sage Publications, 1992), 274.
7 Thomas H. Hammond, 'Agenda Control, Organizational Structure, and Bureaucratic Politics,' *American Journal of Political Science* 30 no. 2 (1986): 382.
8 Office of the Director of National Intelligence, *An Overview of The United States Intelligence Community* (Washington, DC: Office of the Director of National Intelligence, 2007). Available online: www.dni.gov/who_what/061222_DNIHandbook_Final.pdf (accessed April 2, 2007).
9 Egeberg, 120.
10 Howard Aldrich and Diane Herker, 'Boundary Spanning Roles and Organization Structure,' *Academy of Management Review* 2 no. 2 (1977): 217–230; and Herbert Kaufman, *Time, Chance, and Organizations*, 2nd edn (Chatham, NJ: Chatham House Publishers, 1991).
11 Egeberg, 120.
12 Ibid., 121.
13 Hammond.
14 Henri Fayol, 'General Principles of Management,' in *Classics of Organization Theory*, ed. Jay M. Shafritz and Philip H. Whitbeck (Oak Park, IL: Moore Publishing Company, 1978), 23–37; and Luther Gulick, 'Notes on the Theory of Organization,' in *Classics of Organization Theory*, ed. Shafritz and Whitbeck, 52–61.
15 Herbert Simon, 'The Proverbs of Administration,' in *Classics of Public Administration*, ed. Jay M. Shafritz and Albert C. Hyde (Oak Park, IL: Moore Publishing Company, 1978), 107–122.
16 Gerald E. Caiden, 'What Really Is Public Maladministration?,' *Public Administration Review* 51 no. 6 (1991): 486–493.
17 Amy B. Zegert, *Flawed by Design* (Stanford, CA: Stanford University Press, 1999), 13.
18 Kenneth J. Meier and George A. Krause, 'The Scientific Study of Bureaucracy,' in *Politics, Policy and Organizations*, ed. George A. Krause and Kenneth J. Meier (Ann Arbor, MI: University of Michigan Press, 2003), 6.
19 Gulick.
20 Max Weber, 'Bureaucracy,' in *Classics of Organization Theory*, 2nd edn, ed. Jay M. Shafritz and Albert C. Hyde (Chicago: Dorsey Press, 1987), 50–55.

21 Nils Brunsson, *The Irrational Organization: Irrationality as a Basis for Organizational Action and Change* (Chichester: John Wiley, 1985).
22 William T. Gromley and Steven J. Balla, *Bureaucracy and Democracy: Accountability and Performance* (Washington, DC: CQ Press, 2004), 54–55.
23 Meier and Krause, 10–12.
24 Jack H. Knott and Thomas H. Hammond, 'Formal Theory and Public Administration,' in *Handbook of Public Administration*, ed. B. Guy Peters and Jon Pierre (London: Sage Publications, 2003), 141.
25 William McKinley Mark A. Mone, 'Micro and Macro Perspectives,' in *The Oxford Handbook of Organization Theory*, eds. Haridimos Tsoukas and Christian Knudsen (London: Oxford University Press, 2003), 345–372.
26 *U.S. News and World Report*, 'Everyone Knows it's Nicer to Share,' May 26, 2006.
27 *The Weekly Standard*, 'The Agency Problem: Will the Next CIA Director be willing to Challenge CIA Careerists and Continue the Reforms of the Dysfunctional Bureaucracy?,' May 15, 2006.
28 Jeff Worsham and Jay Gatrell, 'Multiple Principals, Multiple Signals: A Signaling Approach to Principal–Agent Relations,' *The Policy Studies Journal* 33 no. 3 (2005): 363–376.
29 Susan P. Shapiro, 'Agency Theory,' *Annual Review of Sociology* 31 (2005): 267.
30 Thomas H. Hammond and Jack H. Knott, 'Policy Management, Administrative Leadership, and Policy Change,' in *Advancing Public Management*, ed. Jeffrey L. Brudney, Laurence J. O'Toole, Jr., and Hal G. Rainey (Washington, DC: Georgetown University Press, 2000), 49–74.
31 Shapiro, 267.
32 Tom Burns and George M. Stalker, *The Management of Innovation* (London: Tavistock, 1961).
33 Paul Lawrence and Jay W. Lorsch, *Organization and Environment: Managing Differentiation and Integration* (Boston, MA: Harvard Business School Press, 1988).
34 Anjali M. Sastry, 'Problems and Paradoxes in a Model of Punctuated Organizational Change,' *Administrative Science Quarterly* 42 no. 2 (1997): 237–275.
35 Rob Johnston, *Analytic Culture in the U.S. Intelligence Community* (Washington, DC: Central Intelligence Agency, Center for the Study of Intelligence, 2005): 23.
36 James G. March, *The Pursuit of Organizational Intelligence* (London: Blackwell, 1999).
37 Karen M. Hult, 'Environmental Perspectives on Public Institutions,' in Peters and Pierre, 149–159.
38 Raymond E. Miles and Charles C. Snow, *Fit, Failure, and the Hall of Fame* (New York: The Free Press, 1994).
39 Miles and Snow, 66–69.
40 Amy Sands, 'Integrating Open Sources into Transnational Threat Assessments,' in *Transforming U.S. Intelligence*, ed. Jennifer Sims and Burton Gerber (Washington, DC: Georgetown University Press, 2005), 32–62.
41 Gregory F. Treverton, *Reshaping National Intelligence in an Age of Information* (New York: Cambridge University Press, 2001).
42 Hult, 153.
43 Glenn Hastedt, 'Washington Politics, Intelligence, and the Struggles Against Global Terrorism,' in *Strategic Intelligence: Counterintelligence and Counterterrorism. Vol. 4*, ed. Loch K Johnson (Westport, CT: Praeger, 2007), 99–126.
44 Hult.
45 Herbert Kaufman, *Time, Chance, and Organizations*, 2nd edn (Chatham, NJ: Chatham House Publishers, 1991).
46 Hult, 153.
47 Herbert Kaufman, *Are Government Organizations Immortal?* (Washington, DC: Brookings Institution, 1976).

48 Hult.
49 Richard W. Scott, *Institutions and Organizations*, 2nd edn (Thousand Oaks, CA: Sage, 2001).
50 Jean-Claude Thoenig, 'Institutional Theories and Public Institutions: Traditions and Appropriateness,' Peters and Pierre, 129.
51 Thoenig, 150.
52 Glenn Hastedt, 'Foreign Policy by Commission: Reforming the Intelligence Community,' *Intelligence and National Security*, Vol. 22, No. 4 (August 2007): 443–472.
53 *Commission on the Intelligence Capabilities of the United States Regarding Weapons of Mass Destruction*, March 31, 2005 www.wmd.gov. (accessed April 3, 2007).
54 Robert Vickers, Jr., 'Intelligence Reform: Problems and Prospects,' *Breakthroughs* 14 no. 1 (Spring 2005): 3–9.

8 Intelligence analysis and decision-making

Methodological challenges

Stephen Marrin

All theories of intelligence should specify the contribution they make to knowledge in the field of intelligence studies. But to do this, the process of how knowledge itself is developed, aggregated, and used also needs to be explored. Methodology provides the foundation to any theory, and that makes the study of methodology a precursor to the study of theory. This chapter describes, evaluates, and critiques how the intelligence literature portrays the relationship between analysis and decision-making, and recommends that a new kind of theory be developed to explain how intelligence analysis is actually used by decision-makers.

Starting with the intelligence cycle

The intelligence cycle – a heuristic device to portray the flow of information between intelligence agencies and policy-makers – provides a descriptive theory of intelligence that is a good starting point for the interaction between information (facts), knowledge, and decision. The intelligence cycle starts with decision-maker information requirements levied on intelligence collection capabilities, the processing of the collected raw intelligence and transmission of this processed material to analysts who decipher its meaning, and relay that understanding back to the decision-makers, who then levy additional requirements. This cyclic process provides both scholars and practitioners with a framework for understanding the processes that underlie analytic production.

Because the intelligence cycle starts with decision-maker information requirements, it describes the information pull aspect of intelligence production, or the way that decision-makers "pull" information from the intelligence community. However, the actual implementation of this "pull" process has left a lot to be desired. According to John Lockhart, the importance of the requirements process has been underrated, which has led intelligence services to "decide their own requirements."[1] In doing so, intelligence organizations perform another aspect of intelligence production, known as information push. Rather than driven by specified information requirements, this process involves the push of information from the intelligence collection and analytic agencies to decision-makers. While intelligence agencies are responsive to the requirements process, they also spend a substantial amount of resources on self-initiated information push products. In many cases, the decision-makers themselves do not know what they need to know or will need to know in the future, and – according to Loch Johnson – "the informational needs of policymakers are sometimes never made known, or made clear, to the producers."[2]

As a result, the intelligence community frequently establishes its own collection and analysis requirements based on what the collectors and analysts believe decision-makers should know rather than start with decision-maker requirements. Peter Sharfman has observed that "traditionally, intelligence dissemination has been based on a 'push' architecture – that is, the intelligence analysts select from a vast quantity of information the things they believe the users most need to know, and then send this information to the users they believe need to have it."[3] To illustrate the point, Johnson quotes former US president Jimmy Carter as saying that even though he "felt that the customers – the ones who receive the intelligence information, including the Defense Department, myself, and others – ought to be the ones to say this is what we consider to be most important," in reality, "quite often the intelligence community itself set its own priorities as a supplier of intelligence information."[4] For the push side of intelligence production, which is divorced from decision-maker requirements, the intelligence cycle is no longer cyclic, but rather linear, consisting of collection, analysis, and dissemination.[5]

Following this linear model, many contributions to the intelligence literature that address the intersection of intelligence and decision-making do so from the perspective of intelligence analysts who provide their policy-making or decision-making "consumers" with intelligence analysis. Most efforts to understand the role that intelligence plays start with the external environment, the collection instruments used to acquire information about that environment, and then explore the process of intelligence analysis and how it integrates the information into understandings about the world, and then how that information is relayed to decision-makers. But only infrequently are decision-maker information requirements incorporated into this assessment of the analytic process, despite the key role they occupy in the intelligence cycle.

When contributors to the intelligence literature address the analytic process and the subsequent incorporation of analysis into decision-making, they frequently pay lip service to the importance of the requirements process but then proceed to ignore the role that decision-makers play in tasking at least a portion of the collection resources. In the end, they tend to take the collection process and its aggregated raw intelligence as a given, and proceed to focus on how analysts might derive meaning from it and relay that meaning to decision-makers. They also portray the incorporation of analysis into decision-making in a linear rather than cyclical fashion, and primarily driven by data rather than concepts or values.

Describing the standard model

The intelligence literature portrays intelligence analysis as a precursor to and foundation for policy decisions, perhaps because of the prevalence of the intelligence cycle in the literature. In this standard model of the intersection between intelligence analysis and decision-making, intelligence analysts provide information to decision-makers who then use that information in the course of deciding which policy option to pursue. According to three CIA officers,

> Sherman Kent and other early commentators of the connection between intelligence and policy posited policy makers who consciously and carefully assembled information relevant to their problems, weighed policy options and implications, and proceeded to select courses of action. Intelligence provided part of the factual and interpretative background for this process and aided in the projection of the consequences of alternative strategies. The role intelligence producers were supposed to play was seen as sizable, yet carefully delineated; they were admonished to guard against too intimate an involvement in the policymaking process, lest they compromise their impartiality and objectivity.[6]

An example of how this standard model is operationalized by practitioners is provided by Paul Pillar, a former National Intelligence Officer. Pillar recently observed that

> the proper relationship between intelligence gathering and policymaking sharply separates the two functions. The intelligence community collects information, evaluates its credibility, and combines it with other information to help make sense of situations abroad that could affect U.S. interests. Intelligence officers decide which topics should get their limited collection and analytic resources according to both their own judgments and the concerns of policymakers. Policymakers thus influence which topics intelligence agencies address but not the conclusions that they reach. The intelligence community, meanwhile, limits its judgments to what is happening or what might happen overseas, avoiding policy judgments about what the United States should do in response.[7]

This intelligence analysis is then provided to decision-makers, where it is used in policy deliberations, creation, and implementation. Pillar later implies that the purpose of intelligence in this relationship is "to inform decision-making."

This standard model of the intersection between intelligence analysis and decision-making is very similar to the data-driven approach to intelligence analysis which longtime CIA officer Richards Heuer describes as analysis where "accuracy depends primarily upon the accuracy and completeness of the available data."[8] The apparent assumption is that decision-making is data-driven as well, with intelligence as an important, potentially crucial, input. In the standard model, decision-makers listen to and incorporate intelligence assessments into the decision-making process because the analysts who produce the assessments are considered to be experts on the subject, and it would behoove policy-makers to incorporate that expertise into their decisions. In addition, the expertise of intelligence analysts is considered to be especially important because of their objectivity in terms of the policy process. Because the analysts do not evaluate policy options or recommend courses of action, they do not have a role in advocating one particular policy option over another. In this data-driven view of decision-making where the specific decision made depends in large part on the data availability, analytic objectivity and the ability to speak "truth to power" are particularly prized.

The desire for objectivity on the part of analysts has to do with the knowledge, sometimes heading towards suspicion, that decision-makers can be less than objective in terms of evaluating policies that they may have vested interests in pursuing. Roger Hilsman, for example, observes that some fear

> that the man who is concerned with policy will inevitably become the advocate of a pet scheme. If he collects facts, as well as thinks of policy, he will tend to select facts which support his policy rather than find the true answer by collecting all the facts.[9]

The underlying assumption here is that the failure to find the true answer will lead to suboptimal decisions.

So as a result, intelligence organizations were created separate from decision-makers; to "select facts" and provide an objective assessment of them as an effort to get at that one "true answer" which is then conveyed to consumers to be incorporated into their policy deliberations. The value of independent and objective intelligence collection and analysis is, therefore, to provide a check on decision-makers' judgment. According to Hilsman,

> by having one man collect facts without thinking of policy and another use the facts to make policy, one at least guarantees that the policy man will have to face the unpleasant facts that do not support his policy.... Thus the policy man who has become wedded to an incorrect policy can be faced with the unpleasant facts which he has ignored and be made to see the one right solution.[10]

Or, as ODNI historian Michael Warner put it, independent and objective intelligence analysis provides "a control variable against which to test the intelligence and policy advice coming from the departments."[11] Presumably, this check will improve policy by preventing decision-makers from fooling themselves into believing that their policies are or will be successful when more pessimistic indicators exist. Because of this emphasis on objectivity, intelligence scholar Michael Handel described "ideal intelligence work" as "objective, autonomous, and free of political pressures."[12]

While many intelligence scholars address the importance of an "objective" contribution to national security decision-making as if it were unique to intelligence, in fact it is not. According to Bruce Bimber, the

> idealized image of the scientific expert involves not simply knowledge, but also a large element of objectivity, of being above politics and partisanship. The idealized policy expert brings the neutral authority of science to bear on politics. Experts derive legitimacy from their ability to appeal to non-political professional standards: the use of dispassionate scientific methods of inquiry, validation through peer review rather than mere assertion, and other classic elements of Mertonian science.[13]

The standard model of the role of intelligence in decision-making appears to be based on this image of an "idealized policy expert" bringing neutral authority to bear on policy. Bimber points out that during World War II, "many had come to think of experts as an apolitical corps that could be trusted to help defeat the enemies and then turn its attention to improving life at home"[14] and that when the war ended, it seemed particularly important to create mechanisms for specialized expertise to flow into public policy discussions. It was in this environment that the CIA – and, more broadly, the concept of a peacetime intelligence community independent of policy departments – was created to facilitate an independent, objective flow of information into the national security decision-making process.

As a result, intelligence analysts are like other experts in government in that they provide their "objective" input into an inherently political policy process. According to Glenn Hastedt,

> the professional is an intermediary between abstract knowledge and political action. He or she translates that information into a form which is both understandable and usable by the non-expert. Deference to the professional typically rests upon the presumption that compromise and negotiation, the hallmarks of political deliberation, have no significant impact on the manner by which professionals arrive at their conclusions. Rationality and objectivity are held to guide their analysis of information.[15]

It is for this reason that the word "politicization" is used in many other policy contexts to describe controversial incidents where pressure has been brought to bear on independent experts to provide scientific information supporting particular political or policy agendas pursued by political or administrative decision-makers. For example, charges of politicization have been made in recent years on controversial issues related to both environmental and health policy such as global warming and the legal and regulatory status of reproductive medications.[16]

In the intelligence context, conventional understandings of the meaning of politicization is that it is a corruption of the objectivity of intelligence system;

either through the intentional manipulation of the intelligence process by decision-makers who want the information and analysis to support a particular policy option, or through the actions of intelligence analysts who provide the decision-makers with the information they want to hear. According to Harry Howe Ransom, an intelligence scholar and Professor Emeritus at Vanderbilt University, politicization occurs "when intelligence estimates are influenced by imbedded policy positions. When preferred policies dominate decision making, overt or subtle pressures are applied on intelligence systems, resulting in self-fulfilling intelligence prophecies or in 'intelligence to please' that distorts reality."[17] Politicization is condemned because of the implication that political desires and pressures can push the expert analysis and advice further from the "truth" and that this can result in suboptimal decision-making.

So in the end, the standard model and its praise of objectivity and condemnation of politicization is deeply embedded in the intelligence literature and the normative judgments that scholars and practitioners bring to bear when evaluating how intelligence analysts and decision-makers should interact. But does the literature support the assumptions and premises that underlie the standard model's incorporation of intelligence analysis into decision-making?

No evidence that standard model works

Implicit in the standard model is an assumption that when decision-makers are confronted with assessments from experts that differ from their own, they will change their assessments and, by implication, their policies to bring them into conformity with what the experts believe. If decision-makers were willing to adjust their policies, then perhaps there is some value of "speaking truth to power." But there is little evidence in the literature to indicate that this actually occurs.

Frequently, intelligence analysis provides a perspective that implicitly questions the efficacy of current politics. According to Robert Jervis, intelligence analysts "paint a complex picture filled with obstacles to effective American policy. Only rarely do the analysts unambiguously point toward a course of action; by effect if not intent, often they will point toward caution if not indecision."[18] He goes on to say that intelligence analysis "often casts doubt on any particular course of action by indicating the ambiguities and weaknesses in the prevailing information, if not the possible alternative interpretations of it."[19]

Decision-makers tend not to welcome analysis that implicitly questions their proficiency as policy-makers or provides only negative assessments of current options. Woodrow Kuhns – a political scientist in CIA's Center for the Study of Intelligence – observes that Hilsman "writing nearly 50 years ago ... found that most policymakers were opposed either entirely or in part to having intelligence analysts responsible for estimating and warning. Intelligence was to provide the facts, and the policymakers were to interpret them."[20] Kuhns goes on to say that "policymaker attitudes toward estimating and forecasting apparently have changed surprisingly little since ... Hilsman did his research." Or, as Robert Gates observed, "it is no surprise that few policymakers welcome CIA information or analysis that directly or by implication challenges the adequacy of their chosen policies or the accuracy of their pronouncements."[21] Michael Handel argued that

> the champion of a certain policy often reacts to intelligence estimates and implied or explicit advice with a "Don't tread on me", and "Don't fence me in." He sees intelligence arming his opposition – and no wonder, for it can't keep its analysis from being used against him by his opponents. All this is particularly annoying to the policy-maker with a purpose – to the man who wants to create and change.... The policy maker may find that intelligence can crowd him and his self esteem, frustrate his efforts to take off on a policy, alarm him with its negativism about policies under way and in extreme cases, lead on from persecution to martyrdom.[22]

The literature does not provide many illustrations of situations where intelligence analysis actually influenced policy-maker judgment when the analysis conflicted with policy preferences. Instead, it indicates that most of the time decision-makers will just ignore the analysis, or look for some analysis that is more consistent with their preferences. Loch Johnson included policy-maker "disregard of objective intelligence" as one of his "seven sins of strategic intelligence."[23] He went on to note that "no shortcoming of strategic intelligence is more often cited than the self delusion of policymakers who brush aside – or bend – facts that fail to conform to their Weltschauung."

George Poteat developed a hypothesis to explain this tendency to ignore unwelcome intelligence analysis. According to Poteat, decision-makers will be highly receptive to intelligence analysis when "policymakers are relatively uncommitted" to specific policies, but will tend to be less receptive to intelligence analysis "in the presence of high or heavy commitments."[24] Similarly, Robert Jervis has said that "only rarely will intelligence find particular bits of information that are so powerful and unambiguous that they can alter deeply held beliefs," especially "after the policy has been set in motion and both intellectual and political costs have attached to altering it."[25]

One explanation for this tendency is because there can be consequences to changing policy mid-stream. According to Leon Fuerth, "policymakers are sometimes willing to reverse themselves, but when they do they will be attacked for flip-flopping. There is a penalty to be paid if one is ready to adjust policy to intelligence" because "to be an elected policymaker is to never admit to making an error."[26] So as a result, even in the face of intelligence analysis indicating that the current policy may have flaws, decision-makers tend to persevere in the hopes that they will be able to solve the problems in time.

Excessive optimism may in fact be an occupational hazard for decision-makers. As Jack Davis has observed,

> policymakers more or less have to operate amidst motivated (desire-based) ... biases. Policymakers, for example have to believe they have a reasonable

shot at achieving things against long odds. They may believe a 1-in-5 chance is a good starting point, even though analysts would label such an outcome as "highly unlikely."[27]

So even though decision-makers might receive intelligence analysis providing negative indicators and warning of worse to come if current policies remain constant, the decision-makers themselves might dismiss that analysis as excessively worrisome given their prospects for turning the situation around. However, Michael Handel observes that "the greatest danger" exists in these kinds of circumstances "when the leader supplants serious deliberation with wishful thinking."[28] This can happen periodically, for as three CIA officers observe, "policy makers are, from time to time, quite capable of deciding upon and becoming wedded to seemingly ill-conceived and uncompromising courses of action."[29] They go on to say that in these circumstances, "intelligence in such cases may ultimately help turn around – but seldom quickly or easily."

Another explanation for the apparent irrelevance of intelligence analysis may be due to the duplication of assessment in both the intelligence and policy-making functions. Hilsman speculated that it was "the ease with which the operating divisions can make another preliminary analysis in passing" that explained frequent

> complaints of intelligence people that no one ever pays attention to their "warnings."... Another may be that the operating divisions, having better information sooner, may have made their preliminary analysis first. Still another may be that although the operating divisions have not made their analysis first, they will have to do it eventually, and are too busy to bother with the intelligence version.[30]

In addition, Jervis has speculated that

> one reason why policy-makers paid little attention (to intelligence analysis) was that they thought their own general knowledge of the situation provided an adequate basis for their decisions. As one senior State Department official put it, "A policy-maker usually has some expertise of his or her own, after all. I use the intelligence community as a resource for factual information, but I don't need it for opinions. I have my own."[31]

Or, as three CIA officers put it,

> policy people regard themselves as having certain expertise and ample sophistication. They are accustomed to interpreting, analyzing, and projecting, as well as planning, deciding, and operating.... Intelligence that attempts to do for them what they believe they can accomplish competently themselves generally is less well received.[32]

At bottom, these CIA officers say that

> the impact of intelligence often depends on factors far removed from its intrin-
> sic quality. Among these factors – which may operate singly or in combination
> – are: whether the intelligence message coincides with or runs counter to pre-
> conceptions on the policy side; how intelligence fits in or conflicts with other
> counsels and pressures; the ostensible "hardness" of the intelligence and the
> extent of unanimity of … the intelligence community in advancing it; the state
> of interpersonal intelligence-policy relationships; and whether different policy
> makers are undecided, of the same mind, or divided in their approach to the
> problem. Thus, intelligence quality, the adequacy of communications, and the
> degree of policy receptivity all bear upon the impact of intelligence.[33]

Regardless of the specific reason that decision-makers bypass or disregard
intelligence analysis that conflicts with their policy preferences, their tendency
to do so is well documented in the literature, as is intelligence-analyst frustration
that their analysis can be ignored at will. But none of this should be new to intelligence scholars. Over fifty years ago, Roger Hilsman pointed out that

> when one believes, as most intelligence people apparently do, that correct
> policy – like Pallas Athene from the head of Zeus – springs full-blown from
> the facts, he is not only frustrated when he decides that policy is made
> without benefit of the information supplied by intelligence, but bewildered
> and indignant as well.[34]

Hilsman went on to describe the views of one frustrated (intelligence) official
who said that

> Before they did anything else, policy people should call on intelligence for
> the information and an estimate. Then they should make their policy. In
> reality, however, policy was made without intelligence or was only supple-
> mented by intelligence. Intelligence people always had to analyze what had
> already happened, or merely to give support for policy decisions that were
> already made. Intelligence did nothing but hack work and research. In prac-
> tice, the thing was all backwards.

As Hilsman says, describing intelligence analysts whose analysis is ignored by
decision-makers, "it is, of course, a humiliating experience to feel unimportant."
    A recent illustration of a frustrated, indignant intelligence analyst's response
to policy being made, in Hilsman's terms, "without benefit of the information
supplied by intelligence" is Paul Pillar's evaluation of the Bush Administration's
decision to go to war in Iraq. Pillar's articulation of the decision-making process
was used to illustrate the standard model of the integration of intelligence analysis into decision-making. But after he set the stage, he then critiqued the Bush
Administration for failing to live up to it. As he says, the Bush

administration used intelligence not to inform decision-making, but to justify a decision already made. It went to war without requesting – and evidently without being influenced by – any strategic-level intelligence assessments on any aspect of Iraq.... As the national intelligence officer for the Middle East, I was in charge of coordinating all of the intelligence community's assessments regarding Iraq; the first request I received from any administration policymaker for any such assessment was not until a year into the war.[35]

He goes on to describe the kinds of judgments the intelligence community made that the Bush Administration subsequently ignored, with the implication being that policy outcomes would have been better if policy-makers had listened to the intelligence community. He concludes that "official intelligence analysis was not relied on in making even the most significant national security decisions" and was politicized to boot. Pillar's obvious indignation regarding the Bush Administration's effort to turn the "proper relationship between intelligence gathering and policymaking" on its head illustrates exactly what Roger Hilsman described more than fifty years earlier.

In other words, there may be a disconnect between the "theory" of how intelligence analysis is used in decision-making, and the practice. So if the standard model is inadequate as a model for the incorporation of intelligence analysis into decision-making, what is wrong with it?

Decision-making driven by both concepts and values

The primary flaw in the standard model is that it assumes that the decision-making process is driven by data and analysis rather than concepts or values. In truth, decisions are not derived organically from the information and analysis available, but involve the use of concepts or theories as well as values as a way to organize them.

The standard model's data-driven assumptions, as Hilsman observes, "implies not only that a set of facts contains a self-evident answer (and that every problem does, in fact, have an answer), but also that it contains only one true answer."[36] If that is in fact the case, then the assumption is that "any reasonable man cannot help seeing this single meaning if he is forced to look at *all* the facts,"[37] with objective intelligence analysts providing those facts and that single interpretation derived from those facts. Or, as Yeshoshafat Harkabi put it, if "decisions (are) based only on intelligence data, decisions and policy would simply 'follow' from it and there would be no need for policy makers."[38]

But decision-makers possess concepts, theories, or mindsets that affect their interpretation and use of raw intelligence data as well as analysis. As Thomas Hughes – a former director of State Department's INR – says, information – which he calls "facts" – has no meaning until it enters the "world of ideas" consisting of "opinions, viewpoints, beliefs, values, concepts and judgments."[39] While Heuer was describing the cognitive processes involved in intelligence analysis when he said that they use these mindsets to "form a picture first and then select the pieces to fit" and that "accurate estimates depend at least as much upon the mental model used in forming the picture as upon the number of pieces of the puzzle that have been collected,"[40] these observations apply just as well to decision-making. Similarly, Hilsman says that both analysts and decision-makers have

> a number of assumptions and expectations (regarding how and why things happen) which lead (them) to believe that when certain things are done, certain results follow. A decision, otherwise, would never be made, an action never taken. And these assumptions and expectations, even when they are only implicit, are just as much "theory" as the hypotheses of science, social or physical. It is this "theory" that helps a problem-solver select from the mass of facts surrounding him those which he hopes are relevant.[41]

The fact of the matter is that there are any number of conceptual frameworks that can be used to filter the data and find meaning in them. As explained previously, because of the complexity and ambiguity inherent in many kinds of national security and foreign policy situations, many different explanations, or hypotheses, regarding the meaning of the data can exist at the same time. While it may be possible to falsify some of these hypotheses through scientific methodology as per Isaac Ben Israel's procedural recommendations,[42] frequently this will not be possible and in the end the decision-maker will be faced with multiple possible versions of the "truth." And it is the decision-maker's conceptual framework, or mindset, or theories, which provides the rationale for choosing one explanation over another, which is why Heuer called this kind of analysis "conceptually-driven."

Frequently, these mindsets are derived from the values that the decision-maker is trying to achieve. According to Dan Sarewitz, professor of science and society at Arizona State University, "the scientific finding never tells you what to do. That is always determined by what you are trying to achieve; and what you are trying to achieve is always guided by values and interests."[43] Or, as Abram Shulsky and Gary Schmitt say, "social science can provide the facts ... but policy makers have a monopoly on choosing the values to be pursued."[44]

The differentiation between fact and value has a long and distinguished history in the philosophical literature as a part of the discussion over epistemology. In the 1700s, philosopher David Hume articulated the importance of differentiation fact from value, which was subsequently adopted by Max Weber and Martin Heidegger. One strand of the fact/value differentiation that has made it into the intelligence literature has come by way of students of political philosopher Leo Strauss who critiqued Weber's take on the implications of the difference between fact and value.[45] A separate strand of the fact/value discussion was adapted by Karl Popper and others involved in distinguishing the positivist and constructivist interpretations of knowledge at the foundation of social science as an academic discipline in the mid-1900s.[46]

Values are important because they provide the decision-maker with the normative objectives that their policies are intended to achieve. Because of this, values themselves can be seen as a determining factor on the adoption of conceptual frameworks or mindsets used to interpret different situations. As Hughes points out, different policy-makers receive information

> within different frames of reference. Impact varied with perception, but the marriage of fact and viewpoint was occurring. These personal receivers reacted to the same fact ... saw it from their differing perspectives, absorbed it into their own value systems, incorporated it into their varying viewpoints, and turned it often into competitive conclusions.... Absolutist notions about facts and their meaning tended to dissolve in this process.[47]

If values drive mindsets and mindsets help the decision-maker organize and interpret information, then values may drive the decision-making process rather than data or expertise based on that data.

Because of this, Shulsky and Schmitt see a more "difficult relationship between expertise and policy – that is, between those who possess specialized knowledge about an issue (such as intelligence analysts) and those who are authorized to determine and implement government policy concerning it."[48] They point out that while

> we want policy to be guided by the best information available; we would be very critical of a policy maker who ignored the available facts and based his actions on his unsupported views of what the world was like. At the same time, we want policy to be made by those to whom the political system (via election or appointment) has given leadership authority; in any case, they must take ultimate responsibility for their policies, regardless of the information on which those policies were based.[49]

The reality is that, as Michael Fry and Miles Hochstein observe:

> the relationship between intelligence and the crafting of policy ... is, essentially, a relationship between two processes, one inductive, the other deductive. Intelligence gathering, ordering and presentation is an inductive process (while) policy formulation is a deductive process whereby policy, guidelines for action, are meant to reflect first principles. The critical interaction occurs when policy communities receive and evaluate intelligence, and judge its value. When intelligence clashes with policy preference, intelligence loses; when information is countered by perception or, more accurately, conception, evidence is discounted. The policy community decides.... That is why critical, quintessential important, calculations about policy legitimation, about domestic support for policy, are made exclusively by the deductionists, by presidents looking inward into society and to political principle as much as outward into the international system, supposedly objectively known.[50]

In the end, however, Shulsky and Schmitt downplay the importance of value-driven decision-making. As they say, the fact-value distinction provides "very little useful guidance in practice" for issues that address national security concerns because while "everyone can easily agree on peace, liberty, and prosperity as goals ... the means to achieve them are debated endlessly."[51] This debate exists because "the social sciences are far from being able to make contingent predictions with any confidence in most areas" and as a result policy debates "deal much more frequently with differing assessments of the factual consequences of policies than with disagreements concerning which values should be sought."[52] So in the end,

> since intelligence analysis can provide the policy maker with only the roughest approximation of what will happen if a given policy is adopted ... in practice, policy makers' choices depend more on their views about the consequences of policies than on their choices of goals.[53]

The reason intelligence analysis can only provide a "roughest approximation of what will happen" is because of the limitations of the "science" of intelligence. For example, Kevin Russell observes that intelligence analysis is like weather forecasting in that its forecasts are at best probabilistic, and that those who make decisions based on these forecasts should keep their probabilistic nature in mind. As Russell observes, if a meteorologist forecasts a 30 percent chance of rain,

> the weather forecaster is giving the viewer enough information to decide whether or not to bring an umbrella. If you don't and it rains, you have no one to blame but yourself – most people would consider a 30 percent significant enough to take precautions in case the scenario does indeed play out. In intelligence analysis it is precisely this element of deciding what the given risks mean in terms of precautions that puts the responsibility of using intelligence in the hands of the policymaker. The intelligence analyst must aid this process. There is simply no other way to get around the uncertainties and necessary subjective elements that are associated with intelligence analysis.[54]

Because of this uncertainty and ambiguity, Shulsky and Schmitt favor a conceptually-driven model where

> what policy makers do is not so clearly separated from what the experts (in this case, the intelligence analysts and estimators) do as it might seem; hence, it is not surprising that the intelligence-policy relationship holds a certain amount of tension. Each side often views the other side's actions as infringing on its territory.[55]

Or, as Richard Betts has observed, the strict separation between intelligence analysis and decision-making may be "an unrealistic application of 'pure science' norms to areas where fact and value are inseparable and judgment must preside."[56]

Challenging the standard model

In the end, both the conceptually-driven and the value-driven models of decision-making provide existential challenges to the standard model. This alternative interpretation of the interaction between intelligence analysis and decision-making turns the standard model on its head; rather than start with the intelligence analyst, it starts with the concepts and values being pursued by the decision-maker which determine the meaning and the relevance of the intelligence analysis that is provided to them.

Conceptually-driven and value-driven approaches to decision-making have the potential to provide decision-makers with multiple interpretations from the same set of information. It is for this reason that Philipp Steger argues that the "textbook model of how science in policymaking works" is unrealistic. Steger argues that the textbook model "fails to consider the real-world phenomenon of 'an excess of objectivity'" a phrase developed by Dan Sarewitz to describe the plentiful sources of scientific information that can be used to support any particular policy agenda.[57] For example, it is possible that the intelligence analysis that most closely matches the policy-maker's preferences will be chosen and those which do not conform to his or her preferences – or underlying sense of how the world works – rejected. According to Hughes, this is "the predicament of 'objective' intelligence. In the absence of context, order and structure imposed on the facts, they can be chosen, arranged and accommodated to the preconceived ideas of opinionated men."[58]

In an intelligence context this process is derided as cherry-picking, where decision-makers specifically take parts of the analysis out of context to make decisions or justify decisions previously reached, and it is usually considered to be an abuse of the "appropriate" role of intelligence analysis. A variant of cherry-picking as conducted by intelligence analysts to support particular policy decisions is called "backstopping." Backstopping involves, according to Hilsman, the intelligence analyst's "mechanical search for facts tending to support a policy decision that has already been made" in order to protect the decision-maker by "supplying him with facts to defend his position."[59] Hilsman goes on to observe that decision-makers "seemed most pleased" with backstopping.

In an environment where multiple inferences can be derived from the same set of data, and no mechanism exists to test the accuracy or reliability of the different interpretations, cherry-picking or backstopping may seem to be a natural way to use information in the decision-making process. In addition, it is completely consistent with Heuer's reference to conceptually-driven analysis involving the choice of a concept or hypothesis and then selecting the information to fit that hypothesis. Yet the occurrence of cherry-picking and backstopping is almost universally condemned by those who believe that decisions should be made on inferences derived from the data rather than for other reasons, including values embedded in political ideologies.

Despite the criticism that exists when intelligence is cherry-picked or used to backstop a particular decision, it is generally accepted that elected or appointed leaders are free to ignore the information and advice of their experts. According to Handel,

> the very fact that a leader is elected to implement a specific policy gives him the right and duty to make political decisions contrary to the evidence or advice provided by the intelligence community. The "primacy of politics" or political control in the strict sense of hierarchy of importance must be recognized. "Intelligence must be the servant and not the master of operational policy."[60]

The three CIA officers acknowledge this when they say that

> intelligence, of course, often is only one among a number of information sources available to policy makers, and they are under no obligation to be guided solely by its light. Policy may, in fact, be shaped by personal, bureaucratic, political, or other factors having little or no relation to intelligence input.[61]

Or, according to Percy Cradock, decision-makers "have the privilege of interpreting the facts differently or ignoring them altogether" based on factors that include "party politics, economic interests, public opinion, personal convictions and vanities" which "can prove decisive."[62]

But just because decision-makers can do something does not mean they should. Handel goes on to say that

> political primacy should be clearly distinguished from political interference, a task which is not always easy. There is a thin line between the right and duty to formulate a policy based on subjective political values, and the conscious or unconscious temptation to abuse or ignore the intelligence process. It is one thing for a statesman to listen carefully to his intelligence advisers, then make a decision counter to their best judgment; and another for him to wield his political strength and authority in the interest of receiving only that information which conforms to his preconceived ideas and political biases. The danger is, in Hughes' words, that "policy-makers quickly learn that intelligence can be used the way a drunk uses a lamp post – for support rather than illumination."[63]

In addition, as Steger observes, a consensus has developed in the general scientific community around the idea "that it's the politician's prerogative to make the final call, even if it happens to be contrary to what the scientific information would indicate" but that the politician would then have to explain a decision if it is made contrary to the science, which usually means "taking recourse to some other scientific information that supports their point of view."[64]

Yet, because of the ambiguity inherent in intelligence analysis and the resulting proliferation of alternative interpretations of the facts, this is not very difficult for an enterprising policy-maker. As Handel points out,

> it is this inherent ambiguity, the lack of objective criteria for analysis, and absence of common analytical standards, that render the intelligence process so susceptible to political interference. Ambiguity legitimizes different interpretations, allowing politically-motivated parties to select the one they prefer. The absence of clarity may also strengthen the tendency of some statesmen to become their own intelligence officers.[65]

In other words, if the interpretation of intelligence analysis is either conceptually- or value-driven, then this pushes the evaluative responsibility to the level of decision-making, and decision-makers must be their own intelligence analysts, too. Hypothesis testing in this environment requires different procedures; rather than an objective search for "truth," the goal is to create mechanisms for the competition of different concepts or theories. This process is frequently described as multiple advocacy, and evaluating different perspectives against each other is considered to be an important part of the decision-making process.

Even if the proponents of different policy options are by necessity optimistic about the prospects for the success of their preferred policy option, as Jack Davis says, "despite this profession-based optimism, policymakers need to be realistic in taking account of ground truth."[66] This need to be grounded may explain why Fuerth believes that

> despite all of [the negative consequences resulting from changing policy], a key responsibility of intelligence producers is to tell truth to power. One shouldn't trade integrity for access. It is better to deal with honest people who tell you where they think the world is going to be.[67]

Presumably he says this because there is value to hear the assessment of independent and nominally objective analysts as a check on one's own judgment; a way to obtain greater "ground truth." Even if contradictory assessments from intelligence have little direct effect in terms of policy creation and implementation, perhaps the impact is more indirect – on the decision-maker's creation of policy alternatives and adjustments rather than directly on the policy itself.

Accordingly, Robert Jervis has argued that a value of nominally objective intelligence analysis may not be in provision of the "truth," but rather in "keeping [the] policy makers somewhat honest" by "pointing out to all domestic combatants in the foreign policy-making process the weaknesses and flaws in the arguments and information that are being relied upon" as a way to counter the "powerful vested interests that supplement, if not displace, the national interest" and lead them to regard "truth" instrumentally.[68] As Jervis goes on to say, intelligence analysis

> may not be able to find the truth; still less may it be able to persuade others that it has found it. But keeping the players honest, not permitting disreputable arguments to thrive, pointing out where positions are internally contradictory or rest on tortured readings of the evidence would not be minor feats.

While this analytic contribution to decision-making may in fact be valuable, it is in direct contradiction to the presumed value of intelligence analysis as per the standard model. According to Handel, the standard model – what he calls the ideal relationship between intelligence analysis and decision-making –

> can only rarely be approximated. Not only do ambiguity and uncertainty plague intelligence work, but political concerns permeate every aspect of its higher and, at times, even lower echelons. It is practically impossible to distinguish between policy-making on the one hand and intelligence input on the other. Indeed, it has been suggested that "the unresolveable tension between policymaking and intelligence rests in fact on an unresolveable definitional problem. For no one agrees on what is policy and what is intelligence."[69]

Or, put more succinctly, Handel says "this 'purely rational decision-making model' and belief in the viability of a 'strictly professional intelligence process' is nothing but an idealized normative fiction."[70]

Need for a new kind of theory

The standard model of the relationship between intelligence analysis and decision-making needs to be re-evaluated and replaced. Rather than a bottom-up approach looking at how data influences, or fails to influence, decision-makers, perhaps a top-down approach would work better. Jennifer Sims notes:

> Because information must be tailored to consumer needs, the process is correctly thought of as more two-way than unidirectional. The intelligence analyst should understand the needs, perspectives, and working constraints of the consumer, including the types of contingencies he faces.... The decision maker, in turn, must understand the limits of knowledge on which the intelligence is based, and factor them into a realistic assessment of the intelligence received.[71]

In other words, the prevalent but false vision of a predominantly unidirectional information flow places conceptual blinders on scholars who have produced accurate descriptions of the inherent complexity of the intelligence production procession but have subsequently failed to integrate the intelligence literature into that of foreign policy decision-making more generally. As a result, the literature that describes and evaluates the information flow between intelligence and decision-making has for the most part not adequately incorporated policy-maker information needs into the subsequent analysis of the process. A side effect of this conceptual failure is an emphasis on the accuracy of the intelligence product with correspondingly less emphasis on assessing whether that product is actually useful to the policy-maker.

Removing the conceptual blinders requires that intelligence scholars replace the intelligence production model with one that more accurately reflects the role of intelligence in policy-making; an interaction entailing continuous two-way communication to facilitate decision-making. Doing that requires starting from a different perspective; that of the decision-maker, and understanding how intelligence fits within a more accurate model of a decision-making process.[72]

Notes

1 John Bruce Lockhart, "Intelligence: A British View," *British and American Approaches to Intelligence*, ed. K.G. Robertson, 1987: (37–52), 38.
2 Loch Johnson, "Making the Intelligence 'Cycle' Work," *International Journal of Intelligence and CounterIntelligence*, Vol. 1 No. 4, 1986: (1–23), 5.
3 Peter Sharfman, "Intelligence Analysis in an Age of Electronic Dissemination," in *Intelligence Analysis and Assessment*, eds. David A. Charters, A. Stuart Farson, and Glenn P. Hastedt. London: Frank Cass, 1996, (201–211), 201–202.
4 President Carter press conference, November 30, 1978; answer to question No. 16. As quoted in Johnson, "Making the Intelligence 'Cycle' Work," 5.
5 At least in its first self-initiated iteration. Based on the intelligence provided, decision-makers might then send feedback and additional requirements, thus initiating subsequent cycles. But that first iteration is linear, and will remain linear if no additional requirements are levied based on it.
6 Ramsey Forbush, Gary Chase, and Ron Goldberg, "CIA Intelligence Support for Foreign and National Security Policy making," *Studies in Intelligence*, Vol. 20, No. 1, Spring 1976: 1.
7 Paul R. Pillar, "Intelligence, Policy, and the War in Iraq," *Foreign Affairs*, March/April 2006.
8 Richards J. Heuer, Jr., *Psychology of Intelligence Analysis*, CIA: Center for the Study of Intelligence, 1999: 59.
9 Roger Hilsman, Jr., "Intelligence and Policy-Making in Foreign Affairs," *World Politics*, No. 3, April 1953: 12.
10 Ibid., 12–13.
11 Michael Warner, "Intelligence Transformation and Intelligence Liaison," *SAIS Review*, V, XXIV, No. 1, Winter/Spring 2004: 85–86.
12 Michael Handel, "The Politics of Intelligence," *Intelligence and National Security*, 1987: 7.
13 See chapter 2, "A Theory of the Politicization of Expertise," in Bruce Bimber, *The Politics of Expertise in Congress: The Rise and Fall of the Office of Technology Assessment*, Albany, NY: State University of New York Press, 1996, 12.
14 Bimber, 13.
15 Glenn Hastedt, "The New Context of Intelligence Estimating: Politicization or Publicizing?," in *Intelligence and Intelligence Policy in a Democratic Society* (ed. Stephen J. Cimbala) Dobbs Ferry, NY: Transnational Publishers Inc., 1987: 54.

16 "Rewriting The Science: Scientist Says Politicians Edit Global Warming Research." March 19, 2006. Available online: www.cbsnews.com/stories/2006/03/17/60minutes/main1415985.shtml (accessed July 11, 2006).

17 Harry Howe Ransom, "The Politicization of Intelligence," in Cimbala (ed.), *Intelligence and Intelligence Policy in a Democratic Society*, 26.

18 Robert Jervis, *Strategic Intelligence and Effective Policy. Security and Intelligence in a Changing World: New Perspectives for the 1990s*, ed. A Stuart Farson, David Stafford, and Wesley K. Work, London: Frank Cass, 1991 (165–181): 173–174.

19 Ibid.

20 Woodrow Kuhns, "Intelligence Failures: Forecasting and the Lessons of Epistemology," in *Paradoxes of Strategic Intelligence* (ed. Richard Betts and Thomas Mahnken) London: Frank Cass, 2003, (80–100), 94–95.

21 Robert M. Gates, "The CIA and American Foreign Policy," *Foreign Affairs*, Winter 1987–1988, Vol. 66 No. 2, (215–230), 221.

22 Handel, "The Politics of Intelligence," 28–29.

23 Loch K. Johnson, "The Seven Sins of Strategic Intelligence," *World Affairs*, Vol. 146 No. 2, Fall 1983: 182.

24 George Poteat, "The Intelligence Gap: Hypotheses on the Process of Surprise," *Intelligence Studies Notes*, No. 3, Fall 1976: 15.

25 Jervis, *Strategic Intelligence and Effective Policy*, 171–172.

26 Leon Fuerth interview (December 5, 2005).

27 Jack Davis. Comments posted to CIA Alternative Analysis Database, November 24, 1999.

28 Handel, "The Politics of Intelligence," 33.

29 Forbush *et al.*, "CIA Intelligence Support for Foreign and National Security Policy Making," 13.

30 Hilsman, 34.

31 Jervis, *Strategic Intelligence and Effective Policy*, 171–172.

32 Forbush *et al.*, 3.

33 Ibid., 12–13.

34 Hilsman, 23–24.

35 See Pillar, "Intelligence, Policy, and the War in Iraq."

36 Hilsman, 12.

37 Hilsman, 12–13. Emphasis in original.

38 Yeshoshafat Harkabi, "The Intelligence–Policy-maker Tangle," *The Jerusalem Quarterly*, No. 30, Winter 1984, (125–131), 128. As quoted in Handel, "The Politics of Intelligence," 14.

39 Thomas L. Hughes, "The Fate of Facts in a World of Men: Foreign Policy and Intelligence-Making," Headline Series #233 New York: Foreign Policy Association, December 1976, 10.

40 Heuer, 62.

41 Hilsman, 13.

42 See Isaac Ben-Israel, "Philosophy and Methodology of Intelligence: The Logic of Estimate Process," *Intelligence and National Security* 4, No. 4, October 1989: 660–718.

43 Philipp Steger, "Pandora's Box – Bringing Science into Politics: The Debate on Scientific Integrity in U.S. Policy-making," *Bridges*, Vol. 5, April 2005. Available online: www.ostina.org/content/view/387/149/ (accessed July 6, 2006).

44 Abram N. Shulsky and Gary J. Schmitt, *Silent Warfare: Understanding the World of Intelligence*, Washington, DC: Brassey's Inc., 1991 (3rd edn, 2002), 134.

45 Gary J. Schmitt and Abram N. Shulsky, "Leo Strauss and the World of Intelligence (By Which We Do Not Mean Nous," unpublished paper, 1998. Available online: turcopolier.typepad.com/sic_semper_tyrannis/files/leo_strauss_and_the_world_of_intelligence.pdf.

46 For specific references to Popper and social science methodology, see Kuhns and Ben-Israel.
47 Hughes, "The Fate of Facts," 9.
48 Shulsky and Schmitt, 133.
49 Ibid., 133–134.
50 Michael G. Fry and Miles Hochstein, "Epistemic Communities: Intelligence Studies and International Relations," *Intelligence and National Security*, Vol. 8, No. 3, 1993, 20.
51 Shulsky and Schmitt, 134.
52 Ibid.
53 Ibid.
54 Kevin Russell, "The Subjectivity of Intelligence Analysis and Implications for the U.S. National Security Strategy," *SAIS Review*, Winter–Spring 2004: 147–163.
55 Shulsky and Schmitt, 134.
56 Richard K. Betts, "American Strategic Intelligence: Politics, Priorities, and Direction," *Intelligence Policy and National Security*, ed. Robert L. Pfaltzgraff, Jr. and Uri Ra'anan, London and Basingstoke: Macmillan, 1981, (245–267), 256–257.
57 Steger, "Pandora's Box."
58 Hughes, "The Fate of Facts," 10.
59 Hilsman, 6.
60 Handel, "The Politics of Intelligence," 14.
61 Forbush *et al.*, 3.
62 Percy Cradock, *Know Your Enemy: How the Joint Intelligence Committee Saw the World*, London: John Murray, 2002, 297.
63 Handel, "The Politics of Intelligence," 14.
64 Steger, "Pandora's Box."
65 Handel, "The Politics of Intelligence," 14.
66 Jack Davis. Comments posted to CIA Alternative Analysis Database, November 24, 1999.
67 Leon Fuerth interview (December 5, 2005).
68 Jervis, *Strategic Intelligence*, 179.
69 Handel, "The Politics of Intelligence," 7. Embedded within this quotation is a quotation from Hughes, "The Fate of Facts," 16.
70 Handel, "Intelligence and the Problem of Strategic Surprise," 235.
71 Jennifer Sims, "What Is Intelligence? Information for Decision-makers," Roy Godson, Ernest R. May, and Gary Schmitt (eds.) *U.S. Intelligence at the Crossroads: Agendas for Reform*, Washington, DC: National Strategy Information Center, 1995, 7.
72 For more on this theory of intelligence, see Stephen Marrin, "Intelligence Analysis Theory: Explaining and Predicting Analytic Responsibilities," *Intelligence and National Security*, 22:6, December 2007: 821–846.

9 Defending adaptive realism

Intelligence theory comes of age

Jennifer Sims

Since September 11, 2001, US intelligence reform has been energized by a public at last attentive to the role of intelligence in international politics. Following al-Qaeda's spectacularly deadly attacks, traumatized families brought Washington's handling of critical national security information to national attention and held it there until reforms passed Congress.[1] Similar, closely watched inquiries regarding intelligence-related matters have been held in Britain and Canada and have also generated reforms.[2]

Oddly, however, scholarship has been slow to catch up with this public interest or its implications. Of the top 13 universities awarding 96 PhDs in international relations from 2001 through 2006, none awarded a doctorate for work on intelligence.[3] Over the past ten years, only about 10 percent of the articles in the top scholarly journals for international relations, such as International Security and International Organization, mention intelligence terms; far fewer have intelligence as their primary topic.[4] The International Studies Association (ISA) treats intelligence studies as a category distinct from the more accepted disciplines of international relations or national security studies and few IR scholars seem to attend intelligence related sessions at the ISA's annual conference. Until 2007, the American Political Science Association treated intelligence lightly, if at all, in the context of other disciplines.[5] One leading IR scholar tenured at a major university has said he regards intelligence as irrelevant largely because it deals primarily with intentions, which he believes are unknowable. In fact, the predominant school of IR theory, structural realism, assumes uncertainty to be a constant in international politics. So, though theories of intelligence should ideally guide efforts at its reform – and not emotions or the politics of the moment – governments plagued by surprise and failure seem to have few intellectual tools to guide them.[6]

Nevertheless, out of the world of intelligence practice and study, a group of scholars has recently emerged intent on defining this new field and offering propositions about its boundaries and importance.[7] Several of the most notable of these scholars have been around a while, drawing attention to the secret affairs of governments for decades. Their work has achieved new relevance and, following the era of intelligence openness of the 1990s, new depth as well. They are not, for the most part, members of traditional schools of international relations theory. And they do not necessarily regard themselves as foreign policy scholars; they are focused on a support function that spans military and civilian operations. Instead, most are theorists who root their approaches in the intelligence field itself and describe their work as an effort to understand the causes of intelligence failure, a circumstance that renders their potential contributions both highly creative and potentially problematic – a judgment that will be discussed below.

It is not my intention in this chapter to review all the work offered by scholars in the field of intelligence today. Rather, my intention here is to celebrate the apparent formation of schools of thought in this young field and second, to defend my own theory which, in the context of broader international relations theory, I refer to as Adaptive Realism. This defense is not meant to suggest that this theory is the only useful one. Rather, by replying to critics, I hope to be able to explore more deeply the insights it offers while better clarifying the theory's limitations.

The nature and utility of theory

Theory involves generalization for the purpose of explaining a phenomenon, such as the rising and setting sun, the trajectory of an arrow, or the nature and behavior of a species over time. One approach to theory building involves collecting data on all these phenomena for some time and then looking for a pattern in the results. By generating hypotheses based on these patterns, one can begin to discern relationships among variables. Indeed, with sufficient data, one can develop laws to predict when the sun will rise, where an arrow will fall, or what color a foal will be when crossing a black stallion with a bay mare. In any case, this kind of inductive theorizing categorizes the phenomenon and reduces it to its most essential characteristics.

This last requirement – that a theory not only explain and predict, but that it do so as simply as possible – is the hallmark of the most elegant and useful theories. As one leading econometrician has put it:

> (T)heories can be so complex that they do not actually allow important data reduction, even though a naive hypothesis-testing approach might accept them as 'true.' More commonly, theories can differ less in whether they pass tests of match with the data than in the degree to which the theories are themselves simple. Planetary motions could be predicted quite accurately before Kepler; Kepler nonetheless had a better theory.[8]

But data reduction and prediction are not all that good theory should offer. Good theory should offer explanations.[9] How, after all, can the accumulation of data on the trajectories of arrows explain why they fall to the ground at all? According to this view, hypothesis testing is a naïve way to build theory. The best kind of theory is, in this view, more than an elegant compression of known data about, say, units in a system.[10] It is an explanatory framework that provides insights into why the units behave as they do.

Indeed, Kenneth Waltz argues that the best theories *explain* laws as simply as possible. Absent a larger theoretical context, the aggregation of data from testing hypotheses about where arrows will fall may help with description and prediction under certain circumstances. But one relies on such predictions at one's peril. Absent explanations of causes, a descriptive theory can fail unexpectedly. Hypotheses that 'fail' may not mean that the theory underlying them is false, only incomplete. For example, the hypothesis that a shopping cart will move when pushed will appear to fail if the cart gets too heavy for the kinetic force applied or is positioned on an incline. While the data from this test is important, what one wants to know is why these results obtained and under what circumstances they would not. What is the simplest overarching explanation for why things move the way they do in relation to a given application of force?

If, therefore, we wish to get at the larger questions of intelligence, such as why it is perhaps the world's second oldest profession (i.e. ubiquitous) and why it is retained as an instrument of statecraft despite evidence of its repeated failures, then we need to consider more than an inductive approach. As Kenneth Waltz has argued, the laws themselves need explanations (If A becomes B only after C intervenes, why does C matter so much?).[11] To answer these larger questions, good theorists come up with notions. Grounded in data, these ideas nonetheless spring more from imagination than from experience. In physics, one doesn't find a 'string' or a 'quark'; one comes up with string theory and then considers whether it fits with the data. A good theory does fit but it also generates interesting insights about the data that you couldn't have discerned without it.

In social science, theory has quite practical applications that are notable most often in their absence. In human affairs, workers lacking a theory for what they do may get confused about their mission or what success looks like. Employees uncertain how they contribute to success, may act at odds with one another or in frustratingly repetitive ways, despite the best of intentions. They work, in effect, like uneducated gardeners, confusing weeds with flowers and moving fence posts for borders that seem constantly to change. Handed a plan, they may grasp the strategic vision, but fail at its execution because they have no sense of the theory behind their contribution to the enterprise. Vigorously pulling up weeds according to the map, they only scatter more seeds, making their work ever more laborious.

To solve this kind of problem, good managers seek to convey the nature of the enterprise and the relationships among its essential features. When they go on to ask why the function exists (generalization) and how it can be done better (causation), they engage theory. When they master theory, they can go beyond incremental change and use it to bring about revolutionary approaches to their business. These managers have the capacity for genius that can be communicated to others. When leaders lack this capacity, bureaucrats or gardeners who work for them may want to give up. Richard L. Russell, who once worked among such gardeners plowing the fields of intelligence, has noted that CIA analysts tend to become obsessed with incremental knowledge, such as the next cable or human intelligence report.[12] Unable to see the larger picture, these analysts and the CIA writ large fail repeatedly, in his view, to think strategically or sift their successes from their failures.[13]

For our purposes then, good intelligence theory should both simplify and explain; in achieving the former, it seeks to preserve the latter. Given that no theory can account for everything, the next task is to ask precisely what it is one wishes to explain. Economics simplifies by assuming that actors are rational and then employs the theory of the firm to explain economic behavior in the market-place and macro theory for understanding trade and comparative advantage among large-scale economies.[14] It does not choose to explain the financial decisions of the idiosyncratic. Most intelligence theories to date attempt less to simplify than to describe comprehensively – a fault driven by the fetish for accuracy over insight. But most theorists will also agree that the model of the intelligence cycle, while a simplification, offers no explanation of the purpose of intelligence. It is not a theory in the sense of the term used here.

A theory of intelligence

With this understanding of the nature of theory, we can now consider a theory of intelligence and international politics I have offered elsewhere.[15] This theory of intelligence is important because it purports to explain why states go to war when calculations of raw power suggests they will lose and why some states win contests despite being militarily inferior. According to this theory, intelligence is 'the collection, analysis, and dissemination of information for decision-makers engaged in a competitive enterprise.' A variety of competitions involve intelligence – business, sports, bureaucratic 'warfare' and international politics – but the purpose of intelligence for each competitor remains the same: to gain a decision advantage over rivals. This can be done by either giving one's own side superior information or by purposefully degrading the adversary's information so that his decision-making suffers relative to one's own. In any case, success is achieved less by finding 'truth' or perfect accuracy, than by gaining better information for one's own side than is available to the opponent at crucial moments in the competition. Similarly, failure is defined, not by 'getting it wrong' but by the loss of these advantages. The crucial moment for advantage is the moment of decision, when idea and intent become action. For this reason, intelligence is an activity that involves decision-makers and is paced by them; indeed, it begins and ends with the decision-maker who, should he decide not to delegate the function at all, may perform it on his own.

So much for simplicity; what about causation? When does intelligence matter and how? An intelligence system is more likely to gain advantages for its decision-makers if it optimizes four critical functions: collection, transmission, anticipation, and leveraged manipulation, or counterintelligence. Regarding the first, the more collection systems deployed and the wider their operating range, the better intelligence is likely to be against any given target. This judgment is intuitively sensible, though it rests on the assumption that the other three functions stay constant, of course. Less well understood is the need from a management standpoint for collection's critical components to be tightly linked. When command and control, platform sensors, processing and exploitation, protection and data exfiltration are all well integrated, the collection manager can make valuable trade-offs as she probes a target. For example, she may reduce the protection given to a platform in order to induce an adversary to strike and expose himself to the sensor. With authority over all components, the collection manager can acquire sensors and platforms tailored to each other, such as satellites orbiting at the right altitude to host cameras designed to photograph and transmit from space. In this way, collectors are able to maximize access to the target at lowest cost and risk, and to do so smoothly, swiftly and with agility.

When management of collection assets is not integrated, officials purchasing cameras (sensors) for emplacement on an aircraft (platform) may discover that others have retired the aircraft or refitted it for another mission; spies (sensors) trained to deploy to a country may be unable to go because of budget cuts affecting the government facility (platform) at their destination; or new satellite sensors may be obtained but the increased data is lost because managers at a separate agency cut the ranks of photo-interpreters (processing and exploitation). Given that integration of collection's components requires vertical command and control, collection 'stovepipes' may actually be good.

But stovepipes also can be bad if managers play favorites among their 'customers,' perhaps because of the way they are funded or other dependencies. In theory, collected information makes a difference to the competition only if it gets to the right decision-makers in time, regardless of their relationship to the collector, or if they are ready and willing to receive it. And the 'right' decision-makers are the ones who, given the intelligence, are in a position to gain a decisive advantage over adversaries.

For this reason, the second critical function of intelligence, transmission, is as important to success as collection. It requires trust among providers and decision-makers that, though difficult to measure, may be estimated by the proximity of intelligence functionaries to policy-makers and the depth and breadth of their communications prior to decisions. The more the intelligence functions are delegated in order to enhance collection, for example, the greater the importance of trust and the more at risk it will be. Obviously, when a decision-maker gathers his own intelligence, he will trust it. But his own eyes and ears reach only so far; he has severe limits to what he can know. So the decision-maker's incentive is to create an intelligence service that can extend his eyes and ears and assess the data gathered on his behalf. Such extended awareness must, however, not diminish confidence in what is acquired. Here is where intelligence analysts and their tradecraft become significant. If analytic tradecraft is to add value to collection, it must give the data meaning in the context of policy. It must be more concerned with making unbiased assessments of the competition relevant to decision-makers than with finding some objective truth in the facts themselves. If 'seeing is believing,' then professionalized intelligence involves an implicit contract: decision-makers convey their strategy and objectives so that intelligence professionals can collect, analyze, and convey what they see in the data *to help their own side win*.

Unlike news services, intelligence is therefore biased. It favors one side because its purpose is to help decision-makers succeed. But how should this 'good' bias be measured and distinguished from the bad kind? The existence of mutual trust and the ability of both decision-maker and intelligence professional to transmit information may best be measured not by qualitative evaluations of analytic product, which is after all a subjective measure, but rather by the health of the oversight process for all decision-makers involved. If decision-makers can review, test, and probe the intelligence that serves them, they will tend to trust it; when they cannot, they will tend to distrust it. If decision-makers no longer believe that intelligence works for them, then trust breaks down. When a professionalized intelligence service conceives its mission as independent and isolated from the mission of the decision-makers who employ it, the contract is broken and intelligence becomes a rival source of power. The transmission of intelligence into action will falter or fail.[16]

Nevertheless, excessive proximity to decision-makers is also a problem if it leads to an inability to anticipate their errors. Excessive proximity can blind an intelligence service to policy-makers' weaknesses or prevent it from imagining policy failures, collecting against the worst case, and providing adequate warning. Ideally, intelligence systems warn about known dangers, such as cheating on an arms accord, but also about undesirable developments for which decision-makers should be ready but do not wish to be, such as new adversaries that will distract them or complicate their plans, or events that suggest their policies are failing. This anticipatory function of intelligence rests on two essential capacities beyond trust: first, the ability to generate collection independent of current policy-makers' preferences; second, the ability to provide warning of unexpected adversaries and new competitions to new customers with a need to know about them. In other words, decision-makers served by a sound intelligence system will have mechanisms to test and probe it, but they will not have a capacity to control it totally.

Not surprisingly, most leaders at some point find this idea objectionable if not mutinous. The Bush White House, intent on its own initial agenda, was reportedly irritated by counterterrorism coordinator Richard Clarke's insistent demands that intelligence on terrorism receive high level and urgent attention and that it be shared more widely with law enforcement before 9–11.[17] According to Clarke and now former DCI George Tenet, the White House didn't listen and decision advantage was lost.[18] President Kennedy disliked hearing from Director of Central Intelligence (DCI) John McCone about the troubling possibility that Khrushchev was placing offensive missiles in Cuba and about McCone's desire to fly risky U2 missions to test the hunch. Kennedy nonetheless listened, the flights were flown, and decision advantage was achieved.[19] Later, President Lyndon Johnson disliked hearing from McCone about troubling developments in Vietnam. Johnson shut McCone out of his inner circle, forcing the DCI's decision to resign.[20] If decision-makers cannot accept the anticipatory functions intelligence must perform, the intelligence process will fail. Good warning therefore requires an intelligence service to be at least somewhat independent of decision-makers. Evidence of such independence in an intelligence service includes, for example, an ability to collect against targets without decision-makers' approval.

The art of intelligence is thus a balancing act. Successful intelligence requires decision-makers and intelligence officials to balance trust and proximity with distance and watchfulness. Such balancing need not be as hard as it seems. If intelligence is bold enough and decision-makers tolerant enough to allow collection against the possibilities of surprise, mistaken choice, misjudgment, and failure, then repeated decision advantages will build trust over time. But this carefully nurtured relationship is not one in which intelligence just 'speaks truth to power' – an excessively simplistic and misleading formula. Power and truth exist on both sides; the question is whether intelligence officials and policy-makers can bring these assets together so that winning decisions can be made. The need for good intelligence to balance independence with proximity to policy-makers renders institutionalized intelligence oversight a key indicator of relatively strong intelligence capabilities.

The fourth and final ingredient for successful intelligence is a capacity for creating weaknesses in an opponent's intelligence system and leveraging these into gains for oneself. In a competition there are two ways to achieve decision advantage: either by collecting better information on the contest than your opponent, or by degrading your opponent's information while protecting your own. The latter is called counterintelligence and it comes in two forms, offensive and defensive. Defensive counterintelligence includes any effort to protect one's own national security from the operations of competitors' intelligence efforts. It includes the security function insofar as that function relates directly to competitively relevant threats; security measures designed to protect information only for reasons of privacy or proprietary gain, for example, do not fall into the counterintelligence arena. In its passive form, defensive counterintelligence may include the development of classification systems, the employment of guards, the use of vaults and the like. In its active form, defensive counterintelligence involves following foreign spies or teasing the adversarial service into revealing its methods through 'dangles' – loyal officers pretending to offer to work for the other side.

In contrast, offensive counterintelligence involves twisting the adversary's intentions by messing with his mind. Its purpose is to defend one's own operations by disrupting or deflecting the other side's information – ideally in ways that leave your own decision-makers not just better protected, but better off in competitive terms. In its passive form, offensive counterintelligence employs camouflage or 'cover.' What the adversary's intelligence system sees is manufactured for the purpose of skewing what he 'knows' and thus his decision-making. The interpretation is left to the adversary. In active offensive counterintelligence, the perpetrator aids the deception by leading the adversary to false judgments through the use of, for example, double agents. Because of the importance of manipulating the meaning of events to successful deception schemes, societies and cultures that value the arts, and intelligence services that recruit those proficient in music, choreography, painting, and improvisation, will tend to be better at this key function than societies and organizations that do not.

Offensive counterintelligence will not work, however, without the other features of strong intelligence in place: collection, transmission, and anticipation. This is because the user must have a way to know if the deception is working (collection) in order to take advantage of it; intimate knowledge of the decision-makers' strategy (transmission) is necessary or deception risks complicating or worsening the contest; and the user must, in order to exert influence on the opponent, emplace assets for effective offensive operations well in advance of their need (anticipation). For this reason, counterintelligence or the ability to degrade an opponent's intelligence system cannot, over the long term, make up for weaknesses in positive intelligence. Nevertheless, for competitors seeking a big impact in a short timeframe, offensive counterintelligence can be especially appealing because it employs the adversary's own intelligence service against it. Indeed, one may hypothesize that the better an intelligence service's collection and transmission functions are, and the weaker its counterintelligence function, the more other governments' may seek to deceive it.

This latter point is especially important when considering the impact this theory of intelligence has on theories of international politics. The theory of intelligence outlined above suggests that the international system, which is highly competitive and anarchic, will tend toward transparency as each state or actor seeks to achieve decision advantage over others. Indeed, if information is a 'force multiplier' that offers ways to gain advantages in diplomacy and war, then it is also a form of power. With the essential ingredients of sound intelligence understood, states and transnational actors should have an incentive to build this power and share it with allies much as they do military equipment. Otherwise weak states may gain advantages against strong ones by using intelligence for asymmetric warfare. Competitors' desires to blind their opponents will also cause disparities in intelligence power, but the international system will nevertheless tend toward transparency because actors gain nothing from blinding others without clear vision themselves, so positive intelligence will always be the priority for all.

If this is true, then those theories of international politics that assume uncertainty is a given in international politics are fundamentally flawed. Some states are more savvy than others in understanding the distribution of power in the international system. Intelligence, as I have written elsewhere, 'turns the lights on' in international politics, permitting member states to choose strategies more effectively, balance against adversaries more efficiently, and ally with the right states at the right times. Intelligence theory renders states relatively 'smart' actors that use knowledge to maximize their power and security. When all states maximize this power, the predictions suggested by neorealist theorists are more likely to pan out. For this reason, I call this theory of intelligence, lashed to the dynamics of international politics, 'Adaptive Realism.'

The critiques

Compelling as this theory may be to its author, others have raised objections. Three of the most serious will be mentioned here, along with rebuttals.

The theory is too narrow

First, some critics have said that the definition of intelligence offered above excludes too much. After all, over the thousands of years of its existence, intelligence practice has involved covert action. How can any useful definition of intelligence exclude its most persistent manifestation?[21] A similar critique has an ethical twist: Since intelligence services in some if not all governments employ methods of aggressive interrogation, torture, and kidnapping, how can a comprehensive definition of intelligence leave aside these darker attributes of the business?

The easy answer to the first question is that covert action, defined as efforts to change political, economic, or military conditions while hiding the sponsoring government's hand, is better understood as secret policy-making. Intelligence may provide decision-advantage to this form of policy-making just as it does for diplomacy or war-fighting. But secretly sponsored efforts to overthrow regimes, support foreign political parties, or tinker with military equipment, are conceptually distinct from supporting functions such as information gathering, which is the essence of what intelligence is about. Indeed, that intelligence services conduct covert action would seem to be more a matter of convenience than anything else. Equipped with stealthy platforms and personnel trained in deception, intelligence institutions are well positioned to play this role. Yet, the more often an intelligence service is asked by policy-makers to perform this function, the weaker intelligence (directed information gathering) is likely to become because assets, such as sources and front companies that could have been used for the core collection function, will be put at greater risk than they were.[22] In any case, Adaptive Realism, including the intelligence theory it embraces, does not seek to describe what intelligence services may or may not do in an institutional sense, but rather to explain how directed information acquisition affects the outcomes of competitions in general and national security contests in particular. It is a theory of causation, not description alone. Thus, while some intelligence agencies execute policies of terror on behalf of a tyrant, such policies are not intrinsic to the function of interest here. That said, sometimes intelligence shows a darker side when decision-makers ask for information to be extracted from sources at any cost; but one of the interesting aspects of the theory presented here is that a service adept at terrorizing to gain information, risks losing the trust of those who employ it – weakening the service over time.

As far as it goes, this discussion may be interesting but not completely satisfying. The argument that intelligence cannot, by definition, involve secret policy-making would still seem to exclude too much. What about intelligence liaison, for example? Certainly intelligence services engage in the secret trading of political favors and even military training and hardware for information. Sources sometimes request political goods in return for their spying. Insofar as these activities change political and economic conditions without revealing sponsorship to all those affected, aren't these commonly accepted intelligence functions in fact secret policy too? And what about offensive counterintelligence, particularly deception? Twisting the minds of an adversary to control their decisions involves gaining an information edge but it would also certainly seem to be covert action by another name. So why exclude covert action from a definition that already embraces secret policy-making?

The answers to these last questions are similar to previous ones and turn on the purpose of theorizing. For the purpose of theoretical clarity one must distinguish among functions. For example, when intelligence liaison shifts from bartering goods for information to exchanges principally designed to affect political, economic, or military outcomes, it becomes policy. Assisting in the capture and interrogation of individuals in an allied country can therefore be understood to be 'intelligence' if it is done principally for the purpose of information acquisition; it is 'policy' if it is done principally to aid the ally in fighting an insurrection. Indeed in the latter case, information loss may outweigh gains. Though the differences are difficult to discern in practice, the proximity of the functions of policy and intelligence in these secret niches suggest that this is an area where policy oversight of intelligence operations is most crucial – especially in democracies. Theory helps us understand this boundary problem because it sensitizes us to the distinctions.

It bears repeating here that theory simplifies and explains; comprehensive description of what today's intelligence agencies do, simply muddies the waters. 'Adaptive Realism' is not designed to explain why states torture their people using secret means; rather, it seeks to explain the impact of information and its management on the outcome of contests among states or other actors in the international system. To explore this latter question, theory demands that we define intelligence systems as the tools competitors hone for this purpose, whether they are called 'intelligence' or not. Some activities performed by intelligence institutions will not, strictly speaking, be intelligence activities according to this definition. Other activities performed by non-intelligence institutions (such as commercial attaché, legal attaché or Foreign Service reporting) will fall within the definition.[23] This is the blessing of theory: it provides clarity of function when human practices and semantics get murky. Although matters of policy importance may be delegated to intelligence officials, such as when DCI George Tenet engaged in brokering negotiations in the Middle East, such delegations of authority do not change the nature of what the theory discussed here suggests intelligence is about at the conceptual level. Similarly, if a Foreign Service officer locates Osama Bin Laden and passes this information to the Secretary of State, he is providing actionable intelligence as surely as if he were an intelligence officer. What distinguishes the intelligence function conceptually from others is its unwavering focus on getting and delivering information for decision advantage.

The theory is too broad

A second very different critique is that the definition of intelligence used here is too broad. Abram Shulsky made this argument when a prototype of the theory presented here was first roughly sketched in the early 1990s.[24] His essential point was that nothing in the above definition mentions secrecy, which he and others believe to be the rather obvious core characteristic of intelligence endeavors. Michael Warner, the historian in the Office of the Director of National Intelligence, has made a similar argument: Including all information that provides decision advantage risks losing the focus on what makes intelligence special. After all, if commercial attaches and diplomats become, by definition, intelligence functionaries, doesn't this dilute the concept of intelligence to the point of ridiculousness?

The answer to these questions is a qualified 'no.' If intelligence is defined as the collection, analysis and dissemination of information on behalf of decision-makers engaged in a competitive enterprise, then the essence of intelligence is dedication to the competitor's cause. Those who perform this function of gaining a competitive edge for their side may indeed include from time to time, diplomats, commercial attachés and even, as 9/11 demonstrated, law enforcement officials. Newspaper reporters, however, are not part of the US intelligence system because they do not conduct their collection and analysis at the direction of the government or with the purpose of gaining advantages for policy-makers. In other countries, however, reporters and newspapers play precisely this role, collecting and writing information in service to the state. And for this reason it is fallacious to derive what intelligence is by the nature of the work intelligence institutions do, or to assume that only people who have intelligence in their titles perform intelligence functions. The activity itself must be understood conceptually first.

With respect to secrecy, the theory presented here treats it as an essential part of manipulating the adversary – a characteristic capability of a high-quality intelligence service. Indeed, the more competitive an enterprise, the greater the likelihood that decision-makers will demand that their decisions and all supporting information be kept secret. Intelligence in service to national security is almost always cloaked in secrecy because, in international politics, the competition is a matter of life and death. Misreading events can lead to lost security and war. In these conditions, the state demands secrecy in all aspects of its decision-making – especially the most intimate knowledge of what leaders know, don't know, and want to know.

Nevertheless, secrecy is not integral to the concept of intelligence and it is certainly not a defining characteristic of all intelligence systems. In a game of cards, a parent may help a child by revealing her hand. In sports, talent searches may be secret, but often they are not in order to attract recruits. And, while bureaucratic competition involves a certain degree of ruthlessness, the masters at it generally use superior knowledge of the rules, relationships among people, and timing rather than systematic secrecy to gain their edge.[25] In business, where competition often involves acting on mutual interest, and in accordance with the law and regulation, secrecy can be either unwise or illegal. Even in competitions involving high stakes, actors may choose speed to accomplish their purposes. Open efforts to collect against an adversary may reveal, through his reactions, more about him than secret collection would.

Intelligence for national security involves great stakes; yet failure to understand that secrecy can be traded for gains in other areas can lead intelligence officials to approach the risk-management problem from a 'worst-case' standpoint and underestimate the role open sources play in intelligence. In certain competitive situations it makes sense to favor speed or efficiency over stealth.

Can intelligence capacity be measured?

A third critique of Adaptive Realism has come from the ranks of IR theorists who assume intentions cannot be known and intelligence capacity cannot be measured. This critique rests on the faulty assumption that intelligence is essentially about divining the unknowable as opposed to illuminating the battlefield. Intelligence is not prophecy. It is training the senses to be more acute for the purposes of bettering decisions, not finding truth. Understood this way, Adaptive Realism amends neorealist theories of international politics by suggesting that the impact of the structure of the international system on outcomes will vary to the degree that the system is transparent; and it asserts that transparency will be determined by the intelligence capacities of states. The more ill-equipped a state is with respect to its intelligence capacity, the more unpredictable will be its actions in the international system and the less useful will be realist theories for explaining outcomes. Alternatively, the better is a state's intelligence system, the more influence it will have; that realist theories are generally good at predicting outcomes has to do with their focus on great powers which almost always have at least better than average intelligence capabilities.

It is also worth noting that structural theories which assume uncertainty as a given in international politics also oddly presume good knowledge if not certainty about the distribution of power among states. In this way, system structure explains outcomes despite collective ignorance of it. Adaptive Realism eliminates this apparent contradiction by suggesting that only systems in which most actors have good intelligence will exhibit dynamics as predicted by neorealist theory, such as balancing and bandwagoning; in conditions of significant imbalances in intelligence, anomalous results will obtain – such as the launching of asymmetric wars and the defeat of militarily dominant states. Adaptive Realism also permits analysts to consider the international system as a whole, not just the proclivities of great powers.

Conclusion

With respect to the question of measurement, more work needs to be done. But the general qualities essential to good intelligence have been outlined above. As political scientists work to operationalize the theory, questions will inevitably arise. For example, decision advantage, a key concept, requires refinement. Presumably one can identify the critical 'decision moments' for a strategy such as the battle of Midway during World War II and, within that battle, key decisions that could have changed the outcome. At those junctures, one must ask which side had better instruments for collection, transmission, anticipation, and leveraging and whether they were geared toward support of the decision-makers. One would look for well-integrated, wide-ranging sensor systems and close working relationships between the managers of those systems and the decision-makers involved. The broad indicators of what to look for are clear. What precise instruments provide decisive advantage within each indicator is not. Yet, as work of this kind develops and data is collected relevant to the theory, it will be useful to keep in mind that precise measurement of intelligence capability is unnecessary to predict outcomes. What matters are the relative intelligence capability of states.

Notes

1 Judge Richard Posner has lamented the role private citizens have exercised in shaping public institutions in this instance, arguing that speed and politics have been allowed to trump good judgment. See Richard Posner, *Preventing Surprise Attacks: Intelligence Reform in the Wake of 9/11* (Lanham, MD: Rowman & Littlefield Publishers Inc., 2005), 55–57.

2 *Review of Intelligence on Weapons of Mass Destruction: Report of a Committee of Privy Counsellors* (London: House of Commons, HC898, 2004); Commission of Inquiry into the Actions of Canadian Officials in Relation to Maher Arar (Arar Commission): *Report of the Events Relating to Maher Arar* (Ottawa: Government of Canada Publications, 2006).

3 Annual rankings of top PhD programs are published by the magazine *Foreign Policy*. Rankings and methodology available at www.foreignpolicy.com/story/cms.php?story_id=3718&page=1.

4 Journal rankings based on the 2005 Journal Citation Reports published by the Thomson Institute for Scientific Information. Search terms included 'intelligence,' 'secrecy,' 'espionage,' 'covert action,' 'spy [or] spies,' and 'paramilitary operations.'

5 This year's change in APSA's policy was the result of the persistence of Loch Johnson, who has worked tirelessly on advancing the discipline of intelligence scholarship.

6 Every generalization has its exceptions including this one. And in general, historians, such as Christopher Andrew and Nigel West, have given the topic more coverage than have political scientists. Michael Handel has written superb books discussing Intelligence theory. See in particular his *War, Strategy and Intelligence* (New York: Routledge, 1989). Scholarly books by former or current practitioners include *inter alia*, Gregory F. Treverton, *Reshaping National Intelligence for an Age of Information* (Cambridge: Cambridge University Press/RAND, 2001); R. V. Jones, *The Wizard War: British Scientific Intelligence 1939–1945* (New York: Coward, McCann & Geoghegan, 1978); John C. Masterman, *The Double-Cross System in the War of 1939 to 1945* (New Haven, CT: Yale University Press, 1972); Abram Shulsky, *Silent Warfare: Understanding the World of Intelligence*, 2nd edn rev. by Gary Schmitt (New York: Brassey's, 1993); Richards J. Heuer, *Psychology of Intelligence Analysis*

(Washington, DC: Center for the Study of Intelligence, Central Intelligence Agency, 1999); and Mark Lowenthal, *Intelligence: From Secrets to Policy*, 3rd edn (Washington, DC: CQ Press, 2006). I am grateful to Andrew Sawka for his research assistance in preparing this article.

7 See, for example, Loch K. Johnson, *America's Secret Power: The CIA in a Democratic Society* (Oxford, UK: Oxford University Press, 1989); Arthur S. Hulnick, 'What's Wrong with the Intelligence Cycle?', in Loch K. Johnson, ed., *Strategic Intelligence Volume 2: The Intelligence Cycle – The Flow of Secret Information from Overseas to the Highest Councils of Government* (Westport, CT: Praeger Security International, 2007), 1–22; Michael Herman, *Intelligence Power in Peace and War* (Cambridge, UK: Cambridge University Press, 1996); Peter Gill and Mark Phythian, *Intelligence in an Insecure World* (Cambridge, UK: Polity Press, 2006); Michael Warner, 'Wanted: A Definition of "Intelligence",' *Studies in Intelligence* 46, no. 3 (2002): 15–22; Michael Warner, 'The Divine Skein: Sun Tzu on Intelligence,' *Intelligence and National Security* 21, no. 4 (August 2006): 483–492; Stephen Marrin, 'Adding Value to the Intelligence Product,' in Loch Johnson, ed., *Handbook of Intelligence Studies* (London and New York: Routledge, 2006), 199–210; and Jennifer E. Sims and Burton Gerber, eds., *Transforming US Intelligence* (Washington, DC: Georgetown University Press, 2005).

8 Christopher A. Sims, 'Macroeconomics and Methodology,' *Journal of Economic Perspectives* 10, no. 1 (Winter 1996): 106. Kepler observed that the data collected on planetary orbits described elliptical paths with the sun at a focus 'thereby accomplishing a sharp data reduction.' See Sims, 105–106.

9 Political scientists may assemble relationships of causation (A becomes B if C intervenes) and articulate them as laws. Such inductive theorizing can help with prediction (If A and C are present, B may show up).

10 See Kenneth N. Waltz, 'Laws and Theories,' in Robert O. Keohane, ed., *Neorealism and Its Critics* (New York: Columbia University Press, 1986), 27–46.

11 Ibid., 27–46.

12 Richard L Russell, *Sharpening Strategic Intelligence: Why the CIA Gets it Wrong and What Needs to be Done to Get it Right* (Cambridge, UK: Cambridge University Press, 2007), ix.

13 He is now professor of national security affairs at the National Defense University's Near East and South Asia Center for Strategic Studies.

14 Both large-scale theories are based on a bold simplification: that man is a rational actor and makes choices in his own self-interest.

15 'A Theory of Intelligence and International Politics,' in Gregory F. Treverton and Willhelm Agrell, eds., *National Intelligence Systems: Current Research and Future Prospects* (Cambridge, UK: Cambridge University Press, 2008).

16 In the US system, oversight is conducted by both the Executive Branch and the Congress. While this splitting of the function makes sense given Congress's own oversight role, Congress's growing decision-making responsibilities in national security policy have introduced problems for an intelligence service seeking to support this decision-making while maintaining trust with the administration of the day. This provides an interesting case for considering the effects of having one intelligence service working for two competing institutions at one level (national politics), while at the same time doing so for the purpose of advancing one competitor's position (the US state) in a different competition: international politics.

17 Richard A. Clarke, *Against All Enemies: Inside America's War on Terror* (New York: Free Press, 2004), 227–238.

18 Ibid., 235; George Tenet, *At the Center of the Storm: My Years at the CIA* (New York: HarperCollins, 2007), 153.

19 Christopher Andrew, *For the President's Eyes Only: Secret Intelligence and the American Presidency from Washington to Bush* (New York: HarperCollins, 1995),

281–284; Graham Allison and Philip Zelikow, *Essence of Decision: Explaining the Cuban Missile Crisis*, 2nd edn (New York: Addison Wesley Longman, 1999), 332.

20 Andrew, 321.

21 Roy Godson, *Dirty Tricks or Trump Cards: U.S. Covert Action and Counter-intelligence* (New Brunswick, NJ and London: Transaction Publishers, 2001), 1–18.

22 The degree to which it is weakened will depend on whether, by performing covert action, the intelligence service tightens its relationship of trust and cohesion with policy-makers. If so, then the loss in collection may be balanced by an increase in trust, improving the transmission function.

23 That this is a useful way to think about intelligence was reinforced by 9–11, in which it became clear that FBI memos should have been treated as critical intelligence and shared as such, but were not.

24 Abram Shulsky, 'What Is Intelligence? Secrets and Competition Among States,' in Roy Godson, Ernest R. May, and Gary Schmitt, eds., *U.S. Intelligence at the Crossroads: Agendas for Reform* (Washington, DC: Brassey's, 1995), 17–27; Jennifer E. Sims, 'What is Intelligence? Information for Decision Makers,' in Godson *et al.*, 3–16.

25 When secrecy is sanctioned, however, it can play a malicious role in bureaucratic competitions otherwise governed by openness. Officials seeking to influence decisions within a bureaucracy can attempt to manipulate the classification system in order to keep out other bureaucrats who have opposing points of view. In this way, competitive bureaucrats can hijack a system designed to protect intelligence from foreign disclosure for the illicit purpose of keeping their own bureaucratic competitors relatively uninformed and weak. When the purpose of such activity is private advantage over the public good, this may be called the privatization of intelligence – a less well-known distortion of the intelligence function than its sibling, politicization, which is any effort to skew intelligence to support policy preference.

10 Policing, intelligence theory and the new human security paradigm

Some lessons from the field

James Sheptycki

Introduction

The chapter briefly reviews some recent discussions concerning intelligence theory and suggestions that we are in the midst of a revolution in intelligence affairs. Taking a page out of the sociology of surveillance literature it is argued here that, while it is possible to say that we are in the midst of technological revolution in intelligence affairs there has not, as yet, been a revolution in intelligence theory.[1] Rather, a dominant intelligence paradigm, referred here to here as the 'national security intelligence paradigm', prevails. This paradigm is predicated largely on the assumptions of international relations realism: *Realpolitik.* An alternative conception is here offered, namely the 'human security intelligence paradigm'. The tenets of this approach to intelligence security will be briefly outlined following which, by way of illustration, two case-study vignettes of contrasting intelligence-led police interventions are presented. These examples pertain to UK domestic police operations and they represent two quite different ways of organizing intelligence-led operations which analogically map onto the national-security/human-security distinction. Throughout the chapter it is suggested that the sociology of policing literature offers a useful touchstone in thinking about the re-orientation of transnational security issues. This is so because the institutions of liberal democratic policing offer a different kind of institutional basis for thinking about security intelligence than do the bases of the currently dominant national security paradigm which are the military and secret intelligence institutions. The chapter concludes by arguing that human security doctrine offers a way out of the impasse that the now dominant paradigm persists in.

Critical debates on the meaning of security have, since the end of the Cold War, been stuck on the cleft stick that is the realist–idealist distinction, with the result that the national security intelligence paradigm has remained largely unmoved.[2] This chapter is a contribution to these discussions, but it is a contribution with its empirical and theoretical roots in the literature on the sociology and politics of policing, rather than that of the military institutions that are the traditional reference points for the 'intelligence community'. This is useful for at least two reasons. Firstly, as I and Andrew Goldsmith have argued elsewhere, it is the case that there has been a blurring of policing and military functions over the recent past and so, for good empirical reasons, it is important to understand how policing theories and capacities alter the conditions and nature of security discourse and practice.[3] Secondly, the impasse that has been reached in critical debates about the nature of security is, it seems to me, at least partly because that scholarship has not identified an alternative to the traditional means – military ones – that have been the sine qua non of international security practice. Both policing and military institutions may muster coercive capacities and, despite the 'militarization' of policing that is undoubtedly taking place in western liberal democracies, this chapter will argue that these institutions may yet do so in very different ways.[4] The argument suggests that the broad scope of human security is both theoretically comprehensible and practically realistic when encompassed by democratic policing means, whereas the broadening security agenda is simply incoherent and unrealistic to a mind-set beholden exclusively to military ones.

The national security intelligence paradigm

Elsewhere in this volume a variety of perspectives on intelligence are offered. This chapter is a contribution to attempts to shift the focus away from the traditional concerns of the 'intelligence community'. It draws on the sociology of policing literature and the emerging doctrine of human security in order to show the practical potential of a genuinely new intelligence doctrine both in theory and in practice. Lessons from the police sector look rather promising in helping to establish theoretical accounts about the nature, purpose and normative basis of intelligence and security practice. This is so for a number of reasons. Firstly, intelligence practice in the police sector is long established, not only with regard to crime, as may be supposed, but also for a variety of other purposes. The use of intelligence by UK police agencies is well known, if not always well understood by the public at large. For many years, police services in the UK, and elsewhere in Europe, have made use of intelligence for a variety of purposes which may be grouped under three headings: crime control, political policing and public safety.[5] Thus, not only is the security agenda of policing already quite broad, there is also a reasonable track record of empirical study.

A second reason why it is worth turning to the scholarly literature regarding police for lessons on intelligence practice is that the academic empirical study of policing in liberal democracies has been substantial for several decades. Crucially this literature includes a rich vein of scholarship combining historical awareness, together with a critical analytical and empirical focus on intelligence theory and practice.[6] It is true to say that policing with intelligence was, for a considerable period, an analytical and research backwater in Police Studies.[7] However, at the turn of the millennium things seemed to change. The pace of organizational transformation in policing institutions (and every other major social institution) was ramped up as a result of the so-called 'information revolution'.[8] Not un-coincidentally, policing scholars saw a resulting shift in policing vocabulary with the introduction of new terms such as 'strategic' and 'pro-active', together with 'intelligence-led policing'.[9] Other policing scholars coined the term 'surveillant assemblage' to describe the concatenation of surveillance technologies and techniques that are currently deployed by police agencies and other security providers in the governance of individuals and populations.[10]

So, the empirical study of policing and security intelligence practices is, by now, both well established and theoretically sophisticated. Another reason why the academic literature on the sociology of policing is useful in this context is that, within it, there is an interesting strand of work concerning the historical manifestations of *transnational* policing in its many guises.[11] This point is worth stressing since the dominance of the national security intelligence paradigm partly rests on its historical lineage and global reach. It is therefore pertinent to point out that policing has been an important aspect of world affairs for some time now and that the academic study of policing has been useful in understanding the trajectory and contemporary circumstances that make up the transnational world order.

A final reason to be mentioned here is that scholars working on policing have long been aware that, largely due to the transformative thrust of neo-liberal philosophies of governance, the state has been losing its classic Weberian claim to the monopoly of legitimate use of force. Consequently, theories about policing in the contemporary period cast considerable light on the 'governance of security beyond the state'. This is important because, as has been belatedly acknowledged in at least some of the IR literature, one of the distinctive features of the contemporary transnational system is that the State *qua* State is no longer the structural key-stone; the world system is a polycentric power system where non-state, supra-state, and sub-state actors all play roles in the governance of security that are equal to, and perhaps even more central than, the roles played by state actors.[12]

For all of these reasons the scholarly literature on policing offers alternative points of insight regarding intelligence theory and security practices more generally. This is crucial because the dominant perception of intelligence practice is largely shaped by the assumptions of *Realpolitik* and all the signs are that this paradigm is not working in the sense that political and human insecurity has only increased since the end of the cold war.[13] Grounded in the literature on policing, a discussion of theoretical innovation for intelligence may be cut loose from its current paradigmatic moorings without running the risk of becoming too theoretically abstract.

There are many contributors to the currently dominant paradigm and so there are some subtle variations in emphasis. One recent attempt to draw together the various threads into a comprehensive theory of intelligence was a workshop undertaken by the RAND National Security Research Division – henceforth the RAND workshop.[14] If there can be any doubt that the mainline of thought in the 'intelligence community' strictly concerns national security under the assumed conditions of IR realism, this document lays them to rest. The keynote speaker was Ernest May, who is Charles Warren Professor of American History at

Harvard University. According to his biography, he has been a consultant at various times to the Office of the Secretary of Defense, the National Security Council and other similar agencies and, at the time of the workshop was a member of the DCI's Intelligence Science Board and of the Board of Visitors of the Joint Military Intelligence College. His address to the experts at the RAND workshop concerned the stories of the German invasion of France in 1940 and the al-Qaeda attacks of 11 September 2001. He used these examples to explain not only the nature of intelligence success/failure (a distinction which depends on which side you are on in a conflict), but also to argue that the intelligence community needed to exercise more 'imagination': 'Asking these 'what ifs' needs to be done regularly and routinely in all steps of military and political planning. It was done on a regular basis during the cold war, a practice that needs to be reinstituted.'[15]

Clearly, the national security intelligence imagination remains within specific parameters, but those parameters are interesting. As Michael Warner, a representative of the United States Office of the Director of National Intelligence and another speaker at the RAND workshop put it: 'intelligence is secret state activity designed to understand or influence foreign entities'.[16] According to him, 'intelligence for states can mean life or death'; the driving impulse 'dates from the earliest days when sovereign powers decided to war with one another for control of territory and populations (and to exclude traitors who divulged their secrets)'.[17] Among the workshop's 41 participants a number of other points of discussion were raised. This included the apparently limited basis of knowledge for understanding cross-national variation in approaches to intelligence and also the extent to which there is, or was, a specifically American theory of intelligence. It also considered such matters as the appropriate mix of 'human intelligence' (HUMINT) and 'signals intelligence' (SIGINT), the effects of technological change on intelligence craft, the psychological dimensions of intelligence collection and dissemination, the politicization of the intelligence function, various aspects of organizational theory as it pertains to intelligence processes and the potential for measurement of intelligence success and failure. But again and again, the discussion drifted back to the changes to the international system since the end of the cold war and concomitant changes in the internal, and especially external, threats to the nation state.

Another invited speaker at the workshop, Loch Johnson from the Department of International Affairs at the University of Georgia argued strongly that

> For too long, the role of intelligence in world affairs has stood in the shadows of traditional research on international relations. What a pity that it takes events like Pearl Harbor in 1941, the revelations of Operation Chaos and COINTELPRO in 1974, the terrorist attacks of 9/11, and the mistakes about weapons of mass destruction (WMD) in Iraq in 2002 to underscore the importance of intelligence. But at last the public (and perhaps even hidebound international relations theorists) seem ready to acknowledge the need to understand the hidden side of government.[18]

Johnson is an international relations theorist and his proclivities are clear, just as the central message of the RAND workshop report as a whole is clear in its depiction of the international state system as a Hobbesian war of all against all. According to this view, and looked at in psychological terms, if states were persons they would be paranoid, if not also schizophrenic. This brings to mind a famous passage from R. D. Laing's *The Politics of Experience:*

> As long as we cannot up-level our 'thinking' beyond Us and Them, the goodies and baddies, it will go on and on. The only possible end will be when all the goodies have killed all the baddies, and all the baddies all the goodies, which does not seem so difficult or unlikely since to Us, we are the goodies and They are the baddies, while to Them, we are the baddies and they are the goodies.[19]

This tangential reference to existential psychoanalysis is not entirely fanciful. Directing our thinking back to the realm of theories about the nature of the contemporary world system, David Held traces the historical ascent of the Westphalian model, which entrenched, for the first time, the principle of territorial sovereignty in inter-state affairs but argues that, although many of the assumptions underpinning it are still operative in international relations today, the contemporary applicability of the model is dubious.[20] Held's point has been, by now, well established by a host of other globalization theorists; that the stretching of social relations across space and time along a variety of institutional dimensions (technological, organizational, legal, cultural) is evidence of the intensification of transnational connections which changes the nature of the global system.[21] These transnational institutional domains create new challenges, not least of which concerns the governability of the global social order, and raises urgent questions about how the whole project might be made democratic. Crucially, Held also observed, that the logic of national (in)security permeates the transnational condition, pointing especially to the behaviour of what Fred Halliday referred to elsewhere as 'seigneurial states'.[22] Held warned that the continuing 'logic of state security has created a cycle of violence and preparation for violence in the international system which hinders the development of policy for a durable peace – whether national, regional or global'.[23] Stuck in the national security intelligence paradigm, the underlying structure of self-perpetuating insecurity remains intact. Confronted with such a knot, it is tempting to want to untie it for as Laing – himself no stranger to knots –suggested: 'As long as we cannot up-level our "thinking" beyond Us and Them, the goodies and baddies, it will go on and on'. This brings us to the question: what is the practical alternative to the national (in)security intelligence paradigm?

Human security

If the roots of the national security intelligence paradigm can be traced back to the Westphalian Peace established in 1648, the roots of the human security paradigm are much more recent, dating to the period just after the cold war ended.[24] Whereas national security focuses on the defence of 'the state' and is organized especially around the fear of an external attack directed against the state, human security is about protecting individuals and communities from any form of political violence and, in its broadest conception includes both freedom from fear and freedom from want.[25] The human security paradigm focuses on political violence, its causes and consequences, and it does so from the perspective of individuals and communities. Further, the broad concept of human security articulated in the UN Development Programme's 1994 *Human Development Report*, and the Commission on Human Security's 2003 report, *Human Security Now*, moves the 'threat agenda' beyond incidents of political violence and disorder to include poverty, hunger, disease and natural disasters because these kill far more people than war, genocide and terrorism combined.

Because the fundament of the human security paradigm is that of universal human rights, rather than state sovereignty, it offers up an obviously very different discourse than national security doctrine. But it is also one that may be all too easily derided from the standpoint of the now dominant paradigm – based on IR *realism* – on the grounds that it is good in theory but it is not realistic. That is where practical lessons from the sociology of policing might be used to make a case for a different intelligence paradigm. In the existing sociology of policing literature much of the discussion about human security doctrine is centred on fear and violence where the 'duty to protect' is articulated with reference to such principles such as 'community policing', 'harm minimization', 'problem solving', 'strategies of minimal force' and the 'constabulary ethic'.[26] 'Good policing is minimal policing – minimally intrusive and carefully controlled in its use of force'.[27] Some of this literature is intended to create an awareness of the police role in natural and man-made disasters giving it even wider applicability. Of course, national security type doctrine is much in evidence in the policing literature as well. The point being stressed here, however, is that practical and realistic alternatives to the national security paradigm which exhibit the characteristics of a new way of thinking – the human security paradigm – can be found in the policing literature.

Human security doctrine, however nascent, is part of a conscious effort to shift the discourse pertaining to global security away from one which focuses on national-state (in)security to the point of view of individual persons and local communities. Under this doctrine the success of policing intelligence can be ultimately judged according to criteria concerning the general health of society and the overall public good, but not narrow law enforcement outputs or military-style pacification criteria. The human security agenda shares close affinity to liberal democratic policing ideology because, although it may occasion the use of coercive force in the maintenance of general social order, it does so only on the basis that the community being policed and secured broadly understands and endorses the mission. This approach aims to be proactive about the causes of insecurity and not simply a reaction to manifestations of insecurity. Further, the doctrine holds that its own legitimacy can only be secured through transparency and public engagement with the political processes of the civil society in which it operates.[28]

At a United Nations summit in September 2005 a portion of the human security agenda was accepted into the discourse on 'humanitarian intervention', that portion which aims at 'security first' and 'freedom from fear' (but, significantly, one that does not aim at 'freedom from want'). The responsibility to protect as defined in this document was limited to a concern with populations at risk from genocide, war crimes, ethnic cleansing and crimes against humanity. At the UN summit it was accepted that

> Each individual State has the responsibility to protect its populations from genocide, war crimes, ethnic cleansing and crimes against humanity. This responsibility entails the prevention of such crimes, including their incitement, through appropriate and necessary means. We accept that responsibility and will act in accordance with it. The international community should, as appropriate, encourage and help States to exercise this responsibility and should support the United Nations to establish an early warning capability.

There was some controversy about this. Catherine Dumait-Harper, *Médecines sans Frontières* delegate to the summit, warned that 'In [terms of] *realpolitik*, the protection of populations is still a secondary objective for most Member States, in particular [those of] the Security Council, unfortunately less important than other concerns like "national interest"'.[29] Critical commentators of the responsibility to protect point out, not without good reason, that there is a real danger that seigneurial states might use the idea to justify furtherance of narrow national interests rather than human security needs more broadly. Nevertheless, ideas about human security, however inchoate and contested, could signal a step away from national (in)security doctrine, and as such could provide some opportunity to change the thought-style that determines security intelligence thinking globally. Interesting in theory, but how might we understand the practicalities of this new thought-style?

Two case vignettes; search and disrupt *versus* problem solving

What follows are two short case studies concerning two differing approaches to 'intelligence-led policing' as it was being practised in England circa 2002. The material that constitutes the data for these vignettes was gathered as part of two larger research projects and full discussion of research methods and data collection involved can be found there.[30] Readers are also advised that these case studies gain added meaning when read against the backdrop of the literature on intelligence-led policing more generally.[31] But before outlining the two cases, it is well to explain to the reader that the academic literature concerning police work routinely contrasts two styles of policing.[32] On the one hand there is community policing along the 'Peelian model', which emphasizes *inter alia*: the police officer as a mere citizen in uniform, the strategy of minimal force, the social service role of police, crime prevention, the rule of law, efficiency and the effective bureaucratic control of operations, legitimacy and democratic account-ability. The second style is the paramilitary policing style of 'zero tolerance', which emphasizes the police officer as an enforcer empowered to use decisive force within and against communities that are conceptualized as uncivil and largely ungovernable. The two cases considered here map onto this theoretical distinction reasonably well and, analogously, also map onto the human security/-national-security distinction discussed previously. These empirical examples serve to illustrate that differences in theoretical orientation can have fundamen-tal consequences for intelligence and security practice.

Case 1: search and disrupt in Northern Town

Opiate usage in the north of England is a matter of long historical practice going back into the nineteenth century. It became a matter of policing concern only in the 1970s when legislative change led to its criminalization.[33] By the 1980s the police in Northern Town had developed an active drug squad that had been thor-oughly inculcated into drug enforcement discourse. An informal practice of crime disruption had developed whereby officers in the drug squad made a point of destroying injecting equipment whenever they found it. This was at a time when the HIV/AIDS virus was still relatively new and little understood as the 'gay plague'. It was not until sometime later that it became evident that the prevalence of the HIV virus (along with hepatitis) in the northern drug-injecting community had come about because of the scarcity of injecting equipment and the adaptive behaviour of 'sharing works'. Some twenty years later the strategic intelligence indicators showed only that drug use in the UK had escalated and the prices for most illicit drugs had fallen. *The Economist* reported in 2002 that the UK had the highest mortality rates due to illicit drugs in Europe.[34] At that time, according to documents circulating within the National Criminal Intelli-gence Service (NCIS), purity-adjusted retail prices (the price-purity level) for heroin had fallen from just over £300 per gramme in 1990 to about £150 in 2001.[35] British Crime Survey (BCS) data showed some interesting trends in drug use, including significant rises in the reported use of cocaine and ecstasy and significant rises in reported lifetime use of cannabis up from 36 per cent in 1994 to 45 per cent in 2000. Use of hard drugs, including heroin and methadone, had remained fairly stable with only slight increases in reported use 'over the previ-ous month' up from 3 per cent to 5 per cent between 1998 and 2000.[36] These trends remained largely stable and in 2005 it was reported that BCS indicators over the previous decade had shown a significant increase in the use of illicit drugs, primarily cannabis, cocaine and ecstasy, with heroin and methadone use remaining fairly constant nationally over the period but with slight falls in the use of amphetamines, steroids and glues.[37]

Patterns of consumption and supply were being ethnographically documented in the north-east of England during the period, as was the nature and structure of the so-called 'middle market' which revealed that there was not so much a national drugs market, but rather a series of loosely interlinked local and regional supply networks.[38] The patterns of drugs and crime in the locality were laid on the historical foundations of previous generations' habits of drinking and public disorder amid the post-Fordist desolation of de-industrialization.[39] Some of the ethnographic research revealed drug use to be chronic in particular local public housing estates in the north-east with, at times, seemingly ubiquitous mass consumption of cannabis among adolescents. Moreover, a strong poly-drug-using subculture was well established among young adults, who fuelled their participation on the pub-and-club circuit with powder cocaine, ecstasy, amphetamines, magic mushrooms and LSD, depending on availability and season. From the mid-1990s smoking 'brown' came to be perceived by many young users as an extension of the already standard drugs menu, sometimes as a 'chill-out drug' after periods of bingeing on party drugs and alcohol. In the midst of this was a small population of several hundred hardcore heroin addicts – stigmatized, distrusted, labelled and excluded as 'junkies', 'skaggies' and 'smackheads' – dispersed and living in small groups.

According to police intelligence analysis, the region had been experiencing a renaissance of heroin use since the early to mid-1990s and the indicators of more widespread heroin use, in terms of drugs seizures and police arrests, were pointing upwards. Recorded crime rates were, however, not rising and the view was that most drug-related crime remained hidden in shoplifting and user-dealer income generation. Crime pattern analysis at divisional level was, in some instances, capable of revealing clusters of burglaries along the routes strung out between user-dealers and their customer base. An analysis of mortality statistics revealed a problematic spike in heroin-related deaths that was attributed to a 'bad batch of heroin' and which may in fact have been due to rapid changes in price-purity levels during the period.

Confidential police intelligence sources in Northern Town identified a local white man in his late thirties, who had a long but undistinguished record of violence, as the main local supplier. This individual, who had a record of one prior arrest (for cruelty to animals) was thought to be the key player in a larger 'family firm'. His younger brother, who also had a reputation for violence but no previous convictions, was also known to be part of the distribution network. Discussions with the National Crime Squad (NCS) revealed that an undercover operation would only be considered based on an analysis of the volume of business. Undercover operations are expensive and rough cost-benefit 'rule of thumb' had evolved whereby only 'Class A' suppliers wholesaling in excess of two-and-a-half kilos per week were deemed to justify the mobilization of these resources. It might therefore do to stress that it was on the basis of the presumed volume of business, and not the reputations for violence, that an undercover operation was mounted.

Thus, based on the available local intelligence, the decision was taken to run an undercover operation using outside operatives. The NCS arranged to have two undercover officers (one male and one female) brought in from the south of England. With the co-operation of local housing officials they were placed in accommodation on the housing estate where the hub of the network was known to be located. The two undercover officers employed a cover story regarding domestic violence – she had supposedly fled the violence of her former boyfriend and run away to the north with her new lover. Within two days local street dealers had come to know the female undercover officer as a heroin user and she began to make small purchases. After a three-month operation it was concluded that the case had indeed identified a multi-kilo dealer who was laundering money through a casino and had invested heavily in local property, including a pub. It was thought his supply originated in Manchester. At this point, the decision was taken to disrupt the local heroin market by making arrests; the subsequent trial led to the conviction of 25 people and the original target received a sentence of seven years.[40] According to a local drug squad officer, 'Bosses want immediate results and they wanted the operation repeated in another venue'. Within months of the trial senior police in the region admitted that illegal drugs were still cheap and plentiful on the streets, that the stark reality was that police could not, by themselves, contain the situation and that the region was being swamped by the demands and pressures arising from the illicit drugs market. The operation, intelligence-led and largely driven by covert means, had been another tactical success in a long history of strategic failure.

Case 2: problem solving in Coastal County

The frontier marked by the English Channel has been associated with a variety of forms of transnational criminality and associated policing practice has been documented back to 1968.[41] However, the opportunities for illicit gain through smuggling extend back to the time of the Stuart monarchs when, in 1642, the Boards of Customs and Excise were first introduced in England and Wales. This was the first UK government department with police-type powers (search, seizure, arrest) and so, in a sense, crime in the region has been marked for centuries by the attempt to enforce trans-boundary trade restrictions. Such enforcement restrictions effectively create an illicit market opportunity and smuggling in various guises has long been an aspect of the regional informal economy. Largely unbeknownst to the primary actors involved in the intelligence-led operation described below and, similarly, unbeknown to many others involved in cross-border policing issues at the time, Her Majesty's Customs and Excise (HMCE, as it was then called) was systematically involved in a whole series of mismanaged undercover operations both nationally and transnationally. The extent of incompetence was made public explicitly in a series of newspaper articles beginning in early 2001.[42] However, the media had been reporting on the attendant criminogenic potential of the massive illicit market in alcohol and tobacco from rather earlier.[43] The full social ramifications of this have not been much studied, but there has been at least some academic scrutiny of these illicit markets.[44] Briefly stated: the principle illicit market in the English Channel region at the turn of the millennium concerned bootleg tobacco, cigarettes and alcohol as a profitable criminal economy evolved in the interstices of the internal European market because of something as mundane as national tax differentials, a criminal economy made all the more robust because of the administrative inefficiency and incompetence of the agency responsible for enforcing the rules.

Coastal County Constabulary, which facilitated the operation considered here, was fully committed to a set of principles articulated under the rubric of intelligence-led policing by the early 1990s and these commitments were sustained over the entirety of the decade and into the next. Concomitant with the commitment to ILP was a concern to abide by the strictures of the European Convention on Human Rights, adopted into UK law in 1998.[45] One training officer in the force described the organization's power as

> awesome, when you consider the surveillance capabilities we have, and the range of information we can draw on, plus we also have the power to arrest, search seize etcetera etcetera. So you've got to be sure that it [intelligence-led policing] is both done under human rights and for human rights. Which can be very difficult in the practical run of things.
>
> (Personal communication to author)

Both human rights and ILP are sets of abstract principles and, in combination, they equate admirably well with the notion of human security intelligence. The case arose from a community safety audit which pinpointed a problem with truanting youths causing a nuisance, engaging in acts of vandalism and small-scale public-order disturbances. Discrete mobile and static surveillance revealed that these youths were frequenting a particular address. The surveillance also discovered that the address in question was a point in an illicit alcohol and tobacco distribution network.

HMCE intelligence liaison officers confirmed that the address was known to be part of a broader network of distribution. For police intelligence analysts the issue was a local crime and disorder problem, but the ultimate causes of this social problem were beyond local influence and therefore could not be fixed. Rather than unilaterally mount a police law enforcement operation, however, the analysts looked for a more comprehensive approach to the problem, and they did so by involving a number of other agencies. The first of these was the local Education Authority. The issue initially came to light as an issue of truanting youths and the questions that this posed included concerns for their health and safety as much as the nuisance they were causing in the community. Disengaging the group from their low-key but nonetheless nefarious pursuits logically required that they be engaged in more legitimate ones and the school system was the line of first resort. Surveillance of the network had revealed that the principal retail outlet for the illicit goods was a less than salubrious café. Local Trading Standards and Environmental Services officers inspected the premises which were found to be in breach of a variety of health and safety regulations. Subsequently, the business licence was revoked due to reasons of food hygiene. Background checks on vehicle ownership details revealed a number of inconsistencies due to fraud and vehicle licences were suspended. Further checks revealed that members of the network were also involved in housing benefit fraud and related activities and so the local Housing Department and the Benefits Agency were also brought in.

In planning and execution of the response the emphasis was on working with the local responsible authorities to alleviate manifestations of social harm embedded in aspects of the illicit market operating in the area. Those guiding the operation continually emphasized the cross-benefits that the various agencies involved would accrue and the overall benefits to community safety. The problem originally identified became an occasion to strengthen local capacities across a range of governmental services and the guiding objective was trying to find ways of reducing crime and improving the quality of life in the area. This broad-based approach was attractive to Coastal County police because it allowed them significantly to dismantle the criminal group's ability to conduct business without pursuing prosecutions in court. Punishment was not the aim. Rather, the aim was preventing, as much as possible, criminal enterprise deemed damaging to the community. In the circumstances, none of the intelligence analysts and others involved in the operation could have expected significantly to impact on the illicit alcohol and tobacco market. What is significant is that the solutions sought aimed primarily at maintaining and strengthening regular routines of good local government and minimizing harm and, in both these regards at least, the strategy met some success.

Understanding this small operation in the context of the broader strategic architecture of national policing in the UK at the time is important. Looked at in terms of the sociology of organizations, the national crime intelligence system was riven by a number of 'organizational pathologies'. The root cause of these pathologies lies in the attempt to centralize policing intelligence leading to a direct clash with the transformative power of information technologies which tends to flatten hierarchies and empower social networks, a trend which runs counter to the organizational expectations of rank-structured bureaucracies.[46] These pathologies give rise not only to internal problems of command-and-control but also external problems of accountability and legitimacy. The language of strategic intelligence analysts is peppered with concepts that denote organizational pathology: information silos, intelligence gaps, linkage blindness, noise, compulsive data demand, information black holes, and other concepts are exhibits in a lexicon of institutional failure. And yet, undeniably, the technological power of intelligence-led policing, for good or for ill, is awesome, as the case of Maher Arar amply demonstrates.[47] What this short case vignette illustrates is how policing intelligence capacities can be used to muster non-punitive responses to identified problems which aim at changing the circumstances that produced the problem in the first instance without unintentionally amplifying social harms. In short, it shows the possibility of an intelligence theory of realistic and practical action, tempered by broader thinking about how to solve problems.

Case-study discussion

Debates regarding theories of intelligence tend toward abstractions and so it is good to ground deliberations about the limitations of currently exiting intelligence paradigms in practical examples. This is especially the case because the currently dominant intelligence paradigm, one built around the suppositions of 'national security', lays claim to roots in 'realism' –international relations realism – and so any challenging paradigm lies open to the charge of being idealistic, or at least not realistic.[48] Although it is true to say that the case material being discussed here is partial and particular and that difficult issues regarding generalizeability are not properly addressed, that they are in some sense real should not be in doubt. The vignette concerning the case of search and disrupt in Northern Town is used here as a stand-in for the national security paradigm. Like the paradigm it exemplifies, this example is based on assumptions about utility of clandestine means to unilaterally achieve a knockout blow that will achieve a specified end; in the case of drug enforcement and interdiction that end being the eventual demise of the illicit drug economy. The approach valorizes above all else secret surveillance and hard coercive capacities in order to identify suitable targets and neutralize them by enforcement means. Its measures of success are abstract ones that are actually measures of agency process and not measures of impact in the real world. In the instance discussed here, cost-benefit calculations were made with regard to the financing of a medium-term undercover operation balanced against the number of arrests and successful prosecutions and associated outcome measures such as sentence length. The unwarranted assumption is that these enforcement and disruption measurement outcomes will translate into improved conditions in the community where the operations take place, but the strategic intelligence picture should continually remind practitioners that this assumption is incorrect. Indeed, the historical record shows that opposite is the case and the replication of tactical law enforcement 'successes' has, over time, actually accompanied an escalation of the problem, indeed these tactical successes actually seem to exacerbate it. The logic can go on repeating itself indefinitely because the outcome measures used to judge success are abstractions. That a case of drug law enforcement is an exemplar of the national security intelligence paradigm cannot be in doubt, since Richard Nixon explicitly made it so in his remarks to media executives at the Flagship Hotel in Rochester New York in 1971.[49] Although it is scientifically improper to generalize from a single case, the case certainly suggests that the dominant paradigm is not only falsifiable in theory, but also in practice, which surely raises doubts about the realism inherent in national security thought-styles.

The vignette concerning problem solving in Coastal County represents a significantly different way of thinking. The predicted outcome of the operation was not based on any measures of agency process – indeed it would have been very difficult to organize the intervention on such a basis given the variety of agencies involved, each with quite different functions. Instead the outcomes were intended to be highly tangible ones felt directly by the community and were aimed at improving public safety and fostering the local capacities of governance that underpin the general public good. This operation was orchestrated in the clear recognition that the ultimate causes of the immediate problem – differentials in 'sin taxes' across the territory of the European Union – were beyond local influence. Then too, the top-heavy structure of the national crime intelligence system and its varieties of organizational pathology rendered it an unsuitable resource. The case discussed reveals how intelligence analysts working at the divisional level of the local constabulary could serve to mobilize the capacities of a variety of actors in the broad governance of community security. Through acting as an analytic resource these actors helped to animate what the eminent policing scholar Clifford Shearing has called dispersed 'nodal' security.[50] Consciousness of human rights legislation provided a normative underpinning to the operation – a constabulary ethic – but the theory of intelligence mobilized was grounded in the local conditions of possibility; as seen in this example, human security practice is realistic.

Conclusion

A central task in this chapter has been to argue that the literature from the sociology of policing provides a useful alternative basis on which to consider theories of intelligence. The dominant intelligence paradigm has its institutional basis in the military and, for want of an alternative organizational touchstone, intelligence theory has languished there. There is a key difference between democratic policing practice and the practices of any military. Democratic policing capacities are exercised on behalf of people who, on the whole, both understand and endorse the police mission; even when it might entail the use of force in those limited circumstances where general social order and the public good are undermined by the actions of the few. The military are trained for the 'killing job' and the role is not so constrained by considerations of legitimacy among subject populations; and if it becomes so, the military function has begun to shade over into policing.[51] This chapter has glossed over the point that the policing apparatus in many jurisdictions is rapidly becoming militarized in order to make the point that sustained empirical and theoretical efforts to understand and theorize the intelligence function, and thereby change its practices, can be found in the sociology of policing literature. A fortiori, because of the emphasis on minimal use of force, human rights and democratic legitimacy, the sociology of policing opens up an alternative and realistic vantage point from which to view the possibility of a set of intelligence practices suited to the apparently idealistic notion of human security. Of course, the policing sector has its version of the national security mind-set, what Jean-Paul Brodeur (1983), theorized as 'high policing'.[52] It is also true to say that this thought-style has amplified itself during the recent past.[53] Irregardless of these trends, democratic policing has, since its historical inception during the nineteenth century, effectively depended upon community legitimacy in order to carry out its mandate. The two lessons from the field related here illustrate the point that it is not hopelessly idealistic to advance a human security intelligence paradigm to replace the old one and that the policing sector offers realistic prospects for testing the practicability of human security intelligence in a sustained programme of action research.

For too long the national security intelligence paradigm has been allowed to prevail because of its pretensions to realism. Despite, or perhaps because of, the danger that both the policing sector and notions of human security could end up providing cover for the continued imposition of national security intelligence doctrine, it is necessary to find a way out from under this is a failed way of thinking which, by any realistic assessment, has gone on making matters worse for long enough.

Notes

1 Kevin Haggerty and Richard Ericson, *The New Politics of Surveillance and Visibility* (Toronto: University of Toronto Press, 2006).
2 Keith Krause and Michael Williams, 'Broadening the Agenda of Security Studies: Politics and Methods', *Mershon International Security Studies Review*, Vol. 40 1996, pp. 229–254; Keith Krause, 'The Research Program of Critical Security Studies' in *Cooperation and Conflict*, Vol. 33 No. 3 1998, pp. 298–333, available at: cac.sagepub.com/cgi/content/abstract/33/3/298; M. C. Williams, 'The Practices of Security: Critical Contributions', *Cooperation and Conflict*, Vol. 34 No. 3 1999, pp. 341–344; Ken Booth, 'Security and Self: Reflection of a Fallen Realist', in *Critical Security Studies. Concepts and Cases*, ed. Keith Krause and Michael C. Williams (Minneapolis, MN: University of Minnesota, 1997), pp. 83–120; Simon Dalby, 'Contesting an Essential Concept: Reading the Dilemmas in Contemporary Security Discourse', in *Critical Security Studies. Concepts and Cases*, ed. Keith Krause and Michael C. Williams (Minneapolis, MN: University of Minnesota, 1997), pp. 3–32.
3 A. Goldsmith and J. W. E. Sheptycki, *Crafting Transnational Policing: State-building and Police Reform across Borders* (Oxford: Hart, 2007).
4 Research concerning the 'militarization of policing' is substantial and impossible to do justice to in a single footnote. Peter Kraska's *Militarizing the American Criminal Justice System: The Changing Roles of the Armed Forces and Police* (Boston, MA: Northeastern University Press, 2001), is a *tour de force*, but is largely confined to the American scene and scholarly literature. P. A. J. Waddington's *The Strong Arm of the Law: Armed and Public Order Policing*, (Oxford: Clarendon, 1991) offers an excellent, although somewhat dated, starting point from which to take in the corresponding British literature. Most pertinently to the interests of this chapter, Kevin Haggerty's and Richard Ericson's article 'The Militarization of Policing in the Information Age', *The Journal of Political and Military Sociology*, Vol. 27 1999, pp. 233–255, provides empirical insights into the cross-fertilization of theory and practice from the military to the policing sectors as facilitated by innovations in the adaptation for use of a vast array of information and surveillance technologies.
5 See, for example, H. Bruisma and J. G. A. van der Vijver (ed.), *Public Safety in Europe* (Twente: Twente Police Institute, 1999); and H. Bruinsma, H. Effers and Jan de Keijser, ed. *Punishment, Places and Perpetrators: Developments in Criminology and Criminal Justice Research* (Cullompton: Willan Press, 2004).
6 Robert Reiner's *The Politics of the Police*, 3rd edn (Oxford: Oxford University Press, 2000) remains the standard reference work for the literature on Anglo-American policing. Mark Mazower's book *The Policing of Politics in the Twentieth Century* (Providence, RI: Berghahn, 1997) gives a good international overview of important

aspects of police history that are relevant to contemporary discussions about policing and intelligence. Tony's Bunyan's *The Political Police in Britain* (London: Julian Friedmann, 1976) is a classic work on the subject and his contemporary work with StateWatch (www.statewatch.org/) is extremely relevant. Gary's Marx's *Undercover: Police Surveillance in America*, (Berkeley, CA: University of California Press, 1988) traces a morass of ambiguities in American undercover police work before eventually concluding that it is a 'necessary evil'. Some years later, Cyrille Fijnaut's and Gary Marx's edited collection *Undercover: Police Surveillance in Comparative Perspective* (The Hague: Kluwer Law International, 1995) did much the same thing, but with added cross-jurisdictional variations. Marx's recent work continues to stress the 'double-edged' nature of policing intelligence and surveillance practices (web.mit.edu/ gtmarx/www/garyhome.html). Pete Gill's *Rounding up the Usual Suspects; Developments in Contemporary Law Enforcement Intelligence* (Aldershot: Ashgate, 2000) offers a remarkable descriptive empirical analysis of developments in several North American jurisdictions and in Britain, and Australian scholar and former police officer Jerry Ratcliffe's edited collection *Strategic Thinking in Criminal Intelligence* (Anandale, NSW: The Federation Press, 2004) provides further international scope.

7 J. W. E. Sheptycki, *Issues in Transnational Policing* (London: Routledge, 2000), p. 9.
8 See Manuel Castell's three-volume monumental work on the network society: *The Rise of the Network Society, The Information Age: Economy, Society and Culture*, Vol. I (Cambridge, MA; Oxford, UK: Blackwell 1996; 2nd edn 2000); *The Power of Identity, The Information Age: Economy, Society and Culture*, Vol. II (Cambridge, MA; Oxford, UK: Blackwell 1997; 2nd edn 2004) and *The End of the Millennium, The Information Age: Economy, Society and Culture*, Vol. III (Cambridge, MA; Oxford, UK: Blackwell 1998; 2nd edn 2000).
9 Mike Maguire 'Policing by Risks and Targets: Some Dimensions and Implications of Intelligence-led Crime Control', *Policing and Society*, Vol. 9 No. 4 2000, pp. 315–336.
10 Kevin Haggerty and Richard Ericson, 'The Surveillant Assemblage', *The British Journal of Sociology*, Vol. 51 No. 4 2000, pp. 605–622.
11 Again, the substantial literature on this topic cannot be summarized in a footnote. Ethan Nadelmann's 1993 book, *Cops across Borders: The Internationalization of US LAW ENFORCEMENT* (University Park, PA: Pennsylvania State University Press) offers a useful starting point which has, more recently, been updated and supplemented by reference to European developments in a book written with Peter Andreas entitled *Policing the Globe* (Oxford: Oxford University Press, 2006). M. Anderson, M. den Boer, P. Cullen, W. C. Gilmore, C. Raab and N. Walker, *Policing the European Union: Theory, Law and Practice* (Oxford: Oxford University Press, 1995) is the authoritative work on the subject. Matt Deflem's *Policing World Society* (Oxford: Oxford University Press, 2002) offers a Weberian sociology of transnational policing in the industrial world, while D. M. Anderson's and David Killingray's rich two-volume edited collection *Policing the Empire, 1830–1940* (Manchester: Manchester University Press, 1991) and *Policing and Decolonisation, 1917–1965* (Manchester: Manchester University Press, 1992) offers many historical insights into the policing of the British empire.
12 This vein of scholarship can be traced back three decades. See: Steven Spitzer and Andrew Scull, 'Privatization and Capitalist Development: The Case of Private Police', *Social Problems* Vol. 25 1977, pp. 18–29; Clifford Shearing and Philip Stenning, 'Private Security: Its Implications for Social Control', *Social Problems*, Vol. 30 No. 5 1983, pp. 493–506; Clifford Shearing and Philip Stenning, 'From the Panopticon to Disney World: The Development of Discipline', in A. N. Doob and E. L. Greenspan (ed.), *Perspectives in Criminal Law*, Toronto: University of Toronto Press; Nigel South, *Policing for Profit: The Private Security Sector*, London: Sage, 1988. Recent articulations have gone beyond mere 'privatization' of the policing function

and have reconceptualized governance and security entirely. See David Bayley and Clifford Shearing, *The New Structures of Policing*, Washington, DC: National Institute of Justice, 2001; Clifford Shearing, 'Thoughts on Sovereignty', *Policing and Society*, Vol. 14 No. 1 2004, pp. 5–12; Clifford Shearing, 'Reflections on the Refusal to Acknowledge Private Governments', in J. Wood and B. Dupont (ed.), *Democracy and the Governance of Security* (Cambridge: Cambridge University Press, 2006).

13 Important recent contributions to the literature which bear out this point include P. H. J. Davies, 'Intelligence Culture and Intelligence Failure in Britain and the United States', *Cambridge Review of International Affairs*, Vol. 17 No. 3 2004, pp. 495–520; L. K. Johnson, 'Bricks and Mortar for a Theory of Intelligence', *Comparative Strategy*, Vol. 22 No. 1 January 2003, pp. 1–28; D. Kahn, 'An Historical Theory of Intelligence', *Intelligence and National Security*, Vol. 16 No. 3 2001, pp. 79–92; Sir Steven Lander, 'International Intelligence Co-operation: An Inside Perspective', *Cambridge Review of International Affairs*, Vol. 17 No. 3 2004, pp. 481–493; and K. O'Connell, 'Thinking about Intelligence Comparatively', *Brown Journal of World Affairs*, Vol. 11 No. 1 Summer/Fall 2004.

14 G. F. Treverton, S. G Jones, S. Boraz and P. Lipscy, *Toward a Theory of Intelligence: Workshop Report*, Santa Monica, CA: RAND Corp, 2006.

15 Ibid., p. 18.

16 Ibid., p. 2.

17 Ibid., p. 3.

18 Ibid., p. 12. The cyclical recurrence of scandal is a systemic feature of national security intelligence doctrine but Johnson interprets these events as evidence that the guardians of intelligence apparatus – 'two standing intelligence oversight committees on Capitol Hill' (p. 13) – are doing their jobs. As further evidence that these committees are suitable guardians, he notes that 'the staffs of the intelligence committees have regularly queried intelligence professionals about their activities and pored over annual budget requests line-by-line' (p. 14). Vigilance in the details does not seem to provide an antidote to recurring scandal because, as the record shows, periodically new scandals arise and the guardians are again caught off-guard. To be fair, elsewhere Johnson has taken a more critical view of intelligence oversight (Johnson 2003, *op. cit.* at 13 ff.), but again there is another interesting and worthwhile intersection with the scholarly literature on policing. Similar cycles of scandal and reform have also been observed in the police sectors of a number of liberal democracies and have been studied in close empirical detail; see, for example, Peter Manning's and J. Redlinger's important and insightful essay, 'Invitational Edges to Police Corruption', in P. Rock (ed.), *Politics and Drugs* (Rutgers, NJ: Dutton, 1977) and Larry Sherman's now dated *Police Corruption: A Sociological Perspective* (Garden City, NY: Anchor Books, 1977). These studies tend to show that secrecy is the structural sine qua non of police wrong-doing and thus, in his ground-breaking book, *Conduct Unbecoming* (London: Tavistock, 1985), Maurice Punch came to the conclusion that 'the most we can expect is a cycle of deviance, scandal, reform and repression, gradual relaxation and relapse into former patterns of deviance, followed by new scandal' and, in the end, 'when the sound and fury die away, it is all too often a case of returning sooner, or later, to business as usual' (p. 200). And so it remains, as long as official and unofficial secrecy prevails. So too it is with the intelligence sector writ large, and for the same reason. The scholarly literature on policing strongly indicates that any complete theory of intelligence would need to take account of these recurring and negative features of secret intelligence practice because of the unforeseen consequences of de-legitimation and de-securitization they bring with them. Such questions are difficult, if not impossible, to ask from within the dominant paradigm of national security intelligence where secrecy is understood to be the most valuable asset.

19 R. D. Laing, *The Politics of Experience* (Harmondsworth: Penguin, 1967), p. 135.

20 David Held, *Democracy and the Global Order; From Modern State to Cosmopolitan Governance* (Cambridge: Polity Press, 1995), pp. 77 and 78).

21 See also Michael Mann's iconoclastic 2003 book *Incoherent Empire* (London: Verso) and Leslie Sklair's influential book *The Sociology of the Global System*, 2nd edn (Baltimore, MD: Johns Hopkins University Press, 1995).

22 F. Halliday, *Rethinking International Relations* (Vancouver: University of British Columbia Press, 1994). Elsewhere I have sought to refine this term with specific reference to debates in the sociology of policing and globalization; see Andrew Goldsmith and James Sheptycki, *Crafting Global Policing* (Oxford: Hart, 2007). Briefly put, the world system is a complex polycentric power system. Differentially empowered state actors are part of this system which is, by no means, restricted to state actors. A variety of state-actors are participants in the contemporary world system including failed, broken or weak states, states which are 'middle powers', and seigneurial states. The latter may deploy all varieties of hard and soft power along political, economic, ideological and military vectors in an attempt to assert lordly independence and freedom of action upon the world stage, thereby contributing to continuing cycles of insecurity.

23 Held 1995, op. cit., p. 120.

24 Interestingly, the human security paradigm has been championed by middle power states. See R. Christie, 'Human Security and Identity: A Securitization Perspective', in *Theory and Practice: Critical Reflections on Global Policy*, ed. K. Grayson and C. Masters (Toronto: York Centre for International and Security Studies; G. MacLean, 'Instituting and Projecting Human Security; A Canadian Perspective', *Australian Journal of International Affairs*, Vol. 54 No. 3 2000, pp. 269–276; and G. MacLean, '(Re)Defining International Security Policy; Canada and the New Police of Human Security', in *Canadian International Security Policy: Reflections for a New Era*, ed. D. Mutimer (Toronto: York Centre for International Security Studies, pp. 11–24).

25 ICISS 2001, *The Responsibility to Protect*, International Commission on Intervention and State Sovereignty (ICISS), International Development Research Centre, Ottawa. Available online: www.iciss-ciise.gc.ca; Report of the Secretary General (2005) *In Larger Freedom: Towards Development, Security and Human Rights for All*, UN General Assembly 59th session agenda items 45 and 55; A/59/2005 available online: daccessdds.un.org/doc/UNDOC/GEN/N05/270/78/PDF/N0527078.pdf?OpenElement.

26 Goldsmith and Sheptycki 2007, op. cit.; see also Jean-Paul Brodeur, *Violence and Racial Prejudice in the Context of Peacekeeping* (Ottawa: Minister of Public Works and Government Services Canada, 1997); N. Pino and W. D. Wiatrowski, *Democratic Policing in Transitional and Developing Countries* (Aldershot: Ashgate, 2006).

27 Peter Neyroud and A. Beckley, *Policing Ethics and Human Rights* (Cullompton: Willan Press, 2001), p. 21.

28 Cf. G. E. Berkely, *The Democratic Policeman* (New York: Beacon Press, 1969); Alistair Henry and David J. Smith, *Transformations of Policing* (Aldershot: Ashgate, 2007).

29 The full text of Dumait-Harper's speech and an overview of the summit itself can be found online at: www.msf.org/msfinternational/invoke.cfm?component=article &objectid=388662F3-FB8F-4F12-B6D4ECB69A1A3D64&method=full_html.

30 J. W. E. Sheptycki, *In Search of Transnational Policing* (Aldershot: Avebury, 2003); J. W. E. Sheptycki, 'Review of the Influence of Strategic Intelligence on Organized Crime Policy and Practice' (London: *Home Office Special Interest Paper* No. 14, 2004, 48 pages).

31 In addition to previously cited work, see also Nina Cope, 'Intelligence-led Policing or Policing-led Intelligence?' *British Journal of Criminology*, Vol. 44 No. 2 2004, pp. 188–203 and Martin Innes and J. W. E. Sheptycki, 'From Detection to Disruption: Intelligence and the Changing Logics of Police Crime Control in the United Kingdom' *International Criminal Justice Review*, Vol. 14 2004, pp. 1–24.

32 Reiner 2000, op. cit. By now the reader will appreciate the breadth of the scholarly literature on policing. Two books which prominently contrast these styles are Jean-Paul Brodeur's *How to Recognize Good Policing* (London: Sage, 1998) and Herman Goldstein's book, which was widely influential in progressive police management circles in the United States, *Problem Oriented Policing* (Philadelphia, PA: Temple University Press, 1990).

33 Martin Plant, *Drug Takers in an English Town* (London: Tavistock, 1975); Jock Young, *The Drug Takers* (London: McGibbon and Kee, 1971).

34 'Britain's Bad Score', *The Economist*, 10 January 2002.

35 Prices adjusted for real purity levels show a different trend to nominal unadjusted purity prices. Nominal street prices have remained largely stable, while purity has risen over time which means there has been a fall in real purity-adjusted prices.

36 Self-report surveys concerning drug use deploy both 'lifetime use' and 'use over the previous month' as alternative measures of use-prevalence. Lifetime use measures in the UK show more consistent trends than do measures of use over the previous month, but what is important is that use-prevalence trends have been generally upwards since the 1970s. See Malcolm Ramsey, P. Baker, C. Goulden, C. Sharp and A. Sondhi *Drug Misuse Declared in 2000: Results from the British Crime Survey* (London: Home Office Research, Development and Statistics Directorate, 2001).

37 N. Chivite-Mathews, A. Richardson, J. O'Shea, J. Becker, N. Owen, S. Roe and J. Condon, *Drug Misuse Declared: Findings from the 2003/04 British Crime Survey* (London: Home Office Research, Development and Statistics Directorate, 2005).

38 Kate O'Brien's *Dealing Tac: Young People, Gender and Neighbourhood Drug Markets* (Cullompton: Willan Press, 2006) is a marvellous anthropological 'thick description' regarding drug culture in the north-east of England; Howard Parker's report (written together with C. Bury and R. Egginton), entitled *New Heroin Outbreaks among Young People in England and Wales* (London: Home Office Police Research Group, 1998), is a carefully researched study of UK heroin markets specifically, while Geoff Pearson's and Dick Hobbs' study *Middle Market Drug Distribution* (London: Home Office Research, Development and Statistics Directorate, 2001) offers empirical evidence as to the locally grounded nature of transnational illicit markets in a variety of drugs.

39 Dick Hobbs, Paul Hadfield, Stuart Lister and Simon Winlow, *Bouncers: Violence and Governance in the Night-time Economy* (Oxford: Oxford University Press, 2003).

40 Disruption was a key performance indicator for the NCS at this time. This indicator existed alongside traditional outcome measures, such as arrests leading to prosecution and crimes cleared up. Measures such as 'disruption' had been heavily criticized by the House of Commons Public Accounts Committee for being based 'to a significant degree on the subjectivity of the investigating staff involved in the individual cases. Even Her Majesty's Inspectorate of Constabulary (HMIC) had observed that "the current method of assessing performance did not adequately reflect what was being achieved and there was concern regarding the quality of disruption"' (cited in Sheptycki, 'Review of the Influence of Strategic Intelligence on Organized Crime Policy and Practice', pp. 31–32).

41 J. W. E. Sheptycki, 'Police Co-operation in the English Channel Region 1968–1996', *European Journal of Crime, Criminal Law and Criminal Justice*, Vol. 6 No. 3, 1998, pp. 216–236; J. W. E. Sheptycki, 'Patrolling the New European (In)security Field: Organizational Dilemmas and Operational Solutions for Policing the Internal Borders of Europe', *European Journal of Crime, Criminal Law and Criminal Justice*, Vol. 10 No. 2 2001, pp. 144–158.

42 See D. Hencke, 'Customs Blunder Led to the Loss of £620 Million', *Guardian*, 9 February 2001. Available online: www.guardian.co.uk/uk_news/story/0,,435578,00.html; D. Hencke '£1 Million Duty Frees a Week Stolen from Warehouse', *Guardian*, 19 November 2001. Available online:www.guardian.co.uk/

guardianpolitics/story/0,,597202,00.html; and D. Hencke and J. Oliver, 'Customs Losing 15bn a Year', *Guardian*, 12 December 2002. Available online: www.guardian.co.uk/uk_news/story/0,,858245,00.html.

43 N. Hopkins, 'Freddy Laker got a knighthood for providing cheap flights. I don't suppose I'll get one for providing cheap fags', *Guardian*, 17 December 1999. Available online: www.guardian.co.uk/g2/story/0,,250064,00.html.

44 Rob Hornsby and Dick Hobbs, 'A Zone of Ambiguity: The Political Economy of Cigarette Bootlegging', *British Journal of Criminology*, 2006 digital object identifier: 10.1093/bjc/azl089.

45 Henry and Smith 2007, op. cit., p. 119; see also *House of Lords Select Committee on The European Communities*, 23rd Report Session 1998–1999, London: The Stationery Office HL Paper 120; see also www.publications.parliament.uk/pa/ld199899/ldselect/ldeucom/120/12004.htm.

46 J. W. E. Sheptycki, 'Organizational Pathologies in Police Intelligence Systems; Some Contributions to the Lexicon of Intelligence-led Policing', *The European Journal of Criminology*, Vol. 1 No. 3 2004, pp. 307–332; see also J. W. E. Sheptycki, 'Police Ethnography in the House of Serious and Organised Crime', *Transformations of Policing*, ed. A. Henry and D.J. Smith (Aldershot: Ashgate, 2007).

47 See www.maherarar.ca.

48 Krause, 'Critical Theory and Security Studies: The Research Programme of Critical Security Studies', 2 ff.

49 At the briefing Nixon stated that 'drug traffic is public enemy number one domestically in the United States today and we must wage a total offensive, worldwide, nationwide, government-wide, and, if I might say so, media-wide' (www.presidency.ucsb.edu/ws/index.php?pid=3049).

50 C. Shearing, 'A Nodal Conception of Governance: Thoughts on a Policing Commission', in *Policing and Society: Special Issue on Policing in Northern Ireland*, Vol. 11 No. 3/4 2001, pp. 259–272.

51 Brodeur, op. cit. 26 ff..

52 J.-P. Brodeur, 'High-Policing and Low Policing: Remarks about the Policing of Political Activities', *Social Problems*, Vol. 30 No. 5 1983, pp. 507–520.

53 M. Webb, *Illusions of Security: Global Surveillance and Democratic in the Post-9/11 World* (Toronto: City Lights, 2007).

11 Theory and intelligence reconsidered

Philip H.J. Davies

For every complex problem there is a simple solution which is wrong.

H.L. Mencken

Cognitive contagion[1]

Canadians are fond of saying that when America catches a cold they get the flu. Much the same might be said of the world at large. On the other hand, there are times when the epidemiology of US-originated crises appears to be more along the lines of Thurber-esque hypochondria than a genuine politically airborne pandemic. And so, at a moment when officials, legislators and commentators alike in America are calling for fundamental change in thinking, methods and management of intelligence, even calling it a 'revolution in intelligence affairs',[2] the Rest of the World needs to consider its position carefully. If there is any contagion at work here at all, we must be sure that the vector diagnosed is the genuine culprit and that we are not dealing with something more reminiscent of the adolescent hysterics recounted in Arthur Miller's *The Crucible* than anything found in a quarantine ward.

At the centre of this latest furore is the role of *theory*. But even here we must move with caution because in this field the notion of theory entails at least two entirely different ideas. As Peter Gill has pointed out, we need to distinguish between theories *about* intelligence and theories *for* intelligence practitioners[3] – although the latter of these is probably better known as the theory *of* intelligence. As I shall endeavour to show, both theories of and about intelligence experience serious risks and pitfalls, albeit of profoundly different kinds and with equally different consequences.

In expressing serious doubts about the net value of theories of and about intelligence, I am acutely aware of the paradox of my circumstances. My work on the British Secret Intelligence Service (SIS, aka MI6) was extensively concerned with theories of bureaucracy and management structure,[4] and my comparative work on national intelligence communities in Britain and the United States has also rested on many of the same theoretical foundation, and been, moreover, directed towards articulating aspects of a 'theory of intelligence culture'.[5] And so it might easily appear that the thesis I shall develop is of the form 'do as I say and not as I do'. I hope to convince the reader, that this is not the case. My goal is not to argue that there should be no attempts to theorize at all but, rather, that theory – like any activity with a real and pervasive risk of counterproductive and even self-defeating blow-back – be turned to only as the means of earnest last resort. And when used, it should be employed for its conceptual and logical rigour, and not as an intellectually pretentious synonym for either metaphor or analogy.

It is commonly assumed that theory is an integral feature of scientific reasoning, but one should never forget Thomas Huxley's aphorism that science is 'organised common sense'. The physical sciences' reputed emphasis on numerical and quantitative techniques derives from the fact that physical phenomena are usually best examined, correlations identified and evaluated, in such measurable, numerical terms. Theory in the physical sciences is not a basic element but an emergent property, almost a side-effect, of more fundamental processes and methods. One of the least appreciated things about science is that there are entire fields of inquiry that are effectively entirely without theory – at least in the physics sense of complex systems of axiomatic, rigorous inference. Most biochemistry, cell biology and even genetics are virtually atheoretical. Chemical pathways, receptors and interactions are really just sequences or maps of observed reactions and interactions. Not all of the sequences are completely understood – but these are questions of scrupulous and scrupulously verified observation, not a priori speculative reasoning. Indeed, cell biology also entails only a minimum of mathematical expression.[6]

Therefore there is no a priori need for the social sciences (in which I include history) to have theory in order to be 'scientific', any more than there is an absolute necessity that they be quantitative either. Much of what we examine in the social sciences can and should have a fairly rigorous logical underpinning, but that is perhaps best envisioned in terms of Aristotelian and Boolean inference rules. Unfortunately, however much the social scientist or historian may try to retain consistency and avoid the pitfalls of informal fallacy, the dependency on ordinary language always carries an inherent risk of ambiguity. That uncertainty within ordinary language can distort inferences, subtly imbue arguments with unrecognized potential contradictions, and provide readers and commentators with the opportunity for opportunistic interpretations and misinterpretations to suit argumentative ends. Unfortunately, there are two particularly persistent problems in the social sciences. The first is the *inherent* opportunity for front-loading biased judgements in formulating propositions and collecting evidence then assessing it. The second is unwillingness in the profession, chiefly in the name of 'academic freedom', to strictly police the kinds of informal fallacies that are so often employed to argue disingenuously.[7]

Theory is, of course, a hugely ambiguous idea in its own right. It is sometimes used to refer to an over-arching logical scheme and sometimes a general model of how things work usually in their simplest form. An example of the latter is basic price theory in economics, which is empirically easy to validate. If there is a coffee blight and much of the crop dies, the price *will* go up. Likewise, if collectively farmers produce too much milk, the price *will* drop, potentially to the point where it is no longer economical to produce milk. Economic theory is often criticized for dealing only with the simplest assumptions and problems, while pushing most of what other social sciences are interested in into the residual category of 'externalities'. However, anyone who has ever had to work with problems of statics and dynamics in physics will be familiar with just such a situation. All too often a simple problem in dynamics becomes desperately complex when one tries to include additional 'real world' factors such as static and dynamic friction on the surfaces in question, atmospheric drag, vibration, environmental factors and so forth. The term 'theory' is also employed (less accurately) to refer to hypotheses amenable to some form of empirical demonstration, and often to more speculative assertions about the 'deep structures' or 'essential' natures of things. In the social sciences, an important distinction is drawn between 'grand theories' and what Robert Merton called 'theories of the middle range'. While the former are attempts at comprehensive narratives concerning the putative nature of society and history, the latter are less ambitious models, templates and typologies usually intended to describe fairly concrete empirical patterns and observations.[8] Another such conception is that of 'implicit theories' that people hold about the world in day to day life rather than the conduct of scientific inquiry. In practical terms, however, what the idea of implicit theory refers to are loosely associated assumptions, premises and conventional wisdoms that do not typically involve the kind of effort at comprehensive logical consistency that the use of the term theory normally implies. Indeed, the very term 'implicit theory' is misleading, and prone to disingenuous usage.

Another important distinction is between 'theory' and what I would term *conceptual* analysis. The need to parse meanings carefully in order to avoid self-contradictions arises from the sort of ordinary language ambiguity that I discussed earlier. Careful parsing of language is essential for any exercise of reason, and so while I propose to argue that theory itself is for the most part of limited value to the social sciences and in both the practice and study of intelligence, conceptual thoroughness is *vital*. It is also essential to draw a distinction between 'theory' and the notion of 'doctrine', something that entails two very different ideas itself. The first of these is what I would call doctrine in the military sense, of a set of standardized conventions and procedures. The other sense of doctrine refers to the partisan ideological sense of a set of normative beliefs about the world that are essentially a priori, based on articles of faith and premises that are treated as inherently and unassailably true regardless of either any weight of evidence to the contrary or lack of compelling evidence in favour. For the purposes of the present discussion I shall refer to the former as *doctrine* and the latter, for lack of a better term, as *dogma*.

Theories of intelligence

Some years ago, Michael Warner suggested that 'If you cannot define a term of art, then you need to do some rethinking.'[9] On the face of it, this is an entirely reasonable assertion, and Warner was quite understandably concerned about the lack of any real consensus about how intelligence was defined, and in what fashion that might affect the conduct of intelligence as an activity. Indeed, in the United States, there has evolved a very extensive body of literature trying to define what intelligence is and what it is not, how it works and how it should not, what it should do and what it should not do. The theory of intelligence arguably begins to take shape with Sherman Kent's seminal 1949 *Strategic Intelligence for US World Policy*,[10] and his subsequent debate with Willmoore Kendall.[11] This has since evolved into various controversies about what the correct definition of intelligence ought to be – whether it ought to be broad, emphasizing all-source analysis, or narrowly concerned (as Warner suggests) with covert collection – the relative merits of the idea of the 'intelligence cycle', the value and risks of 'competitive' and 'alternative' analysis' (not necessarily the same thing), intelligence-producer/policy-maker proximity and so forth. The goal of such work, on the whole, is not really an analytical or descriptive theory of intelligence so much as a doctrine concerning what intelligence is and how it ought to be done.

Examined on its own, the American 'theory of intelligence' appears an entirely reasonable idea and something worth emulating – until one looks at the matter comparatively and asks what the net benefits and costs of intelligence theory actually appear to be. If one puts the US intelligence community alongside that of the UK, one immediately finds two significant differences. The first is that, on the whole, the UK has fewer coordination problems at both the executive and working levels than the United States. The second is that there has, historically, been virtually no attempt to articulate any theory of intelligence and even, at times, a positive aversion to such an effort. Entire volumes have been written about rivalry and friction between CIA and the FBI over counter-intelligence and counter-terrorism,[12] as well as the divided nature of the US intelligence community at large.[13] To be sure, the Secret Intelligence Service (SIS, aka MI6) and the Security Service, MI5, have at times been at loggerheads over exploitation of common sources (such as Enigma), shared operations (under Double Cross) and concerning vetting and security in the early Cold War. But since the 1960s (at least), as I showed in my study of SIS, their relationship has been dominated by joint working-level units and collaborative executive-level participation in the machinery of the Joint Intelligence Organisation.[14] And studies of the JIC machinery itself have revealed a similar picture of interlocking interdependence throughout the overall UK intelligence community.[15]

While Britain's original joint intelligence coordinating body, the Interservice Intelligence Committee, may have been stillborn, its successor, the JIC, has operated continuously since 1936.[16] There have been tweaks and reforms to its associated machinery, usually as short- to medium-term attempts to resolve specific inconveniences.[17] By comparison, the history of US national intelligence coordination is a litany of failed ventures. At the height of wartime pressure, the civilian Coordinator for Information (COI) was refused authority over armed service intelligence,[18] while the service-dominated American Joint Intelligence

Committee was a forum for interservice dispute rather than jointness. Indeed, the only real consensus on the US JIC between the armed service representatives concerned the exclusion of the civilian members representing the State Department and Office of Strategic Services (OSS) from the committee's most important sources and deliberations.[19] After the war, the Director of Central Intelligence was never provided with authority equal to the position's responsibilities,[20] hobbled still further by double duty as head of CIA as well, effectively trying to act as referee while also managing one of the competing players (a practice known as 'double-hatting').[21] At the same time, a whole succession of collegial arrangements – the Intelligence Advisory Board, the Intelligence Advisory Committee, the United States Intelligence Board and the National Foreign Intelligence Board were established and then abolished amid dispute and acrimony.[22] To make matters worse, those disputes and acrimony arose persistent divisions such as ongoing tension between the DCI's national intelligence remit and the Department of Defense's control of some 85 per cent of the intelligence budget, and persistent opposition of armed service intelligence branches to CIA involvement in areas like imagery intelligence, or Defence Intelligence Agency rivalry with the national intelligence produced by CIA and the interagency analytical teams working under the Board of National Estimate and its successor the National Intelligence Council[23] (as well as the gaps between domestic and foreign intelligence already mentioned).[24] The 2004 Intelligence Reform and Terrorism Prevention Act (IRTPA) may have resolved double-hatting, but yet another, still weaker incarnation of the executive-level committee has had to be reconstituted as the National Intelligence Board and the functions of the working-level interagency committees taken over by the Director of National Intelligence's assorted Deputies in the burgeoning machinery of the Office of the DNI.[25] With the limitations on the authority of the DNI, and the persistence of the basic interagency disputes that have characterized the US intelligence community since its inception, it seems unlikely that the new scheme will prove much more successful in the long term than its assorted predecessors.

In contrast with America's running debates over intelligence theory, British officials have rarely paused to worry about how to define or delimit the work on which they were engaged. The first time that there is any actual discussion of what intelligence is or ought to be appeared towards the end of the Second World War. During discussions of possible post-war intelligence arrangements, one official described intelligence as a process 'beginning with the collection of simple facts and ending with the appreciations of complex situations'.[26] During the same exchange, JIC Secretary Denis Capel-Dunn defined intelligence 'in the military sense' as something that 'covers all kinds of information required for the conduct of war'. He added that 'total war' meant that intelligence needed to be conceptualized more broadly to include economic, psychological and political conflict as well.[27] The matter then lapsed until Cabinet Secretary Sir Burke Trend's campaign for JIC reform during the 1960s. At this time, British officials first began to draw a clear distinction between 'information' drawn from open sources and 'intelligence' drawn chiefly from secret sources, or from sources difficult to acquire. The former was envisioned as being primarily the work of the overt civil service, and the latter the task of the intelligence and security agencies and was, therefore, the chief concern of the JIC.[28] Subsequently, conceptual discussion fell once again into abeyance in official circles. At most one might expect to hear officials intone the mantra 'intelligence is about secrets and not mysteries', but typically there has been, and remains, very little patience with conceptual ruminations.

To be sure, during the 1980s and early 1990s Michael Herman and Ken Robertson – the former a retired intelligence officer and the latter an academic – tried to initiate conceptual and analytical discussions of intelligence in an effort consciously inspired by American precedent.[29] However, in the UK the study of intelligence was, and remains, dominated by narrative historical research relatively uninterested in either broad theoretical schemes or fine conceptual distinctions. During the furores surrounding Iraq, the Butler inquiry and Intelligence and Security Committee both offered similar definitions of intelligence as the use of 'more information than is openly available' to inform decision-makers.[30] But their goal was descriptive explanation of how a process was already operating and prescriptive, normative reasoning.

One is forced to conclude, therefore, that contrary to Warner's seemingly reasonable argument, with reference to comparing Britain and America *the development of intelligence theory and the achievement of intelligence order and coordination are actually inversely correlated.*

If there is an inverse correlation between theory-building and institutional order, is the relationship somehow one of cause and effect, and in which direction? One can discern a range of different motivations that are at work in American theoretical discussions, reflecting different aspects of American political and management cultures. In the first place, for example, it seems likely that some of the impetus towards building theories and doctrines of intelligence reflects the fundamental role of legally formal constitutions in US political culture, and the precedent of building them on a specific political philosophy.[31] And this does stand in sharp comparison with a historical British aversion to a single written constitutional document, and to any body of law that might be above the authority of Parliament and therefore potentially prohibitively difficult to alter in the face of changing circumstances and needs.

There are also certain spheres of intelligence theory debate that appear to be attempts to make a virtue out of necessity. The running debates over alternative and competitive analysis, formal dissent and 'footnoting' on interagency estimates is just such a case. A great deal has been made over the decades of the virtues of trying to prevent pathologies such as 'group think' and 'layering' through the challenge of alternative analysis to probe different possibilities. Similarly, the idea of competing analysis between departments – typically between the Department of Defense and putatively 'national' bodies such as CIA and the National Intelligence Council – has been defended on the basis of placing the many interpretations before policy-makers so that they can have as many options before them as possible.[32] There are, to be sure, counter-arguments dealing with questions such as the risk of confusing the policy-maker who may suffer 'analysis paralysis' arising from not knowing whom to believe – or instead simply cherry-pick the appreciation that matches their preconceptions or policy preference.[33] But all of these discussions *post date* the competitive intelligence ethos that they defend or decry.

In fact, the practices of competitive analysis, formal dissent and footnoting *never arose for any of the reasons used to justify the practice today*. The origins of competitive analysis and formal dissent lie in the unwillingness of the various US government departments – especially State and Defense – to cede any of their autonomy or right independent access to and influence on the president to any nominally 'national' intelligence system.[34] That insistence can be traced back as far as the National Intelligence Authority created by original 1946 Truman Memorandum which also established the DCI and Central Intelligence Group.[35] The procedure was then reiterated in 1948 in National Security Council Intelligence Directive 1.[36] As a result, much of the subsequent theoretical doctrine really appears to be the *post hoc* rationalization of something US government departments would do anyway, with or without some sort of 'intelligence theory' rationale. By stark contrast, the JIC's assessment process evolved to pool information and provide a common knowledge base required by an emerging doctrine of joint service planning and operations.[37] A process geared to establishing what is collectively known among various departments rather than 'coordinating' what is already believed by each department – for reasons either sincere or self-serving – as an end in itself is much less likely to generate contention or competition. This is probably the main reason why the UK assessment process has never entailed formal dissent procedures. Admittedly, the recent post-Butler reforms created a new dissent process as part of what can only be seen as a spin-doctor's show of reform.[38] However, at the time of writing that new procedure had yet to be invoked, and JIC officials preferred to re-examine the evidence and drafting to find ways to incorporate doubts expressed by members through artful wordsmithing.[39] In contrast, the US has now gone so far as to place departmental dissent on a *statutory footing* within the 2004 IRTPA.[40]

A significant portion of the intellectual effort behind US intelligence theory also appears to be an attempt to substitute some sort of intellectual, doctrinal order for real-world institutional order. The irony of this is that pursuing intellectual coherence seems more likely to create divisions than resolve them. Rather than generating any actual consensus, the real consequence of seeking a common doctrine has been an assortment of keenly felt, earnestly argued running debates which has achieved very little except to set advocates and ideologues against one another. The believers in competitive analysis are not likely to be convinced by their opponents, and the advocates of broad and narrow conceptions of intelligence are unlikely to change one another's opinions. US government departments are unlikely to sacrifice their short-term self-interest for collective order, and so there will always be a market for competitive analysis advocates. Consultants, open-source researchers, lobbyists and other 'beltway bandits' are unlikely to hang up their shingles, and so there will always be a demand for the advocacy of a broad, maximally inclusive definition of intelligence. After all, a Warner- or UK-style narrow definition that emphasizes covert collection makes the intelligence community a very small one with a more limited budget that is almost completely spoken for in terms of operational priorities and capabilities. In other words, a narrow definition implies less loose money to be spent on consultants and contractors. It is, therefore, profoundly unlikely that any new way of thinking about intelligence is ever likely to make any appreciable difference to the conduct of intelligence in America.

Theories about intelligence

The application of 'theory' to the study of intelligence, rather than its practice, represents an entirely different range of issues. On the one hand, there is the sheer diversity of types or levels of theory that could be applied to intelligence from the behavioural and social sciences. Figures like Richards Heuer,[41] Roberta Wohlstetter,[42] and Harold Wilensky[43] all pioneered the use of tools from sources like psychology, management theory and organizational behaviour to try and develop a deeper understanding of processes at work in intelligence. Likewise, in the UK, Ken Robertson[44] and Peter Gill have sought to apply ideas from political sociology.[45] Most recently and innovatively, ethnography and anthropology have been applied to intelligence analysis at CIA.[46] One of the most useful sources of theory for the study of intelligence has been economics, broadly understood. The organizational politics cum 'neoinstitutional' approach employed in my own work on the UK intelligence community[47] and by Amy Zegart to the US system[48] derives originally from Richard Cyert and James G. March's 1963 *Behavioral Theory of the Firm*,[49] while Richard Posner and Luis Garicano have experimented still further with micro-economic theories to address current issues of intelligence reform.[50] In a similar vein, Michael Herman has briefly considered the application of William Niskanen's bilateral monopoly model of public expenditure to technical intelligence costings, as well as contingency theories of management.[51] Thus there can be no question that some theoretical, or rather, *conceptual* armatures can provide a depth of understanding and recognition of wider patterns and trends that simple narrative history cannot offer. On the other hand, all behavioural and social science theories really should be issued with health warnings in large, ominous letters printed on the packaging. This because, for the most part, they appear more likely to drift from theory to dogma than not.

One can see trajectories of this sort on both sides of the political spectrum. On the left, the evolution of Marxism into post-modernism is a cautionary tale. By the turn of the twentieth century, a central conceptual tenet of Karl Marx's economics, the surplus labour theory of value, had been wholly discredited and supplanted by Alfred Marshall's price theory. At the same time, the predicted immiseration of the working classes failed to materialize as the capitalist class structure began to bulge in the middle with the rise of the professions, mechanization and emerging service industries. The evolution of institutions such as joint stock firms increasingly decoupled ownership from control. On the one hand, this created increasingly distributed rather than concentrated ownership and on the other devolved control to new managerial and technical professions.[52] As the political economy of the twentieth century became more complicated, the attempts to describe it became comparably difficult, and as power became more distributed vertically and horizontally what political economy lost was the ability to isolate culpability for social ills in any one group. A key appeal of Marxism was always the ability to point the finger of blame at a visible class or status group. Marxism therefore, had to shift its intellectual base.

With poverty becoming less and less a central issue,[53] many Marxist scholars shifted away from concrete socio-economic evidence (which did not really support the appealing, Mencken-esque simplicity of historical materialism and class theory any longer) to questions of ideology, false consciousness, and hunting for obscure fragments of Marx's earlier writings that allowed the left to move away from the inconvenient economic evidence of the day. This gave rise to schemes such as Antonio Gramsci's theory of 'hegemony',[54] Louis Althusser's obscurities and wholly notional claim to 'rigour' in his structural Marxism and monolithic concepts of repressive and ideological state apparatuses in which the idea of state power subsumed everything;[55] and the mercurial Hegelian Marxism developed by the Frankfurt School.[56] Most of these approaches became bogged down in versions of Mannheim's paradox[57] which argued, in a loose paraphrase, that if all discourse was conditioned by the prevailing ideology and false consciousness then the theory of ideology itself must be a manifestation of the same ideology and false consciousness. In other words, either the new form of Marxist theory did not exist, or it was wrong. Another problem was that the new approaches depended on an informal presuppositional fallacy: the case for ideology only made sense if one assumed the accuracy of a Marxist account of political economy that was no longer empirically defensible.

The result was a retreat further and further away from evidence-based studies of actual social structure and economic welfare to approaches increasingly dependent on the anecdotal subjectivity of 'interpretation'. Out of this emerged the various schools of post-modernism (chiefly from Germanic Hegelian Marxism) and post-structuralism (from French structuralism or structural Marxism). New interpretative approaches fell foul of the problem of trying to identify the relative merits of one interpretation over another. Interpretations could only ever be *possible* interpretations, and even acknowledging that was an interpretation in itself. The resulting infinite regress was termed the *hermeneutic circle* with reference to a quite antiquated practice of interpreting religious scriptures in order to try and discern their supposedly real meaning.[58] This new problem was, in many respects, Mannheim's paradox resurrected.

There were other more concrete and mechanical problems with this school of thought. For example, disproportionately influential scholars such as Michel Foucault cherry-picked evidence, detaching critical items from their historical context. By way of illustration, Bentham's notorious Panopticon – the basis of Foucault's widely adopted notion of 'panopticism' – was never actually built and the idea was rejected roundly by both parliamentarians and penologists of the day.[59] This misuse of historical evidence to construct a misleading account of penology and social surveillance was possible in a large part because the very idea of interpretation permits a kind of free-wheeling self-indulgence that empirically more rigorous methods do not so easily accommodate. The Panopticon did not actually ever have to have been built, it merely needed to serve as a metaphor. Consequently, theory became no more than metaphor and reasoning merely 'discourse' and, quite bizarrely, the template for a great deal of supposedly social science reasoning became that last bastion of sententious and subjective speculation, literary criticism.[60] What matters in the last analysis for these traditions of thought is not and has never been an empirically accurate description of the world but, rather, a politically correct posture of opposition to what is imagined to be the political order of the day.

On the right one can point to a similar trend in the evolution of 'neo-liberal' thought out of the findings of neo-classical economics. During the 1970s, dissatisfaction with the misapplication of Keynesian economics and the associated ills of sustained inflation and stalled economic growth – 'stagflation' – triggered an opposition to the emerging doctrines of national economic and social management.[61] William Niskanen's diagnosis of the inefficiencies of public sector expenditure,[62] Harold Laffer's concern about diminishing returns above certain threshold rates of taxation, and free-market advocacy led by the likes of Milton Friedman prompted a political doctrine of market-discipline, privatization and private sector management practice that fundamentally informed the economic and public management policies of a number of western administrations. These included Margaret Thatcher's Conservatives in the UK, Ronald Reagan's Republicans in the United States and Brian Mulroney's Progressive Conservatives in Canada, among others. Here again, however, despite the intellectual, often logically and mathematically formal rigour of economics, the political theory fell prey to the Mencken effect as it became dogma instead. For example, the enthusiasm for transferring key public services into the private sector in order to secure 'market discipline' in their financial management flew in the face even of neo-classical economic wisdom. Actually, wholesale privatization ran counter to the findings of neo-economic theories of market failure in the provision of public and collective goods.[63] To make matters worse, privatization also willfully created an assortment of monopoly supply situations. As any first-year student of economics learns in some detail, monopolies and oligopolies are not very good things for either cost efficiency or equilibrium pricing. But market theory as rigorous analysis had become market theory as dogma.

The problem is, therefore, how to tell theory that is analysis based on, and contingent on, evidence apart from theory that is dogma defended with the selective use of evidence. But standing in judgement too often passes for critical reasoning, and condemnation is always an easier task than comprehension – but advocacy is not equivalent to analysis. Theory therefore resembled a sort of intellectual medication, essential to solve certain kinds of problems in the right dosage, but both toxic and additive in the wrong circumstances or the wrong dosage. Put another way, while one might benefit from making use of selected *tools* of theory, one is always best off avoiding *schools* of theory.

There are already signs that the application of theory to the study of intelligence is beginning to import or replicate some of the more destructive tendencies of theory in the wider social sciences. Andrew Rathmell's 2002 thought experiment in post-modernism as applied to intelligence studies[64] displays many of the worst features of post-structural and Hegelian Marxist critique and, at the end of the day, proves more misleading than enlightening. Another problematic foray at the other end of the scale is David Kahn's exploration of grand historical narrative theory in his 2001 attempt to articulate a 'historical theory of intelligence'.[65] In mainstream political science and sociology, the goal of grand historical theories had more or less been abandoned as impracticable by the end of the 1940s (Merton's notion of 'middle range' theory cited above was part of this development), and by 1960s it was common practice to deride or dismiss theories by accusing them of constituting 'grand theory'. There were very good reasons for the retreat from grand theory, although many making the criticism were more than likely to be using the criticism to sneak their own preferred alternative tacit grand theory (usually one stripe of Marxism-derived radicalism or another) into the argument sidelong.[66] Finally, it has been suggested that the study of intelligence might benefit from importing the concepts and 'insights' of international relations theory, and from a more elaborated discussion of 'intelligence ethics'.[67] These latter options are not much more promising than post-modernism or grand theory.

Rathmell is an accomplished historian whose work on intelligence in the Middle East has been some of the finest work done in the area.[68] And yet, his exercise in post-modernism entails all of the vague free-association, reliance on informal fallacies (especially of the straw man variety) and evidence-free handwaving that make the post-modern posture so pernicious. Consequently, he tries to combine the post-modernism in the sense of critical theory (as discussed above) with post-Fordian models of industrial management with the idea of globalization into a single amalgamated 'post-modernism' – which they are not. In fairness, the term 'post-modern' is often confusingly used in management literature to refer to post-Fordian network-based models of manufacturing and management in contrast with the kind of hierarchical, mass-production formula typified by the Ford motor company and its use of developments like the assembly line.[69] And Rathmell does acknowledge the idea of post-Fordism as such.[70] The trouble is that he treats it as part and parcel with the post-modernism of social theory examined above. The result is a conflationary fallacy, treating two profoundly different sets of ideas and values as if they were one and the same. This is especially problematice because, as a dollar-counting, bottom-line-watching method for maximizing profit in a fast moving marketplace, post-Fordism has more in common with old-fashioned 'modernist' epistemologies, behavioural theories and free-market-oriented political economy than it could ever have with post-modernist or post-structural social theory.

Besides a 'conflationary fallacy', Rathmell's characterization of the existing intelligence systems as being machines of mass-production intelligence appears a particularly implausible straw man fallacy as well as factually wrong. At the level of analytical production, most intelligence assessments are produced on a relatively limited scale by comparatively small teams of specialists. The US National Intelligence Council and UK Assessments Staff produce national estimates on the basis of interdepartmental drafting teams working collaboratively – i.e. on a peer-group network basis – with intelligence elements of their respective intelligence communities. Historically, the NIC and Assessments Staff were roughly the same size, between thirty and forty people.[71] Both produced a very varied range of appreciations on the basis of equally varied customer requirements. In the UK especially, collegial, networked interagency operation has been the norm since the 1930s – indeed, peer-group collaboration is the defining characteristic of the Joint Intelligence Committee and the attendant Joint Intelligence Organization.[72] As I have shown at some length, SIS has had a highly networked management structure at least since the inter-war years.[73]

To be sure, some of the technical collection systems such as signals and imagery produce huge quantities of raw intelligence in a manner reminiscent not merely of mass production but of what management theorists call 'continuous flow' production. But hybrid management structures exist for larger organizations in complex or fluid environments, such as matrix management which combines network and hierarchical arrangements. Matrix management, interestingly, was pioneered by TRW who have manufactured many of America's intelligence satellites. In order to cope with both large-scale and flexible requirements, a matrix scheme draws specialist staff from across a conventional bureaucracy and brings them together in task-specific project teams. On completion of the project, the team can be either re-tasked, or the members returned to their home divisions and reassigned to new project teams.[74] Indeed, with its emphasis on small, cross-functional teams in both operations and analysis, a much stronger case for arguing that intelligence – especially in the UK – has often been at the forefront of post-Fordian management.

By the same token, Rathmell's advocacy of the greater use of open sources is another straw man of the first water – as it has been when advocated by other open source advocates consistently and repeatedly over the last decade and a half.[75] For starters, people have been quoting Allan Dulles to the effect that some 80-plus per cent of all information used in intelligence assessments comes from open and diplomatic sources for decades. Much the same estimate of the overt/covert balance was also expressed by Reginald Hibbert during his debate with Michael Herman at the turn of the 1990s.[76] Indeed, the core of the UK's MO5 Special Duties section at the turn of the last century was a library of open sources, including foreign-language publications and relevant industrial and trade journals.[77] The idea that the intelligence community has not historically been aware of, or centrally concerned with, exploiting open-source materials is simply a myth promoted by consultants, partisan critics and other 'beltway bandits' over the decades. A similar straw man is at work in his critique of supposedly positivist concepts of absolute truth.[78] On the one hand, virtually none of those accused of 'positivism' over the last three-quarters of a century has actually been an advocate of the kind of absolute concept of truth imputed to them.[79] And, of course, as we have already seen the roots of the critique of positivist empiricism lay in disingenuous claims by various schools of Marxism that empiricists were instruments of 'domination' simply because they failed to take as their point of departure a Marxist – or right sort of Marxist – critique of ideology and consciousness.[80] As noted above, empiricist doctrines such as positivism are politically wrong whether or not they are factually wrong.

The problems with Kahn's foray into grand theory are subtler. The eventual abandonment of grand theories in sociology and political theory arose chiefly because of a basic dilemma in large-scale historical theories. That is, the scale, sweep and diversity of social evolution on the macro scale is so complex that either one is forced to cherry-pick fragments of the evidence resulting in a skewed and selective account *or* one has to confine one's propositions about that evolution to a level of broad generality that reduces most of them to the status of things which are trivially true. Karl Marx, for example, was never adequately able to incorporate the 'Asiatic mode of production' and ability of tribal societies to sack and conquer more developed civilizations like Rome or Byzantium into his theory of social evolution.[81] The other alternative can be seen in Parsons' 'cybernetic hierarchy'[82] or its later reformulation by Jeffrey Alexander,[83] and really amounts to saying that human actions are conditioned by material factors on the one hand and ideational factors on the other on a sort of sliding scale between the two depending on the kind of activity in question.[84] This is hardly an earth-shaking discovery, however elaborate the theoretical language in which the finding is framed.

To a very real degree, Kahn's historical theory runs into both difficulties. On the one hand one ends up at a truth which is little more than trivial, and on the other makes generalizations that become vulnerable to challenge by negative example. The first difficulty arises because, confronted with the intractable question of how to define intelligence at the outset, Kahn decides to define intelligence excessively broadly 'as information' because, he asserts, '[n]one of the definitions that I have seen work'.[85] In so doing, Kahn falls prey to what I like to call 'Agrell's Limit' after Swedish SIGINT practitioner Wilhelm Agrell. Agrell pointedly observed in 2002 that 'when everything is intelligence nothing is intelligence.'[86] Thus, if one substitutes Kahn's definition of intelligence for the *word* intelligence in the title, Kahn's essay becomes a 'historical theory of information', rather than a historical theory of anything more specific, arcane or fraught. With that in mind, it seems virtually inevitable that he should end up with a principle painfully familiar to any first-year economics student – that information is essential to optimizing resources.[87] His subsequent findings, that information is auxiliary in war and that information is essential only to defence have their own problems. In the case of information being auxiliary in war, one would assume this to be virtually automatic, since by definition, the primary distinguishing feature of war is *force*.[88] But the assertion that information is more essential to defense than attack strikes me as being vulnerable to empirical challenge. The role of intelligence in the 2000 rescue of British soldiers held by members of the West Side Boys gang in Sierra Leone[89] occurs to me as the sort of negative example that Kahn's final hypothesis invites. Indeed, Kahn caveats this latter assertion by saying that intelligence 'rarely' serves the aggressor 'directly'. The question with all such historical generalizations must always be: how many exceptions can they sustain before they are no longer useful as generalizations?

There have also been suggestions that the study of intelligence should import concepts and insights from international relations theory.[90] In many respects, IR theory amounts to little more than an assortment of normative dogmas about how international politics *ought* to be conducted rather than explanations of how it *is* conducted. The so-called idealist- or liberal-internationalists have always had their roots chiefly in normative political philosophies drawing on Hugo Grotius,[91] Immanuel Kant[92] and Jeremy Bentham,[93] arguing little more than the desirability of some sort of international civil society and rule of law. The realist approach evolved in antiquity from Thucydides' cautionary account of Athens' sustained war with Sparta,[94] and in the twentieth century from Hans Morgenthau's[95] and E.H. Carr's[96] cautionary accounts of why the League of Nations failed, leading to the Second World War. Indeed, in that first post-war generation of realist thought, the ultimate practical goal – a stable and viable system of international order and institutions – was not so very different from the goals of the liberal-internationalists.

However, by the 1970s and 1980s, such internationalist realism had become supplanted with a 'neorealism' that represented little more than a succession of politically partisan foreign-policy scholars advocating various forms of unilateralist, hawkish national exceptionalism.[97] Some attempts at descriptive rather than prescriptive theorizing concerned with the various national and cultural frames of reference with regards to international relations began to develop in an approach known as constructivism. But with constructivism's emphasis on culture and ideology, the approach rapidly fell prey to the partisan dogmatic temptations of post-modernism and post-structuralism and devolved into various exercises in sanctimonious 'critical analysis' based on one oppositional special interest or another.[98] By the second half of the 1990s, IR theory appeared to be retreating in disarray. In the UK, at least, it was seriously suggested that the entire enterprise of IR theory as a distinct discipline should be abandoned. Instead, it was suggested that the topic should be re-integrated into the broader tradition of political theory and political philosophy.[99] With such developments in mind, IR theory seems one of the last places intelligence studies and intelligence practice should look for ideas that will not prove either valueless or actually dangerously self-defeating.

One final sphere of 'theory' which has been receiving increased attention in recent years has been the question of ethics. Advocated as a crucial concern by Len Scott and Peter Jackson,[100] ethics has in recent years grown to become a major intellectual industry in intelligence studies. One of the earliest forays into this field was made by Michael Herman in 2001[101] and then again after 9/11,[102] with other British figures such as Sir Michael Quinlan[103] and Angela Gendron[104] experimenting with formulations based in varying degrees on the notion of 'just war' developed by Sir Thomas Aquinas and Hugo Grotius. A similar programme of debate has been taking shape in the United States, sharpened by legal debates over the use of torture in the interrogation of terrorists.[105] On this trajectory I would be inclined to make two points. The first is the somewhat pedantic one that this field is more properly a subdomain of moral and political philosophy rather than theory in the empirical-analytical sense, and not really covered by the kinds of theoretical concerns dealt with here. But this appears an approach vulnerable to partisan antinomies between ethical pragmatism and absolute dogmas of human rights, civil liberties and so forth rather than any useful solutions to the intellectual problems it entails.

Conclusion: theory in intelligence

How seriously should we therefore take Sherman Kent's notion of intelligence as a social science, or Willmoore Kendall's idea of intelligence practitioners trained, and work, in terms of state-of-the-art social science theory? Speaking as one educated in the social sciences and their theoretical tradition, it is hard to imagine anything more blood-chillingly alarming. The idea that the individuals advising the chief executives of nuclear armed states might become bogged down or divided in their assessments over the relative merits of Marxism, functionalism, Lacanian psychoanalysis or whose viewpoint was false or emancipatory consciousness, simply does not bear thinking about. Worse still is the prospect that they might simply throw up their hands in despair at the impossibility of gauging capabilities or (more likely) *intentions* because the whole exercise was no more than a social construct and any interpretation confined to indeterminacy or arbitrary preference by the hermeneutic circle. No doubt conceptual clarity is to be encouraged at all times, and likewise there is no question that there exist theories of the middle and short ranges of significant potential use to observer and practitioner alike. But theory in a more ambitious sense is all too easily a slippery slope into metaphorical speculation, woolly reasoning and disingenuously-packaged dogma. Indeed, I would argue that an axiom of any properly valid and validated social sciences effort should be that all of the most important questions about society are empirical ones, as are the most important answers. This is as true of the study of intelligence as of any less esoteric sphere of inquiry.

If there is any 'revolution in intelligence affairs' that needs to happen in America, it needs to be a less arcane affair. Any such revolution must take as its first task bringing an overweening and too rarely challenged and checked Department of Defense to heel. Intelligence at the national level has always been far too beholden to military interests. But more fundamentally and more importantly, there needs to be a revolution in governmental corporate ethos that puts collective national effort and well-being ahead of the narrow and short-term departmental pursuit of barrels of political and financial pork. The traditional obsession with jurisdictions and boundaries needs to be supplanted with a pre-eminent concern among that nation's practitioners with how the whole system fits together. The British experience, which has been no less dependent on inter-departmental integration, but is far less characterized or hobbled by interdepartmental confrontation, shows that such a depth of division and difficulty need not be the case. Benjamin Disraeli once observed that '[n]ext to knowing when to seize an opportunity, the most important thing in life is to know when to forego an advantage'; America's bickering and divided government departments and intelligence agencies would do well to take that maxim on board. Until that lesson is learned, no amount of effort bent to finding new ways to think about intelligence, no revolution in intelligence theory or anything else will make any difference at all. And in the meantime, the other allies in the Four Eyes community need to avoid confusing America's unique problems with their own.

Notes

1 Acknowledgements are due to the many people who commented on earlier versions of this paper presented at the University of Aberystwyth in the summer of 2006 and the British International Studies Association conference in Cork that December. They include Len Scott, Martin Alexander, Peter Jackson and Paul Maddrell; at BISA, Robert Dover and Mark Phythian. For comments on the original draft of this chapter I am indebted to Peter Gill. Research for this chapter was made possible in part by a Leverhulme Research Fellowship.
2 Deborah G. Barger, *Toward a Revolution in Intelligence Affairs* (Santa Monica, CA: RAND, 2005).
3 Gregory F. Treverton, Seth G. Jones, Steven Boraz and Philip Lipscy, *Toward a Theory of Intelligence: Workshop Report* (Santa Monica, CA: RAND, 2006), p. 64.
4 Philip H.J. Davies, *MI6 and the Machinery of Spying* (London: Frank Cass, 2004).
5 See variously Philip H.J. Davies, 'Ideas of Intelligence: Divergent National Concepts and Institutions', *Harvard International Review* 14: 3 (Fall 2002) and 'Intelligence Culture and Intelligence Failure in Britain and the United States' *Cambridge Review of International Affairs* 17: 3 (October 2004). This is also the frame of reference employed in my forthcoming book, *They Come Not Single Spies: Intelligence and Government in Britain and the United States*.
6 Apart from the elementary arithmetic of physical chemistry or measuring and correlating cell populations with particular laboratory protocols and associated statistical techniques.
7 It always strikes me as odd that radically stricter policing of logic or evidence in the hard sciences is never seen as a threat to academic freedom on those disciplines.
8 Robert K. Merton, 'Theories of the Middle Range', in *On Theoretical Sociology: Five Essays, Old and New* (New York: The Free Press, 1967), pp. 39–72.
9 Michael Warner, 'Wanted: a Definition of Intelligence', *Studies in Intelligence* Vol. 46 No. 3. Available online: www.odci.gov/csi/studies/vol46/article02.html (accessed 16 December 2004).
10 Sherman Kent, *Strategic Intelligence for American World Policy* (Princeton, NJ: Princeton University Press, 1949).
11 Jack Davis, 'The Kent–Kendall Debate of 1949', *Studies in Intelligence* 36:5.
12 See, for example, Mark Reibling, *Wedge: From Pearl Harbor to 9/11: How the Secret War between the FBI and CIA Has Endangered National Security* (New York: Touchstone, 2004); Michael A. Turner, 'CIA–FBI Non-Cooperation: Cultural Trait of Bureaucratic Intertia?', *International Journal of Intelligence and CounterIntelligence* 8:3 (Fall, 1995).

13 Some examples include Amy B. Zegart, *Flawed by Design: The Evolution of the CIA, JCS and NSC* (Stanford, CA: Stanford University Press, 1999); William E. Odom, *Fixing Intelligence for a More Secure America* (New Haven, CT: Yale University Press, 2003) or the regular occurrence of this theme in Christopher Andrew, *For the President's Eyes Only: Secret Intelligence and the American Presidency from Washington to Bush* (London: HarperCollins, 1995).

14 Davies, *MI6 and the Machinery of Spying*, pp. 265, 275–278.

15 For accounts of the development and operation of the JIC system see, in particular, Percy Cradock, *Know Your Enemy: How the Joint Intelligence Committee Saw the World* (London: John Murray, 2002) or F.H. Hinsley *et al.*, *British Intelligence in the Second World War: Its Impact on Strategy and Operations*, esp. vols 1 and 2 (London: HMSO, 1979, 1981).

16 F.H. Hinsley, E.E. Thomas, C.F.G. Ransom and R.C. Knight, *British Intelligence in the Second World War*, Vol. 1 (London: HMSO, 1979), pp. 34–36.

17 For discussions of the post-war reforms of the JIC, see, in particular, Cradock, *Know Your Enemy*, pp. 260–270.

18 Bradley F. Smith, *The Shadow Warriors* (New York: Basic Books, 1983), p. 67.

19 'State Representation on the Joint Intelligence Committee and/or Joint Intelligence Group', 24 July 1950, Box 3, Lot File 58D776, National Archives and Records Administration (NARA); Larry A. Valero, 'An Impressive Record: The American Joint Intelligence Committee and Estimates of the Soviet Union, 1945–1947', *Studies In Intelligence*, Unclassified Edition No. 9 (Summer 2000), p. 77.

20 Michael Warner, *Central Intelligence: Origins and Evolution* (Washington, DC: Central Intelligence Agency, 2001), p. 7.

21 William E. Odom, *Fixing Intelligence for a More Secure America* (New Haven, CT: Yale University Press, 2003), *passim*.

22 The rise and fall of the various executive – and working-level – collegial bodies in US intelligence is a significant untold story and a central feature in my forthcoming book monograph from Praeger.

23 See, variously, Loch K. Johnson, 'The DCI vs the Eight Hundred Pound Gorilla', *International Journal of Intelligence and CounterIntelligence* 13:1 (2000), Odom, *Fixing Intelligence*, all but *passim*, and discussions of the limitations of the Director of Central Intelligence in United States Congress, *Joint Inquiry into Intelligence Community Activities Before and After the Terrorist Attacks of September 11, 2001: Report of the Senate Select Committee on Intelligence and US Permanent House Select Committee on Intelligence Together with Additional Views* (Washington, DC: United States Government Printing Office, 2002) and National Commission on Terrorist Attacks Upon the United States, *The 9/11 Commission Report: Final Report of the National Commission on Terrorist Attacks on the United States* (New York: W.W. Norton & Company, 2004).

24 See note 11 above. See also Richard A. Posner, *Remaking Domestic Intelligence* (Washington, DC: Hoover Press, 2005).

25 Office of the Director of National Intelligence, *An Overview of the United States Intelligence Community 2007* (Washington, DC: Office of the Director of National Intelligence, 2007).

26 'Centralised Intelligence', n.a., n.d., foliated with papers *c.*1945–1946, CAB 163/6, TNA.

27 'The Intelligence Machine: Report to the Joint Intelligence Sub-Committee', 10 January 1945, in CAB 163/6, TNA. I am indebted to Christopher Murphy, now at the University of Salford, for bringing this report to my attention, and, indeed, photocopying it and sending it to me during my brief career exile abroad in Southeast Asia.

28 See, for example, comments of Permanent Secretary of the Treasury Sir William Armstrong, Misc. 155(68), 1st Meeting, 8 January 1968, CAB 163/124, TNA.

29 Michael Herman has made a succession of contributions in this regards, at greatest length in his seminar, *Intelligence Power in Peace and War* (Cambridge: Cambridge University Press, 1996), *passim*, but with particular attention to defining intelligence in his exchange with Reginald Hibbert in the pages of *Intelligence and National Security*, see 'Intelligence and Policy: A Comment', in 6:1 (responding to Hibbert's 'Intelligence and Policy' in 5:1). Robertson's key contributions on intelligence theory include 'Accountable Intelligence: The British Experience', *Conflict Quarterly* 8:1 (Winter 1988); 'The Politics of Secret Intelligence: British and American Attitudes' ed. Ken Robertson, *British and American Approaches to Intelligence* (London: Macmillan, 1987), and 'Intelligence, Terrorism and Civil Liberties', *Conflict Quarterly*, Vol. 7 No. 2 (Spring 1987).

30 Butler, *Review of Intelligence on Weapons of Mass Destruction*, p. 7; Intelligence and Security Committee *Annual Report 2003–2004* (London: The Stationery Office, 2004), p. 9.

31 As articulated in documents such as the *Federalist Papers*, James Madison, Alexander Hamilton and John Jay (London: Penguin, 1987), and the record of debates held at the 1787 Constitutional Convention.

32 The pre-eminent advocate of 'competitive' analysis is arguably Harold P. Ford in his *Estimative Intelligence: The Purposes and Problems of National Intelligence Estimating* (Langham, MD: University Press of America, 1993); an abbreviated defence of competitive doctrine can be found in Johnson, 'DCI vs the Eight Hundred Pound Gorilla', pp. 46–47.

33 Kenneth P. Stack, 'Competitive Intelligence', *Intelligence and National Security*, 13:4 (1998). More recently, former Senate Select Committee on Intelligence chairman Bob Graham has expressed doubts about the value of alternative or competing assessments with reference to the Department of Defence 'cherry-picking' cells prior to the 2003 invasion of Iraq, Bob Graham with Jeff Nussbaum, *Intelligence Matters: The CIA, the FBI, Saudi Arabia and the Failure of America's War on Terror* (New York: Random House, 2005), p. 158.

34 Frank Church *et al.*, *Final Report of the Select Committee to Study Governmental Operations with Respect to Intelligence Activities* Book 1 Senate Report No. 94–755 (Washington, DC: US Government Printing Office, 1976), p. 101.

35 NIA Directive No. 1, 'Policies and Procedures Governing the Central Intelligence Group', reproduced in Michael Warner, ed., *CIA Cold War Records: The CIA Under Harry Truman* (Washington, DC: Center for the Study of Intelligence, 1994), p. 34.

36 'National Security Council Intelligence Directive Number 1: Duties and Responsibilities', 12 December, 1947, reproduced in Warner, *The CIA Under Harry Truman*, pp. 169–171.

37 F.H. Hinsley *et al.*, *British Intelligence in the Second World War*, vol. 1, pp. 35–36.

38 For a discussion of the UK government's post-Butler reforms, see Philip H.J. Davies, 'Spin Versus Substance: Intelligence Reform in Britain After Iraq', *WeltTrends* (Germany), 51 (Summer 2006).

39 Private information.

40 2004 Intelligence Reorganization and Terrorism Prevention Act (IRTPA) Sec.1023.

41 E.g. Richards J. Heuer, *Psychology of Intelligence Analysis* (Washington, DC: Center for the Study of Intelligence, 1999), and the frequent use of the group-psychology notion of 'groupthink' originated by Irving Janis, *Victims of Groupthink.* (New York: Houghton Mifflin, 1972) in inquiries into intelligence failure such as the Senate Select Committee on Intelligence report, *Report on the US Intelligence Community's Prewar Intelligence Assessments on Iraq* (Washington, DC: United States Congress, 2004).

42 Roberta Wohlstetter, *Pearl Harbor: Warning and Decision* (Stanford, CA: Stanford University Press, 1962).

43 Harold Wilensky, *Organizational Intelligence: Knowledge and Policy in Government and Industry* (New York: Basic Books, 1967).

44 See note 28 above, also his work on public secrecy such as *Public Secrets: A Study in the Development of Public Secrecy* (London: Macmillan, 1984) and *Secrecy and Open Government: Why Governments Want You to Know* (London: Palgrave Macmillan, 1999).

45 Peter Gill, *Policing Politics: Security, Intelligence and the Liberal Democratic State* (London: Frank Cass, 1994); and with Mark Phythian, *Intelligence in an Insecure World* (Cambridge: Polity, 2006).

46 Rob Johnston, *Analytic Culture in the US Intelligence Community* (Washington, DC: Center for the Study of Intelligence, 2005).

47 'Organisational Politics and the Evolution of Britain's Intelligence Producer/Consumer Interface', *Intelligence and National Security* 10:4 (October 1995).

48 *Flawed by Design: The Evolution of the CIA, JCS and NSC* (Stanford, CA: Stanford University Press, 1999).

49 Richard Cyert and James G. March, *A Behavioral Theory of the Firm* (Englewood, NJ: Prentice Hall, 1963).

50 Luis Garicano and Richard A. Posner, *Intelligence Failures: An Organizational Economics Perspective* Centre, for Economic Policy Research Discussion Paper No. 5186 (London: Centre for Economic Policy Research, 2005).

51 Michael Herman, *Intelligence Power in Peace and War* (Cambridge: Cambridge University Press, 1996), pp. 295–296.

52 These developments were charted by scholars like Max Weber in e.g. 'Class, Status and Party', in Hans Gerth and C. Wright Mills, *From Max Weber: Essays in Sociology* (New York: Oxford University Press, 1979), pp. 180–186; Ralph Dahrendorf, *Class and Class Conflict in Industrial Society* (Stanford, CA: Stanford University Press, 1973) and Alvin W. Gouldner, *The Future of Intellectuals and the Rise of the New Class* (Toronto: Oxford University Press, 1979).

53 As compared with the very low lower bound standards of income in industrial revolution and nineteenth century Britain, for example.

54 Antonio Gramsci, *Selections from the Prison Notebooks* (London: Lawrence and Wishart, 1971).

55 The quintessential version of Althusser's approach is articulated in 'Ideology and Ideological State Apparatuses: Notes Toward an Investigation', *Lenin and Philosophy and Other Essays* (New York: Monthly Review, 2001), and also 'Contradiction and Overdetermination', in *For Marx* (Harmondsworth: Penguin, 1966).

56 See, for example, volumes like Marcuse's *One-Dimensional Man* (Boston, MA: Beacon, 1964) or Horkheimer and Adorno's *Dialectic of the Enlightenment* (London: Allen Lane, 1973). A valuable route of entry to the arcane and internecine world of critical theory is provided by Martin Jay, *The Dialectical Imagination: A History of the Frankfurt School and the Institute of Social Research 1923–1950* (Toronto: Little, Brown and Company, 1973).

57 A summary discussion of the paradox, albeit from the partisan position of trying to rescue something of the Marxist perspective, see Willard A. Mullins, 'Truth and Ideology: Reflections on Mannheim's Paradox', *History and Theory: Studies in the Philosophy of History* 18:2 (1979).

58 This formed much of the central discussion in the debate between Jurgen Habermas and Hans Gadamer. An overview of this exchange can be found in Alan How, *The Habermas–Gadamer Debate and the Nature of the Social* (Aldershot: Avebury, 1995).

59 Richard Hamilton, *The Social Misconstruction of Reality* (New Haven, CT: Yale University Press, 1996), chapter on Foucault. Hamilton notes that a small number of facilities were built along the lines of the Panopticon (chiefly in America) but the idea never acquired a wider acceptance.

60 See, for example, Jacques Derrida, 'Structure, Sign and Play in the Discourse of the Human Sciences', in *Writing and Difference* (London: Routledge, 1978) and Paul Ricoeur, e.g. *Interpretation Theory: Discourse and the Surplus of Meaning* (Fort Worth, TX: The Texas Christian University Press, 1976), or Michel Foucault, *The Archeology of Knowledge* (London: Tavistock, 1982).

61 The managerialist trend was most notably encapsulated by thinkers like Daniel Bell in his *The End of Ideology: On the Exhaustion of Political Ideas in the Fifties: With a New Afterword* (Cambridge, MA: Harvard University Press, 1988).

62 William Niskanen, *Bureaucracy: Master or Servant?* (n.l.: The Institute of Economic Affairs, 1973).

63 See, for example, Mancur Olsen, *The Logic of Collective Action: Public Goods and the Theory of Groups* (Cambridge, MA: Harvard University Press, 1988).

64 Andrew Rathmell, 'Towards Postmodern Intelligence', *Intelligence and National Security* 21:3 (2002), pp. 87–104.

65 David Kahn, 'An Historical Theory of Intelligence', *Intelligence and National Security* 16:3 (Autumn 2001), pp. 79–92 and in this volume, pp. 4–15.

66 A prime example would be Alvin W. Gouldner's polemic against Talcott Parsons' supposed 'grand theory' (which, in fact, it was not) in his *The Coming Crisis of Western Sociology* (New York: Basic Books, 1970).

67 Len Scott and Peter Jackson, 'The Study of Intelligence in Theory and Practice', *Intelligence and National Security* 19:2 (Summer 2004), pp. 146–149.

68 Andrew Rathmell, *Secret War in the Middle East: The Covert Struggle for Syria, 1949–1961* (New York and London: Tauris, 1995); Andrew Rathmell, 'Copeland and Za'im: Re-evaluating the Evidence', *Intelligence and National Security* 11, no. 1, pp. 89–105.

69 For post-Fordism, see variously Ash Amin, *Post-Fordism* (Oxford: Blackwell, 1994) or Stuart Clegg, *Modern Organisations* (London: Sage, 1990). There is, to be sure, a wealth of post-modernist writing in the post-structuralist sense on organizations, typified by Gareth Morgan's notion of 'imaginisation' which is little more than a radical constructivist account that verges on solipsism; *Images of Organisation* (London: Sage, 1986).

70 Rathmell, *Towards Postmodern Intelligence*, p. 96.

71 Counting, as it were, NIC Chair, Deputy Chairman, roughly a dozen NIOs and the same number again of Deputy NIOs and the NIC Staff, but not including drafters seconded for particular projects (albeit not in particularly large numbers). The Assessments Staff consisted traditionally of a Chief of Assessments Staff, Deputy Chief and three teams each under an Assistant Chief of Assessments Staff, with a new team added under the Butler reforms.

72 M. Herman, 'Assessment Machinery: British and American Models', *Intelligence and National Security*, 10:4 (October 1995).

73 Davies, *MI6 and the Machinery of Spying*, esp. chapters 1 and 7, but *passim*.

74 S. Davis and P.R. Lawrence, *Matrix* (Reading, MA: Addison-Wesley, 1977).

75 Such as Stephen Mercado, 'Sailing the Seas of OSINT in the Information Age', *Studies in Intelligence* 48:3 (2004), and the various contributions over the years by Open Source Solutions entrepreneur Robert Steele.

76 Hibbert, 'Intelligence and Policy', p. 113.

77 Davies *MI6 and the Machinery of Spying*, pp. 28–29.

78 Rathmell, 'Towards Postmodern Intelligence', p. 95.

79 The Gouldner–Parsons debate might serve as a good example here also. Gouldner, writing very much in the Marcuse-esque critical theory idiom coming into fashion at the time, attacks Parsons as a positivist, but defining positivism not as an unsophisticated empiricism but as a political conservatism based on faith in the 'certainties of science' and which 'counseled patience and warned of premature commitments to social reconstruction', *Coming Crisis of Western Sociology*, p. 101. Parsons had, of

course, written his first monograph, *The Structure of Social Action* (New York: The Free Press of Glencoe, 1969, 2 vols), as an extended critique of anti-theoretical positivism. Much the same point might be made of Zygmunt Bauman's description of Durkheim's epistemological stance.

80 This is essentially the argument made by Horkheimer and Adorno in *Dialectic of the Enlightenment* (New York: Continuum 1982) *passim*, but made particularly explicit in Horkheimer's 'The End of Reason', in Andrew Arato and Elke Gebhardt, ed., *The Essential Frankfurt School Reader* (Oxford: Basil Blackwell, 1978), p. 39.

81 This is particularly apparent in his *Pre-Capitalist Economic Formations* (International Publishers, 1965).

82 As articulated, for example, in *The Evolution of Societies* (Englewood Cliffs, NJ: Prentice-Hall, 1977, ed., Jackson Toby, pp. 8–10.

83 As developed in his multi-volume *Theoretical Logic in Sociology* but chiefly vol. 4, *The Modern Reconstruction of Classical Thought: Talcott Parsons* (Berkeley, CA: University of California Press, 1983).

84 Subsequent neo-Marxist formulations of the relationship between material conditions of production on the one hand and ideology on the other have tended to end up in much the same place. See, for example, much of Jurgen Habermas' opus, initially in his *Legitimation Crisis* (Boston, MA: Beacon, 1975) but in greater and more arcane length in his two-volume *The Theory of Communicative Action* (vol. 1, Boston, MA: Beacon, 1984; vol. 2, Cambridge: Polity, 1989).

85 Kahn, 'An Historical Theory of Intelligence', p. 79.

86 Wilhelm Agrell, *When Everything Is Intelligence Nothing Is Intelligence: The Sherman Kent Center for Intelligence Analysis Occasional Papers* 1:4 (October 2002).

87 Kahn, 'An Historical Theory of Intelligence', pp. 84–85.

88 I might well be accused of being a naïve Clausewitzian with such an assertion, but if one were to define the difference between war as a mode of conflict and other distinct modes of conflict (as opposed to war as an evocative metaphor, such as on poverty or crime) what would one not resort to other than force?

89 See, for example, Damien Lewis, *Operation Certain Death: The Inside Story of the SAS's Greatest Battle* (London: Arrow, 2005).

90 Len Scott and Peter Jackson, 'The Study of Intelligence in Theory and Practice', *Intelligence and National Security* 19:2 (Summer 2004), pp. 146–149.

91 Hugo Grotius, *The Rights of War and Peace: Including the Law of Nature and of Nations* (New York: Hyperion Press, 1979).

92 Immanuel Kant, *Kant's Perpetual Peace* (Bristol, VT: Peace Books Co. 1939).

93 Jeremy Bentham's *Principles of International Law* can be downloaded at: www.la.utexas.edu/research/poltheory/bentham/pil/index.html (accessed 14 November 2007).

94 Thueycydides, *History of the Peloponnesian War* (J.M. Dent, 1983).

95 Hans Morgenthau, *Politics Among Nations: The Struggle for Power and Peace* (New York: Knopf, 1985).

96 For example, E.H. Carr, *International Relations between the Two World Wars* (London: Macmillan, 1947).

97 One might look here to figures John Mearsheimer or Stephen Walt.

98 For an overview of these issues, see Jack Snyder, 'One World, Rival Theories', *Foreign Policy* (November/December 2004).

99 Brian C. Schmidt, 'Together Again: Reuniting Political Theory and International Relations Theory', *British Journal of Politics and International Relations* 4:1 (April 2002).

100 Scott and Jackson, 'The Study of Intelligence Theory and Practice', pp. 156–157.

101 Michael Herman, *Intelligence Services in the Information Age* (London: Frank Cass, 2001) pp. 201–227.

102 Michael Herman, 'Ethics and Intelligence after September 2001' *Intelligence and National Security* 19:2 (Summer 2004).
103 Michael Quinlan, '"Just Intelligence": Prolegomena to an Ethical Theory', *Intelligence and National Security* 22:1 (February 2007), pp. 1–13.
104 Angela Gendron, 'Just War, Just Intelligence: An Ethical Framework for Foreign Espionage', *International Journal of Intelligence and CounterIntelligence*, Vol. 18 No. 2 (2005).
105 See, for example, the collected essays by various leading figures in the field in Jan Goldman's *Ethics of Spying: A Reader for the Intelligence Professional* (Lanham, MD: Scarecrow Press, 2006), and the debates surrounding Alan Dershowitz's 'Is There a Torturous Road to Justice?', *Los Angeles Times*, 8 November 2001.

12 Theories of intelligence
Where are we, where should we go and how might we proceed?[1]

Peter Gill

Introduction

If it is commonly accepted that intelligence represented the 'missing dimension'[2] of historical accounts of international and domestic politics for many years, at least until the end of the Cold War, circumstances since then have changed significantly. During the 1990s a variety of inter-linked factors brought intelligence blinking out of the dark, if only into the twilight, for example, the perception that insecurities took a greater variety of forms such as organised crime and trafficking, the interest in intelligence methods of a wider variety of state and corporate agencies and the rapid growth of technologies facilitating the gathering, processing and storing of information. These factors were all massively reinforced by 9/11, and by further attacks in Bali, Madrid, Istanbul and London. The impression given by these 'failures' is that intelligence is unable to ensure public safety just as security problems seem to be escalating.

In some countries, perhaps especially the US and UK, this seems to have given rise to an unbridled security panic, in which intelligence agencies and processes are necessarily implicated, and which has called into question issues of human rights that were previously assumed to be settled.[3] Therefore, the importance of intelligence currently is not just that there is more to study but also because its performance is central to the possibility of maintaining security and safety by democratic means. This demands that social science examines it more systematically than in the past.

In part this is facilitated by the rapid growth of publicly available intelligence documentation in recent years, for example, in the US the continued use of freedom of information laws, in the UK the policy of releasing files to the public archives and, in some former authoritarian states in Europe, the release of files as part of lustration has been a sometimes painful aspect of democratisation. Various US, UK and Australian inquiries into the Iraq fiasco have published further materials and, most recently, the Canadian judicial commission into the rendition of Maher Arar has provided insights into information sharing in the current counter-terrorist climate.[4] But while the increase in the availability of materials for study is very important, it is not enough.[5] We must consider carefully how we use those materials.

In this chapter I attempt to summarise the main implications of the contributions to this collection for the future of theorising about intelligence by considering the general role of theory in social science, more specific issues involved in theorising about intelligence, including key definitional questions, the broader context of social and political theory and how all this can inform research at the different levels at which intelligence takes place. In doing so, I have in mind the need for theory that seeks to explain intelligence as it is practised everywhere, not just in Western states, and that is developed in the context of social scientific examination of intelligence from, as it were, the outside. There *are* similarities between what intelligence scholars and practitioners do but the theoretical ideas discussed here are directed more to the former. This is a necessary basis for any consideration of how intelligence might be improved and/or made more democratic.

What has theory ever done for us?

When the paper from which this chapter has developed was first delivered at BISA, another panellist commented that the central focus for students of intelligence should be, not theory, but history: 'figuring out exactly what happened'. Of course, theory and history were identified by Wesley Wark as two of the eight 'projects' that he identified in intelligence studies in 1993 (Phythian, p. 54 – text references in this chapter refer to chapters in this volume) and it would be idle to argue that any one was necessarily superior. For example, any claim that research is 'simply' empirical – telling the world 'as it is' – is bogus. Stephen Marrin's chapter reminds us that the 'inductive fallacy' of simply accumulating facts in the belief that the truth would emerge was exposed many years ago (pp. 140–141). Even the fact that some areas are selected for research and others are not will be based on ideas of 'significance' plus the availability of access and funds that depend on a broad 'politics' of research.[6]

In selecting areas for research (or, as Graham Allison put it, the ponds in which we fish[7]), we make assumptions that are based on some theory of the world. The choices we make have important implications for our work, for example, if one were to follow James Sheptycki (pp. 166–172) and adopt a 'human security' rather than the traditional 'national security' paradigm for intelligence studies then the implications are considerable. Then, organising our materials so that they 'make sense' to us in terms of pre-existing scholarship and help others to understand our work requires at the very least a clear conceptual framework. There is no other way to cope with complexity (cf. Betts, pp. 103–104); a problem faced not just by intelligence analysts and scholars. We choose conceptual frameworks on the basis of some existing literature and body of ideas. Inevitably these contain (more or less explicit) theoretical assumptions. Good research work will consider those, make them explicit and, as part of its work, address the issue of how far new findings change or reinforce prior thinking. In this way, we move our business forward. The theories we seek provide the means by which we can identify and isolate key factors from the mass of surrounding information (Phythian, p. 55).

We seek to develop our understanding of causal mechanisms so that we can explain events. For positivists, this is the core objective of theory on the road to the further goal of prediction (cf. Kahn, p. 11; Sims, p. 152). Many would doubt the possibility of developing a predictive social science – a point made by several contributors – and, of course, there are those who would dispute even the possibility of identifying causal mechanisms.[8] If the findings of our research are to have any impact on policy or practice, then they must be based on some form of theoretical thinking, some prior effort to *generalise* from experience.[9] Too often the gap between 'theory and practice' is exaggerated into a significant barrier to any useful conversation between theorists and practitioners. In the short run, the concern of the latter is with results and their reactions may be based on a hard-headed pragmatism that seems far removed from the leisured contemplation of theory in the seminar room. But the gap is much more about the occupational interests of different groups engaged in intelligence or its study rather than anything essential to our understanding of the intelligence process per se.

Further, the once significant division between empirical and normative work diminishes: as Zygmunt Bauman argued, the aim of the social sciences is to develop 'responsible speech' about their objects of inquiry and thus ethical issues associated with the conduct and potential impact of research must be contemplated from the outset.[10] Therefore, we must make these assumptions explicit. Intelligence is capable of bringing great benefits and causing great harms; the pretence that somehow our work can be conducted free of normative considerations is unsustainable.

Developing theory in intelligence studies

The term 'intelligence studies' is quite commonly used to describe the rapid development, especially in the last six years, of our field of interest. It has a rather pre-scientific ring to it in comparison with political *science* or soci*ology* but it does accurately describe what is going on, that is, researchers located in longer-established disciplines such as politics, history, IR, criminology focusing on intelligence as a field of study that was, prior to 9/11, largely ignored by mainstream social science (cf. Sims, p. 151). There are pluses and minuses associated with this burgeoning interest and we need to acknowledge that current work is taking a variety of perspectives and directions. This collection is a self-conscious effort to move theory forward since, compared with others among Wark's projects, especially history, memoirs and journalism, it has been relatively neglected.

Let us consider some theoretical efforts to date. David Kahn (pp. 8–10) suggested three principles to be offered by a theory of intelligence: that intelligence optimizes one's resources, that intelligence is an auxiliary, not a primary element in war and that while it is necessary for defence it is only contingent for offence. Kahn argues that these are testable propositions but the problem is their restriction to particular sorts of traditional battlefields; for example, there seems little doubt that intelligence is a primary element for both defence and offence in counter terrorism. Loch Johnson (herein) also provides a set of testable propositions, this time more wide-ranging across the field of intelligence and, although developed primarily within the US context, they are clearly capable of being used comparatively.

Not surprisingly, given our subject matter, everyone is agreed on the impossibility of prediction (e.g. Kahn, p. 87) for a range of reasons. As with all other social sciences this is in part because of the sheer complexity of what we seek to explain and, of course, the fact that our subject matter is people who are reflexive and may change their predicted behaviour for any reason, including the fact that we are studying and making predictions about them! This is not a problem faced by physical scientists, though even there, excellent explanations cannot be simply translated into predictions – earthquakes and weather being classic examples. Isaac Ben-Israel noted twenty years ago the underdevelopment of 'intelligence science' of which a symptom was inexact estimates. Since successes usually remain secret from outsiders, it is impossible to assess whether things have improved overall in this respect though the analytical failures regarding Iraq provide evidence to the contrary. Inevitably, estimating will remain an inexact science (or, art?) and the efforts of outsiders to develop theories of intelligence will remain similarly 'primitive'.[11]

One specific reason for this that comes through in several chapters is the number of paradoxes to which intelligence is subject. Johnson's first propositions (p. 36) suggest that the more affluent and globally oriented a nation, the more likely it is to enjoy intelligence successes because of its coverage; yet points to the paradox that it is also more likely to experience failures because its global objectives cannot be met in a world of such complexity. James Wirtz reminds us of Handel's paradox that subverts the usual risk calculation of likelihood multiplied by impact[12] and which lies at the heart of the theory of surprise: 'The greater the risk, the less likely it seems, and the less risky it becomes. In fact, the greater the risk, the smaller it becomes' (cited in Wirtz, p. 77). Then, there is the well-known warning paradox: if an agency detects an imminent attack and takes counter measures which lead to the abandonment of that attack so that 'nothing happens', this might be taken as evidence that the initial warning was wrong.[13]

Richard K. Betts (pp. 87–88) pointed out thirty years ago that there was no lack of descriptive theory regarding failure but a lack of normative theory as to how this knowledge could be turned into reforms. He identifies paradox as one of the main problems in developing normative theory for reform so that curing some organisational pathologies produces others, for example, the development of a more sensitive warning system will result in more cases of 'crying wolf' and therefore warnings are more likely to be ignored thus *increasing* the risk of failure. Glenn P. Hastedt and B. Douglas Skelley (pp. 126–127) provide a more detailed analysis of the organisational paradoxes besetting reform that can be summarised as: the structures required to improve the control, accountability and security of the intelligence process impede the free flow of information on which the process depends for success.

Many of these paradoxes afflict specifically those working *within* intelligence, especially on organisational matters. Now, it was noted above that there are similarities between what intelligence scholars and some practitioners do, but theories *of* intelligence and theories *for* intelligence have different roles. Those working within intelligence deploy multifarious theories in relation to their specific interests and operations. Some will be highly technical in respect of, for example, detecting evidence of radiological and chemical devices; some behavioural, for example, profiling and some sociological, such as studying motivations and dynamics of groups using violence. As outsiders, on the other hand, our theories of how intelligence 'works' will be drawn from a range of psychological, economic, anthropological, organisational, political science and social theories (Johnson, pp. 51–52).

Clearly, it would be idle to suggest the possibility of some unified field theory of intelligence, given the differences between foundationalist and anti-foundationalist ontologies, on the one hand, and positivist and interpretist epistemologies, on the other.[14] However, Mark Phythian and I have recently suggested that the most productive approach will be a 'critical realism' that seeks to avoid the hobbling effect both of positivism and its anti-foundationalist critics.[15] With positivism, it believes that causal statements can be made while, against positivism, it accepts that not all social phenomena can be observed and therefore research must also seek out underlying mechanisms of events.[16] This is manifestly the case in intelligence studies. Critical realism does not entail any specific model of intelligence (or anything else) but prefers causal explanations based on the interaction between actors ('agency') and structures[17] (see further below p. 219).

Davies (p. 200) asserts forcefully that the most important questions and answers about society are empirical ones. But there are two main reasons why theoretical frameworks are required: first, as suggested above, we need them in order to make sense of masses of data; in the words of Ben-Israel '*The main function of conceptual frameworks is to arrange and interpret facts wisely.*'[18] Second, it is precisely the extent of factors that are unobserved and, possibly, unobservable in the intelligence process that *require* us to develop speculative hypotheses as the basis for research. Now, Davies is correct to warn us against deploying theory that is 'dogma defended with the selective use of evidence' (p. 195) but the answer to that, as for the intelligence analyst, is to seek refutation not just confirmation of initial propositions.[19]

We seek new connections and relations by a creative process of redescription or 'abduction' that is akin to what investigators or doctors do as they test out different hypotheses or diagnoses.[20] Thus, by applying alternative theories and models in order to discern connections that were not evident, what intelligence scholars are doing is what good intelligence analysts do – but in doing so neither group is merely describing reality as if through clear glass. They are seeking to make sense of and thus actively 'create' the worlds of intelligence and government.[21]

Of course, policy makers are no more obliged to listen to academic researchers than they are to their own practitioners (cf. Johnson, pp. 46–48;

Kahn, pp. 11–12), but even if we find our recommendations ignored, another reason why we must develop our explanations of intelligence processes is public education. The normal exclusion of the public from any knowledge or debate about intelligence – other than selected historical episodes – was brought to an abrupt end on 11 September 2001 and reinforced by the subsequent Iraq controversy. There are clear dangers in a security panic – 'intelligence-led' or otherwise – and, as academics, we have a responsibility to interject our findings into debates about the proper and improper uses of intelligence and the problems of its 'failure', however that is manifested. For example, Phythian (pp. 62–63) suggests failure as one focus of theoretical work because it can perform an important educative function for citizens and legislators as well as the agencies themselves; it is also more feasible because more material becomes available to outside scholars as a result of inquiries compared with more routine matters. Sims (p. 152) and Johnson (p. 34) make similar points while Wirtz (p. 79) notes the relative lack of literature on the converse issue of surprise.

Defining the field

In a recent contribution to the definitional debate, Kristan Wheaton and Michael Beerbower argue that the lack of a clear definition of intelligence is the 'primary problem' for the US intelligence community rather than any organisational, leadership or professional issues.[22] Now, far be it from me to intrude on the private grief of Americans seeking to improve their nation's intelligence, but this does sound like a wild over-statement. It seems to reinforce Davies' (p. 192) argument that the lack of any institutional coherence in the US intelligence community has given rise to a compensatory quest for definitional and theoretical coherence.

Be that as it may, if we cannot agree on what we are discussing, then we shall struggle to generate understanding and explanation in an important field of political and social activity with the potential for both much good and much harm, even if practitioners and most decision makers will continue to rub along with the well-known 'duck' definition of intelligence. In this section I distil key elements of the debate, as evidenced especially by the chapters herein, and offer some suggestions. This will not settle all disagreements but, hopefully, it will clarify the key issues. Disputes will remain but that does not matter as long as they are understood when research is compared and people talk *to* rather than *past* each other!

We need, first, to distinguish 'intelligence' from all the other information-processing activities engaged in by almost all social actors – Davies (p. 198) and Warner (p. 18) both remind us of Wilhelm Agrell's article: 'When everything is intelligence – nothing is intelligence.'[23] Second, the concern is to identify the key elements of the process in order to facilitate understanding with a view to improving both its efficacy and ethics.

Wheaton and Beerbower endorse the definition recently provided by Robert Clark: 'Intelligence, then, is a process, focused externally and using information from all available sources, that is designed to reduce the level of uncertainty for a decisionmaker.'[24] This is satisfactory in many respects but, I suggest, can be improved on, with particular reference to the absence of reference to secrecy and action, the limited focus and begging of the question: uncertainty with respect to what? Accordingly, I propose the following: *mainly secret activities – targeting, collection, analysis, dissemination and action – intended to enhance security and/or maintain power relative to competitors by forewarning of threats and opportunities.*[25]

Mainly secret: there has been some debate as to whether or not secrecy is a necessary condition for intelligence. Certainly it is not the case that only information gathered secretly may contribute to intelligence because it is generally recognised that a high proportion – probably over 90 per cent – of information comes from open sources. But at some point in the intelligence process, *some* element of secrecy will be present, for example, covertly gathered information may 'add value' and intelligence, once developed, will be disseminated only to those with a 'need to know'. Competitors (whether actually enemies or not – see below) may attempt to frustrate one's information gathering; therefore another reason for incorporating secrecy is to acknowledge the role of counter-intelligence in protecting the integrity of intelligence. The term 'mainly' reflects the fact that a concern for secrecy (of personnel, sources, methods and product) is manifest throughout the intelligence process. Of course, this is not without cost – we have noted already the paradoxical impact of secrecy, that is, it is seen as essential yet inhibits the free flow of information upon which effective intelligence depends. Also Sheptycki (p. 169, fn. 18) points out the contribution made by secrecy to the apparently inevitable cycles of scandal to which intelligence is subject. The main dissenter to this point of view is Sims who argues that secrecy 'is not integral to the concept of intelligence and it is certainly not a defining characteristic of all intelligence systems', yet it is 'a characteristic capability of a high quality intelligence service' (pp. 161–162).[26] This author's view is that the crucial factor is *security* – secrecy may not be integral to all information or intelligence systems but it certainly is to those with security as their objective (see discussion below, p. 216).

Activities: in a classic work, Sherman Kent pointed out that 'intelligence' may actually refer to three different things: as here, an activity, second, the organisations which carry out those activities and, third, the knowledge that is gained as a result of the activities.[27] The second and third of these can easily be accommodated by prefacing the definition respectively by 'Organisations conducting...' or 'Knowledge gained from....'

Targeting: while contemporary information technologies allow for the collection of masses of information, the intelligence process depends on some element of targeting or prioritising. Foreign countries, for example, will be ranked in terms of their perceived priority as a target and police intelligence will similarly assign priorities according to estimates of amounts of money generated or harm caused by particular organisations or individuals.

Collection: much information will already reside in the organisational memory of agencies and this will be added to by both passive and active forms of collection. Predominantly, as noted above, this will be from open sources but the distinctive feature of intelligence is its covert collection. Collection will take place in a variety of ways, normally characterised as technical, including electronic, communications interception, satellite, imagery etc., and human, involving the use of agents or informers.

Analysis: this is the crucial stage at which 'information' must be evaluated in order to create 'intelligence'. Kahn's definition of 'intelligence in the broadest sense as information' (p. 4) is unhelpful. No matter how much information or 'raw data' is collected, it will not provide answers to the 'mysteries' or 'puzzles' with which intelligence is concerned. Facts do not speak for themselves. Compared with the very large sums of money spent (by those who can afford it) on ever more sophisticated means of collection, the amount invested in improving training and support for analysis is minimal. Analysis is pre-eminently an intellectual activity for which, compared with collection and despite the existence of sophisticated relational software, no technologies exist that can outperform people.

Dissemination: intelligence, once created, needs to be disseminated to those who can do something with it – this may be people within the same organisation or another agency or may be government in general.

And action: there are clearly divisions between scholars as to whether intelligence is just about the provision of useful knowledge to policy and decision makers (cf. Sims, p. 159) or whether it includes also the subsequent taking of action (cf. Betts, p. 106; Warner, p. 19). It is suggested here that a fuller understanding of intelligence activities is obtained if the integral connection with action is acknowledged and that it does not 'make sense' to omit action from the definition.[28] For example, even information collection will be regarded by the targets as a form of action (perhaps hostile) and where the collection is by human means it can be impossible to determine where collection ends and some form of (covert) action begins. Similarly, the nature of any subsequent (in)action may have an important (positive or negative) impact on the future possibilities for collection. Further, the crucial relationship between professionals and political decision makers can only be explored fully by examining how intelligence competes with ideology, values and prejudices in explaining the action. 'Action' will not necessarily follow 'intelligence'; sometimes the desire for action or 'will to power' may determine, if not the whole intelligence picture, certainly the *selection* of the intelligence that 'fits' (cf. Marrin, pp. 144–145).

Analysing 'action' involves, of course, the study of power and we must note that there are two broad theoretical streams of power: sovereign and facilitative.[29] Also, knowledge is both a *form* of power (for example, the 'law of anticipated reactions'[30]) and is a *resource* in deployment of other forms of power (symbolic, material, physical), each of which may be deployed either overtly or covertly, the latter usually involving plausible deniability.[31] A crucial issue is the degree of confidence in 'knowledge' required before it will prompt action. For example, 'intelligence' provides a lower level of confidence than what criminal law defines as 'evidence'. In the UK for example, prosecutors apply a '51 per cent rule' of confidence that their evidence will secure a conviction before prosecuting someone; police will apply a lower level of 'reasonable suspicion' before arresting someone. But what level do police or intelligence agencies apply before acting to disrupt some target group? Probably lower than the police do for arrest but, hopefully, not as low as the 1 per cent rule ascribed to Dick Cheney.[32] These differences lie at the heart of the controversies current in liberal democracies as to the appropriate tools of counter-terrorism policy.

Intended to enhance: intelligence is a goal-seeking activity that seeks to improve on the current situation, whatever it is. Only time will tell whether it is successful or not; intelligence may just 'fail' in the sense of not obtaining needed information or preventing attack or, even more seriously, may 'blowback' as in the case of the provision of stinger missiles to the Afghan mujahedin in the 1980s.[33]

Security: this is the goal that is sought. Security is a sense of safety, reduced uncertainty or of managing risk. It is this which defines the boundaries of our field of interest compared with information gathered for other purposes, for example, football scores, weather reports or train timetables for leisure purposes. Security is always relative to that of competitors (see below); the search for 'absolute' security is a dangerous chimera – it is literally unobtainable and the attempt to obtain it can be highly destructive of social relationships.[34] As Betts points out, the inevitable inadequacies of intelligence demand a 'tolerance for disaster' (p. 107). Given that 'human' is defined more broadly than 'national' security, then our field extends the more we embrace the former paradigm.

And/or maintain power: the literature of intelligence is greatest within the older liberal democracies where intelligence has been seen as providing information for governments in order that they can pursue policies more effectively. However, this ignores the realities of intelligence in many countries (and, indeed, *some* aspects of intelligence within democracies) that is, the defence of specific regimes. While there are significant differences between, say, intelligence as it operates in liberal democratic compared with 'counterintelligence' regimes,[35] the difference is not total since 'political policing' in defence of the regime is evident in some measure everywhere. 'National' security may reflect an ideal in which intelligence serves the protection of a nation's people while 'state security' explicitly refers to the security of a specific regime, often against many of its people but, in practice, the concept of 'national security' has also been used as a cover for the enhancement of the power and interests of certain groups or elites rather than those of the nation as a whole.

As against competitors: living within an entirely consensual environment would do away with the need for intelligence since there would be no reason to feel insecure. 'Competitors' covers a wide range of potential adversaries in order not to limit intelligence to its traditional concern with international relations between states. A key element in the competition is the *resistance* by targets against attempts to gather information and exercise power against them.[36] It is this phenomenon that gives rise to the need for counter-intelligence.

By forewarning: the core objective of intelligence activities is to anticipate, to estimate what is *going to* happen or what might happen. However, once intelligence (as knowledge) is developed, there are a variety of uses to which it may be put. For example, after a violent attack authorities will wish to investigate in order to establish the (domestic or foreign) perpetrators and, to that end, will seek to draw on what, if anything, was known beforehand as well as deploying investigative techniques that are, in effect, *post hoc* intelligence activities.

Of threats: probably the most common and traditional way to view intelligence is as a *defensive* mechanism against perceived domestic and foreign threats and 'threat analyses' are one of the most basic forms of intelligence that agencies produce for their customers.

And opportunities: however, even if defensive intelligence is the basic form, it is not the whole story. Foreign intelligence will be developed in order to inform government in relation to opportunities for the advancement of national military, economic or political interests. Military intelligence regarding the 'order of battle' of enemy's forces will be as useful in the calculation of possibilities of mounting a successful surprise attack as in preventing one by the enemy. Thus, the *offensive* use of intelligence can be witnessed in various forms including propaganda, material support for oppositional groups abroad, or as the basis for physical intervention including undermining the counter-intelligence efforts of competitors.

Developing intelligence theories through the concept of surveillance

In order to develop our theoretical perspectives beyond these basic definitional issues, we should, first, step back from our immediate focus into the broader environment of social and political theory. Acknowledging that intelligence is a pre-eminently social and political phenomenon will help us to avoid reinventing the wheel. For example, Warner (pp. 20–21) shows the importance of paying more attention to the literature discussing how organisations deal with risk because of the similarity with the intelligence process. But at an even more fundamental level, we might make use of the concept of surveillance. Though discussed in different ways by social theorists such as Dandeker, Foucault and Giddens, there is a core of similarity in their definition of surveillance as constituted by two components: first, the gathering and storing of information and, second, the supervision of people's behaviour.[37] In other words, it is concerned with knowledge and power. Len Scott and Peter Jackson have pointed out that 'Much of the study of intelligence concerns the relationship between power and knowledge, or rather the relationship between certain kinds of power and certain kinds of knowledge.'[38] Indeed, all the non-trivial study of intelligence is concerned with this relationship. I claim no originality in deploying this term: Sherman Kent used it in his analysis of US strategic intelligence sixty years ago though he used it only in respect of the gathering/analytical component[39] and it remains common among both practitioners and people more generally to see surveillance in these narrower terms.

In contemporary Western social theory, surveillance is seen both as the central aspect of the establishment of modern 'sovereign' state forms and of the more recent decline of sovereignty as it is replaced by 'governance', including recognising the significance of private forms of governance. Furthermore, studies of non-Western societies show that surveillance is similarly central there: its philosophical basis may be crucially different, for example, rooted in the rejection of individualism, but its core goals – understanding and control – are constants.[40] So, not surprisingly, global surveillance is argued to be an intrinsic part of the general economic restructuring of capitalism that is described as globalisation,[41] and post-9/11 developments have served only to reinforce key aspects of this phenomenon.[42]

Warner (pp. 19–20) reminds us of Adda Bozeman's important observation twenty years ago that the state is often not the decisive working unit in intelligence. If anything, subsequent developments have reinforced this point though, since 9/11, there have been some counter-tendencies. On the one hand, there remain significant parts of the world where militias, criminal organisations, paramilitaries and liberation movements are more significant intelligence actors than the states of which they are formally a part. Albania, Afghanistan, Colombia, Iraq, Palestine and Sudan all provide examples. Also, since Bozeman wrote, the end of the Cold War has seen a proliferation of private security and military companies providing a variety of services, including intelligence, to their contracting principals who may be states, corporations, international organisations or non-governmental organisations.[43] On the other hand, since 9/11 several states have sought to reassert their grip over intelligence matters with enhanced budgets and powers granted to agencies which had shrunk somewhat after the collapse of the USSR. Overall, however, the key element in Warner's argument is that we would be advised to deploy the term 'sovereignties' rather than states to accommodate the variety of 'competitive' intelligence actors we find. The hitherto state-centric nature of intelligence studies must be left behind.

Sheptycki (pp. 170–172) also raises questions about the continued applicability of the Westphalian model given that the dominant interpretation of security in 'national' rather than 'human' terms has militated against the development of policies for peace rather than war. If anything, this tendency seems to have been reinforced since 9/11 by the US defining counter-terrorism in increasingly militaristic terms. Sheptycki argues that examples of the human security paradigm in operation can be found in the policing literature although his examples are not drawn from the 'hard' case of counter-terrorism. But even in this respect it can be argued that police intelligence operations against criminal organisations have more similarity to current counter-terrorist concerns than traditional foreign and military intelligence operations. Further, there is a small but significant literature examining the possibilities of intelligence being deployed in connection with post-conflict and peace-keeping operations.[44]

'Surveillance studies' are also enjoying rapid growth currently as evidenced by the recent launch of an online journal and the publication of several significant books.[45] In the interests of 'leveraging' lessons for our work from disparate fields,[46] we need to familiarise ourselves with this literature even if we do not find it all directly relevant or useful. The core concerns of surveillance – the gathering of information by overt and covert means, its analysis and dissemination and then the application of 'power' (or one of its many synonyms – influence, manipulation, coercion, bribery) in order to discipline, manage or control people are also ours but, in concentrating on the intelligence field, three elements of the earlier definition are crucial: security, secrecy and the resistance of competitors.

Levels of theory and research

Intelligence processes with a view to enhancing security and protected to some extent by secrecy take place at different social *levels*, as evidenced by the literature including the chapters in this collection, although most concentration is on the organisational and national levels. Of course, these levels are constructs developed in part as a means to make social science manageable and as a result of its fragmentation into different disciplines such as psychology, organisational studies and international relations. But, bearing in mind the earlier point about leveraging our field of study through the insights already gained in other areas, in order to inform our research agenda and develop concepts and theory, we need to investigate key knowledge-power processes explicitly at these different levels: individual, group, organisational, societal and international. Doing so does, of course, reinforce some fragmentation in our own field but it is suggested this can be minimised by deploying concepts that are common to and thus link levels: surveillance, knowledge, power, security, secrecy and resistance. Similarly, Wirtz (p. 78) shows how the 'risk paradox' can provide a link between different levels. In other words, just as we seek to avoid ethnocentricity by exploring the validity and applicability of core concepts in cross-national comparative research, so we can compare intelligence across levels and, of course, through time.[47]

Explanation in the social sciences is organised broadly around the respective significance of agency and structure and these levels might be seen as 'nesting' within each other like Russian dolls. As such, individuals are the core example of 'agents' whose actions will be influenced to a greater or lesser extent by the structures of group, organisation, society etc. within which they live and work. But while organisations provide the structure for groups and individuals within them, so they may behave (and be analysed) as agents within broader societal networks.[48] It is customary in the literature to describe the intelligence activities referred to in the definition above – targeting, collection, analysis, dissemination and action – as collectively constituting an intelligence 'cycle' or 'process' (for example, Johnson, p. 34; Marrin, pp. 131–132; Phythian, p. 67). This provides a useful heuristic model[49] for researchers to employ though it should not be taken as a literal description of how things happen. Arthur Hulnick's use of the term 'matrix' provides a better description of the actual relation between these activities,[50] for example, collectors often act as their own analysts or interact with analysts continuously as they try to refine operations.

Some examples follow of how, at different levels, theoretical approaches inform our understanding of knowledge–power interaction in intelligence processes, and of pathways that future work may follow.

Individual: cognitive psychology is the basis for research into practitioners in order to explain how they select or prioritise what information is 'relevant' over that which is not. Then, the role of cognition, perception and psychology in interpretation is crucial in the potential for surprise (Wirtz, pp. 78–79) and failure (Betts, p. 87). There may also be other pressures perceived by intelligence professionals such as those on career prospects when contemplating the potential costs of 'telling (unwelcome) truth to power'.

Group: when small work group is studied, other aspects of cognition and influence enter the frame, for example, 'groupthink' that has already been subject to considerable study in intelligence. But there are other aspects of the significance of small groups, for example, analysts make use of social network theory in mapping criminal and terrorist groups. Researchers might use the same tool as a means of examining how networks of analysts in the same or different agencies cooperate in information sharing that goes beyond formal agreements. This has clear implications not just for improved effectiveness in intelligence but also for mechanisms of control and oversight of intelligence networks.

Organisational: this collection points to a host of questions regarding intelligence organisations and Hastedt and Skelley examine a number of approaches to answering them. Warner (pp. 25–29) demonstrates the link in the US between initial military definitions of intelligence and its organisation. 'Turf wars' between agencies bedevil cooperation and are often presented as the outcome of short-sighted bureaucratic jealousy, but a more thorough deployment of models of 'governmental politics' might well indicate a wider set of issues, for example, competing mandates, adequacy of resources, data protection rules etc. that raise profound policy issues.

Nevertheless, inquiries into 'failure', especially in the US, tend to urge organisational reform. Perhaps if they had had the opportunity to read this collection, their authors may have been less likely to do so. Betts provides a link with other levels when he warns that intelligence failure is more often political and psychological than organisational: reforms cannot transcend the essential ambivalence of analysis or the predispositions and idiosyncrasies of decision makers (p. 104 and cf. Davies, pp. 192–193). A recurring theme that has already been described above as a paradox is the clash between the desire to centralise while maximising the free flow of information. Betts (p. 91) reminds us that Wilensky identified forty years ago the impact of hierarchy, centralisation and specialisation on intelligence and technological developments since then have only exaggerated the problem. Sheptycki (p. 177), similarly, argues that the transformative potential of information networks is too often negated by the continued desire to centralise criminal intelligence at the national level. However, Davies (p. 197) is critical of similar views expressed elsewhere, for example, Andrew Rathmell's characterisation of the way in which the new knowledge economy has rendered the old 'knowledge factories' of intelligence outdated,[51] on the grounds that the small size of assessment groups in US and UK never resembled factories in the first place. But while this may be true for small national assessment groups, the much larger bureaucratic machines upon which they rest, especially for collection, reinforce the relevance of this paradox. The essence of this question is the extent to which the hierarchies into which modern state institutions have been organised since the nineteenth century can continue to provide (if they ever did) a conceptual and organisational framework for effective and accountable intelligence, or whether, as Davies suggests, 'matrix management' provides a more flexible context for the production of intelligence.

Societal: this question is brought into even sharper relief when we consider the growing significance of networks of state, corporate and community 'security' providers, many of which are involved in intelligence. Recent work on the 'governance of security'[52] has started to conceptualise this important development. It is significant, I would suggest, that there is little sign of this work in this current collection (Sheptycki, pp. 178–179 is an exception). This reflects the fact that research on intelligence has concentrated on the state sector and/or the relations between states; it is important that future work broadens to take account of a wider variety of Warner's 'sovereignties'. Johnson's (p. 36) basic propositions about the significance of national wealth to the organisation of intelligence and the growth in private and 'community' sectors also alerts us to the need for a 'political economy' of intelligence, for example, what are the economic factors (both legal and illegal) that condition the development of intelligence organisations? Students of intelligence have important contributions to make to the analysis of developing 'security networks', given their profound implications in terms not only of the funding and provision of intelligence services but also the serious challenges they pose to conventional notions of government accountability. While this has important implications within societies, it also has significance at the international level.

International: this collection incorporates some widely diverging views on the utility of current theorising at the international level for intelligence studies, Johnson (p. 33), for example, considers it 'hidebound' and Davies (p. 199) considers it to be the last place we should look! However, Phythian (pp. 57–61) suggests that, for the purposes of understanding national and international intelligence, neo-realism can explain the conditions that give rise to the full range of intelligence behaviour including why agencies emerge when they do and why the wealthiest states will continue to invest in them, even absent a specific threat. Certainly, existing theories provide the raw material for the development of some interesting and important research programmes. For example, if neo-realism implies that the multiple channels of inter-state contact create further requirements for both intelligence and counterintelligence, Sims (p. 158) suggests that the same highly competitive environment will tend towards transparency because, to the extent that intelligence is a force multiplier, states have the incentive to share with allies. Can these be reconciled? Only by emphasising the normative aspect of Sims argument, that is, states *should* have the incentive to share. We might re-state these different views in terms of the classic Prisoners' Dilemma: in considering intelligence cooperation, any state acting on the basis of rational self-interest, will rank its preferences so that, whatever the other country does – provide intelligence or no – it would be better off not providing information. The logic of this is the fear of getting 'burnt' by the other's (mis)use of the information. If both states follow this course, the result is no sharing, which is clearly the inferior result for both. So, how can states learn more trusting behaviour that will lead both to the optimum outcome of each providing information to the other?[53]

In the light of post-9/11 efforts to improve intelligence sharing these are the central theoretical issues that need addressing, and, of course, they have significant practical significance. Not least is the fact that current nationally-based systems of intelligence oversight are of very limited relevance to transnational sharing. This is clear from recent reports into the scandals surrounding 'extraordinary rendition' from such as the Canadian Arar Commission and the Council of Europe report.[54] But there is also a more fundamental issue to be addressed, that is, the impact of globalisation for intelligence. Discussions about the potential, limits and dangers for transnational sharing are just one issue; now that intelligence is, to some extent, 'beyond the state' within a globalised world of communications, any theory based around the presumed pre-eminence of states will be lacking.[55] Currently, arrangements for global governance lag far behind the globalisation of the threats that intelligence targets but we should not ignore the potential significance of international intelligence also moving beyond the current obsession with terrorism.

Conclusion

There is one important issue that has not been dealt with so far – oversight and accountability. Johnson points out that these supervision efforts should be incorporated in a theory of intelligence 'at least in those open societies where accountability has been attempted in this hidden domain' (pp. 50–51 and cf. Phythian, p. 63). Now, since intelligence is a feature of all organised states and societies and since it has such an intimate relationship with power, I am not sure that oversight can be incorporated into a definition or theory of intelligence *per se*, though it would certainly be an essential part of any theory of *democratic* intelligence. As we saw earlier, the greater legitimacy of liberal democratic regimes is symbolised by the fact that security is defined more in external than internal terms, as it is in authoritarian or counter-intelligence regimes, but internal security and 'political police' intelligence do operate in democracies. Indeed, one of the clearest developments post-1991 and accelerated by 9/11 has been the weakening of this internal/external divide. Therefore, what we have is a spectrum of intelligence on which are ranged many 'sovereignties' from those, at one end, who penetrate entire societies in the search for 'enemies' while themselves enjoying absolute secrecy and autonomy to those at the other whose operations are both much more limited and overseen by ministers, parliaments and/or their appointees. We need a theory that can inform intelligence studies everywhere and, whether we like it or not, many parts of the Americas, Africa, Asia, the Middle East and parts of Europe have some way to go in achieving 'democratic intelligence'. In developing theory and practice to that end, we should note the argument for a shift towards a paradigm of human rather than national security (Sheptycki, pp. 171–172) in which human rights and civil liberties are deployed as principles reflecting accumulated knowledge as to how intelligence might work more effectively yet ethically. Regarding the former, Sims (p. 157) notes the role for oversight in creating the trust between providers and consumers that is necessary. Regarding the latter, patently, the 'competition' between intelligence activities and resistance has profound ethical implications.[56]

The speed of events and the significance of the intelligence-related controversies in the last few years have left academic and other commentators gasping for breath; as observers rather than actors, it is perhaps inevitable that we are condemned to play 'catch-up'. However, in seeking to provide explanations and some enlightenment to the public that goes beyond mere description and speculation, we must take care to develop understandings through integrating theoretical considerations with empirical work. Whatever the 'level', focus or method of our research, we are most likely to develop the intelligence 'interdiscipline' systematically by concentrating on the key interaction of knowledge and power.

Notes

1 Earlier versions of this chapter were presented to BISA, University of Cork, December 2006; ISA, Chicago, March 2007; and Intelligence Governance Section, ECPR Conference, Pisa, September, 2007. In addition to the participants in those panels, I want to thank especially my co-editors, and additionally Rob Dover, Michael Herman, James Sheptycki, Jennifer Sims and Michael Warner for their helpful comments on earlier drafts.
2 Christopher Andrew and David Dilks, *The Missing Dimension: Governments and Intelligence Communities in the Twentieth Century*, London: Macmillan, 1984.
3 These issues are considered by the author in 'Security Intelligence and Human Rights: Illuminating the "Heart of Darkness"', paper given to conference 'Choices for Western Intelligence', University of Wales Conference Centre, Gregynog, April 2007 and forthcoming in *Intelligence and National Security*, 2009.
4 Commission of Inquiry into the Actions of Canadian Officials in Relation to Maher Arar, 2006, *Report of the Events Relating to Maher Arar*, 1. *Analysis and Recommendations*, 2. *Factual background* (two vols), 3. *A New Review Mechanism for the RCMP's National Security Activities*, www.ararcommission.ca.
5 Richard Aldrich, '"Grow Your Own": Cold War Intelligence and History Supermarkets', *Intelligence and National Security*, 17:1, 2002, pp. 135–52.
6 Cf. Gordon Hughes, 'Understanding the Politics of Criminological Research', in Vic Jupp, Pamela Davies and Peter Francis, *Doing Criminological Research*, London: Sage, 2000, pp. 234–248.
7 Graham Allison and Philip Zelikow, *Essence of Decision*, 2nd edn, New York: Longman, 1999.
8 There is a brief discussion of the utility of postmodern approaches to intelligence in

Peter Gill and Mark Phythian, *Intelligence in an Insecure World*, Cambridge: Polity, 2006, pp. 23–25.

9   Cf. Len Scott and R. Gerald Hughes, 'Intelligence, Crises and Security: Lessons for History?', *Intelligence and National Security*, 21:5, 2006, pp. 653–674.

10 Cited in David Garland and Richard Sparks, 'Criminology, Social Theory and the Challenge of Our Times', in Garland and Sparks, *Criminology and Social Theory*, Oxford: Oxford University Press, 2000, p. 4.

11 Isaac Ben-Israel, 'Philosophy and Methodology of Intelligence: The Logic of the Estimate Process', *Intelligence and National Security*, 4:4, 1989, pp. 660–718 at 693–694.

12 Thanks to Rob Dover for pointing this out.

13 For example, Walter Laquer, *A World of Secrets: The Uses and Limits of Intelligence*, New York: Basic Books, 1985, p. 4 fn.

14 David Marsh and Paul Furlong, 'A Skin, Not a Sweater: Ontology and Epistemology in Political Science', in David Marsh and Gerry Stoker, *Theory and Methods in Political Science*, 2002, 2nd edn, pp. 17–41.

15 Gill and Phythian, ch. 2. In its original manifestation this was presented to ISA in 2004.

16 Marsh and Furlong, 'A Skin, Not a Sweater', pp. 30–31.

17 Systematic discussion of the implications of critical realism for international relations can be found in Milja Kurki, 'Critical Realism and Causal Analysis in International Relations', *Millennium*, 35:2, 2007, pp. 361–378 and Chris Brown, 'Situating Critical Realism', ibid., pp. 409–416.

18 Ben-Israel, 'Philosophy and Methodology of Intelligence: The Logic of Estimate Process', *Intelligence and National* Security, 4:4, 1989, p. 711 (emphasis in original.) Ben-Israel was writing about the problems of method *within* intelligence rather than the study of intelligence from outside, as it were, but much of his analysis is equally applicable to the latter.

19 Ibid., 672–697.

20 Berth Danermark, Mats Ekström, Liselotte Jakobsen, Jan Karlsson (eds), *Explaining Society*, London: Routledge, 2002, pp. 91–93. For example, Loch Johnson, 'Bricks and Mortar for a Theory of Intelligence', *Comparative Strategy*, 22, 2003, p. 1; Stephen Marrin and Jonathan Clemente, 'Improving Intelligence Analysis by Looking to the Medical Profession', *International Journal of Intelligence and Counterintelligence*, 18:4, 2005–2006, pp. 707–729; Stephen Marrin, p. 146 above.

21 Michael Fry and Miles Hochstein, 'Epistemic Communities: Intelligence Studies and International Relations', *Intelligence and National Security*, 8:3, 1993, pp. 14–28 at 25. See further Mark Phythian, pp. 65–66 above.

22 Kristan Wheaton and Michael Beerbower, 'Towards a New Definition of Intelligence', *Stanford Law and Policy Review*, 17, pp. 319–330 at 319.

23 Sherman Kent Center for Intelligence Analysis, Occasional papers, 1:4, 2002.

24 Cited in Wheaton and Beerbower, 'Towards a New Definition', p. 329.

25 Adapted from Gill and Phythian, *Intelligence*, p. 7 and to acknowledge important criticisms of that version made by both Shlomo Shpiro and Michael Warner (see p. 4 above).

26 Wheaton and Beerbower similarly exclude 'secrecy for secrecy's sake' but note that 'operational secrecy' is required, 'Towards a New Definition of Intelligence', p. 329.

27 Sherman Kent, *Strategic Intelligence for American World Policy*, Princeton, NJ: Princeton University Press, 1966 (1st pub. 1949), p. ix.

28 As argued by Wheaton and Beerbower, 'Towards a New Definition', p. 327. It *might* make sense to insulate intelligence and policy from each other if one were designing an ideal intelligence system within a government but it does not help us to understand the intelligence process as it actually happens.

29 Jon Scott, *Power*, Cambridge: Polity, 2001 provides an accessible summary of the power debates.

30 Carl Friedrich, *Man and his Government*, New York: McGraw-Hill, 1963, pp. 200–201

31 This is discussed in greater detail in Gill and Phythian, *Intelligence*, pp. 95–101.

32 Ron Suskind, *The One Percent Doctrine: Deep Inside America's Pursuit of its Enemies Since 9/11*, New York: Simon and Schuster, 2007.

33 Steve Coll, *Ghost Wars: The Secret History of the CIA, Afghanistan and Bin Laden, from the Soviet Invasion to September 10, 2001*, New York: Penguin, 2004.

34 The core paradox is that if either state or community is so powerful as to be able to guarantee complete security to citizens then the state or community themselves constitute a massive threat to individual security. R.M. Berki, *Security and Society: Reflections on Law, Order and Politics*, London: Dent & Sons, 1986, pp. 28–43.

35 Christopher Andrew, 'Intelligence, international relations and "Under-theorisation"', *Intelligence and National Security*, 19:2, 2004, pp. 170–184.

36 For example, Gary Marx, 'A Tack in the Shoe', *Journal of Social Issues*, 59, 2003, pp. 369–390, discusses eleven techniques by which information collection may be subverted.

37 Christopher Dandeker, *Surveillance, Power and Modernity*, Cambridge: Polity, 1990; Michel Foucault, 'Governmentality', in Graham Burchell, Colin Gordon and Peter Miller (eds), *The Foucault Effect: Studies in Governmentality*, London: Harvester Wheatsheaf, 1991, pp. 87–104; Anthony Giddens, *The Nation State and Violence*, Berkeley, CA: University of California Press, 1985, pp. 181–192.

38 Len Scott and Peter Jackson, 'The Study of Intelligence in Theory and Practice', *Intelligence and National Security*, 19:2, 2004, p. 150.

39 Kent, *Strategic Intelligence for American World Policy*, 1966, p. 4.

40 Adda Bozeman, 'Knowledge and Comparative Method in Comparative Intelligence Studies', in Bozeman, *Strategic Intelligence and Statecraft*, Washington, DC: Brasseys, 1992, pp. 198–205; James der Derian, 'Anti-Diplomacy: Intelligence Theory and Surveillance Practice', *Intelligence and National Security*, 8:3, 1993, pp. 29–51 at 34–35.

41 David Lyon, *Surveillance Society*, Milton Keynes: Open University Press, 2001, p. 103. Cf. also James der Derian, *Antidiplomacy*, Oxford: Blackwell, 1992, p. 46. Reg Whitaker, *The End of Privacy: How Total Surveillance Is Becoming a Reality*, New York: New Press, 1999 is an excellent survey of contemporary developments.

42 David Lyon, *Surveillance after September 11*, Cambridge: Polity, 2003. Phil Davies (p. 195) may be correct in noting that Bentham's panopticon was never built but that does not undermine the 'empirical reality' of surveillance form CCTV cameras to 'dataveillance' of and by means of computer networks

43 See Gill and Phythian, *Intelligence*, pp. 39–57.

44 For example, Ian Bryan and Michael Salter, 'War Crimes Prosecutors and Intelligence Agencies: The Case for Assessing their Collaboration', *Intelligence and National Security*, 16:3, 2001, pp. 93–120.

45 See Surveillance and Society, http://www.surveillance-and-society.org; Kevin Haggerty and Richard Ericson, *The New Politics of Surveillance and Visibility*, Toronto: University of Toronto Press, 2006; David Lyon, *Theorizing Surveillance: The Panopticon and Beyond*, Cullompton: Willan Press, 2006; Torin Monahan, *Surveillance and Security: Technological Politics and Power in Everyday Life*, London: Routledge, 2006.

46 Cf. Peter Singer, *Corporate Warriors*, Ithaca, NY: Cornell University Press, 2003, pp. ix–x.

47 A 'map' showing the relation between key elements of theory and research is developed in Gill and Phythian, *Intelligence*, p. 37 and applied to comparative work in Peter Gill, '"Knowing the Self, Knowing the Other": The Comparative Analysis of Security Intelligence', in Loch Johnson (ed.), *Handbook of Intelligence Studies*, London: Routledge, 2007, pp. 82–90.

48 Gill and Phythian, *Intelligence*, pp. 27–28.
49 Though Wilhelm Agrell has suggested it be abandoned since it inhibits creative thinking. Greg Treverton, Seth Jones, Steven Boraz and Philip Lipscy, *Toward a Theory of
Intelligence: Workshop Report*, National Security Research Division, Arlington, VA:
Rand, 2006, pp. 21–22.
50 Arthur Hulnick, 'Controlling Intelligence Estimates', in Glenn Hastedt (ed.), *Controlling Intelligence*, London: Cass, 1991, pp. 81–96.
51 Andrew Rathmell, 'Towards Postmodern Intelligence', *Intelligence and National
Security*, 17:3, 2002, pp. 87–104.
52 For example, Les Johnston and Clifford Shearing, *Governing Security*, London: Routledge, 2003. See also Fred Schreier and Marina Caparini, *Privatising Security: Law,
Practice and Governance of Private Military and Security Companies*, Occasional
Paper #6, Geneva: DCAF, March 2005.
53 Don Munton, 'Intelligence Cooperation Meets International Studies Theory: Explaining Canadian operations in Castro's Cuba', paper given to conference 'Choices for
Western Intelligence', University of Wales Conference centre, Gregynog, April,
2007, pp. 14–16.
54 Commission of Inquiry into the Actions of Canadian Officials in Relation to Maher
Arar, 2006, http://www.ararcommission.ca; Committee on Legal Affairs and Human
Rights, *Secret Detentions and Illegal Transfers of Detainees Involving Council of
Europe States: Second Report*, Parliamentary Assembly, Council of Europe, Doc.
11302 rev., 11 June 2007, see esp. Part VI.
55 For example, Richard Aldrich, 'Globalization and Secret Intelligence: Understanding
the Crisis of Intelligence', paper delivered to Intelligence Governance panel at ECPR
Conference, Pisa, September 2007.
56 Discussed further in Gill and Phythian, *Intelligence*, pp. 152–156; see also Michael
Andregg, 'Intelligence Ethics: Laying a Foundation for the Second Oldest Profession', in Loch Johnson (ed.), *Handbook of Intelligence Studies*, Abingdon, Oxon:
Routledge, 2007, pp. 52–63; Jan Goldman (ed.), *Ethics of Spying: A Reader for the
Intelligence Professional*, Lanham, MD: Scarecrow Press, 2006.

Select bibliography

Agrell, Wilhelm, 'When Everything Is Intelligence – Nothing Is Intelligence', Central Intelligence Agency, Sherman Kent Center for Intelligence Analysis, Occasional Papers, 1:4, 2002.

Andrew, Christopher, 'Intelligence, International Relations and "Under-theorisation"', *Intelligence and National Security*, 19:2, 2004, pp. 170–84.

Barger, Deborah G., *Toward a Revolution in Intelligence Affairs*, Santa Monica, CA: RAND, 2005.

Ben-Israel, Isaac, 'Philosophy and Methodology of Intelligence: The Logic of the Estimate Process', *Intelligence and National Security*, 4:4, 1989, pp. 660–718.

Berki, R.M., *Security and Society: Reflections on Law, Order and Politics*, London: Dent & Sons, 1986.

Berkowitz, Bruce D. and Goodman, Allan E., *Best Truth: Intelligence in the Information Age*, New Haven, CT: Yale University Press, 2000.

Charters, David, Farson, Stuart and Hastedt, Glenn P. (eds), *Intelligence Analysis and Assessment*, London: Frank Cass, 1996.

Davies, Philip, 'Ideas of Intelligence: Divergent National Concepts and Institutions', *Harvard International Review* 2002 14: 3, Fall, pp. 62–66.

Cimbala, Stephen J. (ed.), *Intelligence and Intelligence Policy in a Democratic Society*, Dobbs Ferry, NY: Transnational Press, 1987.

Dandeker, Christopher, *Surveillance, Power and Modernity*, Cambridge: Polity, 1990.

der Derian, James, *Antidiplomacy: Spies, Terror, Speed, and War*, Cambridge, MA: Blackwell, 1992.

Fijnaut, Cyrille and Marx, Gary (eds), *Undercover: Police Surveillance in Comparative Perspective*, The Hague: Kluwer Law International, 1995.

Fry, Michael G. and Hochstein, Miles, 'Epistemic Communities: Intelligence Studies and International Relations', *Intelligence and National Security*, 8:3, 1993, pp. 14–28.

Gill, Peter, *Policing Politics: Security, Intelligence and the Liberal Democratic State*, London: Frank Cass, 1994.

Gill, Peter and Phythian, Mark, *Intelligence in an Insecure World*, Cambridge, UK: Polity, 2006.

Godson, Roy (ed.), *Comparing Foreign Intelligence: The US, the USSR, the UK, and the Third World*, Washington, DC: Pergamon-Brassey's, 1988.

Godson, Roy and Wirtz, James J. (eds), *Strategic Denial and Deception: The 21st Century Challenge*, New Brunswick, NJ: Transaction, 2001.

Goldman, Jan (ed.), *Ethics of Spying: A Reader for the Intelligence Professional*, Lanham, MD: The Scarecrow Press, 2006.

Haggerty, Kevin and Ericson, Richard, *The New Politics of Surveillance and Visibility*, Toronto: University of Toronto Press, 2006.

Handel, Michael, 'The Politics of Intelligence', *Intelligence and National Security*, 2:4, 1987, pp. 5–46.

Handel, Michael, *War, Strategy and Intelligence*, New York: Routledge, 1989.

Herman, Michael, *Intelligence Power in Peace and War*, Cambridge, UK: RIIA/Cambridge University Press, 1996.

Herman, Michael, *Intelligence Services in the Information Age*, London: Frank Cass, 2001.

Heuer, Jr., Richards J., *Psychology of Intelligence Analysis*, Center for the Study of Intelligence, Washington, DC: US Government Printing Office, 1999.

Hulnick, Arthur S., 'The Intelligence Producer-Policy Consumer Linkage: A Theoretical Approach', *Intelligence and National Security*, 1:2, 1986, pp. 212–233.

Jackson, Peter and Siegel, Jennifer (eds), *Intelligence and Statecraft: The Use and Limits of Intelligence in International Society*, Westport, CT: Praeger, 2005.

Jervis, Robert, *Perception and Misperception in World Politics*, Princeton, NJ: Princeton University Press, 1976.

Johnson, Loch K., *America's Secret Power: The CIA in a Democratic Society*, Oxford, UK: Oxford University Press, 1989.

Johnson, Loch K., *Bombs, Bugs, Drugs, and Thugs: Intelligence and the Quest for Security*, New York: New York University Press, 2000.

Johnson, Loch K., 'Preface to a Theory of Strategic Intelligence', *International Journal of Intelligence and CounterIntelligence*, 16, 2003, pp. 638–663.

Johnson, Loch K. (ed.), *Strategic Intelligence*, 5 vols, esp. vol. 1, *Understanding the Hidden Side of Government*, Westport, CT: Praeger, 2007.

Johnson, Loch K. (ed.), *Handbook of Intelligence Studies*, New York: Routledge, 2007.

Johnston, Les and Shearing, Clifford, *Governing Security: Explorations in Policing and Justice*, London: Routledge, 2003.

Kent, Sherman, *Strategic Intelligence for American World Policy*, Princeton, NJ: Princeton University Press, 1949.

Laqueur, Walter, *A World of Secrets: The Uses and Limits of Intelligence*, New York: Basic Books, 1985.

Leslau, Ohad, 'Intelligence and Economics: Two Disciplines with a Common Dilemma', *International Journal of Intelligence and CounterIntelligence*, 20:1 2007, pp. 106–121.

Lowenthal, Mark, *Intelligence: From Secrets to Policy*, 3rd edn, Washington, DC: CQ Press, 2006.

Marrin, Stephen, 'Intelligence Analysis Theory: Explaining and Predicting Analytic Responsibilities', *Intelligence and National Security*, 22:6, 2007, pp. 821–846.

Quinlan, Michael, ' "Just Intelligence": Prolegomena to an Ethical Theory', *Intelligence and National Security*, 22:1, 2007, pp. 1–13.

Ratcliffe, Jerry (ed.), *Strategic Thinking in Criminal Intelligence*, Anandale, NSW: The Federation Press, 2004.

Rathmell, Andrew, 'Towards Postmodern Intelligence', *Intelligence and National Security*, 17:3, 2002, pp. 87–104.

Robertson, Kenneth G.R. (ed.), *British and American Approaches to Intelligence*, Basingstoke: Macmillan, 1987.

Scott, Len V. and Jackson, Peter D. (eds), *Understanding Intelligence in the Twenty-First Century: Journeys in Shadows*, London: Routledge, 2004.

Scott, Len V. and Jackson, Peter D., 'The Study of Intelligence in Theory and Practice', *Intelligence and National Security*, 19:2, 2004, pp. 139–169.

Sheptycki, James W.E., 'Organizational Pathologies in Police Intelligence Systems: Some Contributions to the Lexicon of Intelligence-led Policing', in *The European Journal of Criminology*, 1:3, 2004, pp. 307–332.

Shulsky, Abram N. and Schmitt, Gary J., *Silent Warfare: Understanding the World of Intelligence*, Washington, DC: Potomac Books, 2002.

Sims, Jennifer E. and Gerber, Burton (eds), *Transforming US Intelligence*, Washington, DC: Georgetown University Press, 2005.

Treverton, Gregory F., *Reshaping National Intelligence for an Age of Information*, Cambridge: Cambridge University Press/RAND, 2001.

Treverton, Gregory F., Jones, Seth G., Boraz, Steven and Lipscy, Philip, *Toward a Theory of Intelligence: Workshop Report*, Santa Monica, CA: RAND, 2006.

Sun Tzu, *The Art of War*, trans. Samuel Griffith, Oxford, UK: Clarendon Press 1963.

Waltz, Kenneth N., *Theory of International Politics*, Reading, MA: Addison-Wesley, 1979.

Wark, Wesley K., 'The Study of Espionage: Past, Present, Future?', *Intelligence and National Security*, 8:3, 1993, pp. 1–13.

Warner, Michael, 'Wanted: A Definition of Intelligence', *Studies in Intelligence*, 46:3 2002, pp. 15–22.

Wheaton, Kristan J. and Beerbower, Michael T., 'Towards a New Definition of Intelligence', *Stanford Law & Policy Review*, 17:2, 2006, pp. 319–330.

Wilensky, Harold, *Organizational Intelligence: Knowledge and Policy in Government and Industry*, New York: Basic Books, 1967.

Wirtz, James J., 'The Intelligence Paradigm', *Intelligence and National Security*, 4: 4, 1989, pp. 829–837.

Wood, Jennifer and Dupont, Benoit (eds), *Democracy and the Governance of Security*, Cambridge, UK: Cambridge University Press, 2006.

Index

Lightning Source UK Ltd.
Milton Keynes UK
UKOW05f0343271016
286272UK00005B/221/P